The
Community
In America

THE COMMUNITY IN AMERICA

Third Edition

Roland L. Warren
Brandeis University

UNIVERSITY
PRESS OF
AMERICA

LANHAM • NEW YORK • LONDON

Copyright © 1978, 1972, 1963 by
Houghton Mifflin Company

University Press of America,® Inc.

4720 Boston Way
Lanham, MD 20706

3 Henrietta Street
London WC2E 8LU England

British Cataloging in Publication Information Available

University Press of America edition reprinted in 1987

Library of Congress Cataloging-in-Publication Data

Warren, Roland Leslie, 1915-
The community in America.

Reprint. Originally published: Chicago : Rand
McNally College Pub. Co., c1978.
Includes bibliographical references and index.
1. Cities and towns—United States.   2. Community
life.   3. United States—Social conditions.
I. Title.
[HT123.W25   1987]   307'.0973   87-14245
ISBN 0-8191-5494-6 (pbk. : alk. paper)

All University Press of America books are produced on acid-free
paper which exceeds the minimum standards set by the National
Historical Publication and Records Commission.

To Peg, Ursula, David, and Robin,
who ease the strain and pain of difficult work
and help make it all worthwhile.

Contents

Preface

This book is an attempt to explore in a systematic way the common characteristics of the changing pattern of American community life. It does so by placing less stress on a particular geographic area as the focus of analysis than on the types of systemic relationship into which people and social organizations come by virtue of their clustering together in the same location.

The above statement from the preface to the first edition of *The Community in America* is a brief indication of the book's emphasis.

Other statements from earlier editions seem worth recalling, even though it seems superfluous to bore the reader with repeating all that was said in earlier prefaces. Also from the first edition:

This book has abjured richness of description for the more difficult task of analysis. It seeks to present a theoretical conception of community phenomena which takes into account not only the vast changes which are occurring in community life, but also the advances that have been taking place in theoretical analysis. It attempts not to be encyclopedic but, on the contrary, to retain an economy of analytical concepts which, it is hoped, permits adequate analysis of most of the data.

The crying need in community theory, for practical as well as theoretical reasons, is for a relatively simple model of the community which can permit meaningful analysis and testable research hypotheses. Such a model should be capable of accommodating as much as possible of the rich web of social interaction based on common locality that has been the center of interest of community theory, research, and action in the past and will remain so in the future.

The Community in America has grown with each new edition. The reader will notice that chapters 11 and 12, added in the second edition, are an analysis of the turbulent period of the late sixties and early seventies employing analytical concepts developed at length in earlier chapters. In the present edition, a Postscript is added to chapter 12, extending the discussion of the implications of current developments in American communities. While those two chapters constitute an analysis of current history, chapters 13 and 14, appearing for the first time in this present edition, return to a theoretical discussion of the horizontal and vertical patterns of community relationships. They present new, challenging, and—no doubt for some students of the community—debatable alternative approaches to understanding the dynamics of community life today. Quite understandably, they have been inserted before, rather than after, the Epilogue.

The reader will be the ultimate judge of whether this rather unusual procedure of retaining the original ten chapters in their unsullied form with only minor substantive changes and references to more recent publications and adding chapters that reflect changes taking place "out there" as well as the author's further theoretical development is superior to making more radical changes in the original text with each new edition.

At the least, the harried student and occasional researcher will find that the ideas presented are maintained with some degree of stability over time and that passages significant in one edition still appear in the next, even though some moderate updating is involved. Beyond that, the arrangement does give a sense of organic growth, permitting the reader to make his or her own assessment of the extent to which it reflects social changes and intellectual developments adequately over the years.

Although many things change, the following from an earlier preface still reflects the author's disposition:

> My hope for this new edition is that it will continue to be of use not only to those seeking understanding, as I am, but also to those who may find it helpful in their efforts to make our communities more worthy of human beings.

April, 1977   **Roland L. Warren**

Brandeis University

Introduction

The idea of the American community is deceptively simple, as long as one does not require a rigid definition. The term evokes a rich imagery associated with the "country village," the "small town," or the "big city" of an earlier day. One thinks of the country village's Main Street, with its several stores and post office, and the streets, houses, and lawns that immediately surround it in the setting of an enveloping prairie, dairy-farm country, or forest. One recalls the road that traverses the five, ten, or twenty miles—seldom more except in the Far West—connecting it with a small city. Here in the small city is a larger population, a greater variety of shops and services, a daily newspaper, a series of wholesale establishments serving surrounding villages, perhaps a college or university, a hospital, a number of industries. Or one imagines the larger city with its concentration of people, its burgeoning suburbs, its businesses, medical center, museums, department stores, and newspapers that serve a large section of the state or perhaps parts of several states.

One thinks of places large and small, places whose appearances reflect the specialized industrial or other functions they perform, places that vary with climate and topography, with the origin of the people who first settled or later migrated there, with diverse history and traditions—places that differ from each other in a dozen ways and yet with much in common.

One thinks of communities, large or small, as clusters of people living in proximity in an area containing stores and other service facilities for the sustenance of local people and industries whose produce is distributed throughout a much wider area. Surrounding this concentration of people there is usually a much larger geographic area, which is the effective "service area" of that place and whose size varies according to types of "services."

Various criteria thought to characterize communities include a specific population living within a specific geographic area with shared institutions and values and significant social interaction.

Later, we shall develop an analytical framework within which these vague characterizations can be tested against today's American communities. Meanwhile, three broad developments are worth attention. The first is a gradual realization on the part of students of the community that the traditional way of thinking about communities is no longer adequate, if it ever was, to describe American community life. The second is the emergence of a series of circumstances believed to be inimical to healthy community living, the emergence of what may be summarized as "the community problem." The third is the recent development of a number of theoretical and methodological tools, which have increased our knowledge about community structure and processes and hold great promise for future research. The first two developments will be considered in the remainder of the present chapter, and the third will be treated in the following one.

Basic Transformations in Communities

Recent decades have seen an arresting transformation in American community life. The growth of large metropolitan complexes, including the mushrooming of suburbs and the transformation of the central cities, has received wide attention. But even in smaller communities outside the metropolitan complexes, changes are taking place that make older conceptions of community living inadequate. Thus, we find two interrelated developments. One is the actual change occurring in communities; the other is the change taking place in theoretical formulations among students of the community.

Perhaps the most conspicuous development is the constant filling in of large sections of the American landscape with concentrations of people in metropolitan areas. Metropolitan areas consist of large cities and the relatively densely populated territory surrounding them. Standard Metropolitan Statistical Areas, as they are defined for the 1970 Census, must contain at least one city or twin cities of fifty thousand or more inhabitants. Generally they include the city's surrounding county and adjacent counties that have a metropolitan character and are integrated socially and economically with the county containing the central city. The most arresting development, perhaps, has been the closing of gaps between metropolitan areas, particularly on the eastern seaboard where the whole countryside from Portland, Maine, to Virginia is expected soon to constitute one solid metropolitan complex of overlapping and intermingling metropolitan areas. Similar complexes are developing in the Middle and Far West. What happens to traditional concepts of the community under these circumstances?

Even without the overlapping and intermingling, the very growth of the single metropolitan city has placed great strain on older conceptions of the community. While it may have been true that Brooklyn was always transformed into a small town when the old Brooklyn Dodgers were in a pennant race, it is difficult to conceive of Brooklyn as a community, let alone the whole of New York City, with its five boroughs, each a separate county, each large enough to be a good-sized city or metropolis in its own right, each constituting what was formerly a number of relatively independent, though interrelated, communities. A half-century ago Canarsie, Flatbush, Bensonhurst, and Brownsville shared many of the characteristics that are usually associated with a community. Today the concept of community no longer fits them, nor does it fit the Borough of Brooklyn, which contains them, nor does it fit New York City. The concept's extension to the entire Metropolitan New York–northern New Jersey–southern Connecticut area has a certain logic but takes us so far away from earlier formulations of the community as to demand a reexamination of the term.

At the same time the notion of the community as a limited geographic area with relatively definite ascertainable boundaries has become less tenable with the growth of overlapping municipal and other governmental or quasi-governmental units. A host of water districts, public "authorities," school districts, fire districts, and other units has arisen to confuse the picture. The situation is further complicated by the fact that so many people live in one locality but earn their living in another.

How different the situation is from the days when Charles Galpin was able with relative success to delineate communities by traveling along each road out of town and noticing in which direction the ruts in the farmhouse driveways went. This method can still be used meaningfully in many places in the United States and Canada, but the number of people living in the smaller rural communities that retain the semblance of a relatively clearly delineated, relatively self-sufficient geographic area becomes smaller and smaller with each succeeding decade.

3

How different, too, from the studies made by Dwight Sanderson in upstate New York communities in the twenties and thirties. He found that when he delineated the high school area, the hardware area, the grocery area, the church area, and other relevant service areas of a rural community, the lines of all of these closely coincided. Thus, there was one community center serving an area with various types of institutional services, whose service areas generally coincided. One's community for one purpose remained one's community for another. Sanderson's definition of the rural community had both meaning and applicability: "A rural community is that form of association maintained between the people, and between their institutions, in a local area in which they live on dispersed farmsteads and in a village which is the center of their common activities."[1] This definition hardly applies in most of America today.

The development of suburbs created an altered community situation. For the suburb, though in many respects an attempt to recapture the characteristics of small-town community living, is different from the traditional small-town community in several ways. It is dominated to a much greater degree by the neighboring large city than is the nonsuburban small town. This characteristic is true not only of those suburban communities where a large proportion of wage-earners commute to the central city but of other suburbs as well. Commuter suburbs, especially, show this dependence on the central city as a source of daily occupational sustenance, a function traditionally thought of as one of the basic prerequisites of a community. Another important characteristic of the suburb is the transiency of its population, a circumstance that militates against the development of strong community ties among its residents.[2]

On a more fundamental level, certain major changes occurring in American society have been transforming the structure and function of American communities. These changes include: an increasing specialization and division of labor, both within and among communities; the proliferation of differentiated interests among local people who thus associate more often on the basis of specialized interests than on the basis of merely living in the same place; increased interdependence within communities, with other commu-

1. Dwight Sanderson and Robert A. Polson, *Rural Community Organization* (New York: John Wiley & Sons, 1939), p. 50.

2. The percentage of people in 1970 who had lived in a different county the previous year was 7.0 percent for the suburbs (SMSA's outside of central cities) and 5.2 percent for the central cities. This information is based on figures from the U.S. Bureau of the Census, *Current Population Reports*, Series P-20, No. 210 (Washington, D.C., 1970).

nities, and with social systems in the larger society; increased bureau-cratization and depersonalization; the entrance of many formerly local functions into the money-price-exchange-market system; the growth of large metropolitan areas with central cities and suburbs; and finally, a gradual change in many earlier values corresponding to the other changes just enumerated. These changes are sufficiently important to merit separate, extensive treatment. They constitute two additional changes that should be added to the conditions demanding a new formulation of the concept of community.

In the first place, they signalize the increasing and strengthen-ing of the external ties that bind the local community to the larger society. In the process, various parts of the community—its educa-tional system, its recreation, its economic units, its governmental functions, its religious units, its health and welfare agencies, and its voluntary associations—have become increasingly oriented toward district, state, regional, or national offices and less and less oriented toward each other.

In the second place, as local community units have become more closely tied with state and national systems, much of the deci-sion-making prerogative concerning the structure and function of these units has been transferred to the headquarters or district offices of the systems themselves, thus leaving a narrower and nar-rower scope of functions over which local units, responsible to the local community, exercise autonomous power. True, the local office of the state welfare department, the local post office, the local unit of the multibranch bank, the local plant of the national manufactur-ing company, the local unit of the labor union, and the local branch of the supermarket chain are all located within the community and are largely staffed by community people. But the continuation of their very existence in the community, the formulation of their poli-cies, and the determination of their specific behavior are not as sub-ject to local control as they were in earlier decades.

Inadequacy of Older Community Concepts

While such changes as the above transform American communities, making older conceptions of the community less and less appro-priate, a number of points of possible weakness of the older concep-tion itself are appearing on the theoretical level. Students of the community have come to doubt the adequacy of earlier community theory even to describe the situation that existed several decades ago, before the great transformation described above had taken place. Yet there remains much that is valid in the community con-cept. Sociologically, the term *community* implies something both psy-chological and geographical. Psychologically, it implies shared interests, characteristics, or association, as in the expression "community of interest" or the term "the business community." Geographically, it denotes a specific area where people are clustered. Sociologically, the term combines these two connotations. It relates to the shared interests and behavior patterns that people have by virtue of their common locality. Mere similarity of interest does not in itself make a sociological community, nor does mere geographic proximity of residence. In one earlier study of 94 definitions of the term community, it was found that 69 were "in accord that social interaction, area, and a common tie or ties are commonly found in community life."[3]

It was recognized a long time ago that the political boundaries of a village or city did not necessarily coincide with the area of shared life and shared institutions and behavior that constituted the local community. Indeed, one of the most important discoveries of students of the community early in this century was the close interrelatedness of the village or city center with the surrounding countryside, which constituted its "trade area." Here was a social entity that did not appear on a map, and yet its reality could not be denied. Further studies acknowledged that a community must be of sufficient size to contain a fairly broad set of institutions—industry, stores, churches, organizations, schools, government, and so on—so that one could live one's entire life within the bounds of the community, as one sociologist put it. Other characteristics of the community were also identified, as will be indicated in chapter 2. For the moment, let us simply note that this formulation of the community concept arose from a realization that people's lives were intertwined with the institutions that served them locally, that a community was a total framework of living rather than merely a political jurisdiction, and that an interesting though complex network of people, institutions, shared interests, locality, and a sense of psychological "belonging" had been identified and could be further studied with the "community" as the unit for such study.

But the very locality-oriented nature of the community concept encouraged the study of local behavior as though it existed *sui generis,* in its own right, independent of the cultural and social forces from the larger society surrounding it. It is enlightening to observe how often this path was followed in the many community studies written in the first half of the twentieth century. It is likewise interesting to notice how often the investigator acknowledged that, of course, outside forces should be taken into account, but then did not

3. George A. Hillery, Jr., "Definitions of Community: Areas of Agreement," *Rural Sociology 20,* no. 2 (June 1955): 118.

do so. What Steward wrote regarding anthropological studies applied to studies made of American communities as well:

> Most studies, however, have treated the community as if it were a primitive tribe—that is, as if it were a self-contained structural and functional whole which could be understood in terms of itself alone. Scholars are quite aware that any modern community is a functionally dependent part of a much larger whole; but in general they have not yet taken account of this larger frame of reference in community study. Individual communities are often studied as if the larger whole was simply a mosaic of such parts.[4]

Community theory is now in a process of revision, as different types of theoretical approach are formulated to encompass the widespread realization that an adequate description must somehow meaningfully relate the community to the rest of society.

An additional theoretical difficulty confronting students of the community has been the relation of one community to another, particularly communities of different sizes. Let us consider this problem from the standpoint of a small city of fifteen thousand people. Such a city is often the wholesale center for a group of surrounding villages, each of which, *on a particular level of goods and services*, constitutes, with its immediate trade area, a community in itself. As a wholesale center with its hospital, radio station, more specialized shops, and many other facilities, the small city may serve the whole group of surrounding communities, however. In turn, the small city, with its surrounding communities, may be part of the area of service of a metropolis, with its medical center, specialized stores and services, and so on.

Thus, it has long been recognized that American communities do not consist of a number of discrete and separate entities but that there are communities within communities, depending on what level of goods and services and social behavior is under consideration. No one has ever made an adequate systematic classification of these various levels of goods and services and social behavior so that students of the community could speak uniformly about how a community is related to another by being contained within it or by containing it, depending on the order of data being investigated.

Such a classification might help with a related theoretical difficulty: the size problem. Is the term *community* sufficiently flexible to include both a village of two thousand people with its surrounding service area and a city of a million people? Are the same types of

---

4. Julian H. Steward, *Area Research: Theory and Practice*, Bulletin 63 (New York: Social Science Research Council, 1950), p. 22.

relationships involved? Are we still talking about the same phenomenon? Or does the vast complexity of wheels within wheels in the organization of the large city make it more a federation of communities, as it were, than a community itself? There is no consistently acknowledged theoretical resolution of these questions, and some studies have been made of a whole city or metropolitan area as a community while others have taken only one small part of the city for the basis of a community study. When the former is done, the study is typically limited to some one aspect of community life because of the gigantic complexity of the data involved.

Life would be much simpler for students of the subject if communities could be clearly delineated geographically from each other and if there were no overlapping among them. The community concept, based as it is on common life shared by people within a specific geographic area, presents both practical and theoretical difficulties once one attempts to draw lines on a map. It is relatively easy to define and delimit an organization, a business company, or a governmental unit. The community remains elusive, often encompassing one area and one group of people if looked at in a certain way, a different area and different people if looked at in another.

Let us consider still another difficulty: One can point to the formal organization of a business company, or of a church, or of the municipal government on an organization chart; but where is the organization chart for the community? Clearly, it has no formal organization, for it is not formally constituted as a special social "being." Its reality exists only in its constituting a social entity, only in the behaviors and attitudes that its members share, only in the patterns of their interaction. In this respect, it is analogous to a small, informal group of friends. They do not have a constitution or charter, with specified membership requirements, written rules and regulations, specified procedures for choosing leaders, specified duties and privileges of leaders, and so on. Yet they constitute an important social reality. Recent decades have seen great advances in small group research, and some of the most promising theoretical thinking about the community is arising today from theories about the small, informal group.

When all such difficulties are considered, a few sociologists throw up their hands and urge that the whole concept of the geographic community be discarded as a useless theoretical will-o'-the-wisp. Yet the term remains, and community analysis goes forward. The reason is simple. People's lives and their behavior are significantly influenced by their propinquity. Living together in physical proximity requires social structures and social functions that sustain life in the locality and provide the satisfactions that people seek. By living in the same geographical area, even in today's conditions of rapid transportation, people must share common local institutions and facilities. They have a common interest in the local schools, stores, sources of employment, churches, and other institutions and services whose availability to individuals in their own locality is a part of the total pattern of American society. The intertwining of their lives on a locality basis, even in these days of specialized interests, urban anonymity, and depersonalization, provides an important social reality and an important focus of study, even though such study is fraught with theoretical difficulty. In the following chapter, we shall see that several new approaches to community study, as well as the best in some of the older approaches, provide tools for a meaningful analysis of such locality-oriented behavior.

A Community Model

It is the inescapable fact that people's clustering together in space has important influences on their daily activities that perhaps gives us our best clue to a definition of the community as a social entity. We shall consider a community to be *that combination of social units and systems that perform the major social functions having locality relevance.* In other words, by *community* we mean the organization of social activities to afford people daily local access to those broad areas of activity that are necessary in day-to-day living. In this book we shall organize our description and analysis of such activities around five major functions that have such locality relevance. These functions are:

1. Production-distribution-consumption
2. Socialization
3. Social control
4. Social participation
5. Mutual support

While all have locality relevance, they are not necessarily functions over which the community exercises exclusive responsibility or over which it has complete control. On the contrary, the organization of society to perform these functions at the community level involves a strong tie between locally based units such as businesses, schools, governments, and voluntary associations and social systems extending far beyond the confines of the community. Rather than being extraneous to the present consideration of the community, these relationships to extracommunity systems will be an important focus of attention in this book. Nor, as we shall see, does it mean that these functions are not performed by other types of social systems such as informal groups, formal associations, and whole societies.

9

The community, however, is especially characterized by the organization of these functions on a locality basis.

The function of *production-distribution-consumption* relates to local participation in the process of producing, distributing, and consuming those goods and services that are a part of daily living and access to which is desirable in the immediate locality. While it is customary to consider economic entrepreneurs, most typically the modern business corporation, as the principal providers of such goods and services, all community institutions, whether industrial, business, professional, religious, educational, governmental, or whatever, provide such goods and services. Indeed, the conditions under which one such unit or another provides the particular goods or services are an important consideration, and the switch in their provision from one type of auspices to another has important implications, which we shall explore in chapters 6 and 7.

The function of *socialization* involves a process by which society or one of its constituent social units transmits prevailing knowledge, social values, and behavior patterns to its individual members. Through this process the individual comes to take on the way of living of his or her society rather than that of some other. The process is particularly important and noticeable in the early years of the individual, but it extends throughout one's life. In American communities the formal school system is ordinarily considered the principal community institution discharging this function, although it is recognized that individual families have an important role to play, particularly in the early years, and that many other groups are also active in the process.

The function of *social control* involves the process through which a group influences the behavior of its members toward conformity with its norms. Here, too, several different social units perform this function on the community level. Customarily, formal government is considered particularly pertinent, since by definition government has ultimate coercive power over the individual through the enforcement of universally applicable laws. The police and the courts are especially relevant in the performance of the social-control function by local government, but, as we shall see, many other social units, including the family, the school, the church, and the social agency, also play a large part.

An important community function is that of providing local access to *social participation*. Perhaps the most widely prevalent unit for providing this participation is the religious organization—church or synagogue—and we shall consider these organizations in the context of their great importance in performing this function. Ordinarily, one thinks of voluntary organizations of various sorts as the community's most important units for channeling social participation. Nevertheless, many different types of social unit, including businesses, government offices, and voluntary and public health and welfare agencies, provide, through their formal activity, important avenues of social participation to their employees or volunteer workers in the course of the performance of their occupational tasks. Likewise, family and kinship groups, friendship groups, and other less formal groupings provide important channels of social participation.

A final major community function is that of providing *mutual support* on the local level. Traditionally, such mutual support, whether in the form of care in time of sickness, exchange of labor, or helping a local family in economic distress, has been performed locally very largely under such primary-group auspices as family and relatives, neighborhood groups, friendship groups, and local religious groups. Specialization of function, along with other social changes discussed in chapter 3, has led to a gradual change in auspices for many of these mutual-support functions: to public welfare departments, to private health and welfare agencies, to governmental and commercial insurance companies, and so on. Perhaps the present archetype of the community-based mutual-support unit might be the voluntary agency in the field of health and welfare, but the distribution of this function, like others, through a wide range of social auspices is an important aspect of the current situation in American communities. These major locality-relevant functions are considered in detail in chapter 6.

As the above implies, the definition of the community in terms of the systems that perform the major social functions having locality relevance leads to an emphasis on community functions rather than on community institutions. A conventional way of describing the related community phenomena is to consider the various institutional areas of the community: its economic institutions, its government, its educational institutions, its religious institutions, and perhaps its health and welfare, recreational, communicational, or other institutions. As noted, however, these institutional areas correspond only very loosely to the major locality-relevant functions. As already indicated, most of these functions are performed by a great variety of institutional auspices. The present period is characterized by important shifts in the performance of these functions from one set of community auspices to another. Hence, a functional rather than an institutional approach seems to have the greatest potential for bringing out this cross-institutional distribution of important community functions.

A problem facing any student of American communities is how to make general statements that apply widely despite the many gradations in size and other characteristics that differentiate one com- **11** munity from another. One possible approach is to consider numerous different "ideal types" of communities and to make general statements only about each type. Another alternative is to confine one's statements to relationships that are so general that they apply to all communities, regardless of the important differences existing among them. Another possible approach is to consider some of the important dimensions along which communities differ from each other, relate these dimensions to general statements applicable to all communities, and then "locate" any particular community or type of community under discussion at a particular point along each such dimension. Thus, one can set up a dimensional field that is broad enough to encompass all communities and make meaningful statements about them on an appropriately abstract level; at the same time the dimensional field can provide a means for describing the difference between one community and another with respect to location within the multidimensional field. Statements about specific communities can thus have general relevance as long as the location of the community within the field is known. Stein has made an attempt to apply this procedure to the analysis of American communities, employing his three main analytical concepts—urbanization, industrialization, and bureaucratization—as the dimensions of his field.[5] For our present consideration, a somewhat different set of dimensions will be employed. Their relevance and importance will become apparent in subsequent chapters, so they will receive only brief treatment here.

The first of the ways in which American communities differ from each other in their structure and function relates to *the dimension of autonomy.* Our postulate is that American communities differ along this dimension and that this difference is relevant to an approach defining the community in terms of its functions. In considering any community, we shall be interested in the extent to which it is dependent on or independent of extracommunity units in the performance of its five functions.

The second type of difference is in *the extent to which the service areas of local units (stores, churches, schools, and so on) coincide or fail to coincide.* At the one extreme, the service areas coincide and hence everyone within the community service area boundary is served by institutions from the same community. At the other extreme, there is relatively little coincidence of service areas, and people may find themselves living within the school district of a locality to the east, going to church in a locality to the south, trading at a trade center to the north, and so on, without any common geographic center of

---

5. Maurice R. Stein, *The Eclipse of Community: An Interpretation of American Studies* (Princeton: Princeton University Press, 1960).

community activities and without a common geographic area of service.

A somewhat different type of variation concerns the extent of *psychological identification with a common locality.* In some communities a strong sense of local identification is apparent; that is, the local inhabitants consider the community as an important reference group. At the other extreme are communities whose inhabitants have little sense of relationship to one another, little sense of the community as a significant social group, and little sense of "belonging" to the community.

A final dimension will be the extent to which the community's *horizontal pattern* is strong or weak. The horizontal pattern is the structural and functional relation of the various local units (individuals and social systems) to each other (see chapter 5). In some communities the sentiments, behavior patterns, and social systemic interconnections of the horizontal pattern may be strong, in others weak.

In considering community differences, specific instances can be contained within a more generalized frame of reference by using these four dimensions. Putting this graphically, we can say that communities differ on all four of the following dimensions, and we can meaningfully locate each community at some point on each of the lines going from one extreme to another (see Figure 1-1).

Figure 1-1.   Four dimensions on which American communities differ

		0	1	2	3	4	
1. Local autonomy	Independent	└─────┴─────┴─────┴─────┘					Dependent
2. Coincidence of service areas	Coincide	└─────┴─────┴─────┴─────┘					Differ
3. Psychological identification with locality	Strong	└─────┴─────┴─────┴─────┘					Weak
4. Horizontal pattern	Strong	└─────┴─────┴─────┴─────┘					Weak

The Community "Problem"

So far we have discussed some changes that have taken place in American communities, some theoretical difficulties involved in community studies, and the functional conception of the community that we shall use in this book. Let us turn now to a somewhat different type of problem, perhaps much more meaningful to nonsociologists. In their eyes, the problem lends urgency to the study of communities, giving it an importance that mere theoreti-   **13** cal interest would not afford. For through their newspapers and television and through their own experience, discerning Americans have come to the uneasy realization that all is not right with their community living, that undesirable situations appear with growing frequency or intensity and that these are not the adventitious difficulty of one community or another so much as the parts of a general pattern of community living. "Something is wrong with the system"; there is a *community problem*.

It is apparent that certain types of "problems" are broadly characteristic of contemporary American communities. While most noticeable in the metropolitan areas, most of them are apparent in smaller communities as well. They appear in such forms as the increasing indebtedness of central cities, the spread of urban blight and slums, the lack of affordable, adequate housing, the economic dependence of large numbers of people in the population, poorly financed and staffed schools, high delinquency and crime rates, institutional racism, inadequate provisions for the mentally ill, the problem of the aged, the need for industrial development, the conflict of local and national agencies for the free donor's dollar, the pollution of air and water, the problem of affording rapid transit for commuters at a reasonable price and at a reasonable profit, and the problem of downtown traffic congestion. The list is almost endless, and each of the problems mentioned could be subdivided into numerous problematical aspects.

On this level, one can continue naming specific problems almost indefinitely. Are such problems simply a host of disparate plagues with which the modern community, Job-like, is made to suffer? Or are they in some sense interrelated? If so, how? This book is not problem-oriented in the sense of being an analysis of community problems and what might be done about them. Yet no systematic treatise on the community can overlook their existence or neglect to explore their interrelations with each other and with other aspects of community living.

Perhaps we can shed some light by examining community behavior as it has developed and changed in recent decades. A closer look at some of the underlying processes taking place within the community may afford a backdrop against which the community conditions that we interpret as "problems" can be understood as part and parcel of the system of community living that has developed in America. The alternative approach is to take each problem out of its situational context and treat it in relative isolation from the basic community conditions that produced it. To do so is to operate on a superficial and often ineffectual level, as many concerned citizens who have attempted to cope with these problems can attest. In a sense, this entire book represents an attempt to supply such a basic background for these problems, but chapter 3 in particular is devoted to analyzing some of the basic underlying processes to which most of them are related in one way or another.

Meanwhile, it is well to distinguish between the existence of a problem and the existence of the ability to take effective action to resolve it. Looked at another way, if no social system is "perfect," then each system will produce certain "problems." They are, in a sense, the price paid for whatever advantages that particular system of community living entails. We can thus inquire what sorts of problems are generated in American communities and also how effectively they are dealt with.

One sees not only specific problems of one type or another, but also the general problem of inability of the community to organize its forces effectively to cope with its specific problems. Let us consider this last for a moment. The question now becomes: What are the conditions of American community living that make it difficult for people to muster their resources on the community level to cope with their problems?

Certainly, one part of the answer is the fact that many of the problems that are confronted on the community level simply are not solvable on that level, but are *problems of the larger society of which the community is a part.* Any single community's effort is as little or nothing as against the forces of the larger society. Much important behavior that takes place at the community level takes place within units, groups, companies, and other entities that themselves are integral parts of larger state or national systems. It is a thesis of this book that such units often are more closely related to these larger systems than to other components of the local community. Thus, problems of the larger society are not something that are adventitiously imported into the local community like a germ carried by some visitor, but rather they are conditions inhering in the systems of which the community's various units are a part, and the community's units share these conditions as a basic part of their very existence.

Thus, for example, problems of unemployment or of inflation are not amenable to solution community by community, although some palliative action on the community level may attenuate the former. On a somewhat different plain, certain problems are more closely related to the interaction that takes place within the community itself. These problems include those arising from marital and family conflict, from the vicious fund-raising controversy between national and local health and welfare organizations, and difficulties in the central city that are attendant upon the flight to the suburbs of upper- and middle-income groups along with the retail stores that serve them. Nevertheless, such difficulties are a part of the larger cultural patterns of living, which communities share by being a part of American society.

As an example, the problem of family breakdown in the local community is partly, at least, a result of forces in the wider culture, such as conflicting role expectations in marriage, discontinuity in the socialization process, emphasis on hedonistic romantic irresponsibility in the courtship process, decline in opportunities for useful functions performed by children, and separation of the economic sustenance function from the home. Just as communities are not islands isolated from the major social systems of American society, so they are not cultural islands separated from the broad forces of cultural development and change that characterize the major institutions of American society. In sum, many problems that communities face are simply beyond resolving through the effective mustering of resources at the community level alone.

A closely related barrier to effective community action is the *loss of community autonomy* over specific institutions or organizations located within it and closely intermeshed with its welfare. The decision of the absentee-owned company to discontinue its branch plant and the decision of the state highway department to build the new road on the east side of the river rather than on the west represent decisions by community-based units over which the community exercises little control.

To ineffectiveness of possible action at the community level and loss of community autonomy can be added a third barrier to effective community action, one that seems on the surface, at least, to be more nearly under the potential control of community people. This barrier consists of a number of related phenomena that may best be characterized as *lack of identification with the community*.

Perhaps the most widely recognized aspect of such lack of identification of the individual with the community is the much deplored *apathy* of citizens regarding community affairs. People who plunge into community problems with a concern for community improvement often complain with despair that "you can't get anybody interested" in whatever the problem happens to be. So many problems seem to depend for their effective confrontation on sustaining the interest and activity of a large number of people over a sufficient period of time to bring about the remedies thought to be desirable that the alleged apathy of citizens seems to be a paramount stumbling block. The point is often distorted by unrealistic comparisons with overidealized depictions of New England town meetings or by invidious comparisons with some community where "people got together and really did something about it."

Yet there is a valid point here. The increasing association of people on the basis of common occupational or other interests, rather than on the basis of locality alone (as among neighbors), is no doubt a contributing factor. The union man, the banker, and the school administrator often have strong vocational ties to their own groups, and they have less in common vocationally than, say, three farmers living in the same rural neighborhood. Even in recreational and civic activity, association is often on the basis of specialized interest. Thus, the apathy is not complete, for interests often run high in specialized concerns. It consists, instead, of a lack of interest in community-wide concerns that cut across the various specialized interests and thus become "nobody's business."

Over the years, communities have grown larger and larger. The problem of direct as against representative participation arises in large social bodies, not only in government but in various community affairs. Attempts to solve this problem have been no freer of defects in other aspects of community participation than they have in political representation. Community councils, for example, represent an attempt to involve both individuals and organizations in processes of community-wide betterment. They have been extremely sporadic, and even at their best they seldom attain active participation from more than a small minority of the citizenry. Participation in community activities thus usually takes place through participation in some specialized interest group such as a health association, a chamber of commerce, or a better government league, each having its own sphere of interests and activities and its loyal supporters who can generally be relied upon to rally to a cause within their sphere of interests, but not necessarily outside it.

One might ask what else might reasonably be expected, for time does not permit each individual citizen to participate actively in all the concerns that have broad community import. Thus, what is often interpreted as apathy, as "nobody cares," is merely an instance of the hard fact that the number of legitimate community concerns is so great that individual citizens could not actively concern themselves with all of them even if they wanted to and of course many do not.

The increasing transiency of residents of the suburbs has already been mentioned. The constant moving back and forth across the country in search of the better job, as a result of the company's planned policy of personnel rotation, or for whatever reason, puts a premium on the tree that can survive with shallow roots, a point that William H. Whyte has made with great effec- **17** tiveness in his study of The Organization Man.[6] The knowledge that one will probably not remain for many years in the community where one is now living seems unlikely to favor civic participation, and the really remarkable thing is that participation does run so high precisely in the suburbs that show such a great degree of transiency.

Failure to identify with the community takes still another form, which might be called *alienation*.[7] An example is the extent to which useful participation roles are increasingly unavailable to the aged in American communities. Numerous studies of the "problems of the aged" document the point that as people grow older, their roles in family, religious organization, occupation, and voluntary civic endeavor become less meaningful and less active. Compulsory retirement, the friction caused by having older in-laws living with the nuclear family, the fast pace that turns to youthful leadership and new ideas rather than to the wisdom accumulated from another day by older people—all these tend to estrange the elderly from normal avenues of community participation and force them into a state of dependency that is caused less by their inability to function effectively than by the community's inability to make vital use of them. The fact that this estrangement occurs at the very time when shortages in vital community jobs are experienced, particularly in the professions, and when the need for volunteer services in health and welfare agencies is greater than ever, makes the situation particularly ironic.

Groups of people who hold values different from those dominant in the community represent another type of estrangement, which may even constitute a deliberate rebellion against the community's values. These small groups take various forms: splinter sects, practitioners of various cults, members of the "counter-culture," revolutionaries, and so on. Many such groups perform a useful function in challenging the validity of the prevailing values, as gadflies to the conscience of society. Delinquency, vice, and mental illness, on the other hand, represent an order of deviance whose usefulness to the community is far less apparent. They all have in common, though, the estrangement of the individual from the usual values, behavior systems, and satisfactions of the community. There is considerable evidence that such estrangement is widely characteristic of people in the lowest socioeconomic status, the so-called lower-lower class as described

6. *The Organization Man* (Garden City: Doubleday Anchor, 1957).

7. For an analysis of the various meanings applied to this term in the sociological literature, see Melvin Seeman, "On the Meaning of Alienation," *American Sociological Review*, vol. 24, no. 6 (December 1959).

by Warner, Hollingshead, and others.[8] So basically different is their whole pattern of living that they might well constitute a completely different culture.[9]

Estrangement from commonly held values has, since Durkheim, come to be described by the term *anomie*, or normlessness,[10] a situation in which there is little sharing of commonly accepted values and social control over behavior becomes ineffectual. In analyzing the disintegration of a New England community, Homans observes:

> If the good opinion of his neighbors is a reward to a man, then a loss of their good opinion will hurt him, but if this loss does not follow a breach of a norm, where is the punishment? And how can it follow, when the norms themselves are not well defined?[11]

The society-wide character of many problems, lack of community autonomy, and lack of identification with the community are three barriers to the efficient mustering of forces to confront community problems. As a final part of this introductory chapter, it might be well to relate these characteristics to the rise of a process that has come to be called "community development." For one way of describing community development is to say that it is a process of helping community people to analyze their problems, to exercise as large a measure of autonomy as possible and feasible, and to promote a greater identification of the individual citizen and the individual organization with the community as a whole.

8.   See, for example, W. Lloyd Warner and Paul S. Lunt, *The Social Life of a Modern Community* (New Haven, Conn.: Yale University Press, 1941), especially chap. 22; see also August B. Hollingshead and Frederick C. Redlich, *Social Class and Mental Illness: A Community Study* (New York: John Wiley & Sons, 1958).

9.   Different class-based subcultures have given rise to the theme of a "culture of poverty," which has become highly controverted in recent years—not so much over the existence of different lifestyles associated with social stratification as over the relationship of lifestyles to poverty. If the lifestyle of the culture of poverty is presumed to "cause" poverty, presumably the problem should be faced through changing the behavior patterns of poor people through various means of resocialization: psychotherapy, social casework, counseling, and so on. The culture of poverty approach is thus seen by many as an intellectual basis for neglecting deficiencies in the American social structure that are believed by many to be the prime factors.

For an overview of the issues, see Charles A. Valentine, *Culture and Poverty: Critique and Counter Proposals* (Chicago: University of Chicago Press, 1968). The implications of the two alternative approaches to social problems in general and poverty in particular are treated in chapters 11 and 12 of the present book.

10.   Emile Durkheim, *Suicide,* trans. John A. Spaulding and George Simpson (Glencoe, Ill.: Free Press, 1951).

11.   George C. Homans, *The Human Group* (New York: Harcourt, Brace, 1950), p. 366.

Through such a process, communities may be helped to confront their problems as effectively as possible.

The deliberate attempt by community people to work together to guide the future of their communities and the development of a corresponding set of techniques for assisting community people in such a process constitute important advances in the current changes occurring in American communities. They will receive extensive attention in chapter 10. Often, though, different groups of people in the community have different interests and pursue conflicting goals for community change. This diversity of contesting interests is discussed in chapters 11 and 12.

Older and Newer Approaches to the Community   **2**

The systematic study of the community has developed around the general focus of shared living based on common locality. In a sense, the community is the meeting place of the individual and the larger society and culture. It is in his or her own locality, characteristically, that, throughout most of human history and to a very great extent today, the individual confronts society's institutions, its manner of religious expression, its ways of regulating behavior, its ways of family living, its ways of socializing the young, its ways of providing sustenance, its ways of esthetic expression. Fresh eggs in the local store, services at the local church, places to amuse oneself, a source of employment, streets and roads to get to these facilities, a school for one's children, organizations to which to belong, friends and relatives with whom to visit—all these and many other basic ingredients of everyday life remain largely a function of the local arena, and the way people organize themselves to procure them in locality groups is the special subject matter of the study of the community.

The fact that many of these locality-based ways of doing things are patterns provided in a larger regional, national, or international culture and that much of the structure and function of local institutions is influenced from outside the locality is an important topic that this book will treat. But to recognize explicitly the outside influence, the stamp of the mass culture on the individual community, is not to deny the fact that individuals typically have their principal encounters with mass culture through institutions that are deployed on a locality basis so as to be readily accessible to them. The fact that they are so distributed makes these localities, with their clusters of people and institutions, important units of society and significant units for study.

This chapter reviews some of the different ways of approaching communities as objects of study and some of the chief contributions to knowledge about communities that these different approaches have yielded in the past. It also considers some new approaches to supplement the findings that the older ones continue to contribute.[1]

The Community as Space

One question to be raised about the local clustering of people and institutions has to do with their *spatial relationships*. Obviously, people are not found to be distributed evenly throughout geographical space but are sparsely distributed in some areas, thickly clustered in others. The thickly clustered areas tend in the United States also to be centers of institutional services. Generally speaking, the larger the cluster of people, the more numerous and varied the institutional services in the area. What, then, can be ascertained about the way people and their institutions are distributed spatially in communities of various sizes? We shall pursue two approaches that are related to this question, one from studies of rural communities, the other from studies of a large metropolis.

Rural community studies   In 1911 Dr. Charles J. Galpin reported on an exploratory study of an upstate New York rural community. He had investigated the social activity that involved and surrounded the village of Belleville, finding that 27 organizations centered in the village while no organizations other than school districts were found in the open country.

> Village and open farming country form a community of homes which seems to be a sort of social drainage basin beyond whose border every home drains off into some other basin. The big discovery of this survey is the fact of a real rural community and also pretty clearly the area of this community with its bounding lines. It appears that this community takes in parts of

1. Some of the more recent developments will also be discussed in chapters 13 and 14.

four townships, and ignores in its social dealings the voting precincts set by law.[2]

Here, already, are the basic ingredients of the classical conception of the rural community: the trade center and its surrounding area, the realization that villagers and surrounding farmers share common institutions and lead a common life, the delineation of one community from another in terms of a border beyond which people associate themselves with the institutions of a different trade center and thus belong to a different community, and the understanding that communities do not necessarily coincide with the boundaries of governmental units. Galpin went on to make a much more elaborate study in Walworth County, Wisconsin, incorporating and implementing these basic ideas and developing a methodology for delineating the communities of that county.[3]

Since that time numerous studies of rural communities have been made, using essentially the same conceptual approach and essentially the same methodology of delimiting trade areas. Extensive attention has been given to discovering the battery of goods, services, and facilities available in different-sized communities and the interrelation of these different-sized communities in terms of their geographical distribution as well as their trade and other reciprocal relationships. Patterns of settlement have been found to differ in different parts of the country, and the usual American pattern of a village center serving a large area where farmers are settled independently on their holdings has been found to differ markedly from the more widespread type of settlement in Europe and other parts of the world, where tradespeople and farmers live in the village center and farmers or peasants do not live on their land holdings.

Students of the rural community have also found an additional social unit between the individual family and the community: the rural neighborhood. Typically with a place name known to its inhabitants, the neighborhood covers a smaller area than the community; and while it does not have an extensive complement of institutional services, it may have one or a few of them, perhaps a general store, a local district school, in earlier days a grist mill, and so on. But the most important characteristic of rural neighborhoods is the fact that their inhabitants constitute a significant sociological group, showing

2. *Country Life Conference*, University of Wisconsin Bulletin Series No. 472, General Series 308 (Madison, February 1911), quoted in John H. Kolb and Edmund de S. Brunner, *A Study of Rural Society*, 4th ed. (New York: Houghton Mifflin, 1952), p. 211.

3. Charles J. Galpin, *The Social Anatomy of an Agricultural Community*, Research Bulletin 34 (Madison: University of Wisconsin Agricultural Experiment Station, May 1915).

characteristic "neighborly" activities such as borrowing and lending tools and labor, helping each other in times of crisis, friendly visiting, and so on. In this conception physical proximity did not in itself constitute a neighborhood. The process of "neighboring" was its chief criterion. If the neighboring ceased, the neighborhood no longer existed as a significant sociological group, even though people still lived there.

One of the important changes taking place in rural America is the gradual dissolution of neighborhoods as important social groups. In many instances this has arisen from an actual depletion of the population of the countryside as land holdings have grown larger and the village populations have increased. But it also occurs where people remain on the land. The most common development has been that, with the automobile and improved roads, it has been easier for farmers to get into the village center; and a large variety of institutional services have, as it were, been moved to the village from the scattered outlying neighborhoods and become centralized there. The general store, the one-room school, the outlying church, and the like have all moved to the village. Thus, the village has become in numerous ways a center of institutional activities. The lives of people in the surrounding areas are now oriented toward the villages rather than toward their own immediate neighborhoods.

As interest in the rural community grew, a number of ingenious methodologies were developed for its delineation and study. In a sense, the methods for delineating the community were merely refinements of Galpin's original idea of noticing which way the ruts in the driveways turned. It soon became apparent that this approach could be refined by asking the people along each road out of the village centers where they went for certain types of purchases, services, or institutional functions. As one moved out from the village center, one would pass through an area where people overwhelmingly patronized that village center, into a marginal area where they might show a less definite trend, and finally into an area where people went to a different village center. The no man's land between constituted the general area of the community's broad boundary.

One modification of this method was simply to ask the school children for such information, plotting it on a map according to their residence. Still another method was to gather from village stores, schools, weekly newspaper, churches, and so on the actual physical residence of the customers, patrons, clients and plot a different service area for each such service. From these could then be constructed a composite service area, which would constitute the geographic area of the community.[4]

4. For the most usual methods, based on Galpin's work, see Dwight Sanderson, *Locating the Rural Community* (Ithaca: New York State College of Agriculture, 1939).

In the southeast, there was some indication that communities could best be located by taking neighborhoods as units, rather than studying individual families. Thus, neighborhoods were conceived as the building blocks of communities, and essentially the same questions were asked of the neighborhoods as would otherwise be asked of individual families. This method seemed particularly appropriate where neighborhood units were strong or were to be an important focus of the study.[5] Generally speaking, though, rural neighborhoods have been declining in numbers and importance, while social life has come to be more centralized at the village centers.

A corresponding change has been taking place in the villages themselves. There has developed an organization of village functions into national chains, systems, or networks. This development has been accompanied by a diminution of community autonomy as functions still performed at the community level came to be directed from the county, district, state, or national level.

This integration of local community institutions into larger systems outside the local community has presented to investigators a situation wherein much that goes on within the community is only in a superficial sense a community phenomenon. Shall such extracommunity phenomena be studied as though they were integral parts of the community, or shall community study be directed only at those aspects of living that are more integrally a part of the local community's behavior? The "community action" approach, described later in this chapter, is one way in which this question is being answered as a basis for further community research.

Urban community studies   The spatial relationships of the urban community likewise received extensive early attention, but they were studied with a somewhat different approach, by an almost entirely different group of sociologists. While rural sociologists were attached to the large state agricultural colleges and thus tied in with the Extension Service of the United States Department of Agriculture, urban sociologists were based in the large public or private universities located in large cities. The markedly separate paths of urban and rural community studies have led to a consequent isolation, disadvantageous to both groups of students. Working independently becomes progressively untenable as the process of urbanization spreads urban cultural patterns to the rural areas and as suburbs arise, which show marked characteristics differentiating them from the rural communities and from the larger urban centers.

5. For a description of the "neighborhood cluster" method, as it is called, see Irwin T. Sanders and Douglas Ensminger, *Alabama Rural Communities: A Study of Chilton County*, Quarterly Bulletin No. 136 (Montevallo: Alabama College, 1940).

If one is to look, however, for a counterpart to the great spurt in rural community studies, which resulted from the discovery of the rural community as a significant sociological unit, one must go to Chicago, where during the 1920s and 1930s, largely under the leadership of Robert E. Park but nurtured by a whole generation of outstanding sociologists, a creative surge forward was made in the study of the urban community. The city containing the University of Chicago became the best-researched city in the world.

Urban studies have been much more deliberately related to human ecology than have rural community studies. In McKenzie's words,

> The spatial and sustenance relations in which human beings are organized are ever in process of change in response to the operation of a complex of environmental and cultural forces. It is the task of the human ecologist to study these processes of change in order to ascertain their principles of operation and the nature of the forces producing them.[6]

McKenzie went on to define the community in ecological terms: "A community, then, is an ecological distribution of people and services in which the spatial location of each unit is determined by its relation to all other units." He added: "A network of interrelated communities is likewise an ecological distribution."[7]

Park and his associates at the University of Chicago became absorbed with the idea of studying the spatial distribution of people and functions in the urban context. What gave their studies special impetus was their belief that what they were learning in Chicago would apply, with appropriate modifications, to other cities as well. "There is implicit in all these studies the notion that the city is a thing with a characteristic organization and a typical life-history, and that individual cities are enough alike so that what one learns about one city may, within limits, be assumed to be true of others."[8]

It is a common observation that certain parts of various cities are very much alike, even though they are thousands of miles apart. Indeed, they are often more like each other than other parts of the city, which may be just a few blocks away. Alert travelers have noticed the remarkable similarity between such characteristic urban

6. R. D. McKenzie, "The Scope of Human Ecology," in Ernest W. Burgess, ed., *The Urban Community: Selected Papers from the Proceedings of the American Sociological Society, 1925*, p. 167. Copyright 1926 by The University of Chicago Press, Chicago, Ill.

7. "Human Ecology," p. 169.

8. Robert E Park, "The City as a Social Laboratory," in T. V. Smith and Leonard D. White, eds., *Chicago: An Experiment in Social Science Research* (Chicago: University of Chicago Press, 1929), p. 8.

areas as the better-class hotel districts, tenement slum districts, skid-row amusement centers, shopping centers, and so on. Since such similar areas grow up in similar sized cities, regardless of their geographic separation, they must be the product of cultural and ecological forces that operate similarly in all such cities. The Chicago sociologists determined to study the operation of these forces in Chicago, so that their findings could then be applied to other cities and modified if necessary. Basically, they emerged with two important spatial concepts, the urban zone and the natural area. They found Chicago to be describable in terms of five concentric zones, of which the central business district, or Loop, constituted the center. Proceeding outward, one passed through a Zone in Transition, a Zone of Independent Workingmen's Homes, a Zone of Better Residences, and a Commuter's Zone.[9] The zones were found to differ from each other in a number of major ways, some of which became the basis of special studies, such as Reckless's study of the distribution of commercialized vice in Chicago, the study by Faris and Dunham of the ecology of mental disorders, Mowrer's study of types of family disorganization, and his later summary of types of personal and social disorganization as found in Chicago.[10] A host of other studies were made, and numerous other aspects of community living were found to vary characteristically according to the zonal pattern.

Natural areas, on the other hand, were smaller than zones, products of the natural growth of the city, each showing its own customary type of land use, social activity, people, and so on. Natural areas were produced by the natural interplay of social forces, and these were studied in relation to one another. They formed important focuses for investigation in such works as Shaw's study of delinquency areas, Wirth's study of the ghetto, Zorbaugh's study of the Gold Coast and the slum, and many others.[11] Such natural areas constituted important sociological units, standing to each other in an intricate network of spatial and functional relationships as the signif-

9. Ernest W. Burgess, "Urban Areas," in *The Urban Community.*

10. See Walter C. Reckless, *Vice in Chicago* (Chicago: University of Chicago Press, 1933); Robert E . L. Faris and H. Warren Dunham, *Mental Disorders in Urban Areas: An Ecological Study of Schizophrenia and Other Psychoses* (Chicago: University of Chicago Press, 1939); Ernest R. Mowrer, *The Family: Its Organization and Disorganization* (Chicago: University of Chicago Press, 1932); and Ernest R. Mowrer, *Disorganization, Personal and Social* (New York: Lippincott, 1942).

11. See Clifford R. Shaw, *Delinquency Areas* (Chicago: University of Chicago Press, 1929); and Clifford R. Shaw and H. D. McKay, *Juvenile Delinquency and Urban Areas* (Chicago: University of Chicago Press. 1942; Louis Wirth, *The Ghetto* (Chicago: University of Chicago Press, 1928); and Harvey W. Zorbaugh, *The Gold Coast and the Slum* (Chicago: University of Chicago Press, 1929).

icant units whose interrelated aggregate constituted the vast city community.

Concentric zones and natural areas were seen not as static areas whose characteristics were fixed but as the arenas and the resultants of important social and ecological processes. The more specific ecological processes included concentration and dispersion of people, centralization and decentralization of functions, segregation, invasion, and succession. Competition was seen as a basic, if not *the* basic, process underlying the others.

Thus, the Chicago sociologists evolved a dynamic conception of the urban community as the resultant of an ecological process in which there was an interdependence of spatial and social functions through time and according to which a sort of comparative morphology for the study of urban communities could be developed. They provided a basis for subsequent developments in urban sociology, developments that, incidentally, had the effect of disappointing some of the more optimistic hopes of the students of the Chicago community.

For as studies were made in other cities, it was found that these cities did not all follow a concentric zone pattern. Many of the other findings in Chicago seem to have been related more to the peculiar exigencies of time and place, the Chicago of the twenties and thirties, than to American cities in general. In his 1960 book Maurice Stein has made an excellent critique of the Chicago group, pointing out its undeniable contribution but also indicating the extent to which the phenomena that it reported so well were peculiarly influenced by the city's rapid growth and the heavy influx of various ethnic groups during the period of the studies and in the decades immediately preceding them.[12] He points out that one of the difficulties of arriving at scientific generalizations from community studies is the fact that community phenomena vary so much in time and place. In developing an approach that will help community studies to "add up" rather than constitute discrete, noncumulative entities, he calls for a dynamic theory of community change and suggests one based on the interrelated processes of urbanization, bureaucratization, and industrialization. In effect, he maintains that generalization from individual community studies will be facilitated if investigators will first locate their communities within these three dimensions of moving change. In this respect, Stein represents a more recent tendency to come to grips with the two related problems of the difficulty of generalizing from individual community studies and the

---

12. *The Eclipse of Community: An Interpretation of American Studies* (Princeton: Princeton University Press, 1960).

need for an adequate theoretical framework within which to locate the community studied within a change sequence.[13]

The Community as People

Early recognition that a community was more than a mere municipal jurisdiction, but involved an interdependent complex of living patterns on the local level, made appropriate a consideration of the people themselves who made up *the community's population.* The federal Census supplied data on the numbers and characteristics of people according to geographic locality, and the recording of vital statistics for purposes of keeping track of what was happening to people in terms of births, deaths, and marital status provided a constant source of statistical material about the constitution of the population and what was happening to it. The usefulness of such demographic material in community studies became apparent in several ways.

Perhaps most obviously, the individual character of a community is determined to a great extent by the kinds of people who live there. Thus, the high proportion of children and people sixty-five and over in many small villages has its influence on village social life. New mining and lumber communities reflect in their robust vigor the predominance of males in the prime of life and the relative absence of mothers, sisters, and wives. "Cultural islands" of racial and nationality groups stamp their special imprint on a city, as the Irish in Boston and the Mormons in Salt Lake City. Thus, it is customary for studies of individual communities to make a careful analysis of the kinds of people who reside there: the number and percentage in various age groups, the ratio of the sexes to each other by age groups, the numbers and percentage of people of different racial or nationality groups. In communities of any but the smallest size such analysis for different geographical segments of the community is particularly enlightening. Several studies describing the peculiar constitution of the population in various types of natural areas have been made. The differences in age and sex alone between, say, a skid-row section, a middle-class residential area, and an apartment and rooming-house area may be tremendous.[14] An additional aspect

---

13. A broad selection of studies in human ecology, many related to local communities, is given in George A. Theodorson, ed., *Studies in Human Ecology* (Evanston, Ill.: Row, Peterson & Co., 1961). Subsequent work continuing the Chicago School inquiry has emphasized more of the cultural aspects of ecology. See Gerald D. Suttles, *The Social Construction of Communities* (Chicago: University of Chicago Press, 1972) and Albert Hunter, *Symbolic Communities: The Persistence and Change of Chicago's Local Communities* (Chicago: The University of Chicago Press, 1974).

14. Calvin F. Schmid, *Social Trends in Seattle* (Seattle: University of Washington Press, 1944), p. 92.

of the population often studied is that of the mobility of people, both within the community and between communities.

For the study of the individual community, an additional dimension is that of time. Thus, changes and rates of change through a period of time may be established and a picture acquired of what has been happening with respect to the kinds of people who make up the community. Of greater practical importance, projections of population estimates of various groups or of various sections of the community can be made for the future, affording a basis for future planning of community policies, services, and facilities.

Such demographic material has been found useful on a more general level as well. Beyond the task of understanding the precise situation in any particular community lies the larger task of making general statements about communities, with size, functional specialization, spatial organization, growth in population, and so on held constant. Thus, it is possible to make general statements about communities of a particular type. As an example, one might ask, How does the population of the suburbs differ, generally, from that of central cities, or from cities that are independent of metropolitan areas? Here is an earlier answer based on careful demographic research executed in 1950:

> Whether the comparison is with their own central cities or with independent cities, suburbs are distinctive in a series of inter-related traits. The suburban population is relatively homogeneous, ethnically; that is, a high proportion is native white. It enjoys a relatively high socio-economic status, as indicated by occupational composition, average educational attainment, or income. The suburban population shows evidences of a stronger familistic bent than the other urban population, in its comparatively high proportions married and levels of fertility, and its low rate of female labor force participation.[15]

Similar statements can be made about cities with rapid growth rates in contrast to those with slow growth or declining rates; about cities in one region as compared with those in another; about large cities as compared with medium-sized or smaller ones; about manufacturing cities as compared with trade-center cities, and so on.

Demographic analysis thus provides an approach to community studies that enables the student to proceed beyond the limited task of describing a specific community to the scientifically more important task of making general statements about a whole class of

15. Reprinted with permission from Otis Dudley Duncan and Albert J. Reiss, Jr., *Social Characteristics of Urban and Rural Communities, 1950* (New York: John Wiley & Sons, copyright 1956), p.6.

phenomena, in this case, a whole category of cities. Such analysis, as already indicated above, need not confine itself to the more conventional demographic data, but may take into consideration any statistically ascertainable and socially significant variable, such as per capita income, percentage of people on public welfare rolls, percentage of married females working, crime rates, and so on. Thus, Seeley and his associates made interesting analyses seeking to ascertain statistically what variables were positively associated with successful community chest and united fund campaigns.[16] Thorndike made a series of studies of "goodness" of American communities, attempting to establish the existence of significant statistical relationships between such "goodness" and a number of different variables that he thought might be related to it. His method of measuring "goodness" and "badness" was courageous, ingenious, and naive, but his efforts represented a significant attempt to translate such vague but important terms into operational definitions and then to test hypotheses with a number of cities in order to arrive at general, scientifically verifiable statements.[17]

Later, Robert Cooley Angell conducted a series of intercommunity studies using various measures that could be constructed from available statistical material. His purpose was to investigate what factors were associated with high moral integration in American cities, whether positively or negatively. He found that a combined crime index and welfare-effort index constituted the most efficient indicator of moral integration. On this basis, he assigned 43 cities with 100,000 or more population in 1940 an "integration index." He then tested the relationship between nine variables and moral integration in these cities. Four variables proved to show no significant relationship: size, income level, church membership, and percentage of people in small businesses among all business people. The remaining five showed a significant relationship to moral integration, in each case inverse. These were heterogeneity, mobility, rate of city growth, percentage of married women working, and rental spread. Of these, heterogeneity and mobility were crucial in the sense that they alone accounted for about as much variation as all five indicators combined.[18]

16. John R. Seeley et al., *Community Chest: A Case Study in Philanthropy* (Toronto: University of Toronto Press, 1957).

17. See E. L. Thorndike, *Your City* (New York: Harcourt, Brace, 1939), and *144 Smaller Cities* (New York: Harcourt, Brace, 1940).

18. See Robert C. Angell, "The Social Integration Of American Cities of More than 100,000 Population," *American Sociological Review*, vol. 12, no. 3 (June1947), and *The Moral Integration of American Cities* (Chicago: University of Chicago Press, 1951). Parts of both of these reports are incorporated into "The Moral Integration of American Cities," in Paul K. Hatt and Albert J. Reiss, Jr., *Cities and Society: The Revised Reader in Urban Sociology* (Clencoe, Ill.: The Free Press, 1957).

There have been no notable recent studies paralleling in scope and objective those of Thorndike and Angell; however a few writers have considered which characteristics would go into a "good" community.[19]

A somewhat different type of approach permits classification of social areas within the city according to economic, family, and ethnic status. This type of "social area analysis" has been developed particularly by Shevky and Bell.[20]

The Community as Shared Institutions and Values

The community concept, in addition to factors of space and population, includes the notion of *shared institutions and values*. Putting this another way, geographic area and people do not in themselves constitute a community. One must also look for institutions commonly shared and values commonly held by the local population. As we have seen, the area of shared institutional services, far from being secondary, is actually one of the most important ways of delineating communities. But more than this, the shared institutional services are thought to constitute a shared way of life, a level of participation on which people come together in significant relationships for the provision of certain necessary living functions. As indicated earlier, the function of making accessible locally the various institutional facilities for daily living needs is, from the ecological standpoint, the chief reason for existence of the community. If these institutional provisions are conceived broadly, they go far beyond the provision of employment opportunities, stores, and personal or professional services. In aggregate, they constitute a total pattern of living, involving the comprehensive organization of behavior on the locality basis.

The study of communities as a total pattern of living was for a long time largely the interest of anthropologists, whose investiga-

19. Lawrence Haworth, *The Good City* (Bloomington: Indiana University Press, 1963); Roland L. Warren, "The Good Community—What Would It Be?," *Journal of the Community Development Society*, vol. 1, no. 1 (Spring 1970); and "Toward A Non-Utopian Normative Model of the Community," *American Sociological Review*, vol. 35, no. 4 (April 1970); Leonard S. Cottrell, Jr., "The Competent Community," chapter 11 in Berton H. Kaplan, Robert N. Wilson, and Alexander H. Leighton, eds., *Further Explorations in Social Psychiatry* (New York: Basic Books, 1976).

20. See Eshref Shevky and Wendell Bell, *Social Area Analysis* (Stanford, Calif.: Stanford University Press, 1955); Eshref Shevky and Marilyn Williams, *The Social Areas of Los Angeles: Analysis and Typology* (Berkeley: University of California Press, 1949); and Wendell Bell, "Social Areas: Typology of Urban Neighborhoods," in Marvin B. Sussman, ed., *Community Structure and Analysis* (New York: Thomas Y. Crowell, 1959). For a collection of ecological and demographic studies of urban communities, see Leo F. Schnore, *The Urban Scene: Studies in Human Ecology and Demography* (New York: Free Press, 1965).

tions were directed almost exclusively at the relatively "primitive" communities of cultures remote from western civilization. Such communities were relatively small, simple, and self-sufficient, although their relation to the surrounding tribe, society, or culture area was seldom overlooked by ethnographers.

The study of an American community with such a comprehensive frame of reference was embodied in the Lynds' investigations of 'Middletown." Consciously eyeing the work of the cultural anthropologists, the Lynds sought to apply their broad framework of analysis to a small American city. In their words:

> This study, accordingly, proceeds on the assumption that all the things people do in this American city may be viewed as falling under one or another of the following six main-trunk activities: Getting a living, Making a home, Training the young, Using leisure in various forms of play, art, and so on, Engaging in religious practices, Engaging in community activities. . . . By viewing the institutional life of this city as simply the form which human behavior under this particular set of conditions has come to assume, it is hoped that the study has been lifted on to an impersonal plane that will save it from the otherwise inevitable charge at certain points of seeming to deal in personalities or to criticize the local life. . . . Even though such a venture in contemporary anthropology may be somewhat hazy and distorted, the very trial may yield a degree of detachment indispensable for clearer vision.[21]

The fieldwork for the first study was completed in 1925. A restudy of the community was made in 1935, after a decade marked by the violent swing from unprecedented national prosperity to severe depression.[22] This second study likewise used a broad institutional approach to the total community. In addition, it extended the time dimension, which was already included in the first study, by incorporating as much pertinent baseline data from the year 1890 as was available. The Middletown studies marked a milestone in the development of knowledge about American communities, and we shall return to them in greater detail later.

A few years after the second Middletown study, another study was made, even more deliberately anthropological, of a small community in the central part of the United States. For purposes of anonymity, the community was called Plainville, and the author, an anthropologist, did not reveal his own name but used the pseud-

21. Robert S. Lynd and Helen Merrell Lynd, *Middletown: A Study in Contemporary American Culture* (New York: Harcourt, Brace, 1929), pp.4-5.

22. Robert S. Lynd and Helen Merrell Lynd, *Middletown in Transition: A Study in Cultural Conflicts* (New York: Harcourt, Brace, 1937).

onym James West. The fieldwork was done during the summers of 1939, 1940, and 1941. West attempted "to learn specifically and in detail how one relatively isolated and still 'backward' American farming community reacts to the constant stream of traits and influences pouring into it from cities and from more 'modern' farming communities."[23] In the course of the study West came to recognize three aspects of Plainville's development to be of crucial importance, and he gave them special attention. The first was the local system of social stratification, according to which people behaved differently and were differentially treated. Another was the process of socialization, according to which the young were inculcated with the values and behavior patterns of the somewhat distinctive local culture. The third was the "agony of social and economic reorientation" in which Plainville and the surrounding region found themselves as a result of the impact of the recently established federal agencies of the New Deal.

Like the Middletown studies, this study of Plainville represented an attempt to describe the major institutions of everyday living—the ways people get their living, their religious activities, their clubs and organizations, and so on—not only in terms of the structure of their organizations but in terms of the behavior patterns and belief systems that went along with them. Numerous other studies have employed what might be considered an institutional approach to the study of the community. An additional focus of interest and investigation has been the major values that the people in a community hold. Both West and the Lynds had acknowledged the important role of values, the underlying, often unverbalized principles according to which things were judged to be "good" or "bad." The chapter on "The Middletown Spirit" in the second Middletown volume is widely known not only for its deliberate and extensive attempt to articulate some of these principal values held by the people of Middletown, but also because it pointed out many of the self-contradictions in the values themselves.

Shared values are thought of not only as a basic component of what is meant by the community, but also as an important item on which communities often differ greatly from each other. Some years ago a series of studies of six rural communities was conducted under the auspices of the Bureau of Agricultural Economics of the United States Department of Agriculture. One of these communities, El Cerrito, New Mexico, will be considered at some length in chapter 4. The communities were selected not as a strict geographic sampling

---

23. James West, *Plainville, U.S.A.* (New York: Columbia University Press, 1945), p. vii. A restudy two decades later was made by Art Gallaher, Jr., *Plainville Fifteen Years Later* (New York: Columbia University Press, 1961).

of American rural communities "but as samples of, or points on, a continuum from high community stability to great instability."[24] The communities differed from each other in many important ways, not the least of which was the values shared by their inhabitants. Sanders illustrated these differences by summarizing three different types of values in these communities. The values regarding thrift and debt are perhaps the most interesting.

> In the Kansas county, penny pinching is frowned upon and debt is an expected state of affairs. Similarly in Harmony, Georgia, the planter tradition of enjoying life is still so strong that the people say, "Money is made round so that it will roll." On the other hand, the Spanish-Americans of El Cerrito are learning the importance of keeping out of debt, not because they stress thrift but because debt frequently has meant foreclosure and the loss of the home, their most cherished possession. In Iowa there is a promptness in paying one's bills and a general attitude of squeezing the orange pretty dry. It does not duplicate the thrift of Landaff, New Hampshire, which borders on miserliness prompted mainly by the desire to be independent and the difficulty of the economic struggle in the days of settlement, nor is it the thriftiness of the Amish, which by tradition is a part of their religion. It partakes of both of these, however, because pioneer attitudes that were largely Puritan are still strong.[25]

The six communities described above differed drastically in geographical region, type of local culture, and many other factors. Could different values be found to make significant differences in the lives of communities that are close to each other physically and similar in other important respects? Du Wors addressed himself to this question in a study of two adjacent communities, Eastport and Lubec, in eastern Maine. Despite the fact that these two communities were in the same town and were similar in ecology, technology, economics, and population, they showed marked differences in community behavior that could only be understood in terms of their different values.

Eastport was larger and seemed wealthier with its big houses, brick high school, brick library, and brick city hall. Lubec had no library, a tiny town office, and a ramshackle high school.[26] Eastport

---

24. Olen Leonard and C. P. Loomis, *Culture of a Contemporary Rural Community: El Cerrito, New Mexico* (Washington: U.S. Department of Agriculture, 1941), Foreword.

25. Irwin T. Sanders, *Making Good Communities Better*, rev. ed. (Lexington: University of Kentucky Press, 1953), p. 22.

26. Richard E. Du Wors, "Persistence and Change in Local Values of Two New England Communities," *Rural Sociology* 17, no. 3 (September 1952): 210.

went systematically into debt, while Lubec systematically stayed within its budget. Eastport used ten times the amount for WPA, a federal relief program, than Lubec did. Other differences in behavior were noticeably great, all tending to support the general comment of local inhabitants that Eastport was "sporty" while Lubec was "thrifty." At first dismissing these suggestions as unreliable stereotypes, Du Wors gradually became convinced that they were descriptive of actual value differences that were of crucial importance. "At best, Eastport's constellation of dominant values included a high respect for the fine arts and learning. . . . At worst, the community values involved an irresponsible hedonism. Lubec's values, at best, included a high sense of responsibility for community and financial stability. At worst, these values involved a narrowness identified with Puritanism in popular thinking.[27]

A somewhat similar study was made of two communities less than fifty miles apart in the southwestern section of the United States. Though alike in many circumstances, they showed marked differences in behavior, differences that could be summarized by the statement that "the stress upon *community cooperation* in Rimrock contrasts markedly with the stress upon *individual independence* found in Homestead."[28] The investigators attributed this great difference in values underlying community behavior to the fact that Rimrock settlers started early in their habits of cooperation, perhaps because of their common adherence to the Mormon Church, while in Homestead the earlier settlers had come as individual families from various parts of the country farther east and had settled on individual farmsteads, a pattern that tended to reinforce the stress on individualism.

Du Wors stated in his study: "The 'community' originates in the common acceptance of like definitions of recurring life situations. This acceptance of like definitions gives a certain uniqueness, a separateness, a 'personality,' that marks a community as one and not another."[29] Shared values are expressed through such like definitions of life situations and the behavior that results from such like definitions.

This approach to communities can easily overemphasize the extent of value differences among individual communities. In later chapters of this book, it is maintained that the shared values forming part of the "glue" that holds communities together are not necessar-

---

27. "Persistence," p. 211.

28. Evon Z. Vogt and Thomas F. O'Dea, "A Comparative Study of the Role of Values in Social Action in Two Southwestern Communities," *American Sociological Review* 18, no. 6 (December 1953): 648.

29. "Persistence," p. 211.

ily values unique to each community, but are commonly held values of the larger society (see especially chapter 14).

The Community as Interaction

A fourth general area of interest in community studies has been the *interaction* of local people, their association with one another and their behavior with regard to one another. The usual procedure has been to investigate the behavior associated with such major institutional areas as the family, the church, government, education, economic endeavor, and so on, thus considering the processual aspects of the community's institutions as well as their merely structural aspects. Another approach has been to use as a point of departure certain basic social processes such as conflict, competition, disorganization, and dissociation and explore their operation on the community level.[30]

A few decades ago it did not appear particularly difficult to describe the major areas of community behavior and the behavior patterns discernible therein. With the rapid increase in complexity of American communities and the attendant increasing orientation of units within the community toward extracommunity systems, however, the delineation and description of community behavior becomes more difficult. A current resolution of this difficulty being developed by a number of students of the community is called the *community action* approach. These investigators point out that a clear distinction must be made between local behavior that actually is a community phenomenon and local behavior that nevertheless is only remotely related to the community. Let us consider this distinction briefly.

Not all behavior occurring in the local community is a product of the interaction of people at the community level. Behavior within the family, for example, is largely determined by role patterns within the family group that tend to follow patterns in the larger culture rather than patterning themselves community by community. On the other hand, certain organizations operating in the community follow a patterned structure and patterned procedures that are prescribed by a national organization and show little variation by communities. If some local behavior is more relevant to the community as a social entity than other behavior, it becomes important to establish criteria with which one can recognize community-oriented behavior. Behavior meeting these criteria may then be appropriately studied as community behavior, while other behavior may best be

---

30. This was the specific approach of Jessie Bernard's *American Community Behavior* (New York: Dryden Press, 1949).

studied in terms of the extracommunity systems (for example, the United States Post Office) or intracommunity systems (for example, individual families) to which it is most closely related.

Investigators who have followed this community action approach generally agree that there should be no rigid dichotomy between community behavior and other behavior that takes place locally, but that community-relatedness should be considered a variable. Any particular local action should be identifiable somewhere along a continuum from the least community-related to the most community-related. A local referendum on floating a school bond issue would be replete with community relevance and far over toward that extreme of the scale, while the institution of a change in postal rates at the local post office branch would be far over toward the opposite extreme.

Thus, community behavior as such is much narrower than the whole range of behavior that takes place at the local level, and the community should not be considered as embracing all social life in a geographic area, the entire "locality agglomerate," as one writer has called it, but rather as the "interactional community."[31]

Various sets of criteria have been offered as a basis for identifying local actions with community relevance. One student has proposed the following set of dimensions for differentiating community actions: "(1) the degree of comprehensiveness of interests pursued and needs met, (2) the degree to which the action is identified with the locality, (3) relative number, status, and degree of involvement of local residents, (4) relative number and significance of local associations involved, (5) degree to which the action maintains or changes the local society, and (6) extent of organization of the action."[32]

Kaufman has gone further and suggested that community behavior be studied not so much from the standpoint of a circum scribed locality in space as from the standpoint of an "interactional

31. Harold F. Kaufman, "Toward an Interactional Conception of Community," *Social Forces* 38, no. 1 (October 1959): 13. Copyright © 1959, University of North Carolina Press (by assignment from Williams and Wilkins Company). A similar distinction has been made between "community" and "local society." See Willis A. Sutton, Jr., and Jiri Kolaja, "Elements of Community Action," *Social Forces* 38, no. 4 (May 1960): 325.

32. Kaufman, "Interactional Conception of Community," p. 13. A somewhat similar set of criteria is offered by Sutton and Kolaja in "The Concept of Community," *Rural Sociology*, vol. 25, no. 2 (June 1960). See also their "Elements of Community Action." Green and Mayo use five criteria for the classification of community actions: "These are: (1) locale, (2) temporal limits, (3) action orientation, (4) action objects, and (5) the actor," Cf. James W. Green and Selz C. Mayo, "A Framework for Research in the Actions of Community Groups," *Social Forces* 31, no. 4 (May 1953): 321ff. Copyright © 1953, University of North Carolina Press (by assignment from Williams and Wilkins Company).

field," somewhat related to Kurt Lewin's "field theory" analysis.[33] "The interactional field," writes Kaufman, "probably has several dimensions, the limits and interrelation of which need to be determined. The community field is not a Mother Hubbard which contains a number of other fields, but rather is to be seen as only one of the several interactional units in a local society."[34]

Community action sociologists, then, circumscribe the concept of community, making it much narrower than the local society as a whole. Their other special emphasis is on the study of individual actions of the community, rather than on general processes or structure. This represents a radical departure from the usual theoretical approach, one whose possibilities will no doubt be explored more fully in the next few years. In addition, as Green and Mayo assert,

> Even in those studies of communities in which the functions performed by structural elements have been featured, the group or organization itself is the major focus or unit of analysis. . . . Would not a more direct approach be desirable, i.e., to focus attention on action per se rather than on the structure which gave it birth? This, it is believed, can be accomplished by making *an action* itself the unit of analysis. If this is done, however, it is necessary to revise rather radically the customary method of carrying on community research; a revision of the usual sociological framework is required.[35]

Such an approach leads to the consideration of the community not primarily as a locality group but rather as a series of interrelated actions. The full implications of this theoretical orientation have not yet been fully explored.[36]

It has been possible for community-action sociologists not only to develop a set of criteria for identifying community actions, but also a set of criteria for the study of actions through time. Green and Mayo suggest that community actions be analyzed in terms of four

33. See Kurt Lewin, *Field Theory in Social Science*, ed. Dorwin Cartwright (New York: Harper & Brothers, 1951).

34. "Interactional Conception of Community," p. 10.

35. "Community Groups," pp. 320-21.

36. Recently Kaufman has explored further the community interaction approach, and Wilkinson has dealt with the subject using the concept of "field." See, for example, Harold F. Kaufman and Kenneth P. Wilkinson, *Community Structure and Leadership* (Mississippi State University, Social Science Research Center Bulletin 13, June 1967), and Kenneth P. Wilkinson, "The Community as a Social Field," *Social Forces*, vol. 48, no. 3 (March 1970). As indicated in the Epilogue, it is of course possible to emphasize interaction in the concept community to the exclusion of space or locality orientation. Israel Rubin does this in a challenging article, "Function and Structure of Community: Conceptual and Theoretical Analysis," *International Review of Community Development*," nos. 21 and 22 (1969).

stages: "(1) the initiation of action or 'idea'; (2) goal definition and planning for achievement; (3) the implementation of plans; and (4) goal achievement and consequences." They give guidelines for the analysis of action at each of these stages.[37]

Kaufman proposes a five-phase model, pointing out that two or more phases may be carried on concurrently. These phases are: (1) rise of interest, (2) organization and maintenance of sponsorship, (3) goal setting and the determination of specific means for their realization, (4) gaining and maintaining participation, and (5) carrying out the activities that represent goal achievement.[38]

The development of a field of interest around the process of community development has led to an interest in action models that arise in the process of planned social change. The field of community action and community development comprises the subject matter of chapter 10 of this book.

The Community as a Distribution of Power

Few developments in the field of community studies in recent years have made such a vast impact on community theory, research, and practice as the growth of *community power-structure* analysis. This has been a means of coming to grips with the observable fact that certain individuals in the community exercise much more influence on what goes on than do others. Recent study has been concerned with ascertaining the extent to which this is true, just how much influence is wielded, by whom, how, on what issues, and with what results.

The concept of differential ability to influence social behavior is not itself a new one. Thrasymachus, in Plato's *Republic*, gives a vivid description of how members of a ruling group are able to utilize the state and political institutions for their purposes, and a "ruling class" theory has developed through such classic works as those of Machiavelli, Marx, Mosca, and Pareto. The concept of social power is related to this special degree in which some people influence the actions of others. A classical definition of such power was given by Max Weber, who wrote, "In general, we understand by 'power' the chance of a man or of a number of men to realize their own will in a communal action even against the resistance of others who are participating in the action."[39] For centuries it has been realized that such influence over collective action is not confined to the

37. "Community Groups," pp. 323ff.

38. "Interactional Conception of Community," p. 13.

39. *From Max Weber: Essays in Sociology,* trans. and ed. H. H. Gerth and C. Wright Mills (New York: Oxford University Press, 1946), p. 180.

prerogatives of a formal office, such as king, president, general, and so on, but that it can be of other types, as well.

In the second Middletown study the Lynds devoted an entire chapter to "The X Family: A Pattern of Business-Class Control" and pointed out the inordinate influence that members of this leading industrial family exerted in various aspects of the institutional life of that city and the channels through which this influence was exercised.[40] Likewise, in the Yankee City study Warner and his associates described the manner in which concentrated power was wielded by the upper classes in that community, and Hollingshead, in his social class analysis of the youth of a small midwestern city, showed specifically how the school system was controlled by a small number of upper-class people and made to function for their own interests.[41]

The more recent interest and activity in the field of the exercise of social power at the community level was largely set in motion by a study of community power structure by Floyd Hunter. Defining power as "a word that will be used to describe the acts of men going about the business of moving other men to act in relation to themselves or in relation to organic or inorganic things," he studied community power in a southeastern city that is a regional center of finance, commerce, and industry.[42] The book focused its attention on the 40 persons who were found to be the top power leaders in the community. He located these 40 people essentially by canvassing those in a position to know within business, government, civic associations, and "society" activities. From a list of 175 suggested names, 40 were chosen as the top leaders as follows: 11 from large commercial enterprises, 7 from banking and investment, 6 from the professions, 5 from industry, 4 from government, 2 from labor, and 5 classified as "leisure personnel." Although the method of selection was more complex than is indicated above, it nevertheless constituted a relatively simple method that apparently yielded good results and could easily be emulated and refined.

Through carefully planned interviews with these leading power figures and through other community-study methods, Hunter was able to gain a picture of the influence that these individuals wielded, the channels through which they wielded it, the relation of these power figures to each other, and the patterns through which community action in Regional City took place.

40. *Middletown in Transition*, chap. 3.

41. W. Lloyd Warner and Paul S. Lunt, *The Social Life of a Modern Community* (New Haven, Conn.: Yale University Press, 1941); August B. Hollingshead, *Elmtown's Youth: The Impact of Social Classes on Adolescents* (New York: John Wiley & Sons, 1949).

42. *Community Power Structure: A Study of Decision Makers* (Chapel Hill: University of North Carolina Press, 1953), pp. 2-3.

Hunter found that these power leaders generally not only knew each other personally but were in frequent interaction with each other, much more so than chance would allow. Their frequent interaction often involved joint efforts in community affairs. This group of leaders was at the top of the power pyramid, and its influence was found to be exerted through organizational positions and through formal and informal connections with a whole group of subordinate leaders who usually did not participate in making major community policy decisions but were active in implementing such decisions. "This pattern of a relatively small decision-making group working through a larger under-structure is a reality, and if data were available, the total personnel involved in a major community project might possibly form a pyramid of power, but the constituency of the pyramid would change according to the project being acted upon."[43] Thus, though major power was exercised by this group of leaders, they were not all necessarily involved in any single action at the same time.

Hunter emphasized two important characteristics of the power system in Regional City. The first was that economic interests tended to dominate it. The second was that the formal leaders of community organizations and institutions were not necessarily the top people.

> In the general social structure of community life social scientists are prone to look upon the institutions and formal associations as powerful forces, and it is easy to be in basic agreement with this view. Most institutions and associations are subordinate, however, to the interest of the policy-makers who operate in the economic sphere of community life in Regional City.

> The organizations are not a sure route to sustained community prominence. Membership in the top brackets of one of the stable economic bureaucracies is the surest road to power, and this road is entered by only a few. Organizational leaders are prone to get the publicity; the upper echelon economic leaders, the power.[44]

Hunter found that the understructure of leadership through which top power leaders operate is not a rigid bureaucracy but a flexible system, including people described by top power leaders as first-, second-, third-, and fourth-rate. The first-raters are industrial, commercial, and financial owners and top executives of large enterprises. Second-raters include bank vice-presidents, people in public relations, owners of small businesses, top-ranking public officials,

43. Hunter, *Community Power Structure*, p. 65.
44. *Community Power Structure*, pp. 82, 86-87.

and so on. Third-raters are civic organization personnel, petty public officials, selected organizational executives, and so on, while fourth-raters are ministers, teachers, social workers, small-business managers, and the like.[45] Thus, people who hold office in one or another important civic activity may not be those who actually wield power but may be third- or fourth-raters among their lieutenants.

On community decisions of major importance, actions are considered and developed by top leaders and their immediate followers, or "crowds," and then spread out to a wider group of top leaders and crowds for further support and basic decision-making. Only much later, at the carrying-out stage, are the usual civic organization leaders, the press, and interested citizens' groups brought into the picture.

One of the reasons Hunter's book received so much attention was that it challenged much current thinking in the field of community organization and development, which tended to follow such procedures as "encouraging participation in policy-making by the people who will be affected by the policy," "letting plans arise from the felt needs of community people," "basing programs on grass-roots decisions," and so on. If basic community decisions are not made primarily at city hall or at the community welfare council but at the country club and even more exclusive clubs as well as in informal conferences among a small group of top leaders, then important community actions must be supported and approved by these top groups. Community planning agencies and professional leaders in such fields as public welfare and public health recognize this situation.

Actually, however, like other significant books, Hunter's left a number of important questions unresolved. Their resolution has led to a lot of research activity in the community field, and some of the answers are now beginning to appear in research reports.

One question that can be raised with regard to the concept of community power structure as developed by Hunter is, If the power structure is so important, how does it happen that it so often loses in the contest to determine a public issue? For example, in controversies involving the decision to fluoridate a community's water supply, the "power structure" is usually on the side of fluoridation, yet it often loses. Does the power configuration surrounding any particular community issue invariably take the form that Hunter describes, with top policy being determined by members of essentially the same small power group? Or is it not possible that on some community issues, decisive power is exercised by organizations and minor officials as prime movers, rather than merely as the henchmen of a

45. *Community Power Structure*, p. 109.

small power group? There are actually two issues here. One relates to the possible multiplicity of power pyramids, depending on the area of the community activity involved in the issue. The other has to do with the extent to which power on specific issues may fluctuate according to specific organizational campaigns, as against the more or less permanent structure of power wielding that Hunter described.

Turning to the first, a number of studies have been made bearing more or less directly on the question of one versus a number of power structures.[46] With few exceptions, these studies indicate that the picture is much more complex than the one Hunter described, and they indicate a multiplicity of power structures with the power pyramids being much less a tightly knit group of leaders in close interaction than was found in Regional City.

Regarding the more or less flexible aspects of power, as opposed to the concept of a fixed structure, the question would seem to be, To what extent is any particular community issue open to genuine contest, and to what extent is it already determined by the structure of existing power leadership and the attitudes of these leaders with relation to it? Many students of the community are willing to assign much more potential effectiveness to citizen campaigns, organizations promoting particular civic actions, newspaper opinion, and so on, than Hunter would allow. Putting this another way, the power situation surrounding a particular community decision is believed to be influenceable by the organizational activities of various citizens' groups. As Kornhauser asserted, regarding fluoridation controversies, "The anti-fluoridation forces often win in spite of their general lack of power and prestige, because in many cases they are able to mobilize people who, like themselves, are only poorly attached to the community."[47]

46. See Alexander Fanelli, "A Typology of Community Leadership Based on Influence and Interaction within the Leader Subsystem," *Social Forces*, vol. 34, no. 4 (May 1956); Roland J. Pellegrin and Charles H. Coates, "Absentee-Owned Corporations and Community Power Structure," *American Journal of Sociology*, vol. 61, no. 5 (March 1956); Robert O. Schulze and Leonard U. Blumberg, "The Determination of Local Power Elites," *American Journal of Sociology*, vol. 63, no. 3 (November 1957); Robert O. Schulze, "The Role of Economic Dominants in Community Power Structure," *American Sociological Review*, vol 23, no. 1 (February 1958); Nelson W. Polsby, "The Sociology of Community Power: A Reassessment," *Social Forces*, vol. 37, no. 3 (March 1959), and "Three Problems in the Analysis of Community Power," *American Sociological Review*, vol. 24, no. 6 (December 1959). The literature is, of course, too voluminous to list exhaustively here. Several of the above contain additional references to other studies.

47. William Kornhauser, *Power and Participation in the Local Community*, Health Education Monographs, no. 6 (Oakland, Calif.: Society of Public Health Educators, 1950), p. 33.

Investigators have also explored other aspects of power than just the making of decisions and obtaining of consent. These other important leadership activities might include initiating formal community proposals, supporting or fighting proposals through such visible means as fund raising, endorsing, public speaking in behalf of an issue, mobilizing extracommunity pressures, articulating, defining, and suppressing issues, and actually making decisions as a community official.[48]

Another question often raised regarding community power structure relates to the "conspiracy" dimension, that is, to what extent the power structure represents a self-consciously functioning group of people in league with each other to control the community and to manipulate subordinates and formal organizations in their own narrow interests. Most community sociologists who have investigated the question do not believe that such a conspirational dimension is operative to any considerable extent. Hunter himself seems to be somewhat ambivalent on this question, but in a later work on which he collaborated there was an excellent example of such cold, self-conscious manipulation. The issue involved the transfer of title of some public playground land from the city of Salem to a power company, a proposal that had generated considerable popular opposition. In the words of a leading attorney,

> In the electric plant situation the city council was on the spot because they had to stand up and be counted before a large group of citizens. To many of them it seemed like political suicide to vote for the land transfer, but the big brass in the community had been working on the city councilmen individually, "*reasoning*" with them, and they voted for the measure in spite of the fact that most of the civic associations, the veterans organizations, and a good many individual and substantial citizens were against it. One by one they voted as they were told to vote. It isn't very often that we have to have such a test of strength as this, but when the chips are down the interests that I am talking about will throw their weight around.[49]

A final question appropriate to the present discussion is that of the deliberate development and coming prominence of new sources of power through formal organization of such interest groups as organized labor, Blacks, and other racial or ethnic groups. There is considerable indication that officials of these and other voluntary organizations, whether representing special interests or promoting

---

48. Polsby, "Sociology of Community Power,". 233.

49. Floyd Hunter, Ruth Connor Schaffer, and Cecil G. Sheps, *Community Organization: Action and Inaction* (Chapel Hill: University of North Carolina Press, 1956), pp. 104-5.

broad planning or health and welfare goals, are exerting increasing power by virtue of their official positions and the strength of the organizations that they represent.[50]

The Community as a Social System

One of the most promising developments in community studies is the attempt to apply social-system analysis to community phenomena. The social-system concept is based on the idea of structured interaction between two or more units. In sociology these units may be persons or groups. Although the process of interaction among units is basic to the concept, the term social system is not applied to all instances of interaction but to structures of interaction that endure through time and can be recognized as entities in their own right.

Parsons described the social system as "a plurality of individual actors interacting with each other in a situation which has at least a physical or environmental aspect, actors who are motivated in terms of a tendency to the 'optimization of gratification' and whose relation to their situations, including each other, is defined and mediated in terms of a system of culturally structured and shared symbols."[51] Thus, a social system might be an individual family, an industrial company, a hospital, a football team, or a street-corner gang. All social systems according to Parsons are characterized by the following four coordinates: (1) goal attainment, or the gratifica-

---

50. More recent explorations of the "power" concept have taken three important emphases. The first is the continued pursuit of many of the questions raised by the earlier studies. Claire W. Gilbert made a systematic attempt to summarize the numerous findings in "Community Power and Decision-Making: A Quantitative Examination of Previous Research," in Terry N. Clark, ed., *Community Structure and Decision-Making: Comparative Analyses* (San Francisco: Chandler Publishing Co., 1968). Willis Hawley and Frederick M. Wirt, eds., provide a valuable collection of important articles in this field in *The Search for Community Power* (Englewood Cliffs, N.J.: Prentice-Hall, Inc., 1968, 1974), which also contains an extensive bibliography. There is also recent emphasis on multicity studies of community power configurations, especially as they affect decision-making. Clark, *Community Structure*, has this emphasis. A more recent example is Michael Aiken and Robert R. Alford, "Comparative Urban Research and Community Decision-Making," *The Atlantis*, vol. 1, no. 2 (Winter 1970). See also Clark's *Community Power and Policy Outputs: A Review of Urban Research* (Beverly Hills: Sage Publications, 1973). A third vein of elaboration has been associated with social action for a transfer of power from existing structures to sectors of the population who exercise little power. A popular example is Stokely Carmichael and Charles V. Hamilton, *Black Power: The Politics of Liberation in America* (New York: Vintage Books, 1967). John Walton has reviewed the development of community power studies since Hunter with a critical eye. See his "Community Power and the Retreat from Politics: Full Circle After Twenty Years?," *Social Problems*, vol. 23, no. 3 (February 1976). Chapters 11 and 12 of this present book treat some aspects of community power within the context of community change.

51. Talcott Parsons, *The Social System* (Glencoe, Ill.: Free Press, 1951), pp. 5-6.

tion of the units of the system; (2) adaptation, or the manipulation of the environment in the interests of goal attainment; (3) integration, or the attachment of member units to each other; (4) tension, or the malintegration of units seen as themselves systems.[52]

Over a period of years, Parsons has developed a comprehensive theory of social systems. Largely through his influence, social-system analysis has developed in connection with small-group structure and the structure of large organizations and entire societies. Although neither Parsons nor his followers have made a specific application of the theory to communities, they did carry social-system analysis to the point that it is now applied to the community as well.[53]

Meanwhile, Loomis has developed a theory of social systems and a set of tools for their analysis that he has been applying in rural sociological studies for many years.[54] Loomis pointed out that as interaction persists over a period of time it develops certain orderly and systematic uniformities and thus becomes a social system. "It is constituted of the interaction of a plurality of individual actors whose relations to each other are mutually oriented through the definition and mediation of a pattern of structured and shared symbols and expectations."[55]

For Loomis, social systems can be analyzed in terms of nine elements. These are: (1) *belief* (knowledge)—"any proposition about any aspect of the universe that is accepted as true"; (2) *sentiment*—

52. Talcott Parsons, Robert F. Bales, and Edward A. Shils, *Working Papers in the Theory of Action* (Glencoe, Ill.: Free Press, 1953), chap. 5. The above statement is taken from a codification of this work by Morris Zelditch, Jr., "A Note on the Analysis of Equilibrium Systems," in Talcott Parsons and Robert F. Bales, *Family, Socialization and Interaction Process* (Glencoe, Ill.: Free Press, 1955).

53. This statement is probably unfair to Mercer, who applied a modest form of Parsonian analysis in a book written in the 1950s. See Blaine E. Mercer, *The American Community* (New York: Random House, Inc., 1956). More recently, two other books have made direct application of Parsonian analysis to specific communities: Lois R. Dean, *Five Towns: A Comparative Community Study* (New York: Random House, 1967), and Harold Kaplan, *Urban Political Systems: A Functional Analysis of Metro Toronto* (New York: Columbia University Press, 1967). The social-system approach based on general systems theory rather than on Parsonian analysis specifically is beginning to find its way into the urban literature. See, for example, James Hughes and Lawrence Mann, "Systems and Planning Theory," *Journal of the American Institute of Planners*, vol. 35, no. 5 (September 1969), and Robert R. Mayer, "Social System Models for Planners," *Journal of the American Institute of Planners*, vol. 28, no. 3 (1972).

54. See Charles P. Loomis and J. Allan Beegle, *Rural Social Systems* (New York: Prentice-Hall, 1950), and *Rural Sociology: The Strategy of Change* (New York: Prentice-Hall, 1957). Loomis' recent, most thorough exposition of the social-system concept is to be found in *Social Systems: Essays on Their Persistence and Change* (Princeton: Van Nostrand, 1960), from which the description given here is taken.

55. Loomis, *Social Systems*, p. 4. Copyright © 1960, D. Van Nostrand Company, Inc., Princeton, N.J.

47

"sentiments are primarily expressive and represent 'what we feel' about the world no matter why we feel it"; (3) *end, goal, or objective*— "the change (or in some cases the retention of the *status quo*) that members of a social system expect to accomplish through appropriate interaction"; (4) *norm*—"more inclusive than written rules, regulations, and laws; they refer to all criteria for judging the character of conduct of both individual and group actions in any social system"; (5) *status role*—"that which is expected from an actor in a given situation"; (6; *power*—"the capacity to control others"; (7) *rank*—"equivalent to 'standing' and always [has] reference to a specific actor, system or sub-system"; (8) *sanction*—"rewards and penalties meted out by the members of a social system as a device for inducing conformity to its norms and ends"; (9) *facility*—"a means used to attain ends within the system."[56]

These are structural elements. One or more processes corresponds to each one. For example, the first element, belief knowledge), is characterized by the processes of cognitive mapping and validation, while the fourth element, norm, is characterized by the process of evaluation.

In addition, a social system involves certain comprehensive or master processes: (1) *communication*—"the process by which information, decisions, and directives are transmitted among actors and the ways in which knowledge, opinions, and attitudes are formed or modified by interaction"; (2) *boundary maintenance*—"the process whereby the identity of the social system is preserved and the characteristic interaction pattern maintained"; (3) *systemic linkage*— "the process whereby one or more of the elements of at least two social systems is articulated in such a manner that the two systems in some ways and on some occasions may be viewed as a single unit"; (4) *socialization*—"the process through which the social and cultural heritage is transmitted"; (5) *social control*—"the process by which deviancy is either eliminated or somehow made compatible with the functioning of the social groups"; and (6) *institutionalization*—"the process through which organizations are given structure and social action and interaction are made predictable."[57]

With such a set of elements and master processes, any social system can be analyzed and understood, whether it be a small group such as a married couple or a group of friends, an organization such as a ship's company or a retail store, or a nation-state such as the United States or China.

Can communities also be analyzed as social systems? This is a question of great theoretical importance, for if they can, if social-sys-

---

56. Loomis, *Social Systems*, pp. 11-29.

57. Loomis, *Social Systems*, pp. 30-36.

tem analysis "fits" communities as well as these other types of social entities, then students of the community do not have to start from scratch, as it were, and describe communities as though they were unique entities unlike other known social units. Rather, communities can be related to a whole class of other social entities—the class of social systems— and it can be ascertained how structural and processual elements, already known from other social systems, apply specifically to the community. What is known about communities can be related systematically to what is known about other social systems, and further, what is known about other social systems may afford rich hypothetical material for further community research.

This question will receive considerable attention throughout the rest of this book. Meanwhile, it is interesting to note certain ways in which communities tend to differ from other social entities designated as social systems, such as formal organizations. Another sociologist Edward O. Moe describes three important differences:

> *The community is a system of systems.* A community, even a small one, includes a great many different institutions and organizations and the formal and informal sub-groups that grow up within them. These organizations and groups are social systems and they are part of the social system of the community.
>
> *The community is not structurally and functionally centralized in the same sense as a formal organization.* The great range and diversity of the needs, interests, goals and activities of people of the community are met through a variety of separate institutions and groups—no one of which holds a completely dominant position in relation to the others.
>
> *The community as a social system is implicit in nature as compared with the explicitness of a formal organization.* This is true both of the community system as a totality, as well as of the various elements such as the goals of the people who live in the community, the prescribed means of achieving goals, and the underlying values.[58]

Strictly speaking, an organization, not only a community, may be a "system of systems." What distinguishes the community from such formal organizations in this respect is not the existence of subsystems, for both have them, but the fact that in the case of the community, these subsystems are not rationally and deliberately related to each other in centralized fashion, as indicated in the second and third points.

---

58. "Consulting with a Community System: A Case Study," *Journal of Social Issues*, 15, no. 2 (1959): 29.

An example of the enormous potential importance of being able to treat the community as a social system is found in the work of Lippitt, Watson, and Westley on the dynamics of planned social change.[59] This book examines various aspects of the process of planned social change involving collaboration between a change agent (consultant, case worker, group worker, and so on) and a "client system." Using the conceptual tools and processes of social-system analysis, the authors describe and analyze the process of planned change as it involves four different levels of client systems: the individual, the small group, the formal organization, and the community.

Sanders produced an excellent text that relates more specifically to the community. It is called, significantly, *The Community: An Introduction to a Social System,* in which he pointed out that "the basic unit of analysis for the study of a community is the subsystem (combined into major systems) and that the behavior of a community as a total system is greatly dependent upon the interaction among these subsystems."[60] Examples of "major systems" are family, economy, and government; examples of subsystems within the major system of government are political party, bureaucracy, and police.

The "systems within systems" relationship mentioned earlier is of crucial importance in system analysis as applied to the community. This matter will be given extensive treatment later but should be mentioned here as one of the potentially fruitful innovations in community study.

Let us compare, briefly, formal organizations and communities in their intersystem relationships. The office of the district sanitarian is a functioning social system, which, along with other such functioning social systems, goes to make up the district office of the city health department. Although a social system, in relation to the entire district office it is a subsystem. And the district office, in relation to the entire city health department, is also a subsystem. The health department in turn is a subsystem of the city government.

Consider a community. As a system, it is made up of different levels of system and subsystem such as the municipal government, the East Side Baptist Church, the branch plant of the ABC Products Corporation, and the American Red Cross chapter. Many of these, in their turn, are integral parts of larger social systems—the Southern Baptist Convention, the national company, the American National Red Cross—which extend far beyond the confines of the

59. Ronald Lippitt, Jeanne Watson, and Bruce H. Westley, *The Dynamics of Planned Change* (New York: Harcourt, Brace, 1958).

60. Irwin T. Sanders, *The Community: An Introduction to a Social System* (New York: Ronald Press Company, 1958, 1966, 1975), p. 192.

community. However the community itself as a social system does not similarly relate in such a direct way to any larger system. It has a diffuse relationship to the large social system called "American society," but this relationship is much more remote and much vaguer than that of one of the community's subsystems to its larger social system. When one looks for the relationship of the community as such (as distinguished from, say, its government) to a larger social system, one finds it related to extracommunity systems through the direct relation of its constituent subsystems, such as the local Cancer Society to the state organization or the local supermarket to its national chain.

Thus, social-system analysis applied to the community must consider not only the interrelation of the community's subsystems but the more direct, rational, and ascertainable relationship of the various subsystems functioning on the local level to social systems beyond the community. A particularly important point is the nature of the systemic linkage between various community-based units and their respective extracommunity social systems. The fact that certain local subsystems, like the U.S. Postal Service or the local chapter of the American Legion or the local supermarket, are simultaneously parts of two social systems—the local community and their national organizations—and that the norms, values, status roles, and so on, of the two social systems, whether mutually supporting or competing or conflicting, may be different is a fact of tremendous importance, which will receive further attention later.

We have now reviewed some of the older approaches to the study of communities, as well as some of the more recent ones. The social-system approach will be considered intensively beginning with chapter 5. Meanwhile, it will be useful to examine in a systematic fashion the changes that are transforming American community life.

3 The "Great Change" in American Communities

Changes on the community level are taking place at such a rapid rate and in such drastic fashion that they are affecting the entire structure and function of community living. How shall we grasp and analyze this vast, complex, manysided, interrelated process of change?

It is a thesis of this book that the "great change" in community living includes the increasing orientation of local community units toward extracommunity systems of which they are a part, with a corresponding decline in community cohesion and autonomy. As the relation of community units to state and national systems strengthens, the locus of decision-making often shifts to places outside the community. Decisions, policies, and programs of local units, although they must conform in some respects to community norms, come to be formulated in centralized offices outside the community and come to be guided more by their relation to extracommunity systems than by their relation to other parts of the local community. Thus, the ties between different local community units are weakened, and community autonomy, defined as control by local people over the establishment, goals, policies, and operations of local community units, is likewise reduced.

Social change is a process of alteration in the structure or functions of the parts of a society or other social system. At the level of community living, important changes have taken place and continue to take place in the structure and function of various parts of the community and in their relationship to one another. Since the specific instances of such change are almost innumerable, it is necessary to group them in some way and to analyze them within some meaningful framework. As mentioned, the overall framework of analysis that we shall use is that of change involving increasing orientation of community units toward extracommunity systems and of the corresponding decrease in community cohesion and autonomy.

The "great change" can be analyzed in terms of the following aspects, which constitute the outline for this chapter:

1. Division of labor
2. Differentiation of interests and association
3. Increasing systemic relationships to the larger society
4. Bureaucratization and impersonalization
5. Transfer of functions to profit enterprise and government
6. Urbanization and suburbanization
7. Changing values

American communities are changing in all these aspects, and the aggregate of these changes is drastic. Not all communities have changed or are changing at the same rate, either in aggregate or in connection with any one of the seven aspects. Thus, it becomes meaningful to attempt to locate any individual community with respect to any of the seven change aspects to be considered. Although these seven aspects are interrelated, change does not necessarily take place at the same rate in all seven, so a community may be retarded in one, advanced in another. In chapter 4 we shall examine four American community settings that represent, among other things, markedly different positions along the direction of change in these aspects.

In using the term *the great change,* we refer to a series of changes that have been taking place over a period of decades and even centuries. In the 1960s and 1970s, there developed in American society a period of turbulence in connection with the civil rights movement, the neighborhood control movement, and the youth revolt. Many aspects of this turbulence can be understood as a deliberate attempt to combat some of the results of the great change and to slow the change or reverse it. The hostility toward technology, the emphasis on participatory democracy, the increasing derogation of bureaucracy, the sense of diffidence toward the proliferation of gimmicks and gadgets, the questioning of competition and the work ethic, the resurgence of a "back to the land" movement in the rural communes—these and other developments signified a growing revolt against various aspects of the great change. Chapters 11 and 12 will treat some of these developments. In the present chapter we shall confine ourselves to delineating the long-term trends, postponing a consideration of these more recent counter-trends until those later chapters.

The seven changes described here are taking place throughout American society and are not confined to the community level. They are not the only changes taking place, but they are particularly significant for the community level. They are so closely interrelated that there is nothing final about the division of the "great change" into these seven aspects. One could have subsumed it all under four, or nine, or any reasonable number of meaningful headings. This outline seems adequate for incorporating the most relevant material, just as the concept of the "great change" is believed to summarize and conceptualize and characterize in a meaningful way the aggregate of these changes as they have transformed American communities.

It may be well at this point to recall certain basic concepts that have been utilized by social theorists to describe the grand direction of change in social relations in modern times. Characteristically, most of these conceptualizations of change are cast in terms of dichotomies, that is, mutually exclusive pairs of concepts. Somewhere between them the possibilities are covered; in most instances these mutually opposite descriptions are extreme points of a continuum. They represent the "ideal types," to use Weber's term, which may not be embodied completely in any single community but are models with which existing communities can be compared and between which existing communities can be ranged.

Henry Maine analyzed the historical change of social relations from those based essentially on family relations—a situation in which status in the family was the central focus of social life—to those based on the individual's relationships to others, which became increasingly independent of family ties and more formalized in the nature of a *contract*.[1]

The French sociologist Emile Durkheim developed the concept of "division of labor" and explored the relation of this process to change in the structure of society. He pointed out that societies with little division of labor are characterized by a type of solidarity that comes from a single set of values and behavior patterns. The cohesion characterizing such societies is derived from shared interests and values among people whose labor is similar, comprehensive, and

1. *Ancient Law* (New York: Charles Scribner, 1864), and *Village Communities East and West* (New York: Henry Holt, 1871-89).

undifferentiated. He described such cohesion as *mechanical solidarity.* With the division of labor, however, comes a splitting of social tasks and a corresponding interdependence of the parts of the increasingly complex society. People are held together not so much by shared values, which, indeed, may have been transformed into a state of "normlessness" or *anomie,* but rather by their mutual interdependence because they perform differentiated tasks within a complex whole.[2]

Likewise, Ferdinand Toennies developed a theory of change and a pair of opposite models of social relations between which to range any possible societies and against which to measure change.[3] He contrasted two basic types of groups. In one, relations of sympathy among the members is a primary feature and emphasis is on the value of the group in and for itself. Examples are family, neighborhood, and friendship groups. He called this basic type *Gemeinschaft.* In the contrasting type, the group's focus is on its purpose, or task; it is more rationally organized to achieve a purpose and shows greater formalization of interaction. Examples of this type of group are the city and the state, and this more rational, formalized, goal-oriented type he called *Gesellschaft.* These concepts represent not only abstract types of groups but also a model for the assessment of change, for in general change takes place from the Gemeinschaft type of human association toward the Gesellschaft type.

Loomis and Beegle have adapted Toennies' concepts to a useful means of comparing two or more social systems or a single system at two different times. They employed a four-dimensional scale, each dimension consisting of one aspect of the contrast between Gemeinschaft and Gesellschaft types. The dimensions are: (1) nonrational versus rational action; (2) functional diffuseness versus functional specificity; (3) community of fate versus limited responsibility; and (4) integration of roles within and outside the systems. In each case, the first-mentioned is the Gemeinschaft-like type, the second the Gesellschaft-like type.[4]

Other helpful conceptualizations of contrasting social types and of major directions of modern social change have been made, including the folk-urban distinction and the sacred-secular polarity. Perhaps it is sufficient at this point, however, simply to note that in

2. *The Division of Labor in Society,* trans. George Simpson (Glencoe, Ill.: Free Press, 1947), and *Suicide,* trans. John A. Spaulding and George Simpson (Glencoe, Ill.: Free Press, 1951).

3. *Gemeinschaft und Gesellschaft,* first published in 1887. For an English translation see Ferdinand Tönnies, *Community and Society (Gemeinschaft und Gesellschaft),* trans. and ed. Charles P. Loomis (New York: Harper Torch Books, 1963).

4. Charles P. Loomis and J. Allan Beegle, *Rural Social Systems: A Textbook in Rural Sociology and Anthropology* (New York: Prentice-Hall, 1950), pp. 18ff.

considering the subject matter of this chapter, we are in company with a great number of social scientists who have given attention to the problem of conceptualizing and describing the major dimensions of social change. While each contribution is helpful, none of them can lay claim to being accepted to the exclusion of all others as the only "correct," final, all-inclusive conceptualization.

Division of Labor

Some years ago, a governmental effort to describe different types of occupations in the United States labor force identified and defined some twenty-two thousand distinct jobs.[5] This figure documents a condition that is readily observable in American communities: a highly elaborate division of labor and specialization of occupational effort. But it is more than a condition; it is a process, for the division of labor continues to take place as functions become more narrowly defined and work becomes more specialized. The continuous process constitutes one of the dynamic elements of community living.

In a penetrating analysis, Durkheim pointed out the obvious concomitant of the process: an increasing interdependence of one person on another for things that one's own specialization does not provide. A complex social system has to accompany the specialization, in order to provide for the coordination of the specialized functions in production and for the distributive allocation of the products. People become united through this complex interdependent network of specialized effort on which they are jointly dependent, united as functionally interrelated parts of a complex system, rather than by virtue of sharing the same type of occupational skills, problems, and points of view.

What Durkheim analyzed in terms of mechanical and organic solidarity is described rather aptly by Hawley in his distinction between symbiotic and commensalistic relationships. The symbiotic relationship (of specialization and mutual interdependence) characterizes the "corporate" group, which is internally differentiated and symbiotically integrated. The "categoric" group, by contrast, is an association of functionally homogeneous individuals. The community, according to this conception, can be conceived as a "congeries of corporate and categoric groups."[6]

5. *Dictionary of Occupational Titles,* 2nd ed. (Washington: U.S. Government Printing Office, 1949).

6. Amos H. Hawley, *Human Ecology: A Theory of Community Structure* (New York: Ronald Press, 1950) pp. 209, 210.

In these terms, the change described here is one from a community based on categoric groups to one based on corporate groups. One might add that the community itself becomes more of a corporate than a categoric group as well. "The dynamics of the community," said Hawley, "as manifested in its day to day operation and in change in response to altered conditions, are traceable mainly to the corporate units. In contrast, the categoric group, by virtue of its homogeneous membership is capable of only the simplest kind of collective activity."[7] Thus a community characterized by more complex corporate groups is capable of a much greater proliferation of differentiated functions.

What does the increased specialization of occupational effort imply for the individual in the community? Most directly, it means that he or she produces a smaller and smaller portion of the things the family consumes. One's productive enterprise is separated almost completely from one's consumption of goods and services by the intervening network for distributive allocation mentioned above. In American society, the family farm has represented the closest type of relationship between the family as a unit of economic production and the family as a unit of economic consumption. The traditional family farm was highly self-sufficient. The trend toward specialization on the farm is of course part of the trend we are describing, and the absolute as well as proportionate number of farm families in the economy has decreased for several decades, a particularly significant instance of the change being considered here.

For the individual, it also means a change in the perception of one's work. The difference between a close relationship of one's work to the final product and a remote and in some instances practically unknown relationship of one's work to the final product is widely recognized. For example, the changing relation of the shoemaker to the finished pair of shoes was found to have important implications for job satisfaction in Yankee City.[8]

But there is another implication of such specialization. It means that people living in the same locality, rather than sharing a common universe of discourse regarding their common occupation, have no such strong occupational bond to unite them. Increasingly, within the locality, the individual wage-earner does not know what his or her next-door neighbor does for a living.

The change toward symbiotic interdependence and the accompanying proliferation of individualized functions have resulted in

7. Hawley, *Human Ecology*, pp. 210-11.

8. W. Lloyd Warner and J. O. Low, *The Social System of the Modern Factory: The Strike: A Social Analysis* (New Haven, Conn.: Yale University Press, 1947).

fewer of these functions being performed within the individual family. Thus, the family becomes less significant as a locus for recreational and service functions, as well as for those of economic production. This shift is illustrated by the transfer of "vocational guidance" functions from the parents to the school guidance specialist, the transfer of recreational functions to the recreational specialist. "I am learning how to climb trees," said one youngster to another in a cartoon. "Who's your instructor?" queried the other. The point can be summarized by saying that within American communities, functions formerly performed within the family have now become the specialized prerogative of functional specialists, such as appliance repairers, psychiatrists, guidance counselors, nurses, homemakers, and playground directors. Under these conditions, the family looks to the community as the significant social grouping within which such functions are available.

On the community level, the division of labor takes the form of the provision of an increasingly complex proliferation of specialized goods and services. It also has an important relationship to the "great change" in community structure and function, for the division of labor has constituted the dynamic of the process of structural differentiation within American communities. Such structural differentiation has resulted in a symbiotic interdependence of the type described by Durkheim. At the same time it has weakened the contribution that shared occupation and occupational interests make toward community cohesion. It is interesting that Durkheim, who documented with some interest and approval the increasing organic solidarity that accompanied the division of labor, made a classic study of suicide in which he observed that division of labor could also be accompanied by a certain normlessness, or *anomie,* a condition in which there was no longer general agreement among individuals regarding the norms that should guide their behavior.[9]

Differentiation of Interests and Association

A number of important community consequences arise from the process of differentiation of interests and association, for in this process the principal basis for social participation shifts from locality to interest. In the locality type of participation, individuals and families who share the same locality associate in neighborly fashion with others in the immediate vicinity. A unifying basis of interest underlying such association is that of the common locality. The fact that people live near each other means that their lives are intertwined.

---

9. Emile Durkheim, *Suicide,* trans. John A. Spaulding and George Simpson (Glencoe, Ill.: Free Press, 1951).

Such important functions as production and distribution, socialization of the young, social control, and mutual support are performed largely within the locality by such relatively undifferentiated groups as family and neighborhood. Further, since relatively little differentiation of labor has taken place, the families share a common interest in that they all are units of economic production, as in the earlier American preindustrial rural community.

The contrasting situation is a differentiation of interests among people in the locality and differential association based on the respective interests. The individual often turns away from other individuals in the immediate locality and associates with individuals from other localities on the basis of selective interests.

Individuals within the same family, or within the same neighborhood, participate in specialized, differentiated aspects of the larger culture and relate to others on the basis of similarity of interests rather than of locality. In this process, social relationships characteristic of the primary group are superseded by secondary-group relationships. In coining the term *primary group,* Cooley referred specifically to such groups as the family, the play group of children, and the neighborhood (note the similarity to Toennies' typical Gemeinschaft groups). He called such groups "primary" because of their fundamental importance in forming the attitudes and behavior patterns of their members.[10] Cooley's followers were quick to adopt another term, *secondary group,* to specify groups in which there is less intimacy, more formality, and less continuous face-to-face association. Where the primary group is intimate, involving the participation of the "whole" personality, the secondary group is more casual, and individuals participate with only that segment of their personality that represents the shared interest. Here again, there is not a rigid dichotomy, but a continuum between these two extremes.

The distinction is a profound one, for a shift toward association of the secondary-group type has characterized the increasing differentiation of interests and association. The implications for the individual and the community are important. For the individual, it means that much of one's time, whether in earning a living or in pursuing leisure-time interests, is spent with people—whether in the office or factory, in the lodge or club, in the union, bowling team, or PTA—whom one does not necessarily know very well but with whom one shares a specialized interest in a particular segment of the larger culture. As association with neighbors declines, individuals often find themselves strangers in their own localities, knowing few if any

---

10. See Charles Horton Cooley, *Social Organization* (New York: Charles Scribner's Sons, 1909).

of the neighbors.[11] They find themselves interacting with people in *categorical* relationships (lawyer-client, salesperson-customer, home owner-plumber) rather than in *personal* relationships.

The differentation of interests that for participation purposes "scatters" the neighborhood has a similar effect on the family. Family members find themselves pursuing their own differentiated interests and associations, in most of their waking hours going their own separate ways. Under these circumstances it is understandable that relationships of a primary-group or quasi-primary-group type often tend to spring up within the more formal, secondary-group settings. The customer gets to know the supermarket employee well enough to call him Charlie, the restaurant customer gets to know the waitress well enough to inquire about her sick mother, and the individual is on a first-name basis with the people in the office or in the plant work unit.

Yet this tendency for impersonal relationships to become more personal does not completely resemble the earlier, primary type of relationship, which has been supplanted. "The modern city, with its multiplicity of organizations of every conceivable sort," wrote Linton,

> . . . presents the picture of a mass of individuals who have lost their bands and who are trying, in uncertain and fumbling fashion, to find some substitute. New types of grouping based on congeniality, business association, or community of interest are springing up on all sides, but nothing has so far appeared which seems capable of taking over the primary functions of the local group as these relate to individuals. Membership in the Rotary Club is not an adequate substitute for friendly neighbors.[12]

Linton wrote these lines during a time when the Chicago school of urban ecology dominated systematic thinking about urban conditions in the United States. Since that time, many investigators have found a more extensive set of informal relationships within the

---

11. There has been a considerable literature on this point, which may be summarized in the following way: although there has undoubtedly been a trend toward increasing anonymity in the neighborhood, it is not complete, and even in the urban neighborhood individuals may know some of their neighbors. In an urban neighborhood study, for example, it was found that 86 percent of the people knew the names of one or more of their neighbors and 47 percent knew the names of four or more. See Marvin B. Sussman and R. Clyde White, *Hough, Cleveland, Ohio: a study of Social Life and Change* (Cleveland: Press of Western Reserve University, 1959), p. 22. See also "A Second Look at the Traditional View," in Harold L. Wilensky and Charles N. Lebeaux, *Industrial Society and Social Welfare* (New York: Free Press, 1965).

12. Ralph Linton, *The Study of Man* (New York: Appleton-Century, 1936), p. 230.

urban environment than was previously postulated. Two aspects are relevant here. One is the discovery of strong networks of kinship and friendship ties.[13] The other has been a resurgence of interest in the urban neighborhood stimulated by low-income residents whose demand for "neighborhood control" represents a deliberate revolt against the "great change" (see chapter 11).

The implications at the community level are particularly important in respect to the community function of social control. It is widely recognized that such primary-group controls as gossip, praise and blame, and ostracism constitute strong restraints on the individual's behavior. These controls, to be effective, presuppose that the individual in *known* by the controlling group and that the approval of the group is *important* to him or her. Such sanctions as praise and blame and ostracism have great effectiveness where the individual is dependent on the group for major life functions, where one has internalized group norms and places value on them, and where the group's opinion is important to one's self-image. On the other hand, where one can function effectively without the group and where the group's opinion is not important to one's self-image, controls of the primary type often lose their effectiveness, and such secondary-group controls as rules and regulations, law, and police action tend to supersede them. The difficulty of trying to apply secondary-group controls where primary controls have broken down or are at variance with the larger society is widely acknowledged by students of delinquency and crime.

At the community level, differentiation of interests and association implies the need for a means by which the different interests and interest groups somehow receive appropriate weight in the process of decision-making. In a most practical way it poses the problem of how to reconcile a representation of interests by locality with a representation of interests (occupational and other) not closely related to locality. Many large cities reflect this problem in various organizational structures that permit representation by neighborhoods as well as by interests. In some respects, the family has ceased to be the unit of operation in the determination of community matters and has been superseded by important interest groups and their representatives.

---

13. See Jane Jacobs, *The Death and Life of Great American Cities* (New York: Random House, 1961); Herbert Gans, *The Urban Villagers* (New York: Free Press of Glencoe, 1962); Paul Craven and Barry Wellman, "The Network City," *Sociological Inquiry*, vol. 43, nos. 3 and 4, (1973); Carol B. Stack, *All Our Kin: Strategies for Survival in a Black Community* (New York: Harper & Row, 1974); Martin D. Lowenthal, "The Social Economy of Working Class Communities," in Gary Gappert and Harold Rose, ed., *The Social Economy of Cities*, UAAR, vol. 9 (Beverly Hills, California: Sage Publications, 1975).

An obvious reflection of the shift in interest and association has been the decline of the neighborhood as a significant social unit in both rural and urban areas. Rural sociologists are questioning whether the rural neighborhood is any longer a significant functioning group.[14] Urban neighborhoods have long since been considered with skepticism in this regard. Nearly 50 years ago one sociologist, in observing the decline in association on a locality basis in urban areas, suggested that people living in the same urban locality might better be called "nigh-dwellers" than "neighbors."[15] And among city planners and urban sociologists, there rages a constant controversy over the extent to which city planning should attempt to incorporate the goal of restoring in the urban neighborhood an emphasis on locality-based participation.

Most important for the community, perhaps, is the fact that by dissolving the significance of interests based on locality, the differentiation of interests has weakened an important basis for cohesion. The locality is no longer the important reference group that it once was, and people tend to identify themselves with various interest groups with which they are functionally much more closely interrelated than with their neighbors. Nisbet puts it strongly: "For more and more individuals the primary social relationships have lost much of their historic function of mediation between man and the larger ends of our civilization."[16]

Increasing Systemic Relationships to the Larger Society

Division of labor and differentiation of interests and association have tended to relate community people and community units of various kinds to systems extending outside the community. As communities have grown more differentiated internally, their differentiated parts have become linked with state and national systems beyond their borders. A thousand threads tie together similar units in different communities into state and national systems organized for various levels of coordination and control. Thus, communities become more interdependent in a type of symbiotic or organic solidarity similar to

14. See, for example, Walter L. Slocum and Herman M. Case, "Are Neighborhoods Meaningful Social Groups Throughout Rural America?" *Rural Sociology*, vol. 18, no. 1 (March 1953).

15. See Bessie A. McClenahan, *The Changing Urban Neighborhood* (Los Angeles: University of Southern California, 1929).

16. Robert A. Nisbet, *The Quest for Community: A Study in the Ethics of Order and Freedom* (New York: Oxford University Press, 1953), p. 52.

that existing on the local level under advanced conditions of division of labor.

But the interdependence of communities is not with each other as homogeneous wholes. Rather, it is through the interrelation of their differentiated units as parts of national systems. Consider the following different kinds of community-based units: the local post office, the local branch bank, the local post of the American Legion, the local Catholic or Methodist church, the local office of the state employment service, the local Social Security office, the local chain-store supermarket, the local plant of the national company, the local labor union, the local disease-oriented health association, the local boy scout troop, the local Salvation Army unit, the local PTA, the local school system, the local public welfare office. These organizations all have in common a sort of amphibious nature. They belong to two worlds: the world of the local community and the world of their own respective state or national systems. As shown in the examples, they straddle the various institutional areas of the community. Many of these organizations are much more integrally a part of their respective extracommunity systems than they are of the community in which they are located. And in many instances, the seat of decision-making is not within the local community but rather on a district or state or national decision-making level, centralized to promote coordination of the various parts of the system operating in communities across the country. This relationship of local units to extracommunity systems is considered extensively in chapter 8, which utilizes the concept of the community's "vertical pattern."

The trend is toward a community that is less and less a locally oriented and coordinated aggregation of functional units, more and more a way station for various branches of national organizations.

Remarking on the proliferation of large-scale organizations, Boulding wrote:

In the United States 15,000,000 workers are organized into labor unions. At least half the farmers are organized into three large farm organizations. Great corporations dominate many fields of industry. Every trade and every industry, almost without exception, has one or more trade associations. Every profession is organized with its professional associations. There are innumerable organizations representing special interest groups, from Audubon societies to Zoroastrians. The national state in all countries is immensely more powerful, and reaches much farther down into the lives and pockets of the individual, than a hundred years earlier. Government departments have multiplied and expanded into huge bureaucracies. Veterans' organizations cover millions of ex-soldiers, and wield immense

63

political power. Lodges and fraternal orders have multiplied.[17]

He pointed out, moreover, that such organizations are more efficient in attracting and holding members than ever before. Referring to such important extracommunity systems by using the term "lateralizations," Aginsky wrote:

> The trend is toward lateralizations superseding communities in America as the "in-group." This pertains especially to those individuals who live in urban centers.
>
> From the foregoing we might suggest that the American community should no longer be considered as an integrated population confined to a definite geographic locus with its members having a majority of like interests in common. Rather, with increasing rapidity the various lateralizations having membership beyond the local community and in the majority of cases being headquartered in distant places have much influence upon some portion of the local population. This tends to make of that portion a semi-distinct component of the population.[18]

It is easy to jump from this point of view to that of considering these parts of extracommunity systems as outside of the local community system, even though they are located there. As stated above, however, such units belong to both worlds, and the fact that they are integrally related to extracommunity systems does not preclude their being part of the local community. They certainly fit within our definition of the community as "that combination of social systems that perform the major social functions having locality relevance." We simply note that on one of the four dimensions outlined in chapter 1, the "local autonomy" dimension, these units tend toward the pole of dependence on extracommunity systems.

This increasing extracommunity tie tends to orient individuals toward specialized, vertical systems as the important reference groups in relation to which they form their self-images. In occupying a status in one of the local units of such a system the individual must be guided by role expectations from that extracommunity system. These expectations conflict on occasion with those of the local community system, as, for example, when a branch-plant manager is

17. Kenneth E. Boulding, *The Organizational Revolution: A Study in the Ethics of Economic Organization* (New York: Harper & Brothers, 1953), pp. 3-4.

18. Burt W. Aginsky, "The Fragmentation of the American Community," in B. W. Aginsky and E. G. Aginsky, *Selected Papers* (New York: Printing Unlimited, 1955), p. 96.

ordered to cut down on production because of the company's national inventory condition.

In many instances, it means that the individual is actually in the community only as a transient. The individual's relation to his or her company may be more permanent than the relation to the community. As William H. Whyte has reported, national company policy often calls for a rotation of young executives, salespersons, and other personnel.[19] Like a member of the Army, the individual finds his or her principal relation to an institution rather than to a community; and no matter where one goes, the norms, goals, rewards, and sanctions of that institution will provide an accustomed environment and a relatively coherent set of demands, which may be much more consistent than those of the succession of communities in which one lives. Another result is that the decision-making locus of the institutions that provide the individual's daily needs is remote, for the policies of these institutions may be formulated hundreds of miles away and a formidable bureaucratic structure may also intervene.

For the community, the implications are equally important. Obviously, to the extent that decision-making is transferred elsewhere, it impairs community autonomy. In many instances, of course, the goals for which the unit works are simply not appropriate to the community level. This goal differentiation is obvious in the case of a local arsenal or Air Force base. But it is also true of a health association whose medical research problems are financed with local money but have no more relevance to one particular community than to any other community in the country. Likewise, the community may be the site of a national university (in contrast to a community college), which sees itself as related not to the local community's needs but to those of higher education and the advancement of learning and research on a national if not international basis. But in other instances, even where the goals of the unit are more relevant to the local community—for example, the branch of a chain of banks, a locally based chain store, or a local public welfare office—the unit may be activated and administered for all intents and purposes from a centralized office, which sets policies for all the communities within its area.

The systemic tie with extracommunity systems has a more subtle impact. If often results in the situation that local areas are cut up differently for different purposes. This is particularly noticeable in the smaller communities, where the school district may encompass one area, the telephone system a slightly different one, the local gov-

---

19. *The Organization Man* (Garden City, N.Y.: Doubleday Anchor, 1957).

ernment still another, and the employment area of the local manufacturing company still another.

In a different vein, the tie of local units to larger systems often provides an avenue for the periodic influx of "experts" and "specialists" into the community. Various experts in the state and federal government are available to local communities for consultation on schools, highways, sewage, urban renewal and so on, and the personnel of private organizations and business companies provide special service or supervision to the local unit in a way that enables it to operate more efficiently in terms of the goals and objectives of the larger system.

Two further questions are raised by the extracommunity ties. One is how units that exist in the community as integral parts of diverse extracommunity systems can be flexible enough to relate to each other on the community level in ways that avoid bitter conflict and enhance the access of community people to the functions of the larger society. The other is the problem of what types of decision and what types of institutional control are appropriate for the local community level, and what types are more appropriate for the respective extracommunity systems.[20] Such questions became particularly pointed in relation to the Great Society programs of the 1960s and were carried over into subsequent federal programs such as revenue sharing.

Bureaucratization and Impersonalization

The development of impersonal bureaucratic structures to coordinate the complex systems growing out of specialization and the division of labor has an important impact on local community life. Bureaucratic organization is virtually essential for the efficient administration of these complex systems, yet its nature is frequently misunderstood and it is considered only in its negative aspects. For the sociologist, "bureaucracy" is a useful term employed to describe a particular type of social organization widely characteristic of the complex extracommunity systems that penetrate local community life.

Max Weber made a penetrating analysis of bureaucratic organization that has formed the basis of current sociological analysis of this type.[21] According to him, bureaucratic organization has the fol-

20. Federal governmental programs influencing developments in local communities during the late sixties and early seventies are treated in chapter 11.

21. See the chapter on "Bureaucracy" in *From Max Weber: Essays in Sociology*, trans. and ed. H. H. Gerth and C. Wright Mills (New York: Oxford University Press, 1946), from which this account is taken. It appeared originally in Weber's *Wirtschaft und Gesellschaft.*

lowing features: There are fixed and official jurisdictional areas. Regular organizational activities are distributed as fixed official duties. Authority is distributed in a stable way and is strictly delimited. Methodical provision is made for the fulfilling of duties by persons having the proper qualifications. There is a hierarchy of different levels of authority, with supervision of lower offices by higher ones. Official activity is connected with an "office" with files, staff, and so on, and is considered to be distinct from the sphere of private life. Office administration presupposes thorough and expert training. Official activity is expected to be a full-time vocation of the bureaucrat. The management of the office is based on more or less stable, exhaustive rules that can be learned. For the bureaucrat, office holding is a vocation of relatively high esteem, usually for one's life, involving a fixed salary rather than wages or fees, and usually involving a career with the possibility of promotion to successively higher positions within the hierarchy.

"Bureaucracy," wrote Weber, "has a rational character: rules, means, ends, and matter-of-factness dominate its bearing."[22] Bureaucratic organization has become widespread in the Western world simply because it is the most efficient means for organizing and administering the complex interrelated institutional systems of contemporary society.

Bureaucracy is highly impersonal. It involves the objective discharge of business according to "calculable rules" and "without regard for persons." "The more complicated and specialized modern culture becomes, the more its external supporting apparatus demands the personally detached and strictly 'objective' *expert,* in lieu of the master of older social structures, who was moved by personal sympathy and favor, by grace and gratitude."[23]

Bureaucratic organization, with its smooth-running hierarchy of regularized, integrated control, has come to be the dominant form of large-scale organization. The reason for its advance "has always been its purely technical superiority over any other form of organization. . . . Precision, speed, unambiguity, knowledge of the files, continuity, discretion, unity, strict subordination, reduction of friction and of material and personal costs—these are raised to the optimum point in the strictly bureaucratic administration, and especially in its monocratic form."[24]

The reader will recognize that bureaucratic organization characterizes not only modern government but also political parties,

22. Weber, "Bureaucracy," p. 244.
23. Weber, "Bureaucracy," p. 216.
24. Weber, "Bureaucracy," p. 214.

labor unions, and other types of organizations. Weber emphasized this point, maintaining in addition that "the very large, modern capitalist enterprises are themselves unequalled models of strict bureaucratic organization."[25] Obviously, he did not mean this in a derogatory sense, for he insisted that his interest was purely value-free (wertfrei), purely objective. Moreover, he considered it impossible to maintain such a degree of complexity and efficiency without bureaucracy.

This view is somewhat different from the popular conception of bureaucracy, which is derogatory. The popular conception differs markedly from Weber's description; it also emphasizes certain disadvantages of bureaucratic organization, particularly its red tape, its inflexibility, its unimaginativeness, and its impersonality. These disadvantages are highly significant, for they also must be considered in assessing the impact of bureaucratization and its accompanying impersonalization on the community.

A widely used analysis of planning and politico-economic systems has drawn up the disadvantages of bureaucratic organization. It has certain "minor costs," including red tape, passing the buck, inflexibility, impersonality, and excessive centralization. Its major costs include the following: the charge that bureaucracy, particularly in the government setting, is often wasteful of manpower, materials, and money; the threat to equality made by the hierarchical principle, the difficulties of popular control of bureaucratic organizations; excessive loyalties by individual bureaucrats to their professions and to the bureaucracies that employ them; and faulty communication up through the hierarchical ranks to the policymakers.[26]

An additional defect, which Weber largely ignored but which contemporary organizational theorists have emphasized, is the process of "goal displacement," according to which bureaucratic

25. Weber, "Bureaucracy," p. 215.

26. Robert A. Dahl and Charles E. Lindblom, Politics, Economics, and Welfare: Planning and Politico-Economic Systems Resolved into Basic Social Processes (New York: Harper & Brothers, 1953), pp. 247-61. See also Robert K. Merton, "Bureaucratic Structure and Personality," Social Forces, vol. 18, no. 4 (May 1940). Recent studies of public decision-making and policy-implementation begin to provide frameworks for understanding the practical effects of bureaucracy on policy and programs. See Gideon Sjoberg et al., "Bureaucracy and the Lower Class," Sociology and Social Research, vol. 50, no. 3 (1966); Anthony Downs, Inside Bureaucracy (Boston: Little, Brown & Co., 1967); Francis E. Rourke, Bureaucracy, Politics and Public Policy (Boston: Little, Brown & Co., 1969); Peter M. Blau and Marshall W. Meyer, Bureaucracy in Modern Society, 2nd ed. (New York: Random House, 1971). Graham T. Allison in The Essence of Decision: Explaining the Cuban Missile Crisis (Boston: Little, Brown & Co., 1971) puts forward an insightful model of the dynamics of bureaucratic decision-making, and Jeffrey L. Pressman and Aaron B. Wildavsky in Implementation (Berkeley: University of California Press, 1973) give an engrossing case study of the local programmatic effects of politics and bureaucracy.

behavior becomes directed toward filling the needs of the organization rather than serving the functions for which the organization was established.

On the community level, whether we confront bureaucracy in the business enterprise, the labor union, the government office, or the voluntary association, its disadvantages are closely related to its advantages, both for the individual and for the community. The bureaucratic form of organization, of course, is a form that accommodates the complex division of labor by instituting an impersonal, secondary-group type of structure to perform functions that are either new or were earlier performed in many instances under the primary-group auspices of family, friendship group, neighborhood, and church.

Bureaucratic organization is important at the community level in another respect. It provides the structural and procedural vehicle through which various types of decision-making behavior can be deliberately "administered" rather than being left to the decisions of individuals in the "market." In subsequent chapters there are numerous occasions where this distinction in types of decision-making will be pointed out.

At the community level, various types of behavior occur that indicate that one choice has been taken rather than another. In some instances, this choice is simply the aggregate of choices made by individuals in the matter—whether or not to give to a certain fund campaign, to apply for work at a particular factory, to see a particular motion picture, to engage in cooperative activity with one's neighbor, and so on. In other instances such decisions are not left to the exigencies of individual choice, but a structure is set up through which such decision-making can take place in a deliberate and organized fashion. Thus, the individual gift choice becomes administered through the United Fund; the individual work choice becomes administered through a union; the individual motion picture choice becomes administered through the censorship activities of a religious organization or patriotic society; the individual activity in cooperating with one's neighbor becomes administered through a neighborhood association. Related to the growth of bureaucratic structures as formal, rational, deliberate administrative bodies there has been a transformation of many types of choices from the "market" type to the "administered" type.

For the individual, bureaucracy demands the price of impersonality for the benefit of just treatment—a fateful exchange which, on balance, may be too high a price. Nevertheless, if the parent does not know the schoolteacher personally as a neighbor, it is important to gain the assurance that his or her child will be treated on an equal plane with any child the schoolteacher may happen to know personally. The same is true of one's relation to the utility company, to the sanitation department, or to the police. Indeed, as L. L. Bernard pointed out many years ago, one of the difficulties in modern community life is the lack of an adequate set of norms to govern secondary ("derivative") group relations, and the inappropriateness of primary-group norms when applied in the secondary-group situation (graft, favoritism, nepotism, and so on).[27] Thus, bureaucratic impersonalization and "dehumanization" are but the reverse of the coin whose other side is favoritism, personal whim, and the misuse of power.

Looked at from the other side of the relationship, the individual is often in a position within a bureaucratic structure in which he or she must "follow the rules" even when doing so means acting in an inappropriate way when the other person is a neighbor. The conflict between the just exercise of official duty and the obligations that a person owes a friend or neighbor is a great human theme running through history but is particularly cogent under modern conditions of community life where so many living functions are performed by impersonal bureaucracies. The primary-group norms seem somehow more appealing than those of the secondary group. Love seems superior to justice. But the theologian Emil Brunner maintained that love must transcend justice, not fall short of it. That is to say, rather than failing to meet secondary-group obligations, love must meet them and then go beyond them.[28] It is perhaps not too much of a digression at this point to recollect that Reinhold Niebuhr pointed out that people often do things in the name of a large organization or "cause" that their moral code would not allow them to do in their personal relations with other human beings.[29]

The individual in a bureaucratic position often confronts situations where "following the rules" seems to be an affront to ordinary human values. Impersonality forbids one to make an exception and indeed to do so would be to show favoritism or at least to place the individuals one is dealing with in a position where they depend on one's personal kindness rather than the impersonal "justice" of the system. Such personal consideration is exactly what bureaucratic organization must avoid, for it is part of its reason for being to avoid it. We shall return to this problem in chapter 8, where it will become

27. L. L. Bernard, "The Conflict between Primary Group Attitudes and Derivative Group Ideals in Modern Society," *American Journal of Sociology*, vol. 41, no. 5 (March, 1936).

28. *Justice and the Social Order*, trans. Mary Ottinger (New York: Harper & Brothers, 1945), esp. chap. 15. The point here is similar to that of the Christian doctrine of the "second mile" (see Matthew 5:41).

29. See *Moral Man and Immoral Society: A Study in Ethics and Politics* (New York: Charles Scribner's Sons, 1932).

apparent that this relationship is one that integrates the bureaucrat with the vertical extracommunity system, rather than with fellow members of the community. From the standpoint of the individual confronting the bureaucracy, its rigidity, impersonality, and coldly rational operation give him or her a sense of powerlessness epitomized in the ironic admonition: "Go fight City Hall!"

Actually, there is one other characteristic of bureaucracy, pertinent here, implied, but not made explicit, by Max Weber. In bureaucratic structure, policy is ordinarily not made in the lower echelons of the organization, but relatively high in the hierarchy. Thus, ordinary citizens confronting the bureaucratic organization are separated from policy-makers by several levels of intervening functionaries, none of whom has the power, even if he or she had the will, to make the exception to accommodate personal situations. The road up through the chain of command typically takes the individual out of his or her own locality to district, state, or national "headquarters." There, an exception may possibly be made with impunity.

But in the lower echelons, the exception, the concession to meet "human" needs, can be made by the bureaucrat only at the risk of going against the "rules." Often here, as in other cases where norms of conduct create points of tension and conflict, the violation of the rules may be winked at, as long as no major disturbance is created or the violation does not receive unfavorable publicity. But in any case the bureaucrat runs the risk that the latter may happen. In violating the rules, the bureaucrat has nothing to win and everything to lose.

The process of bureaucratization takes place throughout the various institutional areas of government, business, religious activity, the helping professions, and so on. While other fields, such as that of medical care, would serve as excellent examples, perhaps the example of bureaucratization in the school will suffice as an illustration. To get some idea of the scope of bureaucratization within the school system consider the following: the increasing specialization of subjects and types of functionary; the proliferation of separate areas of professional competence requiring certification—music teacher, vocational guidance teacher, school psychologist, attendance supervisor, social studies instructor, and so on; the development of tenure and seniority provisions for promotion; the supervision of various specialties by respective divisions and bureaus in the state education department; the proliferation of regulations governing each separate activity or function; the necessity of reports, the precise calculation of state-aid funds based on rigid procedures of control; the increasing professionalization of many functions formerly considered within the competence of any qualified teacher. **71** increasing professionalization of many functions formerly considered within the competence of any qualified teacher.

As noted above, bureaucrats tend to have special loyalties to their professions and to the bureaucratic organizations that employ them. This loyalty is but one of several factors orienting community institutions upward and outward along lines of vertical extracommunity systems rather than across and inward to other institutions in the community.

In another respect, to the extent that bureaucratic policy, as indicated above, is formulated in higher echelons outside the community, community autonomy is weakened in the sense that levels of authority are interposed between the community and the policy-making hierarchy.

Finally, the rationality of organization of bureaucratic structures is a rationality designed to favor the organization's own goals. As in the case of the system's relation to the individual, the system's relation to the community typically precludes making "special exceptions," for the special exceptions are violations of the rationally efficient system whose reason for being is to facilitate the system's goals rather than the community's, where these do not coincide. Nevertheless, exceptions do get made in favor of the community. They constitute minimal adaptations of the ideal system in order to take care of situations that otherwise might develop into potential threats to the system or some part of it, such as complaints leading to disadvantageous modification in the public utility law, or delimiting the power of some bureau, or laying down some basic regulations for an industry.

Thus bureaucratization, with its accompanying impersonalization, performs a vital function but at the same time tends to weaken community cohesion and autonomy and to orient community-based units toward extracommunity systems.

Transfer of Functions to Profit Enterprise and Government

A transfer in the allocation of functions from certain kinds of social auspices to others accompanies other aspects of the "great change." In the process, commercial enterprise and government are allocated many functions that other agencies used to perform. Let us see how this process works.

Any society is confronted with a choice of which type of group or agency or institutional structure it wants to entrust with the performance of various functions. As an example, housing can be provided by the individual family through its own effort, by various neighbors in a neighborhood building effort, by a voluntary association such as a cooperative, by commercial housing contractors, or by government. These represent five relevant possibilities of allocation in the modern American community:

1. Individuals (families)
2. Special ad hoc groupings larger than the family
3. Voluntary associations
4. Business enterprise
5. Government

Where individuals or families perform the function for themselves, there is usually no financial exchange involved. With such special ad hoc groupings as neighbors getting together to perform a function, the relationship is one of either nonmonetary reciprocation (borrowing, lending, doing favors) or, at the most, of barter. Where the function is allocated to a voluntary association, it is often financed through gifts, fees, or membership dues. In business enterprise, it is financed typically by a price paid, and in government, by taxes. The first two methods involve little exchange of money, but in the last two cases money plays a large role in commanding goods and services, either as price or as tax.

Viewed this way, the change we are now considering is a change from the performance of functions by individuals and by simple barter agreements among neighbors to functions performed by business and government involving a direct or indirect payment of money. Voluntary associations often perform as an intermediate stage in the process. The direction of change has the net effect of placing certain functions in the general money-price market and in the governmental arena that formerly involved neither. We shall consider this whole question of the allocation of community functions to different auspices in chapters 6 and 7.

The change is intimately related to the division of labor. As individuals specialize, they depend on other people to perform functions they formerly performed themselves. They pay for them with the money they earn by performing their own specialized functions. They pay directly to individual business enterprises or indirectly, through taxes, for the functions that the government performs. The net result is to get these functions standardized, to get them "into the price system," and to have them financed either through the operation of the market or through taxes.

The individual both receives and spends more money, even assuming a constant level of living. Again, the auspices under which these goods and services are provided are decreasingly those of the primary group of family, friends, and neighbors, and increasingly those of secondary groups such as business and governmental units.

Thus, while farmers once produced the majority of their food, they no longer do so. An early investigation I conducted in a dairy-farm section indicated, for example, that the majority of the dairy farmers bought their butter at the store, that they did not make it themselves. Many other functions that years ago were performed by the family or by the neighborhood are now performed for a price or for taxes, and many new functions have been assumed by business and governmental auspices. Examples of the trend include the growth of restaurants and the increase of semiprepared or fully pre-pared frozen meals, of the canning and frozen-food functions, of haircutting, of dressmaking and clothes making in general, of various types of home repair functions such as appliance repair, house painting, and roofing. More recently, the "do it yourself" movement has altered and in some cases reversed this long-term trend.

Other functions such as parental guidance have been trans-ferred in part, at least, to such tax-paid personnel as guidance coun-selors, teachers, school psychiatrists, and so on. The provision by the family for the dependency of old age has been largely transferred to government through social security payroll deductions. Financial assistance otherwise has been taken over to a considerable extent, earlier by voluntary social agencies, but increasingly by a combina-tion of government units. Much recreational activity has gone from the family and neighborhood to such voluntary organizations as Scouts and Y's, to commercial motion-picture houses and bowling alleys, to governmental youth bureaus, playgrounds, and the like. Increasingly, schools have acquired broad recreational functions, not only through playgrounds and activities for children but also through spectator sports such as basketball and football contests for both young and old to watch and through adult education programs and band concerts.

This transference of activities reduces the vitality of family and neighborhood for the individual by taking away some of their mean-ingful functions and thus some of their reason for being. On the other hand, the individual finds many functions performed in sec-ondary groups, which he seeks out selectively on the basis of interest.

At the community level, many units that perform important functions, whether they be chain stores, local offices of the state welfare department, or schools, are more likely to be oriented to-ward extracommunity systems than were the auspices that they replaced.

Perhaps most important, the price-tax mechanism is particu-larly well adapted to the proliferation of specialized functions and the attendant division of labor and necessary exchange of goods and services involved in the symbiotic interdependence that accompanies the division of labor.

Urbanization and Suburbanization

To say that urbanization has accompanied the community changes so far portrayed would be an understatement, for actually urbanization is so intimately intertwined with these changes as to be inseparable from them. The growth of cities and of social structures and behavior patterns associated with city living has constituted one of the most striking aspects of recent history.

Let us look at some of the quantitative aspects of urban growth and then turn to some of the social aspects, relating them to our analysis of the great change. In 1790 there was no city of as many as 50,000 people in the United States. By 1840 there were only five such cities. A century later, however, there were 199 cities of over 50,000 population, and by 1970 there were 396. Looked at another way, in 1790 only 5 percent of the people of the United States lived in places of 2,500 or larger. By 1970 this figure had risen to 73.5 percent of the population.[30] Standard Metropolitan Statistical Areas, comprising cities of 50,000 or more people and the densely concentrated population in the surrounding county or counties, have grown more rapidly than the country as a whole. In 1940 the principal Standard Metropolitan Areas comprised only 51 percent of the United States population. By the year 1970 there were 243 Standard Metropolitan Statistical Areas with a combined population of 139 million people, comprising 68.6 percent of the country's population.[31]

In recent decades the principal growth has not been in the central cities themselves but in the surrounding areas. Actually, a large number of central cities have declined in population, especially since 1940, despite the growth in the metropolitan area of which the city is the core. Thus, where earlier it was accurate to speak of the growth of cities, it is now more appropriate to speak of the growth of that part of the metropolitan areas outside of the central cities. Hawley describes the sequence:

> Redistribution of population moved toward concentration from 1900 to 1920, and toward dispersion from 1920 to 1950. A conclusion from this as well as from observation of changes in growth rates in central cities and in distance zones, is that met-

30. Donald J. Bogue, *The Population of the United States* (Glencoe, Ill.: Free Press, 1959), pp. 19, 47; and U.S Bureau of the Census, *Statistical Abstract of the United States: 1976,* 97th ed. (Washington, D.C., 1976).

31. U.S. Census of Population, 1970.

ropolitan development in the first half of the 20th century involved, first, a rapid growth of centers at the expense of satellite areas, and, subsequently, a centrifugal movement to satellite areas to the detriment of growth in central cities. It is probable that the maturation of centers is a requisite to the expansion of settlement in satellite areas.[32]

In a sense, then, urbanization and suburbanization are part of the same process, the process of spatial distribution of complex and ever larger concentrations of people in metropolitan areas. The processes, though interrelated, merit separate treatment, and we shall consider urbanization first.

For many decades, sociologists have noted the growth in number and size of cities and tried to characterize their social life. Numerous attempts have been made to capture conceptually the obvious differences that life in the large cities manifests as distinguished from life in smaller rural communities. Louis Wirth, in a classic description of urbanism as a way of life, described three important characteristics of the city: large numbers of people, density of population, and heterogeneity of people. From these three, Wirth, in a brilliant analysis, sought to derive various implications for urban personality and social organization. He noted the accompanying weakening of kinship and other face-to-face ties and the corresponding growth of pressure groups and other interest groups. "Meanwhile," he added, "the city as a community resolves itself into a series of tenuous segmental relationships superimposed upon a territorial base with a definite center but without a definite periphery and upon a division of labor which far transcends the immediate locality and is world-wide in scope."[33]

Many characteristics attributed to urbanism as opposed to ruralism in American communities have been characteristics peculiarly associated with city growth in the United States and Canada. The high percentage of foreign-born, for example, was noted and emphasized by Park, Wirth, and other sociologists of the Chicago school of the twenties and thirties. Graft and corruption have characterized many American cities, but they are not necessarily an exclusive concomitant of city life. Dewey has analyzed the many characteristics assigned to urbanism by different students of the subject and has concluded that the following characteristics are the inevitable product of the three salient aspects of urbanism that Louis Wirth emphasized:

32. Amos H. Hawley, *The Changing Shape of Metropolitan America: Deconcentration Since 1920* (Glencoe, Ill.: Free Press, 1956), p. 161.

33. "Urbanism as a Way of Life," *American Journal of Sociology* 44, no. 1 (July 1938):

1. Anonymity
2. Division of labor
3. Heterogeneity, induced and maintained by points 1 and 2
4. Impersonal and formally prescribed relationships
5. Symbols of status that are independent of personal acquaintance[34]

Variations in these five characteristics thus inevitably accompany variations in size and density, though they can undoubtedly be influenced by cultural and historical peculiarities.

The aspects of the "great change" so far depicted constitute an alternative list of relevant characteristics:

1. Division of labor
2. Differentiation of interests and association
3. Increasing systemic relationships to the larger society
4. Bureaucratization and impersonalization
5. Transfer of functions to profit enterprise and government

Although these were given as aspects of the "great change" rather than as unique qualities of urbanism, there is a close relationship between Dewey's list of essential characteristics of urbanism and these five trends of change, considered as characteristics. This relationship is more than coincidence, for a moment's reflection will indicate that the city as a form of social organization is ideally suited to embody the characteristics that the changes discussed in this chapter have brought forth in American society.

The city as a social form was also given great impetus toward growth by the process of industrialization accompanying the successive waves of industrial and agricultural revolution since the eighteenth century. Factories, the most efficient facilities for taking advantage of large-scale production methods, needed large numbers of workers in their immediate proximity, and they had to be close to sources of power: initially, water power or steam power from coal. Placing the steam engine on wheels and in the hulls of boats involved a great advance in the transportation of raw materials, manufactured products, and foodstuffs for large aggregations of people. Thus, great cities arose at sources of raw materials, at sources of power, or at centers of transportation networks. The development of electric and automotive power subsequently permitted both industrial decentralization and a dispersion of large numbers of people to places of residence at some distance from the city centers.

---

34. Richard Dewey, "The Rural-Urban Continuum: Real but Relatively Unimportant," *American Journal of Sociology* 56, no. 1 (July 1960): 65.

During this long process, the cities were fed by an influx of in-migrants from abroad, first from western and northern Europe, later from eastern and southern Europe. This influx approximated a million a year for several years in the first two decades of the present century, but was considerably curtailed with the restrictive immigration laws of the 1920s. The large numbers of immigrants constituted a cultural-historical addition to the heterogeneity otherwise to be expected in urban life.

The cities were also fed by a great influx of in-migrants from the rural areas. Kolb and Brunner point out that the farm population of the United States decreased by 8,000,000, a loss of practically 25 percent, between the high-point year of 1916 and the census year of 1950, and that the total migration of farm people to cities and towns in the twenty years following 1930 was almost equal to the total farm population of 1940.[35] The urbanward migration has continued since Kolb and Brunner's study.

The same trends that formed part of the "great change" and that were closely related to the growth of cities were also closely related to the developing industrialization of economic enterprise. Each of the five aspects considered has been not so much a cause of industrialization as an integral part of the "great change" of which industrialization is also a part.

It is difficult to consider the more recent changes taking place in city life without simultaneously considering the growth of the suburbs. Cities and suburbs, as mentioned earlier, constitute a symbiotic whole, separated only by the arbitrary jurisdictional lines of the city border. But there is a psychological, as well as an ecological, aspect to their relationship. For the suburbs themselves represent a reaction to the social characteristics of city living, a reaction against the anonymity, division of labor, heterogeneity, impersonality, and formalized status, all of which Dewey considered to be the essence of urbanism. Both aspects converge in a resultant exodus of city people to the suburbs, including those who commute to the central city and those who find work in the suburbs themselves.

The impact of this exodus on the central cities has been three-fold. First, it has tended to draw large numbers of white middle-class people out of the city, leaving the city with increased proportions of its population at the extreme ends of the income scale—the very rich and the very poor—and with an inordinately high concentration of nonwhites. Second, it has meant that the city must maintain essential

---

35. John H. Kolb and Edmund de S. Brunner, *A Study of Rural Society*, 4th ed. (Boston: Houghton Mifflin, 1952), pp. 28-29. The figure is somewhat countermanded, however, by a simultaneous but smaller movement of people in the opposite direction.

services not only for its own residents but also for a great number of commuters who utilize its facilities during the day but are identified with a suburban community of residence. Generally speaking, municipal governmental forms do not recognize or accommodate the fact of the symbiotic interrelatedness of the city and its suburbs. Third, and closely related, it has resulted in the gradual transformation of the central city into a center of various functions related to the metropolitan area and to the larger areas of trade and influence beyond. As the city center has grown, it has displaced residential neighborhoods, thus resulting in the already noted depletion of population in many central cities.

These three implications of the development of the metropolitan area for the central city itself are part of the bewildering background against which specific problems such as urban blight, the need for urban redevelopment and for low-cost housing, illegitimacy and juvenile delinquency, and transportation must be considered. Underlying them all, though not necessarily causing them, is the increasing inability of the city to raise through its tax base the huge sums of money required to provide necessary services for the entire metropolitan area and to confront the problems attendant upon the flight of large numbers of middle-class people to the suburbs.

The process of suburban dispersion has been taking place since 1920. Using the term "metropolitan ring" to denote the portion of a Standard Metropolitan Area which lies outside the central city, it can be said that the metropolitan rings have grown faster than the central cities since that year. Bogue points out that although such metropolitan rings contained only about one-ninth of the United States population early in the century, they accounted in 1950 for one-fourth. The growth rate of population in areas surrounding the central cities has been increasingly greater than that in the cities, almost two-and-a-half times greater between 1940 and 1950.[36] This trend has continued, though at a slower rate. From 1960 to 1970 the central cities increased by 0.6 percent while the metropolitan population outside the central cities increased by 2.4 percent.[37]

The term *suburb* is used in many ways. When speaking of the "population of the suburbs" in general, the metropolitan ring is a useful referent. Actually, though, this concept of suburb does not agree completely with the concept when used to denote a particular type of community. Duncan and Reiss wrote, "in the usage of most

36. Donald J. Bogue, "Urbanism in the United States, 1950," *American Journal of Sociology* 60, no. 5 (March 1955): 481.

37. The U.S. Bureau of the Census, *Statistical Abstract of the United States, 1976*, 97th ed. (Washington, D.C., 1976).

writers the term 'suburb' appears to denote an urban place (usually an incorporated place) outside the corporate limits of a large city, but either adjacent thereto or near enough to be closely integrated into the economic life of the central city and within commuting distance of it."[38] We shall use this denotation when referring to the "suburban community" but shall use the broader concept of the metropolitan ring in referring to the "suburbs" generally.

Suburban communities have often been called "bedroom" communities because they are associated with people residing in such places but commuting daily to the central city for work. Actually, such commutation characterizes many suburban communities, but not all. Schnore has drawn a distinction between "residential" and "employing" suburbs. "The basis for this distinction is whether or not the suburb draws more workers to its confines every day than the number of working people who sleep there every night."[39] If it does, it is considered an employing suburb. On this basis, he found that residential suburbs grew almost twice as rapidly as employing suburbs in the 1940-50 decade.[40] Residential suburbs have not only grown faster but seem to be at least as numerous in population as employing suburbs, if not more so. Duncan and Reiss asserted: "A number of writers have suggested, however, that suburbs tend to polarize into two major types, 'dormitory' communities whose residents work elsewhere in the metropolitan area, and employing or industrial suburbs which have a sizable economic base. The findings on the differences between suburban and other urban populations clearly suggest that the dormitory type is the modal one among the suburbs.[41]

The distinction between residential and employing suburbs suggests the fact that the "suburbs" are not the undifferentiated, homogeneous mass suggested by some popular writers, but that they show great differences in occupation, income, and many other characteristics of their population. Schnore concluded: "The metropolitan community must be undergoing a process of increasingly specialized land use, in which subareas of the community are devoted more and more exclusively to a limited range of functions. The result of this mounting 'territorial differentiation' is increasing

38. Reprinted with permission from Otis Dudley Duncan and Albert J. Reiss, Jr., *Social Characteristics of Urban and Rural Communities, 1950* (New York: John Wiley & Sons, copyright 1956), p. 117.

39. Leo F. Schnore, "The Growth of Metropolitan Suburbs," *American Sociological Review* 22, no. 2 (April 1957): 167.

40. Schnore, "Metropolitan Suburbs," p. 168.

41. *Urban and Rural Communities,* p. 7.

segregation, with similar units and similar functions clustering together."[42]

As Wood has pointed out, particular types of suburbs have attained an extraordinary degree of internal homogeneity precisely because they have tended to segregate out one particular type of people, thus differentiating themselves from other suburban communities. "Industry and people," wrote Wood in a passage describing the growth of suburban communities, "had moved out but they had not moved out together—and the result was that all kinds of communities appeared to ring the city. The suburbs extracted one by one economic and social functions that had previously existed side by side. Each tended to emphasize a particular aspect of society: residential living, industry, recreation, gambling, retail trade. Even slums developed."[43] Berger has emphasized the heterogeneity of the suburbs, pointing out the lack of conformity of the people in the working-class suburb that he studied to the pattern of living generally attributed to "the suburbs."[44]

The great suburban growth is related to other aspects of the "great change." Perhaps the most important relationship, as suggested earlier, is one of reaction. The suburbs represent a reaction of individual families to the very trends of change depicted in this chapter and an attempt to escape from them by re-creating a type of community living in which they or their visible aspects are minimized. If the large city represents the community pattern par excellence for the development of the basic social changes considered here, then suburbanization represents the community pattern par excellence for trying to escape their consequences in residential living. The suburbs are the small town's last stand. They represent the last great hope for preserving small-town values within the ever growing metropolitan orbits.

In so characterizing the suburbs, we are in danger of overgeneralization. We have noted the great differences among suburbs, perhaps the greatest of which is the difference between residential and industrial suburbs. Other differences abound, as we shall see. It is doubtful whether general characteristics of social life applied to "the suburbs" actually are applicable in all cases.

Yet in order to look for the model characteristics, those associated with the greatest number of suburban communities, we must

42. "Metropolitan Suburbs," p. 172.

43. Robert C. Wood, *Suburbia: Its People and Their Politics* (Boston: Houghton Mifflin, 1959), p. 64.

44. See Bennett M. Berger, "The Myth of Suburbia," *Journal of Social Issues*, vol. 17, no. 1 (1961), and *Working-class Suburb* (Berkeley: University of California Press, 1960).

81

conclude, with Duncan and Reiss, that the dormitory suburb, the suburb characterized by a high degree of commuting to work, is the modal type. Here are men and women whose day in the city involves them deeply in the division of labor, in differentiated interests and association, in systemic relationships to large national or international organizations, in vast bureaucratic structures with their attendant impersonalization, and in the functions of profit enterprise and government. They return to their residences, in communities out beyond the city limits, in some cases extremely far out, where they can enjoy a type of association that is, insofar as feasible, the opposite of what they have been experiencing all day. The separation of community of work from community of residence is one of the most significant developments of modern living. It is a basic background condition of the crisis in large city centers, a crisis caused in part, as indicated earlier, by the attempt of commuters to evade the local consequences of the type of metropolitan organization within which they earn their daily living but from which they want to escape nightly.

In suburban localities, these commuters can recapture some of the characteristics of small-town living. "In any given suburban territory," wrote Wood, "small governments, truly local governments, remain to enhance the feeling of the small community in the modern world, to cling to the ideal of the republic in miniature, and to prevent the encroachment of the metropolis. Suburbia is brave to the point of rashness in its struggle for existence; it is resourceful, aggressive and so far successful. Only one question of importance remains; is it right in its decision to remain free?"[45]

Wood maintained emphatically that it is not. Essentially, he claimed, the attempt to escape the consequences of the ecological system of which the suburbs are a part is morally irresponsible. From the standpoint of local governmental economy and efficiency, it is wasteful. Furthermore, according to Wood, it is a barrier to the progress to be made in the direction of developing a truly integrated metropolis, one which seeks to solve its problems rather than escape them, one which affirms the values of urban living and tries to enrich rather than obstruct them.

In this position, Wood represents one possible extreme with respect to the relation of the suburban community to the metropolis. Arthur E. Morgan represents almost the opposite. He was concerned with the necessity of functional coordination of suburbs and city center for some specific purposes, but he was equally emphatic on the desirability of maintaining the autonomy of the suburban

45. *Suburbia*, pp. 254-55.

community in the process. He proposed a loose federation for specific, demarcated joint functions as a solution.[46]

The suburbs seek to preserve or recapture not only the values of the small town but also the values of small-town family living. This trend is indicated by the exodus to the suburbs of couples with young children, the desire to go some place where "there are better schools for the children and a place to play" and where there is a piece of ground, a lawn to mow, and plants to cultivate and complain about. The family cookout, the omnipresent station wagon, the playroom, the romp with the children, the support of the PTA, the "do-it-yourself" activities—all symbolize in one way or another a desperate interest in family living and an act of faith in suburban family life as an equivalent, if not an equal, of life in the old village or on the farm.

Bell summed this up by hypothesizing that "the move to the suburbs expresses an attempt to find a location in which to conduct family life which is more suitable than that offered by central cities, i.e., that persons moving to the suburbs are principally those who have chosen familism as an important element of their life styles as over against career or consumership."[47]

This familism translates itself into such demographic indicators, when compared with central cities, as a higher percentage of people who are married, a higher percentage of people living in their primary families, a lower ratio of quasi-household residents to population in households, higher fertility ratios, and a lower percentage of women in the labor force.[48]

It is, of course, possible to attribute to the suburbs social characteristics that are associated with middle-class people, regardless of where they live. The higher income and other middle-class attributes characterizing suburban families may be the basic factors in their behavior, rather than the fact of their suburban residence. Dobriner has written, "Many of the generalizations referring to the 'suburban man' or 'suburban society' or 'suburban culture' are not

46. *The Community of the Future and the Future of Community* (Yellow Springs, Ohio: Community Service, 1957), chap. 8.

47. Wendell Bell, "Social Choice, Life Styles, and Suburban Residence," in William Dobriner, ed., *The Suburban Community* (New York: G. P. Putnam's Sons, 1958), p. 231.

48. Duncan and Reiss, *Urban and Rural Communities*, p. 131. Recent research has helped provide a more sophisticated understanding of why people live in the suburbs and the quality of life there. See especially Oliver P. Williams et al., *Suburban Differences and Metropolitan Policies: A Philadelphia Story* (Philadelphia: University of Pennsylvania Press, 1965); Sylvia Fava, "Beyond Suburbia," *The Annals of the American Academy of Political and Social Science*, vol. 422 (November 1975); and Barry Schwartz, ed., *The Changing Face of the Suburbs* (Chicago: University of Chicago Press, 1976).

manifestations of an ecological phenomenon, but, rather, a facet of the complex life styles of the middle class."[49] Since few definitive studies delineate the two, we can at least acknowledge that suburban community living differs from that of the central cities and that at least part of that difference can be attributed to the higher proportion of middle-class people in suburban communities.

Suburban neighboring, associational activity, camaraderie, and civic endeavor, while on the one hand a reaction against specialization and impersonalization, nevertheless differ somewhat from the analogous locality-based activity of earlier small-town life. For one thing, in the suburbs there is the sense of transiency, the tendency of people to move around, not only vocationally but geographically and in terms of style of life. For another, there is the tendency to feel at home in a community precisely because one's strong identification is toward the national company or other national organization whose branch is located in the nearby city. The individual and his or her family may move across the country, but the tie to the company remains. There also remains the chain of company-oriented activities, both official and unofficial, which take a large share of one's waking hours. While the company may encourage its employees, and particularly its young middle-class executives, to "get into community activities," the home base, the anchor point, would seem to be the company rather than the community.

"If by roots we mean the complex of geographical and family ties that historically knitted Americans to local society," wrote Whyte, "these young transients are almost entirely rootless."[50] He went on to draw an interesting analogy from a tree-nursery catalogue. In growing its trees, the nursery transplants them several times. In this way, "the longer, more easily damaged roots are reduced so that more small feeder roots develop near the stem. The more feeder roots, the more quickly the tree is established on your land." Whyte pointed out the analogy with transient suburbanites. "Through a sort of national, floating cooperative, they are developing a *new* kind of roots. The roots are, to be sure, shallow—but like those of the redwood tree, even shallow roots, if there are enough of them, can give a great deal of support."[51]

Significantly, the informal association of commuters often takes place among people who have in common their transiency in the community, their preoccupation with interests and associations

49. *Suburban Community*, xxi.

50. From *The Organization Man* (Garden City: Doubleday Anchor, 1947), p. 318. Copyright © 1956 by William H. Whyte, Jr. By permission of Simon and Schuster, Inc.

51. *Organization Man*, pp. 319, 320.

and concerns that reach beyond the local community and that set them off from other, more locally oriented people who are more firmly anchored in the community.[52]

Rootless and transient though it may be, social life in the residential suburb strives desperately toward personalization, toward association on the basis of propinquity rather than differentiated interests, toward minimizing differences—at least among horizontal strata—associated with the division of labor, toward seeking those very characteristics that are the antithesis of bureaucracy, toward sentiment and informality, toward restoration of primary-group contacts, toward a sense of neighborhood and neighboring, and toward restoring to individuals and families, to special ad hoc groupings, and to voluntary associations—functions which in the central city are performed by profit enterprise and government. The car pools, the community clean-up days, the voluntary work on the recreation center, the raffles for a swimming pool, the do-it-yourself—all represent an attempted change in functional auspices away from profit and tax-supported enterprise.

From this standpoint, one can accept the rootlessness, the essential superficiality of first-name friendship patterns, which do not run deep or persist through time, and the artificiality of much of the cookout, do-it-yourself cult of family primitivism as an attempt to preserve and restore values threatened with destruction. Given the "great change," here is adaptive behavior aimed at accommodating it while still preserving the semblance, if not the reality, of basic social configurations that the "great change" otherwise threatens.

But while an attempt is made to preserve older values, these values themselves have been changing, and their transformation constitutes the last basic aspect fo the "great change" to be considered here.

Changing Values

Social scientists use the term *values* to denote the capacity to satisfy a human desire that is attributed to any object, idea, or content of experience. Values are not the specific acts that people perform; rather, they are the underlying principles according to which people make their choices. Such values are products of the culture. Individuals acquire these values, these preferences for one type of condition, quality, or pattern of living rather than another as they grow up within a culture and take on its ways.

---

52. See, for example, Dobriner's study on "Local and Cosmopolitan as Contemporary Suburban Character Types," in Dobriner, *Suburban Community.*

We have already noted the fact that the configuration of values may differ from one community to another (see chapter 2), even though these communities may be part of a larger culture and thus share many similarities in institutions and beliefs. A foreign observer has written:

> The cultural unity of the nation consists, however, in the fact that *most Americans have most valuations in common* though they are arranged differently in the sphere of valuations of different individuals and groups and bear different intensity coefficients. This cultural unity is the indispensable basis for discussion between persons and groups. It is the floor upon which the democratic process goes on.[53]

An excellent four-point outline for appraising the relative importance of different values has been provided by Williams:

> Dominant and subordinate values *for a group or social system as a whole* can be roughly ordered to these criteria:
>
> 1. *Extensiveness* of the value in the total activity of the system. What proportion of a population and of its activities manifest the value?
> 2. *Duration* of the value. Has it been persistently important over a considerable period of time?
> 3. *Intensity* with which the value is sought or maintained, as shown by: effort, crucial choices, verbal affirmation, and by reactions to threats to the value—for example, promptness, certainty, and severity of sanctions.
> 4. *Prestige of value carriers*—that is, of persons, objects, or organizations considered to be bearers of the value. Culture heroes, for example, are significant indexes of values of high generality and esteem.[54]

Keeping in mind that American communities differ in the relative importance that they assign to various values, let us review briefly some basic American values that have relevance at the community level. We shall then be in a position to note important value changes, particularly as these are related to other aspects of the "great change."

One important value, *freedom*, implies that large areas of choice should be left open to the individual regarding the way he or she is going to think, feel, and behave. The roots of this value lie deep in

---

53. Gunnar Myrdal, *An American Dilemma: The Negro Problem and Modern Democracy* (New York: Harper & Brothers, 1944), p. xlviii.

54. Robin M. Williams, Jr., *American Society* (New York: Alfred A. Knopf, 1951), pp. 382-83.

the early settlement of the colonies, many of whose first inhabitants had chosen to migrate to these shores in order to free themselves from various restrictions on their religious, political, or economic activities.

Americans have shown an abiding propensity to place a positive valuation on *individualism*, tending to measure good and bad in terms of the effect on the individual human being. They have been hesitant to restrict the free activity of the individual even when such activity was detrimental to the larger society. Although far from immune from the "tyranny of the masses," which Tocqueville thought was particularly noticeable in informal group pressures to conform to current fashions of thought and behavior, they have hesitated to use the formal controls of the state to govern areas of conduct in ways often found acceptable in Europe.

Related to several other values is a strong emphasis on *democracy* as a system combining responsibility of the government to a majority of the people and a simultaneous protection of the rights of the minority. But the idea of democracy has diffused to other areas of community living, as indicated by such familiar concepts as "democracy in education," "democratic family living," "industrial democracy," and "democratic planning." The diffusion of the concept of democracy to nongovernmental institutions is, in degree at least, an important distinguishing feature of American society.

Simultaneously, Americans are known the world over for their emphasis on *practicality*. "Will it work?" "Is it practical?"—such insistent questioning of a new idea or policy or gadget illustrates this emphasis, which at the same time is reflected in the prestige held by the engineer, the physician, and the businessman, as opposed to the schoolteacher, the clergyman, and the philosopher.

A related characteristic is that of *pecuniary evaluation*, the tendency to evaluate things and people in monetary terms. This tendency is illustrated in the great interest shown in multimillion-dollar film spectacles as well as in the use of monetary income as a measure of personal worth. Indeed, the United States and, perhaps to a lesser extent, Canada may still be the only places where the term "personal worth" brings up in most people's minds a financial consideration rather than a nonfinancial one.

Americans have also emphasized the value of *success,* placing a high positive valuation both on the possibility of succeeding in various types of undertakings ("The difficult we do immediately; the impossible takes a little while longer.") and also on the fact of having succeeded. The premium on success was bolstered by the Protestant ethic which emphasized industry and thrift and whose followers prospered not only in the eyes of the Lord but also in the amassing of personal wealth. It was also bolstered by the fluidity of the class structure and the relative importance placed on achievement as opposed to hereditary wealth or family position as a basis for assigning status.

An important emphasis on *education* is related both to the need for an informed electorate in a political democracy and to other values of success and individualism. Perhaps for this reason, formal education has given more support and impetus to the natural sciences and the social sciences than the humanities. An important aspect of the value placed on education is the often unvoiced assumption that "education is the answer" to various types of social problem such as poverty, alcoholism, preventable illness, and sexual immorality.

Science has come to be almost a magic word in American communities, expressing the growing confidence of millions of people in the results of a rational attempt to understand the world around them. The high status of science is undoubtedly related to the values of success and practicality, for to Americans, science has "paid off." It has lengthened the life span and increased the level of living. More recently, its importance for national defense and for space exploration has been emphasized and dramatized.

Another characteristic belief is that things in general can be made better, along with the belief that, this being the case, things *should* be made better. *Progress* is not only possible, but it is somehow a duty of society. The Enlightenment's faith in the infinite perfectibility of man took deep root in America, with its abundant resources, fluid society, emphasis on science, and aspiration for success. As the present century began, the ideas of Social Darwinism, the doctrine that natural selection was at work in the social world to assure the increasing perfection of the individual and of society—and that the government should not tamper with the process—were a means of reconciling the idea of progress with other American values.

When Jefferson drafted the Declaration of Independence, he modified Locke's natural rights of life, liberty, and property to become "life, liberty, and the pursuit of happiness." With the increasing secularization of American culture, *happiness* has come to be an important value. But happiness as a value in American communities is perhaps best thought of not in terms of the philosophical subtleties into which it fell at the hands of the natural-rights philosophers and the nineteenth-century utilitarians but simply as a belief that life should be enjoyable, that pleasure is better than pain,[55] that

55. Which in itself represents the long path Americans have traversed from the rigorous Puritan ethic of the early colonists.

misery should be avoided, and that everyone should be free to pursue happiness.

A feeling of obligation to "do something about" the more unfortunate people at home or abroad is perhaps best described as the value of *humanitarianism*. Like many other values, this one has its inconsistencies. Americans send billions abroad to help bolster various economies, many of which they at the same time are hampering by various trade barriers. Great interest has been focused on the victims of malnutrition, tuberculosis, or cancer, while alcoholics, psychopaths, and victims of the various vices have received "not bread but a stone." Nevertheless, important changes related to this value will be noted shortly.

We already observed that Tocqueville noticed a tendency for Americans to exercise tremendous pressure toward conformity through informal group pressures. *Conformity* should be included in any list of American values, if only to correct a possibly false impression given by listing such values as freedom and individualism. These various values are obviously at odds with each other, with one or another taking precedence according to the social context, and with communities differing from each other in their long-term tendencies to consider one value as more important than the other.

America has been considered a nation of "joiners." Later we shall discuss the extent to which this notion must be limited to perhaps half rather than all Americans (see chapter 6). Nevertheless, it is significant that the latest edition of *The Encyclopedia of Social Work* that listed national voluntary associations listed 370 national voluntary associations in the United States and Canada in the field of social work alone,[56] and over two decades ago Hamlin estimated that there were more than 100,000 voluntary health and welfare agencies in the United States.[57]

Among the various strains in American culture that are related to this extreme elaboration of voluntary organizations would seem to be a strong emphasis on humanitarianism, a strong faith in progress, a preference for citizen initiative over governmental intervention, a belief in "educating the public," and a series of personal satisfactions that Americans are able to find in formal voluntary associations.

The relative emphasis placed on such values as those described above changes with the topic under consideration and with the community. It also changes through time. Let us consider now some

56. *Encyclopedia of Social Work* (New York: National Association of Social Workers, 1965).

57. Robert H. Hamlin, *Voluntary health and Welfare Agencies in the United States: An Exploratory Study by an Ad Hoc Citizens Committee* (New York: Schoolmasters' Press, 1961), p. 59.

major value changes that are particularly relevant to the community level in American society.

One of the most notable changes is the *gradual acceptance of governmental activity as a positive value in an increasing number of fields*. Functions that only a few decades ago the vast majority of people would have considered as well outside the field of proper government activity or regulation now are accepted as perfectly appropriate governmental activity. The trend applies to all levels: federal, state, and local. The alternative position, that "that government is best which governs least," is rapidly fading as a standard for contemporary judgment. Increased clamor or at least support for increasing governmental activity is evident in such fields as industrial development, social insurance, health and welfare services, housing, education, and scientific research. Similarly, increasing intervention by government to regulate economic enterprise, to regulate charity drives, to settle industrial disputes, to protect consumers, and for many other regulatory purposes is coming to be accepted as a necessary and desirable function.

Obviously, this change in basic value orientation is related to the increasing vertical systemic orientation of many important functions and to the growth of various systems on the state or national level (see chapter 8). It is likewise related to the growth in bureaucratization and impersonalization of many functions, for modern government is expected to administer its vast programs through a system with virtually all the characteristics that Weber ascribed to bureaucracy, and it is related to the transfer of functions from other auspices to profit enterprise and to government mentioned earlier. It represents a gradual transition in the content or relative strength of such values as freedom and individualism, a change that involves contemporary value conflict within which one side, at least, follows John Dewey in asserting that freedom and individualism under present conditions can only be realized through greater, rather than less, governmental activity.[58]

Another important change in values is the *gradual change from a moral to a causal interpretation of human behavior*. There is a growing tendency to react to socially unacceptable behavior as a purely natural product of causes either known or yet to be determined and an increasing tendency to act toward such socially unacceptable behavior not with moral indignation and with punishment for misdeeds but rather with a therapeutic attitude, an attitude of looking for changes in the physical or social environment or in interpersonal or intrapersonal relationships that will remove the cause of the aberrant behavior and make possible the development of socially accept-

58. See John Dewey, *Individualism Old and New* (New York: Minton, Balch, 1930).

able patterns. Examples of deviant behavior that people are considering from the causal and therapeutic standpoint, rather than from one of moral indignation and punishment, are mental illness, alcoholism, prostitution, drug addiction, juvenile delinquency, and many types of crime. The development is not even. Thus, mental illness and juvenile delinquency are more likely to be viewed from the causal-therapeutic standpoint than is prostitution, but even in the latter, great changes in value orientation are apparent.

The changed orientation toward such aberrant behavior is partly, at least, a result of the larger historical development by which a rational-causal explanation for life has come to supplant a theological-moral explanation, part of the larger development from "sacred" society to "secular" society. It has a concomitant that is closely related but sufficiently important to warrant separate consideration.

This is the *change in community approach to social problems from that of moral reform to that of planning.* This change is particularly noticeable in the fields of poverty, slums, vice, crime, family breakdown, and other "problem" areas. Where the great social reformers of a few decades ago, like Jane Addams and Homer Folks, tended to mount great moral crusades to reform the misdoers, to bring social justice to the exploited, and to achieve action through periodic bursts of zealous campaigning to right this or that wrong, their counterparts today are social-agency board members and health and welfare planning-council leaders, who seek to apply rational planning to the community's problems so as to bring the community's resources to bear most effectively to achieve communitywide goals of prevention and control.

Here, too, the influence of the "secular," rather than the "sacred," approach is apparent. The value change noted here is obviously closely related to the growth of bureaucracy and impersonalization. One might refer to the "bureaucratization" of American humanitarianism, except that the name "bureaucratization," if not the reality behind it, still reflects older values much more congenial to the "moral indignation" and "reforming crusade" approach.

Tied in with the acceptance of planning is the acceptance of the specialist, the professional person, whether in public health, labor mediation, community welfare planning, or public housing. The increasing complexity of contemporary problems leads to a further specialization through which citizens delegate to specialists the function of confronting community problems that earlier they would have considered the appropriate arena for all competent and conscientious citizens. One should add that the setting up of special agencies to confront many types of community problem is another instance of the flow of functions away from the primary group, away from individuals and special ad hoc groupings and in the direction of voluntary associations (private agencies) and government as appropriate secondary groups to cope with the problems on a more formal, rational, specialized, and impersonal basis. The acceptance of such modes of confronting community problems represents an important change in values.

A final change is perhaps less closely related to other aspects of the "great change," but nevertheless it should be considered. This is the *change of emphasis from work and production to enjoyment and consumption*. Much of the social dynamism of American society has been attributed to the Protestant ethic, a philosophy of life that emphasized as religious duties such virtues as thrift and industriousness.[59] It has also been noted that just such ascetic concentration on work and thrift with corresponding renunciation of pleasure as sinful paradoxically led those who abided by it to prosper economically and thus become victimized by the plenty and affluence against which their ethic had warned. While the question of the relationship of the Protestant ethic to the rise of capitalism, and more specifically to the alleged industriousness of Americans, has been somewhat controverted, there is little disagreement that recent decades have seen the rapid decline of the older puritanical antipleasure ethic and a corresponding increase in the ethic of enjoyment.

The change has been characterized by a decrease in value placed on producing and an increase in value placed on consuming. A study a number of years back compared the subjects of biographies in a popular magazine during five sample years in the period 1901 to 1914 with the subjects of biographies in the same magazine in the year 1940-41. Among other things, it found that the percentage of subjects who came from political, business, and professional life declined from 74 percent to 25 percent, while the subjects from the entertainment world increased from 26 percent to 55 percent. Similarly, it classified the vocations of 125 popular heroes whose biographies were treated in articles in two popular national magazines in 1940-41. Of these, 2 percent were in the sphere of production, while 55 percent were in the entertainment and sports sphere. "We called the heroes of the past 'idols of production,' " the author wrote. "We feel entitled to call the present-day magazine heroes 'idols of consumption.' "[60]

59. See Max Weber, *The Protestant Ethic and the Spirit of Capitalism*, trans. Talcott Parsons (New York: Charles Scribner's Sons, 1958).

60. Leo Lowenthal, "Biographies in Popular Magazines," in William Petersen, ed., *American Social Patterns* (Garden City: Doubleday, 1956), pp. 66, 74, 75.

The reader will perhaps see an affinity between this change in values and the historic change from "inner-directedness" to "other-directedness," a change that is the theme of *The Lonely Crowd:*

> If we wanted to cast our social character types into social class molds, we could say that inner-direction is the typical character of the "old" middle class—the banker, the tradesman, the small entrepreneur, the technically oriented engineer, etc.—while other-direction is becoming the typical character of the "new" middle class—the bureaucrat, the salaried employee in business, etc.[61]

While the inner-directed person is guided by a strong set of principles implanted early in life, "What is common to all the other-directed people is that their contemporaries are the source of direction for the individual . . . it is only the process of striving itself and the process of paying close attention to the signals from others that remain unaltered throughout life."[62] This transition from an inner-directed to an other-directed society is alleged to be a comprehensive change affecting all areas of American living: schools, industries, government, research, domestic life, voluntary associations, and so on.

Whyte reported an analogous broad change in the gradual abandonment of the Protestant ethic in favor of the social ethic. "By social ethic I mean that contemporary body of thought which makes morally legitimate the pressures of society against the individual. Its major propositions are three: a belief in the group as the source of creativity; a belief in 'belongingness' as the ultimate need of the individual; and a belief in the application of science to achieve the belongingness."[63] As the social ethic comes into ascendancy, it tends to emphasize the values of leisure, installment financing, and consumption rather than those of industriousness, thrift, and production.

In relation to other aspects of the great change, it is interesting to note that Riesman found the other-directed type especially congenial to vocations associated with modern bureaucracy, while Whyte commented in relation to the social ethic: "With reason it could be called an organization ethic, or a bureaucratic ethic; more than anything else it rationalizes the organization's demands for fealty and

---

61. David Riesman, Nathan Glazer, and Reuel Denney, *The Lonely Crowd: A Study of the Changing American Character* (New Haven, Conn.: Yale University Press, 1950). p. 36 in Doubleday Anchor edition (1953).

62. Riesman, Glazer, and Denney, *Lonely Crowd*, p. 37.

63. *Organization Man*, p. 7.

gives those who offer it wholeheartedly a sense of dedication in doing so."[64]

The switch in emphasis to consumption rather than production is related to the transition documented by Riesman and Whyte. It involves not so much a renunciation of earlier values as a shift in their emphasis. In this shift, conformity rises at the expense of individualism. Science and practicality are enlisted in the service of happiness, which comes increasingly to be emphasized as a measure of success; and progess comes to be measured in terms of the leisure and consumer goods available to the individual. More recently, a different kind of value change has made itself apparent in the development of a "counter-culture" which disparages the commercialism, materialism, and impersonality of American society and advocates an emphasis upon personal values and relationships. In chapters 11 and 12 this is treated as a revolt against the "great change."

We have considered seven aspects of the great change in American society and have pointed out how these aspects are related to social organization and process on the community level. In chapter 1 we defined our use of the term *community* and pointed out four important dimensions on which American communities differ from each other. We are now in a position to relate the "great change" to these four dimensions of community. In the process, we shall see that these dimensions are useful not only as a significant framework for classifying differences among contemporary communities, but also as a paradigm of community change, for in each case, the "great change" as analyzed in this chapter has resulted in an overall movement in the same direction on each of the four dimensions. You will recall that the four dimensions are local autonomy, coincidence of service areas, psychological identification with locality, and strength of the horizontal pattern. As we consider the aspects of the "great change" described so far in this chapter, it is apparent that these four dimensions represent not only a static classification but a trend through time. The "great change" implies a movement from left to right along the scale indicated in Figure 1-1. The great change involves a movement through time from independence to dependence on the autonomy dimension; from coinciding service areas to differing service areas; from strong psychological identification with the locality to weak identification; and from a strong horizontal pattern for communities to a weak one.

Obviously, not all communities are changing at the same rate of speed, or have reached the same point in the rightward swing along each of the four dimensions. Indeed, not all parts of any particular community are necessarily to be located at exactly the same point along each dimension. Nevertheless, each community can be considered an aggregate in terms of the distance it has traveled along the four dimensions, and meaningful differences among communities can be observed.

In chapter 4 we shall consider four quite different communities, indicate the extent to which the various aspects of the "great change" have affected their structure and function, and locate them on each of the four dimensions of change.

4 Four American Communities and the "Great Change"

The communities chosen for description and analysis in this chapter represent a broad diversity. From the standpoint of size, they vary from a small village of only a score or so families to the suburb of a large metropolis. In location, they depict the United States Southwest, the Middle West, the Northeast, and southern Canada. Likewise, the people of these communities vary from the Mexican-American farmers of a southwestern village to the well-to-do businessmen of a rich commuting suburb.

The studies made of these communities represent landmarks in community field research. The communities described represent different degrees of development along the dimensions of the "great change" considered in the preceding chapter. El Cerrito, for example, shows little evidence of the various changes depicted in that chapter, while Middletown and Crestwood Heights show them in marked degree. It should be noted that the fieldwork for these community studies was done at different times, some of it as early as the 1930s. Significantly, however, the time each community was studied does not correspond precisely to the degree to which the "great change" is evident. For example, the Middletown of 1935 shows a

96

greater impact of the change than does Springdale in the 1950s. These four cases illustrate different embodiments of the change, some showing much greater development in this respect than others. Although they all change through time, they do not change at the same rate, and El Cerrito, for example, showed relatively little change at the time it was studied.

Shifting from the factor of time to that of size, it is interesting to note that there is a one-to-one correspondence between the size of these communities and the degree to which they experienced the changes involved. Here again, one would expect a rough, though not an unfailing correspondence, because of the concurrent operation of factors other than size.

One other type of variation should be mentioned, relating to the variation in point of view of the investigator. All these studies followed to a great degree the "institutional approach" described in chapter 2, but each was done from a particular theoretical point of view, which characteristically influenced the selection of the data that the investigator considered important enough to gather and analyze and the interpretation that the investigator gave to the data. The Lynds' studies of Middletown, for example, used two cleavages as focal points of interpretation: that between the business class and the working class and that between the two sets of values simultaneously held by Middletowners. Vidich and Bensman, on the other hand, asserted that their Springdale study was "an attempt to explore the foundations of social life in a community which lacks the power to control the institutions that regulate and determine its existence."[1] The Crestwood Heights study was undertaken as part of the Canadian National Mental Health Project, and the data gathered and interpretations given reflect its special interest in the child-rearing process and its implications for mental health.

There is an unavoidable subjectivity in community studies, and while this affects somewhat the data gathered, it affects the interpretations given even more. Hence, one might question whether El Cerrito, for example, might have looked different if the study had been made by Vidich and Bensman, or whether Crestwood Heights might not have been given a somewhat different type of interpretation if the study had been made on one hand by Olen Leonard and Charles P. Loomis or on the other by the Lynds. As Stein pointed out in an illuminating analysis of the subjective aspects of community studies, "Short of reading the field notes, no one can know what the primary observations may have been, and so the published study becomes the

---

1. Arthur J. Vidich and Joseph Bensman, *Small Town in Mass Society: Class, Power and Religion in a Rural Community,* p. viii. Copyright 1958 by Princeton University Press, Princeton, N.J.

sole avenue that the general public or other scientific readers have to the community in question."[2]

There is an interesting instance of a community being studied independently by two different investigators, who came out with remarkably different interpretations of the community involved. Although seventeen years had elapsed between the two studies, the investigators did not believe that the community had changed sufficiently to warrant the great discrepancy in their findings, but both attributed it to the difference in their points of view. Commenting on this difference, Redfield, who made the first study, wrote: "The principal conclusion that I draw from this experience is that we are all better off with two descriptions of Tepoztlan than we would be with only one of them. More understanding results from the contrast and complementarity which the two together provide."[3]

Such fortunate replication of the studies by an independent investigator does not usually occur, however, and it did not with the four communities that we shall consider here. This is usually the case. The reader must therefore be alert to the possibility of distortion caused by the particular point of view of the original investigators and also to the possibility of distortion caused by the present author in his selection of certain aspects from the reports to incorporate into the brief summaries included in this chapter. Certainly, although the hope is to avoid distortion, the selection has been influenced very deliberately by the search for relevant data about the extent to which each of the seven aspects of the "great change" is apparent in the four communities.

El Cerrito, New Mexico

In an arid part of the American Southwest lies the small village of El Cerrito, New Mexico.[4] At the time it was intensively studied in 1939, its population consisted of only a score or so families, all of original Spanish extraction, language, and customs. Its way of life was so drastically different from that f most communities in the United States and Canada that one might question its inclusion in this book. Yet, its citizens were United States citizens and it was an American

2. Maurice R. Stein, *The Eclipse of Community: An Interpretation of American Studies* (Princeton: Princeton University Press, 1960), p. 310.

3. Robert Redfield, *The Little Community: Viewpoints for the Study of a Human Whole*, p. 136. Copyright 1955 by The University of Chicago Press, Chicago, Ill.

4. This description is a synopsis of Olen Leonard and C. P. Loomis, *Culture of a Contemporary Rural Community: El Cerrito, New Mexico* (Washington: U.S. Department of Agriculture, 1941).

community. It serves as a reminder of the great diversity that exists among American communities and the people who inhabit them.

El Cerrito is especially significant as a community that experienced little of the "great change," which is the principal theme of this book. Thus, it constitutes something of an anchor point, a point on which to tie as we consider the rapid change transforming the very nature of American communities. One appreciates the extent and importance of such change when one turns back to El Cerrito and realizes that communities can be like it.

Community characteristics   All the inhabitants of El Cerrito were of Spanish-American stock, descendants of earlier Spanish settlers who intermingled with local Indian peoples. Their language and culture were Spanish, English being spoken only in the local school. The extreme isolation of their location was a barrier against influence from the larger culture. The telephone had never reached as far as El Cerrito, and only five newspaper copies came regularly into the village, all of them printed in Spanish. There were no magazine subscriptions and only two radios in intermittent operating condition. Few families owned automobiles, whose occasional trips to Las Vegas brought their passengers into contact with other Spanish Americans, often relatives. The work of the county agent of the agricultural extension service had not had any impact on the prevailing methods of agriculture. The village was in such a remote section that one would be fortunate to find it without the most detailed instructions.

Two social units dominated the social life of El Cerrito: the family and the church. The family was the basic unit, children having a strong identification with the family, which was also the chief unit of economic production. Even after the sons and daughters were married and living in their own homes, they had strong responsibilities to family members and were expected to help them in any distress and to be present for such important ceremonies as family reunions, first communions, marriages, and deaths, even in the rare case where this involved traveling for hundreds of miles. Most of the considerable amount of visiting and exchanging of work back and forth within the village was between close relatives. Indeed, there were few families in El Cerrito that were not related in a third-cousin relationship, or a closer one, to all the other families in the village.

Complementing the family in the closest reciprocal relationship was the church. Without exception, the villagers were Roman Catholic. Although there was no resident priest, there was a church, and services were held regularly on Sundays and often during the week in charge of a local woman. The church gave the family its   **99** moral sanction and supported it at such meaningful crises as first communion, marriage, and death.

The annual two-day celebration in honor of the community's patron saint was a high point of the year. It took considerable preparation, and a regular system was used to rotate the responsibilities connected with it. The many other holy days were rigidly observed. In a way, the church building itself reflected the importance that the church had in the minds of the villagers, for it was the best-kept building in the village, and hands were never wanting when it needed repairs or a coat of whitewash.

By contrast, the school was an institution of relatively minor importance, reflected in its shoddy appearance when compared with the church. It was not a center of important family and community ceremonies, and family members other than young children had no significant relationship to it. The school was considered important as orienting the young to the world beyond El Cerrito, but such a function was only vaguely achieved in its program. Nor was any great importance placed on the children's learning much more than simple English and arithmetic. State law required English to be spoken in the school, but there was little supervision or regulation from outside, and conversation frequently lapsed into Spanish. The general attitude seemed to be that, except for English and arithmetic, the child could best be taught what he or she needed to know by the family or by the church.

El Cerrito was located in a valley of bottomland formed at a widening in the Pecos River. The bottomland was fertile, but small in area. Livestock was formerly raised on huge tracts of dry land in the surrounding mesa, but most of these holdings were depleted through land sales to pay delinquent taxes and in other ways. During an earlier period, however, it was possible to get wage jobs with the railroad or by working in the area farther north.

With the Great Depression these sources of support had dwindled, and the people were thrown back upon their remaining land for sustenance. At the time of the study, the only additional sources of income were jobs that involved leaving the village, including WPA jobs and a number of other federal relief programs. Economically, the village was extremely depressed, yet in the preceding fifteen years, only two families had moved away with no plans for returning. The village apparently had an extremely strong attraction for its people, despite the economic hardship, for reasons that will be considered below.

The irrigated farmland was worked by prescientific methods, which had changed little over the years. The chief crops were beans, corn, and alfalfa, with additional fresh vegetables during the summer. Farming was on a subsistence basis. Working the land involved considerable cooperative effort, and there was much exchanging and borrowing of labor and tools. The irrigation system was vital to the meager life of the community. Significantly, although none of the more usual farm organizations to be observed elsewhere in the United States was found in the village, the "Ditch Association" had functioned longer than any villagers could remember. Water was distributed according to the size of the holdings, and an appropriate amount of labor on the ditch was expected in return. The system was administered by a ditch boss and a three-man ditch committee, which drew up and enforced such regulations as were necessary. These four were elected annually. Enforcement of compliance with regulations was relatively easy because of the importance of the water for each plot and the possibility of suspending water rights or imposing heavy fines in assessed labor. Although hard work and thrift were recognized as necessary to eke out a bare subsistence, they were not valued as virtues in themselves, as they often have been in many American communities.

There was relatively little differentiation among the villagers as to economic or social status. The three men in the village who were full-time farm laborers were all related in some way to their employer. Indeed, earlier extremes between wealthy cattle-owning dons and lowly peons disappeared with the decline of large holdings.

Recreation in El Cerrito was almost exclusively of the type involving no expenditure of money, pursuits that people can arrange for themselves. These included dances, visits to town, attendance at political rallies, and fishing. There was no commercialized recreation. There were dances each Saturday night in the school, with music supplied locally. Both old and young attended, and often, older people gave announcements or talks on any topic they cared to bring before the group. This interruption of the dancing was a sanctioned prerogative and was accepted courteously.

The old customs received strong support from the villagers. Social control was highly effective. Among the small group of isolated villagers, group approval and sanction constituted the informal means of controlling behavior, facilitated by clearly defined prescribed patterns of behavior and by lack of conflicting or confusing alternative patterns from the larger society. Group norms thus received solid support from the group, and the deviant was assured high visibility and strong disapproval.

An important underlying element in this situation was the entire pattern of high integration that characterized the community. The fieldworkers who studied El Cerrito concluded that the high integration was due chiefly to the following combination of factors.

1. *Families* were strong centers of important activities. Being closely knit, they tended to hold the individual member not only to his or her kinship group but also to the local customs and to the local community.

2. The *church* was an important unifying force in the community, uniting all the villagers in common faith, common moral sanctions, and many common activities that gave color and significance to their lives. It stood toward the family in a close relationship of mutual support.

3. The *sense of belonging to a community* was strongly ingrained in the individual, who knew all other villagers on an intimate, face-to-face basis and shared a closely intermingled life with them.

4. The sense of *one's own people*. The villager did not share fully in the larger Anglo culture. He or she felt most at home with the other villagers who shared a common life: common customs, common values, common language, common religion.

Yet at the time of the field study, this apparently stable community was threatened with disintegration. The economic basis for the support of the villagers had declined through loss of land and loss of nearby job opportunities. Into this situation, various agencies of the federal government had entered to offer economic help. These included the WPA, offering jobs; the CCC and NYA, offering camp experience for youths; the Farm Security Administration, offering loans and grants; and the Agricultural Conservation Program, which financed certain conservation projects. These afforded an important channel to the larger society, both through providing cash and through the effect of the work-camp experience on youths.

Youths who had been at the CCC camps came to learn more about the world outside, and several of them expressed an interest in leaving El Cerrito in favor of some place where the economic opportunity would be greater. They also became impatient and critical of the older customs and values of El Cerrito.

Thus, the economic situation threatened to destroy El Cerrito. Its inhabitants loved the old ways and wanted to stay where they were and preserve them. But they realized that they no longer could support themselves economically. Either the government would have to increase its support, thus changing the traditional basis of agricultural subsistence, or people would have to move away from El Cerrito. It was difficult to conceive of any economic development that would help sustain El Cerrito that would not in some way tie it in more closely with the production and exchange system of the larger American society and thus bring it out of its cultural isolation and relative self-sufficiency.

El Cerrito and the "Great Change" Somewhat abstractly, one might translate the seven aspects of the "great change" for analytical purposes into two extreme types representing, as it were, the ideal types of "before" and "after." If one were to do so, the "before" type would have the following characteristics: It would be a community in which there is very little division of labor, the one widely significant difference being, perhaps, between the sexes. Similarly, there would be little differential association on the basis of specialized interests; rather people would simply associate with each other on the basis of their propinquity. The community would be largely self-sufficient, with a minimum of ties to the surrounding society. Social relationships and the performance of local functions would be on the basis of behavior patterns formed by custom and sentiment in which the people involved had a personal relationship to each other. With little division of labor and all practicing a common method of gaining a livelihood, there would be little need for a market and price system. Such exchange of goods and services as was necessary would be on the basis of gifts, loans, and barter. This simple type of social organization could not, of course, sustain the population of large cities, and communities would therefore be small. Finally, there would be a common set of social values held by all members of the community, values that received little challenge from the world outside the community and that showed little change over a great period of time.

El Cerrito approximated this extreme type of community. It represented little, if any, change away from the type in the directions indicated in chapter 3. All its adult males engaged in essentially the same pursuits, basing their livelihood on a simple, prescientific agriculture. Nor were people separated on the basis of cultural background, since they all shared the same Spanish-American heritage as well as the same religious affiliation and spoke the same language. Isolated physically from the larger culture, they had few ties of communication with it and few systemic ties to it. They were united with each other not only by close ethnic and religious ties, but also by close ties of overlapping kinship. Organized leisure-time activities brought all the members of the community together, and informal visiting and mutual aid patterns brought various members of the community together in many different relationships.

The agricultural agent, the school system, the government, the church all involved ties to the larger society, but in each case the tie was minimal. And in each case, the presence of rational, impersonal administrative machinery was at a minimum. Most services in the church were conducted by a lay person. The schoolteacher was hardly an impersonal representative of distant cultural values, and there was little sign of the proliferation of specialized, bureaucratized personnel characteristic of larger schools with special subject **103** teachers, nurses, guidance counselors, school psychologists, athletic coaches, and administrative and clerical personnel.

Two major events in the annual cycle of community living required a somewhat elaborate organization. The maintenance, repair, and utilization of the irrigation ditch required a specially selected officialdom of three persons. But it is significant that these positions were rotated and that they were unpaid. It is also significant that the Ditch Association functioned without charges, being solely a cooperative endeavor involving the pooling of work, along with a nonmonetary system for assessing duties and enforcing sanctions on those who failed to perform them. The organization for the two-day celebration of the patron saint's birthday also involved somewhat elaborate rules and procedures, and the positions of responsibility were similarly rotated among community members, rather than involving specialists to perform them.

Borrowing and lending of tools, help in time of trouble, provision of recreation, performance of community functions, provision of food and other goods and services — such functions that elsewhere are often provided as a commercial or money-making venture were here provided in a different way, with the coin being not a metal but reciprocation, the customary procedures according to which exchanges, gifts, and loans of goods or of services are so performed and so controlled that over a period of time what is given approximates what is received.

Urbanization and suburbanization were indicated neither by a growth in the size of the community nor by the advent of the classic characteristics of urbanized society: large numbers of people, density of population, and heterogeneity of people.

The old values remained, strengthened by custom and by informal social controls, little challenged by the ideological ferment in the surrounding culture. Physical and cultural isolation, common culture, unchanging technology, and a mutually reinforcing religious and family system were all parts of the strong pattern of community cohesion.

In chapter 1 it was pointed out that communities differ significantly from each other on four dimensions. Considering these dimensions, it is apparent that El Cerrito showed great *local autonomy* both in the control that it exercised over its own community institutions and processes and in its relative self-sufficiency. It encompassed the same people and the *same geographic area* for its school, for its church, and for its other associational activities. Its residents showed a strong sense of *psychological identification* with the community, preferring to remain in El Cerrito even under economically disadvantageous circumstances and maintaining a strong sense of identification even when absent from the community. Its *horizontal pattern* of community relationships, according to which the community is able to hold together and function as a significant social entity, was remarkably strong. On all four characteristics of the scale on page 13, El Cerrito would rate remarkably close to zero.

And yet there were at least minimal signs of the "great change." Perhaps most important of all, the decline in the local economy necessitated various types of governmental financial aid programs that established new systemic ties to state and federal government and some of which brought El Cerrito people, especially youths, into contact with the surrounding money-based culture and with ideas that challenged the older community values. The community dances, though not commercial, nevertheless charged a price for admission. Radios, newspapers, and automobiles gained a foothold, presaging closer cultural ties to the larger society with a corresponding challenge to prevailing values. Most important, the decline in the almost self-sufficient economic base made it virtually impossible for the community to go on supporting its members without further financial subsidy from the larger society (and a closer systemic tie) or without the introduction of economic pursuits that would involve division of labor, entrance into the money economy, and other aspects of the "great change." Another possibility was that the community would decline in numbers as the attempt was made to preserve the community's ways but as economic necessity claimed its toll in migration.

Actually, this past is what occurred. A later account by Loomis indicated that since 1940, when it contained twenty-six families, the population had dwindled to a quarter of that size. The migration was chiefly to Pueblo, Colorado, 263 miles away, and took place through the procedure of men obtaining work, establishing a hold in Pueblo, and then bringing family or relatives. They kept in as close touch as possible with those who remained in El Cerrito.[5]

Springdale, New York

Community characteristics   Springdale is a relatively small village in the general farming and dairying area of upstate New York.[6] At the time of the study, the village of some 1,000 people was the

5. Charles P. Loomis, "Systemic Linkage of El Cerrito," *Rural Sociology*, vol. 24, no. 1 (March 1959).

6. Selections from Arthur J. Vidich and Joseph Bensman, *Small Town in Mass Society: Class, Power and Religion in a Rural Community.* (rev. edn. © 1968 by Princeton University Press; Princeton Paperback, 1968): 200–01, and pp. 269-70. Reprinted by permission of Princeton University Press. Additional material from the Springdale study is presented in an issue of the *Journal of Social Issues*, vol. 16, no. 4 (1960), on the topic "Leadership and Participation in a Changing Rural Community," ed. John Harding, Edward C. Devereux, Jr., and Urie Bronfenbrenner.

center of a rural community of approximately 2,500. It contained no large industry but was a trade center for the surrounding country-side of farms, which varied from 50 to 1,000 acres. About a third of those who were gainfully employed were farm owners or laborers. Almost another third worked in the village, as business proprietors, professionals, clerks, salesmen, skilled and semiskilled workers, or manual workers. Something over a third of the employed commuted to work in towns and cities in the vicinity. These tended to be skilled and semiskilled industrial workers and some sales and clerical workers. Only 25 percent of Springdale people were born in the local area, and 45 percent had moved in since 1932.

Springdale had no motion-picture house, no supermarket, no outside industry. Actually, the largest economic enterprise was the central school, with an annual budget of a quarter of a million dollars and about 60 employees.

Springdale had a number of different voluntary associations, including the Masons and the American Legion and their auxiliaries, the Grange, three book clubs, two volunteer fire companies, a Community Club, Farm Bureau, Home Bureau, Little League Baseball club, and, in season, a variety of fund-raising organizations such as the Red Cross, Cancer, Cerebral Palsy, and Heart associations and the March of Dimes. About half of its organized social activity was connected with the churches.

Springdalers thought of themselves as "just plain folks." They maintained strong ideas regarding the superiority of rural life over city life, thinking of small rural communities as healthy and whole-some places to live and the cities as centers of social problems and political corruption. They showed a good deal of neighborliness, including the propensity to gossip. Their social values were charac-terized by equality, industriousness, self-improvement, and opti-mism. Hard work and self-improvement were believed to be the basis for "getting ahead." These values were somewhat differently regarded by the different social class groups, which were as follows:

Middle class
    independent entrepreneurs
    prosperous farmers
    professionals and skilled industrial workers

Marginal middle class
    aspiring investors
    economically and socially immobile ritualists
    idiosyncratics

Traditional farmers
Old aristocrats
Shack people

The rational farmers were differentiated from the traditional farmers in that they considered farming as a business. They calculated costs carefully, distributing their energy and their costs so as to obtain a maximum yield in relation to prices. Their farming decisions were based on rationality rather than sentiment or tradition. Typically, they put their profits back into expansion, unlike the independent entrepreneurs (merchants, people with small businesses), who did not typically reinvest for expansion. The traditional farmers differed in all these respects. At the other extreme were the shack people, who rejected a rational ordering of their living, rejected the idea of hard work and self-improvement, and sought short-term gratifications. They participated hardly at all in the organized social life of the community. While the social classes differed from each other notably, particularly in such things as investment and reinvestment, hoarding, consumption, and work, "the underlying secular trend indicates a shift from production to consumption values in the community."[7]

The relation of Springdale to the "mass society" was a special focus of attention in Vidich and Bensman's book. They pointed out that outside influences were transmitted directly through specific persons such as the agricultural extension specialist. They might also be expressed through community members who were heads of local branches of state and national organizations, of local businesses dependent on outside resources, or of local church units of larger religious bodies. Decisions about the community were in some cases made by institutional personnel in business or government outside the community, and, of course, the community was affected by impersonal "market" decisions of business and government, which affected the entire economy.

Certain organizations "imported" culture into the community. These included the Farm Bureau, Home Bureau, 4-H Club, Future Farmers, Boy and Girl Scouts, Masons, Odd Fellows, American Legion, Grange, and other local branches of national organizations. New cultural standards were imported by teachers, too, and by a variety of sales people and "experts" from surrounding business, voluntary, and governmental organizations. Culture was also brought in through the mass media and through the curriculum of the schools and Sunday schools, as well as by new people who came into the community to live.

Through their employment, many Springdalers were directly connected with organizations of the mass society. A particularly important vocational group was that of the professions, such as lawyers, ministers, doctors, teachers, engineers. Generally, they were

7. Vidich and Bensman, *Small Town*, p. 78.

not native to the community; they constituted, however, an important link to the culture beyond the community through their knowledge and values. Industrial workers and businessmen, through their employment or through their operation of a franchise, also provided an important link. Rational farmers were closely geared to the price structure and market exigencies of the larger society, while traditional farmers were characterized by their relative self-sufficiency and by their relative isolation from extracommunity farm influences.

Local government consisted largely of the village and town boards and the activities they maintained. They had many stipulated functions and powers, but wherever possible they adapted their own activity to that of state and federal agencies, performing only those functions not provided by such agencies and thus surrendering voluntarily much of local government's autonomy to state and federal agencies. Further, functions within their powers for which there was great local demand and which could not be transferred to larger jurisdictions were often left for nongovernmental action by voluntary agencies or ad hoc community organizations.

Village politics was dominated by the conservative influence of the people in business and reflected their low-tax orientation. To a very great extent the board was dominated by the legal counsel, a lawyer chosen by the board, who dominated largely through his special competence and the contrasting incompetence of the village board members in village matters, particularly those involving the legal and formal aspect of village transactions. The board took as little initiative as possible, preferring to avoid an increase in the village tax rate by letting other, larger governmental units or voluntary associations perform functions. Its proceedings were characterized by an attempt to minimize decision and action, a tendency for unanimity in decision-making, and an abdication of local governmental responsibilities.

While the village government was dominated by businessmen, the town government, whose principal concern was the maintenance of roads, was dominated by prosperous farmers. It, too, willingly transferred much of its power to other agencies of government. Springdale's relation to the politics of state government was in the nature of a political collaboration among rural communities to support the party that dominated the state legislature and succeeded through strong rural support in keeping in check the opposite party, which represented the large cities.

Springdale's links to state and national politics were provided through three channels: the state subsidy, state and national elections, and national agricultural policies. The value of its affiliation with other rural interests on the state level was indicated by the fact that the county in which Springdale was located got back in state aid approximately twenty times the amount it contributed in all state taxes.

The school had some six hundred students in grades 1 through 12. The school board was dominated by the convergence of business and farm interests in a low-tax, low-expenditure ideology. The school principal was an expert who came from outside the community. He represented educational values and goals that did not always agree with those of local business and farm interests, but he was realistic in how far he chose to go, and he was strengthened by his expertness in school matters. He often found support for his own purposes in the Parent-Teachers Association, which he occasionally used as a method of introducing ideas that he favored.

Four different religious denominations had churches in Springdale, with a total of about 300 to 400 active supporters out of the 1,700 adults. Traditional farmers participated little in church life, and the shack people remained completely aloof. The lay leadership of the various church activities came from the industrial and professional groups. The top policy leaders were largely the same people that were key leaders in the community's political institutions. The minister in each case exercised great influence through his link to an extracommunity denominational structure and through his own specialized competence, but like the school principal, each minister had to modify his objectives and policies in relation to his lay board. The churches expressed great interest in the growing ecumenical movement (toward concerted church action in various spheres), but their activity in this respect was largely ceremonial. Actually, important unwritten rules governed the relations between the churches, particularly in regard to the "stealing" of members. Significantly, proselytizing activities of the churches were never aimed at the immoral, irresponsible "unreliable" groups in the non-churchgoing population, even though there was otherwise strong interchurch competition for membership, and even though each church carried on extensive missionary endeavor for non-Christians in various remote places in the world.

Although there were many systemic relations to state and national organizations of all types, "a wide range of community activities are coordinated simply because a small number of individuals are engaged in a wide range of leadership positions."[8] Throughout the institutional structure of Springdale, one came again and again onto four men who occupied various positions of official and unofficial leadership. These were a farm feed and mill operator, the editor of the local paper who was town clerk, a lawyer who was legal

8. Vidich and Bensman, *Small Town*, p. 258. **109**

counsel to the village and other organizations, and a county commit-teeman who was a high-order Mason. In the combination of these four men, "one could gain almost a complete picture of the major activities, plans, personnel and decisions that make up the life of the community at any given moment."[9] They constituted major focuses of community power, and through their reciprocal relationships they provided a rough kind of coordination of community effort. Through their access to county and state bureaucracies and leaders of governmental or nongovernmental activity they exerted consider-able control over the local professional and expert people, such as ministers, teachers, county agent, and so on. While these four men were crucial in decision-making, the leadership in the execution of decisions and in the making of minor decisions was more diffuse, extending to all classes except the shack people.

Springdalers were faced with a basic discrepancy between their image of small village life with its ideal virtues, its self-sufficiency, its reward for hard work and endeavor and the actual facts of life in which local autonomy was surrendered to external systems and in which personal life goals were seldom fully realized. "Life, then, con-sists in making an adjustment that is as satisfactory as possible within a world which is not often tractable to basic wishes and desires."[10]

Springdale and the "Great Change" Springdale provides an excellent opportunity for comparison with El Cerrito. Both were relatively small, rural communities; but the difference is vast, both in relation to local community cohesion and autonomy and in relation to the ties of community units to extracommunity systems. It should be noted that the report by Vidich and Bensman, as its title indi-cates, placed particular emphasis on exploring the ties to the "mass society," and thus such ties featured more prominently in their report than they might in a study of the same community by other investigators. But allowing for this, the difference from El Cerrito was enormous. We shall analyze it in terms of the community's situa-tion with regard to the specific aspects of the "great change." Much of our data has been included in the foregoing account of Spring-dale, which follows, generally, the sequence of description given by the authors of the study. In the following analysis we shall supple-ment these data with other pertinent data from *Small Town in Mass Society.*

In Springdale, the division of labor showed considerable elabo-ration. As far back as 1880, the authors noted, specialization was

9. Vidich and Bensman, *Small Town,* p. 263.

10. Vidich and Bensman, *Small Town,* p. 314.

beginning to take industry out of the home, and even at that time there was increasing emphasis on a cash economy and on specialized farming. As a contemporary example, the production of butter and cheese had been superseded by the specialized production of fluid milk that through an intricate organizational and transportation network was delivered to the urban market. Regarding division of labor, the authors reported that "a wide spectrum of occupations is represented in the community. There are on the one hand business proprietors, farm owners and professionals; on the other hand, clerks, salesmen, farm laborers, skilled and semiskilled workers, manual workers and the odd-job men of many skills and no specialty."[11]

The large number of organized clubs and other voluntary activities, the four different religious denominations, the many different social class groups showing such great differences in values and life styles—all these pointed to a variegated associational life largely based on differential interests, in some cases vocational, in others not.

In connection with vocation, the authors reported that the large group of industrial workers did not fit well into the local society because their jobs took them to other communities on a commutation basis and also because the predominantly rural community of Springdale had no important plants and did not really understand industry and the industrial process. To this extent, the industrial workers represented a somewhat alienated group, as did the shack people. Significantly, these two groups constituted a substantial proportion of the total population. The prosperous or "rational" farmers likewise constituted an operational group distinguished from those in nonfarm vocations but also distinguished from the "traditional" farmers in values, technology, and style of living. Still another type of social differentiation was based on nationality group, since about 15 percent of the community's population was Polish, mixed with some Ukrainians, who came to the community principally in the decade of the twenties.

Thus, though Springdale was a relatively small, rural community, it represented important divisions of labor and important differentiation of interests and association related to occupation, social class, religion, and ethnic group. Despite differential participation based on these factors, there was a good amount of neighborly behavior based on the fact that people found themselves living in proximity to each other. This neighboring was chiefly characterized by help in time of crisis, such as birth, death, illness, fire, or catastro-

11. Vidich and Bensman, *Small Town,* p. 21.

phe, but also included routine borrowing and lending of tools, food, and clothing. Nevertheless, even in such neighborly activity, social differentiation applied, for the authors pointed out that a lawyer's wife was on neighborly terms with others "like herself" rather than with the carpenter's wife. And such groups as farmers and teachers were likely to carry on neighborly relations with each other much more than with members of other groups.

Systemic ties to the larger society were strong, and the authors emphasized them. In their preface they stated: "In summary, this study is an attempt to explore the foundations of social life in a community which lacks the power to control the institutions that regulate and determine its existence."[12] Although this statement tends to put into absolute terms a condition that was more accurately a matter of degree, it serves to summarize the extent to which systemic ties to the larger society dominated the stage on which local actors developed their daily drama. Such systemic ties applied throughout the institutional structure. Vocationally, the farmers illustrated different types of relationships. The prosperous farmers operated their farms rationally and on a cash basis in close adaptation to the national market. Their dairy business was closely regulated under the Federal Milk Price Order in the New York Milk Shed, influenced by agricultural policies of the federal government, such as farm price supports, farm credit programs, and special preferential programs for land improvement and fertilizer, and closely adapted to the exigencies of the national market for agricultural products. Actually, their income, and thus to a large extent their status relative to other groups in the community, was largely determined by forces over which local community people had little control.

In contrast, the traditional farmers, operating largely on subsistence principles rather than on a cash-crop farming basis, were comparatively immune from the daily exigencies of the market. They had thus not benefited so greatly by the recent national prosperity, but by the same token they were not as vulnerable to forces beyond the immediate community, a condition that occasionally made them envied by the prosperous farmer group. The shack people were even more immune to the systemic forces of the larger society.

Likewise, industrial workers depended for their jobs on companies that were largely outside the Springdale community and that in turn were sensitive to national economic conditions. The merchants on Main Street depended on the income of farmers and industrial workers, and fluctuations in national economic conditions were eventually reflected in their cash registers.

12. Vidich and Bensman, *Small Town*, p.viii.

Many of the voluntary associations were but local embodiments of a national organization's prescribed pattern, over which their local community influence was minuscule. In the case of the American Legion, for example, the authors pointed out that "local members have nothing to do with higher levels of organizational activity. Sometimes they hold offices at the district level, but no one from Springdale has ever held a state office."[13]

Local government bodies did not reflect in their own operations the contemporary American trend of expanded governmental activities. On the contrary:

> In almost every area of jurisdiction the [village] board has adjusted its action to the regulations and laws externally defined by outside agencies which engage in functions parallel to its own. State police, regionally organized fire districts, state welfare agencies, the state highway department, the state youth commission, the state conservation department—these agencies and others are central to the daily functioning of the village.[14]

The strengthening systemic ties to extracommunity units were almost invariably accompanied by a growing rational systematization of the corresponding activities and an increased delegation of function to specialized personnel operating within and deriving much of their power from bureaucratic structures. Such bureaucratization was reflected both in the systemic linkage of local units to large extracommunity bureaucracies—the Dairymen's League, the state department of education—and also in the development of bureaucratic relationships among people in different positions within the local community. Thus, though farmers are often considered the very embodiment of individualism, the rational farmers, as described earlier, constituted individually almost a prototype of the rational, systematized, nonsentimental behavior characteristic of bureaucratic organization. In a somewhat related fashion, the village board found itself voluntarily yielding, on the one hand, to various county and state bureaucracies, and on the other hand becoming increasingly dependent on the specialized knowledge of the village counsel, who afforded the necessary competence in threading the village's way through the complex, systematized bureaucratic procedures that state law prescribed for its operations. Through specialized knowledge came a large measure of power for the village counsel.

13. Vidich and Bensman, *Small Town*, p. 24.
14. Vidich and Bensman, *Small Town*, p. 113.

In the case of the school and the church—also structured to a large extent by patterns imposed by state or denominational authorities, although with strong components of local control—specialized knowledge on the part of the principal and the minister was coupled with the linkage position that those officials occupied between the local community unit and a larger extracommunity system. The school itself reflected the growing rationalization and systematization process, having been formed as a more efficient, centralized, and integrated unit out of 26 independent school districts in the thirties and constituting the largest community institution both in budget and in number of employees. The school principal was an outside expert brought into the community to administer the school. His power with relation to the local school board was relatively high because of his specialized knowledge, because of state education department laws, policies, and procedures, which he administered and which provided the explicit legitimation of the power of his office, and because of important forces and trends in the larger society that supported him in many aspects of the local school situation.

Similarly, the minister of a Springdale church was an "outside expert," not considered a permanent resident by Springdalers but exercising considerable influence over local church matters and a considerably smaller influence in general community matters through his competence as the specialized occupant of one of the community's important and highly visible positions and through his linkage position to the church's denominational body. As such, he not only represented the power of the rules and policies of the denominational body, but also had constant access to new pronouncements, to educational literature, and to new program suggestions emanating from his denominational body. Likewise, the county agricultural agent represented a specialized position designed to integrate more rationally a segment of the community's activities into the practices and procedures of the larger society.

It is interesting to pause for a moment to contrast Springdale's special expert school administrator and his school payroll of 60 people with the simple teacher in El Cerrito; to contrast the four different specialized ministers with the part-time priest and the lay person who carried on much of the church ritual in El Cerrito; and to contrast the role of the agricultural agent of Springdale's county with the complete lack of contact of the county agent with the people of El Cerrito.

Although considerable power is delegated to individuals within a bureaucracy and although this power is enhanced by the access that such officials have to the extracommunity systems with which they link the community, such bureaucratic power was definitely limited in Springdale. The authors pointed out that the school principal, the clergymen, the agricultural agent, and the teachers all occupied vulnerable positions. They were hired experts, and they could be fired (although there were certain tenure provisions for principal and teachers). Further, their activities could in part be controlled by certain powerful local people who had access to the administrative superiors of such professionals in the denominational hierarchy, at the state college, or in the state education department.

A major aspect of the "great change" is the gradual transfer in auspices of certain production-distribution-consumption functions, largely from individuals and special ad hoc groupings to business enterprise and government. Little of this transfer had taken place in El Cerrito. Many such functions remained in individual, family, and small-group hands in Springdale as well. The authors pointed out, for example, that "the family garden, the mason jar and the deep-freeze are important parts of Springdale's economy. For many families, in the village as well as in the country, the garden represents an important income supplement."[15] The village board took two recourses in renouncing its proper powers. One was to abdicate functions to county or state government; the other was to turn over important board functions to special ad hoc groupings or voluntary associations. The Community Club, over the past seven years, had concerned itself through various committees with numerous functions and activities that were the proper but unexercised prerogative of the village board. Springdale shared in a youth recreation program in which the state youth commission reimbursed local communities with 50 percent of certain recreation expenditures for children and youths. In another vein, the Springdale farmers, who in an earlier day made their own butter and cheese, now shipped fluid milk to market and with their "milk check" bought the butter, cheese, and other things they needed. This development applied to traditional farmers in moderate degree but even more strongly to the "rational" farmers.

In the trend toward urbanization and suburbanization, Springdale, like El Cerrito, did not follow the national pattern as reflected in increasing growth. On the contrary, the Springdale community achieved its highest population peak in 1880. In another way, though, Springdale did show greater adaptation to the trend than El Cerrito, for part of the reason for the depletion of Springdale's population was the exodus from the community of people migrating to surrounding cities in search of industrial and other work not available in Springdale. Among those who remained, the effects of indus-

15. Vidich and Bensman, *Small Town*, pp. 20-21.

trialization were reflected in the approximately one out of three employed Springdalers who commuted elsewhere for work. A related development was the tendency for individual households to be supported from as many as three or four different jobs, often combining both farm and nonfarm occupations. Thus, urban growth in the vicinity was reflected in adaptations within Springdale's commuting pattern and in the linkage of farm and nonfarm occupations in many of its households.

Although the authors did not treat the subject of value change systematically, they pointed out in several places an increase in the values of consumption over production. Their interesting analysis of values centered on four variables: investment and reinvestment, hoarding, consumption, and work. They found it preferable to analyze these values in terms of the different relation of the various social classes to them at the present rather than in terms of any overall historical change. Perhaps one reason they did not center their analysis on the change in values through time is their reported difficulty in identifying a valid indigenous culture whose gradual change could be charted. Rather, they reported a historical accumulation of residues from the mass culture of earlier times imported into the community through migration or communication at various periods in Springdale's history.

In summary, various aspects of the great change were apparent in the Springdale community in ways that contrast it dramatically with El Cerrito. Associated with this change, Springdale showed much less *local autonomy*, expressed either in economic self-sufficiency or in the control that it exercised over community institutions and processes and a much greater orientation of local activities toward the patterns and programs of extracommunity systems. The *geographical area* in which Springdale people lived and moved and had access to the major activities of daily living was not the same for all of these activities, as indicated by the commuting of approximately one-third of the community's residents to places outside Springdale for the major work that gave them sustenance.

Likewise, the *psychological identification* of Springdalers with their community was far from complete. The community found it difficult to embrace its industrial commuting workers. Its shack people, one out of ten in the community, showed little identification with community interests and activities. Its *horizontal pattern*, through which various community units are kept in functional coordination with each other and through which the community exists as an entity, though not as strong as El Cerrito's, was nevertheless supported in part at least by local village, town, and school district jurisdictions; by an array of local institutions, which bound various community groups together for some purposes at least; and by the

116

local leaders who, through keeping a hand in almost all locality-relevant activity, were able to exert considerable integrating influence.

Middletown, Indiana

A small industrial city in the Middle West was chosen by the Lynds to make their successive community studies because it met two main considerations:[16] that the city be "as representative as possible of contemporary American life" and that it be a place sufficiently compact and homogeneous to be practical for studying the total living situation.

Community characteristics   Middletown affords a good example of growth and change, which are an important focus of attention in the two studies. Back in 1885, it was a small county seat of some 6,000 people. Then the discovery and exploitation of the area's natural gas rocketed it to a population of over 11,000 five years later, and forty factories had moved into the area. Although the cheap gas was depleted in a few years, Middletown had been pushed into the industrial revolution. Its population grew to nearly 37,000 by 1920 and was estimated at 47,000 in 1935.

The first Middletown study used 1924 as its principal reference year but in many places reached back to 1890 as a base year against which to measure change. The second study, in 1935, was able to assess the impact of the Great Depression on Middletown's developing community institutions. In the present description, we shall use the 1935 study unless otherwise stipulated.

Aside from their interest in measuring change and their utilization of the institutional approach as a basis for describing the community (getting a living, making a home, training the young, using leisure, engaging in religious practices, engaging in community activities), the Lynds had two other centers of description and analysis. One was the great cleavage between business-class and working-class styles of living. The other was the conflicts in value that characterized Middletown people.

Although no enumeration of the total number of different occupations was given in the Middletown studies, it certainly numbered at least several hundred by 1935. Its 19,000 gainfully employed workers in 1930 included 9,811, or about half, in manufacturing and mechanical industries. The other most numerous

---

16. This description is based on Robert S. Lynd and Helen Merrell Lynd, *Middletown: A Study in American Culture* (New York: Harcourt, Brace, 1929, reprinted in paperback, 1956), and *Middletown in Transition: A Study in Cultural Conflicts* (New York: Harcourt, Brace, 1937).

categories of industrial occupation were trade, transportation and communication, domestic and personal service, clerical occupations, and professional service. Middletown had 81 manufacturing establishments in 1933, with an average of 80 wage earners per establishment. Because of the Depression these figures were lower than they had been in 1925, but they give some indication of the extent of Middletown's industrialization.

The extent to which division of labor had taken place in the years preceding the Great Depression was given dramatic illustration by the fact that a six-room "ideal home," constructed in the early twenties and used widely for advertising purposes, involved the performance of various functions as follows: The site was developed by a local real-estate man and was laid out by a landscape architect from Chicago. The house was built according to an architect's plan with financial help from local banks by the real-estate owners. It was built under the direction of a construction contractor, and its construction was supervised by an assistant. The foundation was built by a subcontracting bricklayer, and the stone base which topped off the foundation was the work of another subcontractor. Still different subcontractors or specialists sanded and surfaced the floors, stuccoed and plastered the house, installed the electrical wiring, installed the plumbing, painted and decorated the house, installed the tin work, and installed the furnace.

Even by 1924 specialization in industrial plant management had also reached a considerable elaboration. "Thus the 'general manager' of the glass factory of a generation ago has been succeeded by a 'production manager,' a 'sales manager,' an 'advertising manager,' a 'personnel manager,' and an 'office manager'."[17] Similarly, while in 1890 the superintendent was the only person in the whole school system who did not teach, by 1924 there was a great variety of specialized administrative personnel standing between the teachers and the superintendent. These included principals, assistant principals, supervisors of special subjects, directors of vocational education and home economics, deans, attendance officers, and clerks.[18] Thus, as early as 1924 Middletown had developed a degree of division of labor that far exceeded that of the Springdale of the 1950s. Industrial development in the community and an attendant increase in population undoubtedly accounted for much of this change.

Accompanying the division of labor had been a progressive differentiation of interests and association among Middletown people. Even by 1924 differentiation was so great that the Lynds could refer to the multitude of different "worlds" in the city:

17. Lynd and Lynd, *Middletown*, p. 44.

118   18. Lynd and Lynd, *Middletown*, p. 210.

Small worlds of all sorts are forever forming, shifting, and dissolving. People maintain membership, intimate or remote, formal or tacit, in groups of people who get a living together—factory, department of factory, group within department under the "group system" of production, factory welfare association, trade union, board of directors, Chamber of Commerce, Merchants' Association, Ad. Club, and so on; through one's home activities one belongs to a group of relatives, a neighborhood, a body of customers of certain shops, patrons of a bank, of a building and loan association; a student may belong to the high school, the sophomore class, the class pin committee, the managing board of the school paper, the Daubers' Club, History B class—and so on indefinitely through all the activities of the city. Some of these groupings are temporary—a table at bridge, a grand jury, a dinner committee; others are permanent—the white race, the Presbyterian Church, relatives of John Murray. Some are local—depositors in the Merchants' Bank, the Bide-a-Wee Club, friends of Ed Jones, residents of the South Side; others are as wide as the county, the state, the nation, or the world.[19]

The different "worlds" in which Middletown people lived reflected, among other things, an increase in the number of formally organized clubs, both relatively and absolutely. In 1890 there was one club for every 125 Middletowners, but by 1924 this figure had reached one for every 80. Yet the Lynds concluded that although opportunities for social contact were increasing, the contacts were usually more casual than in 1890, and the leisure-time organizations tended to have the effect of setting people apart from others in the community.

Social differentiation could be seen in the different way in which business-class people and working-class people utilized three widely different institutions: their "taverns," their lodges, and their churches. In the working class, shabby households and little money for entertaining friends caused social isolation in which taverns provided a physical meeting place and also "an environment conducive to spontaneous human association," for which there was a need much greater than that experienced by the business-class. Perhaps for much the same reason, working-class lodges were strong while business-class lodges were declining. The Lynds also considered it significant that there was a great contrast between the conduct of the two groups in their separate churches after the service. Working-class people tended to linger in the aisles and on the steps, much in the fashion of El Cerrito, while business-class people left briskly to go about their business.

19. Lynd and Lynd, *Middletown*, pp. 478-79.

Churches involved another marked difference in degree from El Cerrito, or even from Springdale, for in contrast to the one church in the former community and the four different denominational churches in Springdale, there were 65 different congregations in Middletown in 1935, comprising 22 different denominations.

Many groups with an avowed civic purpose represented, nevertheless, the special interests of a particular group as well. These included the Chamber of Commerce, the Merchants' Association, Real Estate Board, Medical Society, the D.A.R. and American Legion, the Teachers Federation, the Public Ownership League, and so on. Noting the formation of a new service club, the newspaper editor commented laconically: "That makes six men's civic clubs here, exclusive of the Chamber of Commerce. . . . Also two women's clubs of the same character. . . . If all were one club, what a power it could be in the city!"[20]

Middletown's people were divided into many different levels of socioeconomic status:

1. An emerging upper class of manufacturers, bankers, corporation executives, and a few attorneys
2. Smaller manufacturers, merchants, professional people, and some high-salaried employees of some of the larger firms
3. Salaried professional people, small retailers and entrepreneurs, clerks, clerical workers, salesmen, civil servants
4. Foremen and highly skilled workers and craftsmen
5. The largest group: the working class of semiskilled or unskilled laborers
6. The lowest class: "poor whites" and other irregularly employed people at the bottom of the economic and social ladder.

Psychologically, at least, the first three classes identified themselves with the business class, and the rest were the working class. Thus, Middletown presented wide differentiation of interests and association.

As Middletown developed over the years, various parts of its structure became tied increasingly with state and national systems. This process was increasingly apparent in economic activity. During the fieldwork for the first study, the pressure of chain stores on local retailing was apparent. In a period of less than a year, three clothing stores and a shoe store were taken over by chains extending beyond the local community, and four additional chain stores entered the community. Of the seven largest industrial plants, three of the presidents resided in other states, dramatizing the remoteness of control

20. Lynd and Lynd, *Middletown in Transition*, p. 285.

from the local community scene. In the later study, two General Motors plants, a Borg-Warner plant, and an Owens-Illinois plant were an important connection with nationwide industrial concerns and a decisive economic influence in the community. The Depression saw a local campaign to "buy in Middletown," which represented in its way an attempt to avoid some of the economic disadvantages of the industrial and commercial links to the larger society while obtaining their advantages as reflected in local factory payrolls.

Like El Cerrito, but on a much grander scale, Middletown experienced the "golden flood" of federal funds coming through work relief and other projects of the federal government.

The growing tie to the larger society was also symbolized by the growth in the number of nationally syndicated newspaper columns, a number that had risen from two in 1925 to over twenty in 1935. Associated with this increase was an apparent decrease in the amount of attention and merit given to the locally originated editorials of Middletown's newspapers.

As industrial plants and other social enterprises grew in size and became closely tied to extracommunity systems, they showed an increased tendency to embody the rational, deliberate, impersonal, specialized, highly intricate administrative characteristics that accompany bureaucratic organization. The Lynds observed in 1924 that "teachers in Middletown's schools today have more formal book training and less experience of dealing with children than those of a generation ago." The increase in professional training is dramatic. In 1921-22, only 29 percent of Middletown's public school teachers had had four years or more of professional training beyond high school; a decade later the percentage had more than doubled.

The "outside expert" tendency, noted in Springdale in the 1950s, was also symbolized in the Middletown of the 1920s by the fact that the eight or nine leading clergymen were all from outside the community. Their background and training differed markedly from those of the great bulk of the clergymen, whose situation was much more similar to that of 1890.

The rational organization of social functions was also apparent in the community's charities. The Community Chest was organized in 1925 as "a centralized, city-wide massing of resources" through which the community supported nine welfare agencies and four additional enterprises, in vivid contrast to "the struggling church mission sewing school and the charity kindergarten supported by 'penny collections' and similar devices that constituted the local organized charity of 1890."

Over the years, there was a generally consistent trend toward the transfer of local functions to government and business and a **121** tendency for these two institutions to gain in the scope of their activities. By 1925, for example, local or state government had acquired such new functions as regulation of industrial working conditions, supervision of workmen's compensation, health care, supervision of food, services for children, and a number of related activities. Such offices and agencies as the Board of Works, Board of Safety, Sinking Fund Commission, City Planning Commission, City Judge, Judge of the Juvenile Court, City Comptroller, and Street Commissioner had all been added in the decades following 1890.

Most dramatic, perhaps, was the Depression-supported tendency for charitable activity to become organized and administered on a community-wide basis through the Community Fund and then for many functions to be taken over from the fund by local government. In the earlier study, the Lynds had noted the development of the Community Fund and had related this to a corresponding tendency reported by local ministers for a decrease in personal tithing (the practice of giving one-tenth of one's income to the church). The Depression need rapidly engulfed the Community Fund with demands for relief that far exceeded the ability of the community to raise the necessary money through voluntary giving, even though centrally organized. The result was the rapid growth of the public relief functions of local government, a growth that went against local values favoring few government functions and the idea that charity was a private and voluntary concern.

"Nobody in Middletown in 1925 dreamed of the extravagant possibility that within seven years tax relief would aggregate three times the entire Community Fund budget, and that the city's major municipal problem would become the financing of tax-supported relief."[21] Here, as in other instances, the Depression intensified a long-term trend of the "great change," as the direct relief expenditures of Middletown's township rose from $21,000 in 1928 to over $304,000 in 1933, with a quarter of the population on relief. The Community Fund was able to contribute a maximum of $50,000 for direct relief in 1930, a figure that declined steadily as public expenditures increased.

Functions were also being assumed increasingly by business, as Middletown people through their individual decisions to perform a function at home or to purchase it from business enterprise decided increasingly for the latter. Thus, Middletowners developed a practice of "eating out," as reflected in growth of restaurants much more rapid than the increase in population. They were buying more readymade clothes, taking less responsibility for performing this func-

21. Lynd and Lynd, *Middletown in Transition*, p. 102.

tion at home. The same tendency was apparent in the growth in numbers of barbers, hairdressers, and manicurists.

Leisure-time pursuits, earlier almost exclusively a function of the family, neighborhood, and church group, were becoming commercialized at the time of the second Middletown study. At the same time, there was a great expansion in organized recreation during the Depression, financed both by individual voluntary agencies and by the Community Fund, and by public moneys. It is interesting to note, however, that the Depression apparently also had the effect of increasing the amount of neighborly visiting and inexpensive leisure-time pursuits in the home and in the back yard.

The field of health care also showed an increase in functions performed outside the home by voluntary agencies and by government. Thus, Middletown's hospital admissions rate increased by 150 percent in the decade 1925-35, while the population increased by about 26 percent. Although some of this discrepancy is attributable to the fact that Middletown's new hospital was attracting people from outside the city, there was a substantial increase in the use of hospital facilities by the sick. An indication of the specific increase in hospital utilization is given in the percentage of live births that took place in the hospital rather than elsewhere, a figure that stood at only 12 percent in 1925 but had more than tripled in the following decade, reaching 39 percent in 1935.

Health care services provided by voluntary agencies or by government increased rapidly during the Depression, though not all of the increased services were given out on the basis of financial need. By 1932 the township was paying over $50,000 for hospital care, doctors' bills, and other items, a figure more than twice the total township expenditure for all types of poor relief in 1928. Thus, a long-term trend of transfer in the auspices of various community functions, particularly the transfer of functions to voluntary agencies and to government, was hastened by the Depression in Middletown.

Middletown's population growth from 6,000 people in 1885 to 47,000 in 1935 was associated with a relatively rapid industrialization, as evidenced by the extensiveness and variety of its industrial pursuits in 1935. There was also evidence that, as the city grew in size, its various business and social service institutions reached out to encompass many people from the surrounding countryside within their orbit. Although they did not claim to have demonstrated all of the following characteristics, the Lynds' study of Middletown led them to suggest that Middletown's growth in industries and in population had brought a number of changes in social relationships often associated with urbanization and the "urban way of life." Specifically, they mentioned that people perhaps had a larger number of casual **123** acquaintances but with a smaller percentage of the total population; acquaintance and association were more selective and more formal: "One's sense of 'belonging' intimately to the entire social group probably tends to decrease with the increased size of the city, with a resulting tendency to a lower average participation in local movements of various kinds." The number of influential leaders increased in numbers but decreased in proportion to the total population; people with low socioeconomic status were more likely to become detached, "untied in any active sense to community-wide life and values." There was a growth in the segregation and homogeneity of residential areas. Status in the group came to be recognized increasingly through symbols, such as wealth and the conspicuous consumption that signifies it. With the growing difficulty of unifying people who are only accidentally together through their geographic propinquity, it became necessary to "invoke gross emotional symbols of a nonselective sort by which masses can be swayed," symbols that tend to be generated at the top of the social structure and imposed on those below.[22]

Changes in values The Middletown of 1935 had emerged, at least partly, from a crucial strain upon its total way of life as a community. The Depression had wrought havoc with its economic system, brought important changes in its institutional functions, and threatened the old values that had supported the pre-Depression era. Throughout their second report, and particularly in the chapters on "The Middletown Spirit" and "Middletown Faces Both Ways," the Lynds documented this threat to the old values, this adaptation of institutions in ways that undermined them further, and this ambivalence of belief through which sincere lip service could be paid to the older values while the newer ones continued, against great resistance, to make noticeable inroads. In the process, Middletowners displayed a "marked tendency in . . . thought and feeling to see the place where remedial change is needed in individual people and not in its institutions." In a period of conflict and change,

> One frequently gets a sense of people's being afraid to let their opinions become sharp. They believe in "peace, but ———." They believe in "fairness to labor, but ———." In "freedom of speech, but ———." In "democracy, but ———." In "freedom of the press, but ———." This is in part related to the increased apprehensiveness that one feels everywhere in Middletown. . .

22. Lynd and Lynd, *Middletown in Transition*, pp. 466-68.

Middletown wants to be adventurous and to embrace new ideas and practices, but it also desperately needs security, and in this conflict both businessmen and workingmen appear to be clinging largely to tried sources of security rather than venturing out into the untried.[23]

The emphasis placed by Middletowners on business, money, and material possessions was very great, and the Lynds at one point characterized Middletown as "this striving, accumulating society, always pulling up stakes from the present in the hope of striking it rich in the future." But the emphasis on the future did not in any way imply a desire or willingness to plan comprehensively for the future of Middletown as a community.

Quite the contrary, Middletowners placed more stress on the improvement of the individual, as indicated above, than on the desirability of cooperative planning for the future. Part of this attitude was related to the conceptions underlying the viewpoint Middletowners had of the scope and potentiality of local government. They tended to think in terms of holding taxes down, of placing proper checks and safeguards on governmental activity. They believed strongly in the competence of the untrained common man in directing community affairs; they distrusted "planners" and "idealists," emphasizing the viewpoint of the practical, workaday world. "In a culture so patterned, the likelihood of the emergence of forthright civic social change through the city's elected and appointed administrators is curtailed almost to the vanishing point."[24]

Yet important shifts in values were apparent. We shall consider two of them. First, times and working conditions had changed since 1890, when the standard work week was sixty hours and when there was less difference between the working hours of the business class and the working class than was apparent in 1935. Even in 1914, 73 percent of the workers labored sixty hours per week or more. Increased leisure and a shorter work day were available for both business and working class in 1935, even disregarding the "enforced" leisure that attended the Depression.

But particularly in the business class, especially among the older families of established wealth and key influence, there was emerging a new generation of people who, though taking their business and civic roles most seriously, nevertheless were coming to emphasize leisure as a positive value in a way that the older generation never had. Social status in these top circles was coming to be determined not only by position in the community's productive

---

23. Lynd and Lynd, *Middletown in Transition*, p. 492.

24. Lynd and Lynd, *Middletown*, p. 125.

structure but by position and behavior in regard to consumption as well. The positive values that Middletown placed on leisure were apparently increasing, though the evaluation of individual work and enterprise remained strong.

A second basic shift in values was related to the impact of the Depression, for Middletowners found themselves having to take steps, particularly in the administration of relief, that went against basic values of individualism and free enterprise and that involved a grudging acknowledgement that there was a causal as well as a moralistic approach to the type of social problem represented by unemployment and ill health. The failure of family, neighborhood, and church group to "take care of their own" had resulted in an organization of voluntary giving through the Community Fund, which in turn failed to meet the demands created by increasing unemployment. Under these circumstances it was difficult to continue to believe that any normal, upright individual could and should "take care of himself" and that merely a trickle of public moneys should go to care for the aberrant and depraved.

The Depression-induced mushrooming of public relief involved an assumption of corporate responsibility for the care of the needy through tax funds unlike any seen before. Although some of this change faded as the economic situation bettered, it left what the Lynds called a "bench mark for social change." Another such bench mark was also Depression-linked. As federal funds became available to communities for public works as a part of the New Deal program of "pump-priming," the community, though largely opposed to the philosophy of government that was implied, grasped at the opportunities for business activity and for employment that were offered it. In doing so, it faced for the first time the process of positive, affirmative planning for civic purposes.

Nevertheless, on balance, there was much less change in basic values than one might have anticipated by the changed conditions and the unprecedented community actions taken to meet them. Although values had been shaken and the inconsistencies in many values seemed more apparent, the Lynds concluded in 1935: "Middletown is overwhelmingly living by the values by which it lived in 1925; and the chief additions are defensive, negative elaborations of already existing values, such as, among the business class, intense suspicion of centralizing tendencies in government, of the interference of social legislation with business, of labor troubles, and of radicalism."[25]

Middletown and the "Great Change"   In the above synopsis of the Middletown studies, the various aspects of the "great change"

25. Lynd and Lynd, *Middletown in Transition*, p. 489.

have constituted a readily useful outline guide for the description of the community. Although the choice of materials from the two lengthy reports has been selective, of course, most of the significant developments they reported have readily been subsumed under one or another of the changes that are part of the systematic analytical approach of this book. The changes have represented a greater progression along the four dimensions on which American communities are distributed than was the case in either El Cerrito or Springdale.

On the first dimension, that of *autonomy*, Middletown's increased systemic ties to extracommunity systems were perhaps most noticeable in the manner in which the city's industrial ties made it even more vulnerable to unemployment in the Great Depression than most American communities, but the ties were also indicated in many other aspects of the institutional structure.

Regarding the extent to which Middletown's various service areas coincided, the data are not as clearly apparent for judgment as in the cases of El Cerrito or Springdale. From what data were given, however, the indication is that the *geographic areas* encompassed by Middletown's various community functions tended to coincide much more nearly than Springdale's, particularly as regards the place of residence and the place of work.

On the third dimension, the extent of *psychological identification* with a common locality, the estrangement of many people from civic participation, particularly on the lower rungs of the socioeconomic ladder, and the bifurcation of the community into the two somewhat separate spheres of business class and working class, while affecting negatively the identification of Middletowners with their community, did not seem to have been disruptive to the extent shown by many communities today.

On the fourth dimension, the strength of the community's *horizontal pattern*, despite the negative orientation toward planning and toward deliberate collective action, the many adaptations made by Middletowners during the Depression indicated an ability for various parts of the community to be brought into and held within a meaningful relationship to each other. In this function, the exceptional influence of a small number of top-level business-class people, including the members of one family in particular, and their permeation of the decision-making boards and bodies of the most diverse aspects of Middletown's institutional life, figured importantly.

Crestwood Heights, Ontario

On the brow of a hill within easy commuting range of a large Cana-   **127** dian city was located the well-to-do suburb of Crestwood Heights.[26] Incorporated separately, the 17,000 residents were so closely tied in with the surrounding metropolitan area that one might question whether this municipality could properly be called a community at all. No clear physical boundaries distinguished it, and it hardly contained that rather full complement of local institutions that are considered by many students to be a distinguishing characteristic of a community.

Community characteristics   As a municipality, it maintained a council, police and fire departments, and schools. In the voluntary field, it had a community council, a community center, and a Home and School Association, along with several less important organizations. But it lacked industry of its own, a hospital, large stores, its own water supply and sewage disposal system, or voluntary social agencies. It had no service clubs and only one church.

For all such functions, it drew on other parts of the large metropolitan area of over a million people and its central city containing nearly 700,000 people. Most of its own population was employed in the central city, where they occupied executive and professional positions in the many commercial and other institutions of the metropolis. Yet the authors believed Crestwood Heights to be a community, despite its intricate interdependence with the other parts of the metropolitan area. "It exists *as a community* because of the relationships that exist between people—relationships revealed in the functioning of the institutions which they have created: family, school, church, community center, club, association, summer camp, and other more peripheral institutions and services."[27]

Although Crestwood Heights existed as part of a spatially interconnected but differentiated congeries of symbiotically related parts of a great metropolitan area, it showed in its own composition considerable homogeneity. Far from being a cross section of the many different groups in the area, it was comprised almost entirely of middle-class people. Its one principal group differentiation followed religious lines, roughly 60 percent being Christian and 40 percent Jewish in 1951. Interestingly, differences in religious belief were not marked, for though there was active associational life in connection with the churches and synagogues, these activities "serve to gird the child with the minimum of spiritual armor, which may be shed easily in favor of other defences, should it be experienced as

---

26.   This description is a synopsis of the book by John R. Seeley, R. Alexander Sim, and Elizabeth W. Loosley, *Crestwood Heights: A Study of the Culture of Suburban Life* (New York: Basic Books, 1956; Toronto: Toronto University Press, 1956).

27.   Seeley, Sim, and Loosley, *Crestwood Heights*, pp. 3-4.

obsolete or cumbersome."[28] The greatest split in basic beliefs and behavior patterns in Crestwood Heights was neither along economic nor ethnic nor religious lines, but along lines of sex,.as we shall see later.

Several points of contrast with El Cerrito are striking. "Should an intruder from outside wander through its streets, he would find little, except a slight difference in sign-posts, to distinguish Crestwood Heights from Big City—or from other suburbs near it."[29] How different from the clearly identifiable close clustering of homes in El Cerrito! The difference in physical characteristics reflected the great difference in social organization, El Cerrito being largely self-sufficient and self-contained, while Crestwood Heights was so interdependent with the rest of the metropolis that it could not exist without it.

Again, while the people of El Cerrito had been there for generations, those in Crestwood Heights were much more transient, consisting almost entirely of "parents who have moved into Crestwood Heights when adult, and their children who have been born or brought up there." This characteristic of relative transiency, along with the impersonality attendant upon large aggregations of people, involved a set of social relationships where people are not known to each other directly, as persons, but rather through status symbols. "Because there are few strong ties of locality or kinship, a man is judged largely by the number and quality of the things he owns. These objects must be seen, approved, and envied by other men—as they are in Crestwood Heights."[30] Or people might have to be known through their formal associations. Exclusive clubs were important for this function, "and if a Crestwooder is successful in ascending through the hierarchy of club membership, he ultimately touches the fringe of the upper class, where family and inherited wealth *do* cast over him a corner of their mantle."[31]

The churches that Crestwooders attended were mostly located outside the community and thus were not a center of community-related activities; the central importance of the church in El Cerrito stands in vivid contrast. Typically, Crestwooders did not linger after the service. As one of the researchers reported: "The moment the last prayer was said, every one stood up and seemed in a great hurry to leave the church, and as the lady sitting beside me seemed particularly anxious to get by me I had little time to look around. Outside again, I noticed there was little loitering or conversation, and every

28. Seeley, Sim, and Loosley, *Crestwood Heights*, p. 215.
29. Seeley, Sim, and Loosley, *Crestwood Heights*, p. 4.
30. Seeley, Sim, and Loosley, *Crestwood Heights*, p. 7.
31. Seeley, Sim, and Loosley, *Crestwood Heights*, p. 295.

one seemed instead to head straight for his car and drive away."[32]

But perhaps the greatest contrast is in the place of the school in the community. In El Cerrito, its functions were shoddy and neglected, as was its physical structure and appearance, for relatively little importance was attached to it. In Crestwood Heights, the school stood at the center of interest of the community. The major institutional focus was on child rearing, and "the community of Crestwood Heights is literally built around its schools."[33] "The virtual co-emergence of school and community, the nature of local class structure and ambition, the relative weakness or weakening of other institutions; new sources of power in the school, and of influence and capacity and concern: all these combine to force the school towards a lone eminence, from which it can hardly be said to have actively fought shy."[34] As one might anticipate, the Home and School Association was the strongest, most active organization in Crestwood Heights, and the Director of Education reported that 30 percent of his time was spent with the work of that organization, a fact that reflects not only the importance that he attached to it, but the extent of parent participation and activity in the association.

The central function of the school was related to a number of other aspects of the community. The community was changing—so rapidly, indeed, that the researchers reported that even during the time of the study, "what was descriptively true in the third and fourth year required substantial revision to fit the state of affairs in the fifth."[35] Corresponding to rapid community change was the rapid change and development through which the children of Crestwood Heights were expected to move in the unfolding of their careers. In the selective process according to which personal and social competence are acquired, knowledge and skills obtained, and occupational goals are formulated and achieved, the school played a decisive role. Given such rapid change and such explicit career demands, the school grew in importance in the socialization process, largely at the expense of the family. "It has become clear as we have studied the school that it is taking over more and more of the responsibility for the socialization of the child, and that it is more certain of its methods than the parents are of theirs."[36] Thus, the authors pointed out:

neither church nor family now possesses enough or suitable

32. Seeley, Sim, and Loosley, *Crestwood Heights*, p. 66.

33. Seeley, Sim, and Loosley, *Crestwood Heights*, p. 244.

34. Seeley, Sim, and Loosley, *Crestwood Heights*, p. 234.

35. Seeley, Sim, and Loosley, *Crestwood Heights*, pp. 23-24.

36. Seeley, Sim, and Loosley, *Crestwood Heights*, p. 284.

means to teach the child many of the necessary roles of adult life; they can be learned only in a prolonged, intensive, and specialized formal training. The one-room school, accordingly, has been transformed into the large, highly specialized educational plant which is the school of today. The training of teachers has also been intensified and diversified; and specialization within the profession has become the norm. The administration of such a complex institution as the school has become a profession in itself. The Principal of a large urban high school, for example, does not now usually teach classes himself. Directors of education, school inspectors, provincial administrators of education, all the members of the vast educational hierarchy, stand over against the local citizen boards of education, which still control the tax-supplied funds.[37]

An integral part in the social system of the school was played by various specialized experts. "These people, 'expert' by local definition and their own consent, find themselves in so intimate an involvement with Crestwood Heights (and communities like it) that together they may almost be viewed as a single social or interaction system."[38] There arose a great demand for experts:

The services of the experts are, as has been indicated, required to obtain or build a house, in the ordinary sense of a shelter or, more particularly, in the new sense of a "matrix of living." The once relatively simple matter of feeding the family requires the services of domestic science specialists; consumers' guides; hygienists and health teachers in general; pediatricians; specialists who can advise on the meaning of food and food preparation in the maintenance of happy married relationships; and communications experts, journalistic and novelistic, who will give clues as to what "the best people" are *really* eating, regardless of all the foregoing considerations. Not only must the body be cared for in the ordinary sense, but cosmeticians are ready to advise on the style of hair-do which is appropriate to a personality (which its bearer does not herself recognize); newspaper columnists will advise on how to get fat or thin, with or without pain. And even within these specializations, further specializations by age levels may be detected: particularly relevant messages may be addressed to those entering their teens, to the adolescents, to the young married couples, and others.[39]

Partly because of their own particular research interests, and partly because of the major focus of community concern on the

---

37. Seeley, Sim, and Loosley, *Crestwood Heights*, pp. 228-29.

38. Seeley, Sim, and Loosley, *Crestwood Heights*, p. 344.

39. Seeley, Sim, and Loosley, *Crestwood Heights*, p. 362. **131**

schools, the authors made an intensive analysis of the place of experts in the school system, particularly those experts in one or another way related to the preoccupation of "human relations." Such experts were differentiated from Crestwood lay people chiefly through the selective process of recruitment, the special training that they had received, and the expert social system that existed in the larger community and with which they formed a vital link.

At the top of this expert hierarchy stood the acknowledged experts of the larger society, their rank often in direct ratio to their distance from Crestwood Heights. Just below them were the top experts of the local metropolitan area, who had a more frequent contact with the school. It is interesting to note that the Director of Education, himself an "expert," stood in a key position as a bridge to these two types of experts. They contacted him when approaching the school, and through his links with principals, teachers, and Home and School Association, he channeled the experts' contacts appropriately.

Another type of expert, on a somewhat similar level but with different status, were various residents of Crestwood Heights who themselves were expert in one of the relevant fields but whose relationship to the local schools was that of expert volunteer rather than paid professional.

Within the teaching profession itself were various functionaries specializing in something other than the general teaching of subject matter. The kindergarten teacher, the remedial reading or vocational guidance teacher, the counselor, the specialist in parent education were all examples of the growing number of such specialists in the schools of Crestwood Heights. These specialists rated higher in the school hierarchy than rank-and-file classroom teachers. Through such specialization, one often rose to higher ranks of administration or "expertness."

The growth in number and kinds of such specialists corresponded, the authors pointed out, to the new social functions that the school was coming to be expected to perform in American culture. The school increasingly was expected to assume functions of facilitating general social adjustment and personality development, of educating "the whole child." Significantly, while specialization in the school in earlier years was almost exclusively in terms of a particular subject matter, "the most recent brand of specialization now centers around the child as object, concentrating more heavily upon his psychological processing."[40]

Specialization of function apparently accompanied fragmentation of other aspects of living. In a fast-moving culture in which

40. Seeley, Sim, and Loosley, *Crestwood Heights*, p. 262.

parents felt less and less adequately equipped (vis-à-vis the specialists) to minister to the needs of their developing children, there was a relation between the proliferation of specialists and changes of function within the home. "When I was a girl," reported one Crestwood mother, "we all worked of an evening around the dining room table. We had a warm fire in the room and we all worked quietly or read in the same room. Now, we scatter throughout the house to follow our interests."[41] By and large, the interests that seemed spontaneous tended to be associated with the activities of the peer group, while those planned as purposeful and preparatory for careers tended increasingly to be allocated to specialists.

But the specialists themselves showed a similar fragmentation. For the school specialist, as for the other experts, "what has been argued so far is that the training process is such—and perhaps increasingly such—as to make for an alienation of the expert from other bodies of knowledge; from any general value-scheme; from insight either into his own motives or into the nature of his culture, or both; and from the understanding of the social situation in which his training takes place."[42]

The research on the community of Crestwood Heights was part of a research, training, and service project with a primary orientation toward mental health, particularly of children. Among its objects were "to experiment with a technique of free discussion with children; to see what could be added to the armament of a good school system that would make its contribution to the mental health of its pupils greater or better; to provide a picture of the growing-up process in one more community, and to evaluate the consequences for mental health of that process."[43] The book Crestwood Heights purported to describe the social life of the community in which the project was conducted. For this purpose, it emphasized a psychological approach.

A by-product of this approach was an interesting analysis of the fundamental psychological and philosophical orientations of adult men and women in Crestwood Heights, an analysis that happily will bring us through one possible gate to the analysis of the community as a social system, the subject matter of the following chapter.

While one could find verbal agreement in Crestwood Heights on such fundamental concepts as discipline, maturity, responsibility, democracy, freedom, and autonomy, there were basic underlying

41. Seeley, Sim, and Loosley, Crestwood Heights, p. 56.
42. Seeley, Sim, and Loosley, Crestwood Heights, p. 349.
43. Seeley, Sim, and Loosley, Crestwood Heights, p. 407.

contradictions. "So marked were these internal contradictions that the possibility of writing a chapter on the system of beliefs of Crestwood Heights seemed virtually to be nil."[44] The contradictions can be summarized as being "the division between those who look at human nature and human behavior from a viewpoint primarily rule-oriented and moralistic, and those whose views are primarily cause-oriented and naturalistic or scientific."[45] The alert reader will note that the change from one type of orientation to the other was given as one of the basic changes in values in the preceding chapter of this book. Roughly speaking, the *Crestwood Heights* authors pointed out, the two points of view were those of lay persons and professionals, respectively, although they noted the exceptions. But more important than the difference between those two groups or between community members based on social class or ethnic differences was the difference based on sex, the "striking divergence in the belief systems of men and of women."[46]

The women of Crestwood Heights took as their supreme value the happiness and well-being of the individual. They tended to have a deterministic viewpoint of human behavior, particularly from the standpoint that behavior is psychologically "caused." They tended to believe in the perfectibility of human beings, placing great stock in the wide cultural variations among different peoples as indications of mankind's flexibility and changeability. They tended to emphasize emotional, rather than rational, considerations as most important.

The men tended to emphasize the opposite values. For the men, the organization or group, rather than the individual, was the primary focus of loyalty. In viewing human behavior, they tended to be voluntarists, believing in free will and individual moral responsibility. They were aware of the variations in human culture, but tended to emphasize people's sameness and immutability as against what they considered utopian aspirations for change. Finally, the men were inclined to view behavior rationally and would subordinate feeling to thought.

In the above contrast, where the points of view relate to the value changes described in chapter 3, the women represented the direction of change, while the men represented ideological positions that, it is asserted, are gradually weakening in American communities. Thus, if we are to add this alleged finding from Crestwood Heights to our own discourse, we would say that values are changing as indicated, and that in places like Crestwood Heights, at least, it is the females who are in the vanguard. The authors noted, inciden-

44. Seeley, Sim, and Loosley, *Crestwood Heights*, p. 379.

45. Seeley, Sim, and Loosley, *Crestwood Heights*, p. 381.

46. Seeley, Sim, and Loosley, *Crestwood Heights*, p. 382.

tally, the correspondence between the female value position and that of the experts. Indeed, at several places they pointed out the important role of females in furthering the ideological views of the experts in the school system.

When we turn from ideological viewpoints to the realm of action, however, a striking contrast was reported in the Crestwood Heights study. In the sphere of practical action, as against belief, it was the men who were individualist, determinist, perfectibilist, and emotionalist, while the women were collectivist, voluntarist, immutabilist, and rationalist. The authors began a long summary of this somewhat paradoxical analysis by saying: "The men seem primarily concerned about the preservation of life against destruction, and they feel and believe accordingly. The women seem concerned about the creative and elaborative processes, and they believe and feel accordingly. The men attend to the *necessary* conditions of living; the women to the conditions that would make life *sufficing*."[47] This dichotomy, expressed in the folk language as the difference between "making a living" and "making a life *worth* living," will receive extensive analysis in terms of task orientation and process orientation in the following chapter, for both points of view apply centrally to the concept of a "social system." Meanwhile, let it be noted that the sex-based differential emphasis in values and behavior has important implications for child rearing, since "to the degree that the picture represented is a true one, every child is assured of the experience of being pulled in two different directions with respect to all important matters."[48]

Summary   We are now in a position to move to an analysis of the concept of social system and particularly to explore its applicability to our understanding of American communities. Before doing so, let us look again at these four diverse communities that have been portrayed. Almost without exception, as we moved from one to another of these four communities we moved along the lines outlined in chapter 3 as the principal aspects of the "great change." And quite appropriately, we ended with a community whose very specialization of occupation and whose close daily interrelation with its immediate environment were so great that one might well question whether there is any sense in which that community really exists as a significant sociological entity. Yet in chapter 1 we defined a community as that combination of social systems that perform the major social functions having locality relevance. Before we examine these locality-relevant functions, it will be helpful to examine in some depth

47. Seeley, Sim, and Loosley, *Crestwood Heights*, p. 393.
48. Seeley, Sim, and Loosley, *Crestwood Heights*, p. 394.

the concept of a "social system" in its possible application to American communities.

The American Community as a Social System   5

Our task in this chapter is to examine the characteristics of social systems and then assess the extent to which communities display these systemic characteristics and can thus be treated as social systems.

In chapter 2 we noted that social-system analysis was beginning to be applied to communities. We pointed out that this development held great promise, for it might relate the community as a sociological entity to various other types of sociological entities that have been analyzed as social systems. It is exactly at this point that the field of community studies has been relatively weak in the past. As a sociological entity the community has been difficult to define and to relate to other important areas of sociological knowledge.

Indeed, these difficulties have been so great that many serious students of the community have tended to question whether or not the very concept is worthwhile. Significantly, Parsons and his followers have never made a major attempt at community analysis in systemic terms.[1] Likewise Loomis, who made a carefully stated analysis of the components of social systems, did not make any systemic analysis of the community as such. His interesting and useful analysis of

---

1. See footnote 53 in chapter 2.

the Old Order Amish as a social system is actually an analysis of a society rather than a community. Further, the type of society portrayed is not at all representative of the great bulk of American communities, for as a total way of life, the Amish society has deliberately tried to cut itself off from the major economic, political, educational, voluntary associational, and other state and national social systems whose growing impact on local community living has presented such a grave challenge to the community concept.

The problem, of course, is whether it is possible to distinguish a sociological entity called *the community* from its environment and, if it is possible, to determine the extent to which it functions as a social system. We have already defined the entity in question as that combination of social units and systems that perform the major social functions having locality relevance. And we have specified these major functions as production-distribution-consumption, socialization, social control, social participation, and mutual support. We turn now to a description of the properties of social systems so that we can then consider the extent to which communities display these properties.

The "Social-System" Concept

A social system is a structural organization of the interaction of units that endures through time. It has both external and internal aspects relating the system to its environment and its units to each other. It can be distinguished from its surrounding environment, performing a function called boundary maintenance. It tends to maintain an equilibrium in the sense that it adapts to changes from outside the system in such a way as to minimize the impact of the change on the organizational structure and to regularize the subsequent relationships.

In considering each of these descriptive statements in some detail, it will be helpful to consider three basic sources of social-system analysis that in my opinion are most useful for our analytical purposes: the contributions of Loomis, Parsons, and Homans.[2]

2. For the contributions of Charles P. Loomis, we shall confine ourselves to his recent definitive book, *Social Systems: Essays on Their Persistence and Change* (Princeton: D. Van Nostrand and Company, 1960). The work of Talcott Parsons on social systems is distributed over a number of publications, perhaps the most important of which, for our purposes, are his book on *The Social System* (Glencoe, Ill.: Free Press, 1951) and chap. 5 of Talcott Parsons, Robert F. Bales, and Edward A. Shils, *Working Papers in the Theory of Action* (Glencoe, Ill.: Free Press, 1953). In the present analysis, Morris Zelditch's "Note on the Analysis of Equilibrium Systems," from Talcott Parsons and Robert F. Bales, *Family, Socialization and Interaction Process* (Glencoe, Ill.: Free Press, 1955) is also used, as is Parsons' chapter on "General Theory in Sociology" in Robert K. Merton, Leonard Broom, and Leonard S. Cottrell, Jr., eds., *Sociology Today: Problems and Prospects* (New York: Basic Books, 1959). George C. Homans's concepts are taken from his book *The Human Group* (New York: Harcourt, Brace, 1950).

According to Loomis, a social system "is composed of the patterned interaction of members. It is constituted of the interaction of a plurality of individual actors whose relations to each other are mutually oriented through the definition and mediation of a pattern of structured and shared symbols and expectations."[3] There are nine elements that constitute a social system: belief (knowledge); sentiment; end, goal, or objective; norm; status role (position); rank; power; sanction; and facility. Each of these is articulated as a process.

For Parsons, a social system is defined most simply as "two or more units, $x_1, x_2, \ldots x_n$, related such that a change in state of any x_i, will be followed by a change of state in the remaining $x_j \ldots x_n$ which is in turn followed by a change in the state of x_i, etc."[4] Or, still more simply, "Two or more units in interaction with each other form a system."[5]

Homans's definition of a social system is derived from his analysis of small groups: "The activities, interactions, and sentiments of the group members, together with the mutual relations of these elements with one another during the time the group is active, constitute what we shall call the *social system*."[6] Homans analyzes systems in terms of three elements: activity, interaction, and sentiment.

A word should be said about the nature of the member units that, in their interrelationship, comprise the social system. There are two types of member units of social systems: individuals and groups of individuals. For example, a club is a social system made up of the individuals who are its members. Within the club, however, there are various subsystems—its various formal committees and its informal cliques—which themselves can be considered social systems.

Strictly speaking, it is more precise to say that the system or subsystem consists of the *roles* that individuals enact within an enduring pattern of interaction, for not all aspects of the individual human being are part of any particular social system; only those appropriate to one's role are part of that system. The same principle applies to groups of individuals forming subsystems within a larger social system. Keeping this limitation in mind, we can avail ourselves

---

3. Loomis' *Social Systems*, p. 4.

4. This quotation from Zelditch's codification of Parsons may be misleading. It suggests that any change in any part of a social system will be reflected in changes in all the other parts of the system. But Hillery pointed out that various parts of the community may change without bringing about corresponding changes in all other parts, in George A. Hillery, Jr., *Communal Organizations: A Study of Local Societies* (Chicago: University of Chicago Press, 1968).

5. Parsons and Bales, *Family, Socialization and Interaction Process*, p. 402. See the more complicated definition on p. 46 of this book.

6. *Human Group*, p. 87.

of the more frequently used terms *individual* and *group* in the subsequent discussion.

When systems comprising groups of individuals, whether formally or informally structured, are considered in their interrelationship as units of a still larger social system, they are often designated as subsystems. This term indicates that they themselves are social systems but parts of a larger social system at the same time. This "wheels within wheels" phenomenon is, of course, a commonplace occurrence seen in the most divergent social contexts. As Georg Simmel pointed out, it appears as soon as a group numbers three persons.

We need only note this phenomenon here and make a mental resolution to be as explicit as we can when using the words *system, unit,* or *subsystem* about precisely which grouping we are alluding to. For purposes of community analysis, of course, the importance lies in the fact that to the extent that a community is a social system, many of its subsystems are at the same time subsystems of larger systems that extend beyond its borders.

External and internal patterns   In analyzing the external and internal patterns involved in a social system, we shall start with Homans's conception, for he was the first to make a systematic analysis of these terms, and his analysis has to a certain extent been incorporated by both Loomis and Parsons into their more recent statements.

Homans defined the external system as "a set of relations among the members of the group that solves the problem: How shall the group survive in its environment?"[7] Again, more formally, "If we must have a definition in words, we can say that the mutual dependence between the work done in a group and the motives for work, between the division of labor and the scheme of interaction, so far as these relationships meet the condition that the group survives in an environment—this we shall regularly speak of as the external system."[8]

The meaning that Homans gave to the external system becomes clearer when it is contrasted with the internal system, which is

> the elaboration of group behavior that simultaneously arises out of the external system and reacts upon it. We call the system "internal" because it is not directly conditioned by the environment, and we speak of it as an "elaboration" because it

7. *Human Group*, p. 93.

140   8. *Human Group*, p. 107.

includes forms of behavior not included under the heading of the external system. We shall not go far wrong if, for the moment, we think of the external system as group behavior that enables the group to survive in its environment and think of the internal system as group behavior that is an expression of the sentiments towards one another developed by the members of the group in the course of their life together.[9]

Note that for Homans the distinction was roughly that between the *raison d'être* of the group, in terms of what it is supposed to accomplish in relation to its environment (external system), and the spontaneous relations, based principally on sentiment, that arise in the course of the group's activities. Thus, it coincides partly, but not completely, with a widely used distinction between a group's *task functions* and its *maintenance functions*. The relation of these two sets of terms is most important, and we shall pause here to explore some of its implications before going on to consider how Loomis and Parsons conceived the external-internal patterns.

In order to accomplish its purpose with respect to its environment, a group must not only perform goal-oriented tasks, but it must also be able to keep its members so organized with respect to each other that they will continue to function as a group and perform the tasks. There are two important aspects to this process of maintaining the organization of the group. One is what Homans called sentiment. This has to do with the positive feelings that group members develop toward each other and toward the group as a whole as they interact in performing the tasks to fulfill the group's purpose. This Homans included as the basic content of his internal system. Another aspect of the process has to do with the structural organization of the group members within which labor is divided, subtasks are performed, and rewards are allocated. This aspect of the maintenance function Homans included in the *external* system. For example, in treating the men who worked in the Bank Wiring Room in the famous Hawthorne study, he quite deliberately assigned to the external system all the formal organizational structure related to the tasks that the men performed. The term *maintenance functions*, however, otherwise identical with Homans's internal system, is customarily employed by other students to include the type of formal organization of behavior that Homans deliberately excluded from the internal system.

As an example, Thibaut and Kelley defined task functions as follows: "Hence one general problem that confronts this generalized type of group is that of controlling its social and physical environments so that they will yield high outcome for its members. The activities required to do this will be referred to as *task functions*." They then defined maintenance functions: "We refer to these activities by which the interdependence of the members is maintained . . . as the *maintenance functions* of the group."[10]

Although these authors stated the affinity of these concepts to those of Homans, they nevertheless clearly allocated to the maintenance functions certain important group activities that for Homans would fall in the external, not the internal, system. Among these, for instance, are allocating the rewards to the various members, synchronizing reward allocation with cost peaks, and cutting costs by improved communications. These are all largely, though not entirely, determined by the formal structure of the group rather than by spontaneous relationships based on sentiment.

Let us see if we can sum up the distinction at this point. Homans's external and internal systems correspond roughly, though not precisely, to a frequently used distinction between the task and maintenance functions of a system. In his external system, Homans included both the tasks the group performs in relation to its environment and the formal aspects of the group's organization for these tasks. In his internal system, he included the sentiments and spontaneous relationships that arise among members as they perform the group's tasks. In the usual task-maintenance distinction, task functions parallel Homans's external system and maintenance functions parallel Homans's internal system, with one exception: The formal aspects of the structure through which the group is organized to perform its tasks, although included by Homans in his external structure, are customarily considered as part of the group's maintenance functions.

Until recently Talcott Parsons made relatively little use of the internal-external concepts, having developed his own well-known set of concepts associated with the pattern variables. Zelditch codified Parsons's schema into the following four coordinates: *goal-attainment*—"the gratification of the units of the system"; *adaptation*—"the manipulation of the environment in the interests of goal-attainment"; *integration*—"the attachment of member-units to each other in their distinction from that which is non-system"; and *tension*—"the malintegration of member-units seen as themselves systems."[11]

10. Reprinted with permission from John W. Thibaut and Harold H. Kelley, *The Social Psychology of Groups* (New York: John Wiley & Sons, copyright 1959), pp. 274-75.

11. Parsons and Bales, *Family, Socialization and Interaction Process*, p. 404.

These four coordinates are then further reduced as follows:

Instrumental Activity	*Expressive Activity*
Goal-Attainment	Integrative Aspects
Adaptation	Tension Aspects

Clearly, the instrumental activity corresponds to the task functions, and the expressive activity corresponds to the maintenance functions as defined above.

In a later statement, Parsons dropped the term "expressive" and attempted to reconcile this division with that of Homans. He gave the following analysis:[12]

	Instrumental	*Consummatory*
External	Adaptive Function	Goal-Attainment Function
Internal	Pattern-Maintenance and Tension-Management Function	Integrative Function

Thus, he joined together under external and internal the pairs that were joined under instrumental and expressive. But in the process, pattern-maintenance and tension-management, functions that relate to the system's internal structure as distinguished from the sentiments of the integrative function, were listed under internal. Although Parsons stated in this later formulation that his use of the terms external and internal was "very close to that employed by G. C. Homans,"[13] it would appear to depart from Homans's formulation on this highly important decision of whether to include the formal aspects of the structure through which the member units are held together in a functioning system under the internal pattern rather than the external. His usage thus parallels that of the task-maintenance dichotomy, which is, in some ways, more readily adaptable to the social-system analysis of communities.

Loomis followed Homans explicitly and apparently would exclude from the internal *pattern*, as he more appropriately calls it, the formal aspects of the interrelation of the system's member units. He pointed out the relationship of the external pattern to "Gesellschaft-like sequences" and of the internal pattern to "Gemeinschaft-like sequences." And with Homans he clearly ascribed to the *external* pattern the formal aspects through which member units are coordinated as a system:

12. Merton, Broom, and Cottrell, *Sociology Today*, p. 7.
13. Merton, Broom, and Cottrell, *Sociology Today*, p. 5.

143

Whether the internal or the external pattern of a social system receives primary emphasis is very frequently a function of size. To attain maximum returns from the division of labor and the application of technology from the external pattern, the system may of necessity be large. To be normatively integrated large systems must be equipped with authority structures that give primacy to the external pattern. Although small groups may make minimal use of an external pattern and function in a Gemeinschaft-like manner, making relationships ends in themselves, it is difficult for large groups to do so. Large groups tend to give relatively greater emphasis to the external pattern.[14]

Perhaps this is as good a place as any to point out the relevance of the present discussion to our subsequent analysis of the community as a social system. Following Homans and Loomis for a moment, let us first consider a large organization and then a community in their external and internal aspects.

In a large organization, as Loomis indicated above, in order to achieve normative integration there must be a clearly defined and highly elaborate formal authority structure that coordinates the division of labor. This structure is rationally organized (bureaucratic) in order to perform the tasks of the organization with relation to its environment. Hence, its highly formal bureaucratic structure is clearly part of the external pattern. Integration through the communication of sentiment and the development of spontaneous relationships among group members, although an important means of integration at the small-group level, takes on less and less importance for the large organization as a total system. (Indeed, it frequently operates through hostile cliques and gripe sessions to defeat the goal attainment of the system.)

In a community, as we shall see, normative integration is achieved in part through the communication of sentiment among the members, through common values, local loyalties, shared tradition, and so on; it is also achieved in part through the spontaneous relations that arise among unit members as they function in their various tasks as members of the community. But as in other systems, the larger the system, the less effective are these ties of "sentiment" to achieve the necessary integration and coordination of the parts so that the community can function adequately as a system in the performance of its tasks. More and more, the community depends for its integration on formal structures, such as the community press, the municipal government, the council of social agencies, the city planning commission, to achieve at least the minimum of integration

14. Loomis, *Social Systems*, p. 40.

so that the parts of the system can function in systemic relation to one another and so that the locality-relevant tasks can be performed. We shall consider some of these integrative factors, both informal (sentiment, cliques, power structure, etc.) and formal (community councils, municipal government) in chapter 6. The use of the task-function, maintenance-function terminology is particularly suitable for analysis of the systemic aspects of communities, and it will be employed from time to time in subsequent chapters.

Boundary maintenance   By definition, a social system is an organization of interaction of member units, and as such it must be distinguishable from its surrounding environment. That is, it must be possible to ascertain precisely which units are interacting as member units of the particular system to be described. The system endures as long as these units remain in a systemic relationship, as differentiated from the relation of the units to other units in the environment. Such behavior is termed "boundary maintenance." Obviously, if the system cannot retain this relationship, it dissolves, no longer being an identifiable organization of interacting units.

Loomis described boundary maintenance as "the process whereby the identity of the social system is preserved and the characteristic interaction pattern maintained." He offered a helpful description of the variety of types of boundary maintenance:

> They may be primarily physical, as political boundaries, prison walls, zoning restrictions, or prescribed use or nonuse of facilities; or they may be primarily social, as are the life styles of social classes or the preference for endogamy. They may be spontaneously or unconsciously applied, as in the family display of company manners; or they may be planned and rationally applied, as in the travel restrictions imposed extensively by totalitarian states and less extensively by democratic societies. They may be expressed in group contraction as in casting out deviants; or they may be reflected in group expansion, as in the uniting of parallel labor unions, as similar groups find boundary maintenance facilitated by joint effort.[15]

In applying system analysis to communities, an important question related to system boundaries has already been raised in this book: To what extent can contemporary American communities be identified as social systems distinguishable from their surrounding environments? To the extent that they cannot be meaningfully distinguished from their environments, they cannot properly be considered social systems.

15. Loomis, *Social Systems*, pp. 31, 32.   **145**

Equilibrium   Social systems are constantly experiencing changes, both in their formal and in their informal structure. These changes are in part caused by the behavior of the system as it responds to impacts on it from its surrounding environment. Thus, a member of a friendship group moves to another city, or competition from another firm leads to the reorganization of one of the branch offices of a company, or a growing friendship between two members of a football team is reflected in their relationships with the team's captain. Such changes call for adjustments in the systems involved, adjustments that accommodate the change and typically operate to minimize its impact on the system. This process has been codified by Zelditch as follows: We can say that "a change of state of x_i is followed by a change of state of $x_j, \ldots x_n$ such that no further change of state occurs in the system." Thus, by equilibrium is meant "a state of a system such that there is zero change of state of the units of the system relative to each other."[16]

The concept of equilibrium is frequently misunderstood as implying a sort of static conception of social systems. Actually, the opposite is the case, for in order to preserve or re-establish equilibrium, a system must constantly undergo reactions of the dynamic nature indicated above. Thus, equilibrium is not the status quo, for as the system operates through time making adaptive changes to the impacts upon it, the equilibrium that is sustained or restored is seldom precisely the equilibrium that existed before the impacts.

Homans has dealt extensively with the concept of equilibrium. "A social system is in equilibrium and control is effective," he wrote, "when the state of the elements that enter the system and of the mutual relationships between them is such that any small change in one of the elements will be followed by changes in the other elements tending to reduce the amount of that change."[17] It will be recalled that Homans's principal focus of attention as he considered social systems was the small group. He related equilibrium to the process of social control and considered such control in connection with the group's behavior when a member departs from a group norm:

> The individual's behavior is controlled because the results of his departure from the norm are, on balance, unpleasant to him, and because the mutual dependence of the elements of behavior means that a relatively small departure will have relatively large results. When control is effective in this sense we say that the social system is in equilibrium.[18]

16. Parsons and Bales, *Family, Socialization and Interaction Process,* p. 402.

17. Homans, *Human Group,* pp. 303-4.

146   18. Homans, *Human Group,* pp. 311-12.

Putting this another way, a system is in equilibrium (a dynamic state) when it is able to react to a change in such a way as to minimize that change's impact on the relation of the units in the system. Parsons and Zelditch have taken it as axiomatic that systems "seek equilibrium." Homans has preferred to describe the situation without such an assumption, for some responses of a system to a change in one of the elements may be such as to bring about greater change. He pointed out that the group's method of punishing the individual for the violation of a group norm may further estrange that individual and his or her behavior from the group and its norms. Perhaps this type of situation can be most expeditiously handled by accepting the equilibrium-seeking behavior of a system as axiomatic and acknowledging the obvious fact that in many instances a system's behavior concerned with minimizing the impact of a change results in intensifying it, with even greater impact on the equilibrium of the system.

When this last occurs, three typical outcomes are: (1) The system succeeds in absorbing the change but in the process the restoration of equilibrium involves considerable change in the relations of the system's member units; (2) The system is unable to accommodate the change and instead rids itself of the disturbing member unit, for example, as in the splintering of Protestant sects from parent bodies. This second type of outcome is what Loomis described as boundary maintenance by means of group contraction through the ejection of deviants. (3) Or a system may be unable to restore equilibrium as continued changes operate that disintegrate the relations holding the member units together in a distinguishable interaction pattern. The system becomes no longer discernible from its environment, ceasing to exist. This last condition is well illustrated by Homans's analysis of the Hilltown community: "Because Hilltown still has a name, geographical boundaries, and people who live within the boundaries, we assume that it is still a community and therefore judge that it is rotten. It would be wiser to see that it is no longer, except in the most trivial sense, a community at all."[19]

A Digression into Literature and Philosophy

So far we have been discussing some of the main features of social systems with a view toward coping with the question of the extent to which American communities are appropriate subjects for such analysis. Before we tackle the question, let us back off and make our approach by a somewhat different route. Indeed, the route may appear so circuitous as to lose us in the forest rather than lead us to

19. *Human Group*, p. 367.

the clearing where we hope to do some constructive work. But it may be both useful and enjoyable to skirt around a little, looking at some of the contour of the surrounding land and noting some of the different types of flora and fauna in the environment of our clearing. In the process, we shall wander right out of the field of sociology and find ourselves in groves of poetry and philosophy, but it may be an intellectually stimulating trip.

Let us start quite far out, with a poem, Keats's *The Eve of St. Agnes*. In one richly worded passage we are given a colorful picture:

> Full on this casement shone the wintry moon,
> And threw warm gules on Madeline's fair breast.

Beautiful lines. As Thouless has pointed out, much the same meaning might have been conveyed with quite different words:

> Full on this window shone the wintry moon,
> Making red marks on Jane's uncoloured chest.[20]

But is it the same meaning? At least, quite a different feeling is conveyed. Keats described this tableau in a way that evokes vivid pictures, rich with emotional associations. He exemplifies the substance of Max Eastman's description of the poet's function. Eastman said, in effect, that the poet holds up everyday reality to us but shows it in a different light. A poet has the ability to convey some of the rich warmth of the immediate experience, which we prosaic mortals tend to miss as, nose to the grindstone, we go about our daily routines performing life's tasks and solving the problems that life presents to us.[21] It takes a Wordsworth to tell us to stop a minute and look at a beautiful field of daffodils. Indeed, Wordsworth was convinced that we were missing the quality of life in the busy pursuit of mundane tasks:

> . . . late and soon,
> Getting and spending, we lay waste our powers:
> Little we see in Nature that is ours;
> We have given our hearts away, a sordid boon!

We are in very little danger of falling into Faust's fatal snare of saying to the moment, *Verweile doch, Du bist so schön.* "Hold a while; you are so beautiful."

---

20. Robert H. Thouless, *Straight and Crooked Thinking* (London: English Universities Press, 1936; New York: Simon and Schuster, 1932), pp. 13-14.

148 21. *Enjoyment of Poetry* (New York: Charles Scribner's Sons, 1921).

It is but a few steps from poetry to philosophy, and the steps are particularly easy to traverse since, in a sense, many philosophers were poets. Certainly, Plato was poetic, as a reading of the seventh or tenth book of the *Republic* will indicate; but one also calls to mind Democritus writing poetically on the nature of things or Nietzsche writing both poems and philosophical works and, as in *Thus Spake Zarathustra*, making a vivid amalgam. Or, more recently, one might compare the beautiful, almost poetic, prose of a Santayana with the rich but cold and colorless exposition of John Dewey. Dewey, who wrote so lucidly on *Art As Experience*, was unable to give his own writing that happy combination of form and content that might make it meaningful not only logically but esthetically. His philosophical colleague William James was much more capable of engaging the reader in a warm relationship of mutual friendly interest in his subject matter.

Interestingly enough, it was William James who pointed out, in his essay on *The Sentiment of Rationality*, the important difference between two ways of knowing, the one indicated by the Latin word *scire*, the other by *noscere*; the former indicates knowledge about, the latter, acquaintance with: a distinction neatly made by the German *wissen* and *kennen*, by the French *savoir* and *connaître*. The physicist knows a good deal about the light waves involved in the color blue but cannot communicate "blueness" to a blind person. In a sense, the poets are communicating to us some of the immediacy and "taste" of experience as though we were blind, giving us a sense of its dynamic, ongoing vitality.

The philosopher Bergson emphasized that reason tends to proceed by means of analysis, a breaking down of that which it considers, and thus misses the dynamic quality of reality, its *élan vital*, which can be experienced only through intuition, an attempt to see things whole, through "acquaintance" rather than "knowledge about."

But the philosopher who perhaps comes closest to the poets in this respect is Martin Buber, who took another facet of the distinction and asserted that we can look at people, things, the world, as a series of "It's" and relate ourselves to each It in an I-It relationship, or we can look upon them as "Thou's" and relate ourselves to them in an I-Thou relationship. The latter is essentially religious, essentially mystical, a relationship distinguished from the I-It relationship as mutual sympathy and compassion are distinguished from manipulation and exploitation.[22] It is quite a different I, Buber insisted, which is involved in the I-Thou relationship from that which is involved in the I-It relationship, This distinction was also recognized

22. *I and Thou* (New York: Charles Scribner's Sons, 1952). **149**

in somewhat different form by that most unpoetical of philosophers, Immanuel Kant, and is expressed in the third statement of his "categorical imperative": "So act as to treat humanity, whether in your own person or in that of another, never merely as a means but always as an end as well."[23]

But we can turn from the poetic and the philosophical and observe much the same distinction in the most mundane episodes of daily life. (Or should we say that these mundane episodes are infused with rich poetic and philosophical content, if we but stop and observe?) Let us consider a simple business call, where the caller has business to transact but first comes in, sits down, and visitor and host engage in small talk before getting down to work. Or note the custom by which formal speakers so often make introductory remarks, sometimes including humorous stories, before launching into the formal part of their speech. In both instances, is not something poetic occurring? Is not the one person saying, as it were: I know we have business to do, a task to accomplish together; but first, let's hold on just for a moment. We are persons, aren't we? Here we are, together, you and I, engaging in an interchange—and talking to each other as a person would to another person, before we get down to the formal relationship that brought us together and now sets us our task. Well, now let's go. What I want to say to you. . . .

Or take a customer who comes into a supermarket week after week, and even in the impersonal, mechanized, bureaucratized setting of the supermarket (as contrasted with the old grocery store) eventually strikes up a conversation with the checkout clerk: My, what a crowd. You really are busy today. I should think you'd get tired. And after a few more times, it may be: How is your boy? Did he get over his measles all right? The same can happen, but more rapidly, among people who are placed in a common work setting to do a job. They communicate with each other about the job, but they begin to interact with each other as persons, getting to know each other, forming likes and dislikes, finding themselves coming to place more stock in what this person says than that one, perhaps even getting together when not on the job to go bowling together.

We are a long way from the poetic way of perceiving reality as opposed to the philosophical or from the distinction between knowledge about and knowledge by acquaintance. Or are we? Isn't there something that all these situations have in common? On the one hand, the emphasis on the task, the content, rationality, purposefulness, subordinating means to ends; on the other the emphasis on the process, the present relationship, sentiment, deliberate purposelessness, attention to means as somehow ends in themselves.

23. *Metaphysics of Ethics.*

But look—we are back at the clearing! For this type of relationship that springs up within a formal organization is exactly what Homans had in mind, although he described it in different terms, in pointing out that a social system is actually comprised of two systems, the external, which is organized and interrelated on the basis of content, rationality, the task to be performed, the business at hand, and the internal, which is organized on the basis of the realtionships between people as individual personalities. Homans developed the main thread of his analysis using the material that was gathered in the famous study of the men in the Bank Wiring Room in the Hawthorne plant of the Western Electric Company.[24] But he also analyzed other, quite different settings, recognizing that the kind of relationship that he termed the internal pattern actually characterized an extremely wide range of social experience or, in somewhat more precise terms, characterized all social systems.

The relationship has perhaps been most widely probed scientifically in small-group research, where the distinction is often made between task and maintenance functions. It has long been recognized in the sociological distinction between categoric and personal contacts in the interaction process (see page 60). The categoric contacts involve interaction insofar as this is determined by a particular categorical relationship, such as that of storekeeper to customer, lawyer to client, teacher to student, lieutenant to sergeant. Personal contacts, on the other hand, are those in which the relationships are more spontaneous, arising in the free interplay of personalities. And it has long been recognized that personal types of relationship tend to spring up within the categorical ones, as, for example, when storekeeper and customer get to know each other as persons.

The distinction has also been recognized in the differentiation between primary-group relations and secondary-group relations (see pages 58-62), the latter being more rational, more formalized, more specifically task-oriented, less intimate. Here, too, relationships, such as among personnel of a small office, which are formally established as purely secondary-group relationships, often develop into primary-group relationships over a period of time. This development sometimes causes complications, as when the young executive who becomes the boss's golf-playing companion is believed thereby to gain the "inside track" in business matters as well, or when the boss and secretary become "too" intimate.

The terms *formal structure* and *informal structure* have also been widely used to indicate the same distinction. Thus, there is an important sense, deeply rooted not only in the nature of social relation-

---

24. As reported principally in Fritz J. Roethlisberger and William J. Dickson, *Management and the Worker* (Cambridge, Mass.: Harvard University Press, 1939). **151**

ships but in ways of knowing, ways of looking at the world, in which emphasis is placed on task, content, or purpose on the one hand or on maintenance, form, or immediacy on the other. The distinction has many ramifications among contemporary issues. Consider the contrast often drawn between authoritarian leadership, which emphasizes the task, and permissive leadership, which stresses relationships among the participants of the group; between teaching "subject matter" and teaching "children"; between Taylorism, that scientific management movement that attempted to increase productivity through more deliberately rationalizing the tasks to be performed, and the group-dynamics movement, which seeks to increase productivity by emphasizing the relationships that exist among individuals as they participate in the interaction patterns that the system prescribes.

It may be rash to take the distinction too far, but let us at least be courageous. Consider, for example, the alleged transition from the Protestant ethic characterized by industriousness, thrift, diligence (emphasis on the task) to the "social ethic" described by Whyte in *The Organization Man* in terms of scientism, belongingness, and togetherness. Or consider Riesman's distinction in *The Lonely Crowd* between the inner-directed man, essentially the man who pursues his goals according to firm values implanted early in life in the socialization process, and the other-directed man, restlessly scanning the social horizon to pick up cues from his peers as to what he should believe in and how he should behave.

We shall encounter the distinction in a whole complex of forms in the community. Indeed, it is because of this important fact that we are now making this long preliminary excursion. We shall, for example, be concerned with those aspects of the community that are principally involved in the performance of the locality-relevant tasks described in chapter 1 and with those aspects of the community that are principally concerned with the maintenance of the various parts (member units) of the community in a systemic relationship to one another. We shall note that many community-based units perform tasks that relate them to systems outside the community, but that at the same time such units must by definition be systemically related to each other on the local level if the community is to constitute a social system. And on a level much more immediate than definitions, we shall find that the conflicting behavior of different task-oriented groups in the community often poses practical problems of interunit relationships that threaten the persistence of the community by weakening its social control and intensifying to a critical level the problem of maintaining equilibrium.

It was mentioned earlier that the development of social-system analysis has arisen principally in the research done on small groups, only secondarily in that done in more formal organizations like business organizations or hospitals, and hardly at all in work on the community. One of the most significant and widely known research findings in social-system research on the small group is closely related to the present discussion. Robert F. Bales and his associates at Harvard University, in their work on interaction process analysis in small groups, found that as the members of small groups tend to develop a differentiation of roles in the performance of a task, there frequently arises a person who tends to assume leadership in guiding the group in the accomplishment of its task, through making suggestions, proposing courses of action, assigning roles to others, and so on. At the same time, some other person often is found to pay particular attention to the way people are feeling, to the ruffled emotions that often are caused as the group goes about its task-performing function. The one is a task leader, the other a social-emotional, or expressive, leader.

Thus, emphasis on the task accomplishment and emphasis on the social-emotional condition of the group become differentiated through role specialization, usually represented by two different people who assume these respective leadership roles. The distinction appears not only through differential role allocation but also through differential activity of the group through time. In one phase of activity the group may concentrate mainly on task performance, on "getting its work done." At another time, typically after an intensive phase of task performance, the group may concentrate on its members' social-emotional needs, relaxing with small talk after some hard work, or joking, or in other ways reducing tension. As the group's attention shifts from one phase to the other, the appropriate leader, whether task specialist or social-emotional specialist, participates intensively.[25]

Here is an example of moving, fluctuating equilibrium, where phases of task performance tend to create tensions in the members and to threaten the group's equilibrium, which is then restored through activity directed at the group's maintenance functions. Is there an analogue in the community? We shall see, as we explore the suitability of American communities for analysis as social systems.

Applicability of Social-System Analysis to the Community

Let us close in rapidly on our main question: To what extent can social-system analysis appropriately be applied to American communities? Or, phrased somewhat differently, to what extent do Ameri-

25. See Parsons and Bales, *Family, Socialization and Interaction Process*, chap. 5.

can communities display the differentiating characteristics of social systems that they can properly be called such and analyzed accordingly? Notice we are not asking: Are American communities social systems, or are they not? We are putting the question in such a way as to allow for differences in degree. We are definitely reserving the right to point out, for example, that communities may show one systemic characteristic much more clearly than another, and, on a different level, that some communities show the various systemic characteristics to a much greater extent than do others. We are not likely to end up with a clear-cut Yes or No answer to our question. Like the harried executive pressed by subordinates for a definite decision, we may have to pound the desk and declare: I said maybe, and that's *final!*

We can organize our analysis around a consideration of the following questions:

Of what units is the community as a social system formed?

To what extent can the community as a social system be distinguished from its surrounding environment?

What is tne nature of the structured interaction of units in the community as a social system?

What are the tasks that the community performs as a social system?

By what means is the structured relationship among the interacting units of a community maintained?

Can an external and an internal pattern of activities be differentiated in the community?

What is the relation of community social-system units to other social systems?

In turning to these specific questions, we at once encounter a difficulty that itself has relevance to our discussion. How shall one take into consideration the great variation in American communities in answering each question? Can one speak of "the American community" generically, or must one eternally delimit such statements to "some communities thus ... and some communities so ...?" If American communities do not show a sufficient degree of similarity on a sufficient number of criteria so that general statements may be made about them, there arises a question that is prior to the one under consideration. It is not whether the American community can be considered as social system but whether or not there is any value to the concept of the American community at all.

In chapter 1 the community was defined as that combination of social units and systems that perform the major social functions having locality relevance, and five such functions were specified. In chapter 2, several different approaches to the community were considered both from the standpoint of how it is to be conceived and from the standpoint of new conceptual tools for research. While these respective approaches have great value, it should be emphasized that when we now use the term *community*, we are defining it as above. The definition was not formulated lightly, and we shall stick with it if only for the sake of being specific and remaining consistent. We acknowledge that people are involved, that a geographic area is involved, that shared values are relevant, that a sense of psychological identification is relevant, that the demographic approach has value, and so on. But when we ask the extent to which the American community can properly be described as a social system we are asking the extent to which "that combination of social units and systems that perform the (specified) major social functions having locality relevance" can properly be described as a social system. Nothing more and nothing less.

What units make up the "community system"? By definition, the community is comprised of social units and systems. Is it not begging the question to define the community in systemic terms and then proceed to discover that it operates in the manner of a social system? The question is a justifiable one. To qualify the community as a social system, however, we must be able to answer satisfactorily the whole list of questions posed above. We shall not be able to turn the trick by the mere device of substituting some favorably loaded terms. Actually, these terms "social units and systems" are in the definition for a double purpose. They serve to recognize that, in systemic terms, the community's members may be both individuals and groups; and they also serve to keep our terminology consistent. As has been pointed out, social systems frequently are found as subsystems within larger social systems, so there is no particular difficulty here.

The important point is that while a small group consists of member units who are individual people (though of course, cliques within a small group may also be considered as units of the group), a community comprises units that are both individual people and, even more pertinent, social systems into which these individual people are organized. Examples are clubs, business establishments, governmental offices, churches, schools, and so forth.

We have noticed in the preceding chapter that as the "great change" transforms American communities, increasing impersonality and bureaucratization operate, among other variables, to place increasing importance on the organizations to which an individual belongs.

To what extent can the community as a social system be distinguished from its surrounding environment? This is one of the **155**

crucial questions. We stated in chapter 1 that although the concept of the community is fraught with difficult theoretical questions, the term is still used because of the inescapable fact that the spatial location of people's residence does affect their social relationships. Living together in physical proximity necessitates the local access to the major functions that we have listed as "locality relevant."

Our question, in geographical terms, is, To what extent, as we go across the countryside and notice people living in some relation to a population cluster, are there identifiable "bundles" of social interaction that provide locality-relevant functions for people living in the same geographic area? Putting this another way, Do schools, churches, employment opportunities, shopping facilities, local government, local newspapers, and so on serve substantially the same group of people in substantially the same geographic area?

We have observed instances where the locality of gainful employment was a different locality from that of school attendance. We have indicated that in the suburban "sprawl," institutional service areas may overlap in various ways. We noted that Crestwood Heights could not be distinguished visually from its surrounding geographic environment, and we also noted that many of its basic institutions, including churches and major sources of employment, were not located within its confines. Rather, churches were in the immediately surrounding section of the metropolitan area, employment opportunities were principally at the metropolitan center. One wonders whether communities do not represent St. Augustine's definition of God, "an infinite circle whose center is everywhere and whose periphery is nowhere."[26]

Yet, just as obviously, many communities *can* be located geographically from the air, at least roughly. While things may be somewhat vague at the periphery, the person who flies across the United States in most cases has little difficulty distinguishing different clusters of population. Grant that many people cross from one cluster to another for various locality-relevant purposes; grant that some of the clusters taper off into each other imperceptibly; grant that in all cases the borders between the clusters are difficult to determine precisely; grant that a different border might be indicated for one kind of institutional service area than for that of another. The geographical arrangement of the clusters nevertheless remains an important key to the geographic interrelationship of social units and systems.

Before leaving this particular question, we might note that rather than having a geographic area as the principal frame of refer-

26. Scott Greer has pointed out that neighborhoods, at least, are reminiscent of the definition in just this way. See "The Social Structure and Political Process of Suburbia," *American Sociological Review* 25, no. 4 (August 1960): 520.

ence it might be preferable to start with various types of institutional services, such as schools, churches, or local government, and examine the extent to which they show systemic properties, noticing, where it is the case, that for some purposes the system has one spatial extension, for other purposes another. Our definition of community is specifically designed to facilitate this approach.

We have examined the relation of communities to the question of geographic boundaries. Social systems, even more importantly, have and maintain psychological boundaries. Do communities also? The widely reported experience of newcomers finding it difficult to become accepted by local people, particularly associated with New England, is an example of such psychological boundaries on the community level. Since a community as a social system, unlike a formal association, has no formal, rationally defined, hierarchical organization, it is much more difficult to determine who "belongs" to the community and who doesn't.

Let us dwell on this point a moment. The community as a system may be considered to consist of various units and subsystems. Many of these subsystems have clear-cut organizational structures: the church with its board of trustees, clergymen, elders, congregational members; the school with its board of education, principal, teachers, pupils; the bank with its directors, officers, and various employees and depositors. These subsystems have a definitely formulated and identifiable structure.

Not so the community. There is no president of a community, no board of trustees, no officers, no members in any formal sense. Certainly, the mayor of a city can hardly be considered its president. There may be fifty or a hundred people whose position or power makes them more important in the community than the mayor. The mayor is the formal head of one of the community's constituent subsystems, the city government. Likewise, there is a city council, a board of directors of the Chamber of Commerce, of the First National Bank, of the United Fund. But there is no board of directors of the community, in any formal sense. In an informal sense, of course, we must note that the community has a structure: a social class structure, a power structure, a structure of informal cliques and friendships. But we are talking about the formal sense in which membership might be determined. In this sense, communities differ from many types of social entities showing systemic qualities by the fact that communities as such do not have a formally organized structure.

Consequently, community membership is difficult to determine. Further, one must be aware of the great variation in communities in the extent to which "belonging" to the local community is a psychologically important relationship. Yet here again, though membership may be difficult to determine and though its importance may vary, there is often a sense of identification with one's community, and likewise, it is generally possible to ascertain who "belongs" and who doesn't. The newcomer who arrives in the community and immediately sets about trying to get people to do things "the way we did in New City" soon finds out that communities have membership boundaries, and that however unprecise they may be, they are defi nite enough to indicate that he or she doesn't yet "belong."

We can sum up this question of systemic boundaries by saying that for communities, especially, geographic boundaries are particu larly relevant, though often vague and difficult to define, and that psychological boundaries exist and are maintained, even though formal membership is not applicable since the community is not a formally organized system. And, noting the extent to which matters of degree are involved, we are again convinced that our inquiry should ask the extent to which communities manifest systemic characteristics, rather than for a Yes or No answer as to whether or not they are social systems.

What is the nature of the structured interaction of units in the community as a social system?   Let us explore the implications of this question by taking two subsystems of the community: a family and a bank. Generally speaking, we are not interested in the intra-family behavior of people in community social-system analysis, nor do we need to take account of it except as it is relevant to the community as we have defined it and relevant to the performance of the locality-relevant tasks, which will be discussed in chapter 6. The family as a social system, as a "unity of interacting personalities," as Burgess called it a half century ago, is not our concern, and, although much family behavior takes place within the geographic confines of the community, it is not in and of itself relevant to community analysis.

In the case of a bank (and for purposes of interest, let it be a bank with branch offices in various other communities in that section of the country), we have two levels of behavior that, in a sense, are not relevant to the community as a social system. The first, paralleling the family, is the intraunit level—behavior of the various personnel within the bank, including the formal procedures and the informal, the external and the internal system, to follow Homans. But note something interesting: It is the external system that links the bank to its environment, and so we are interested in the bank's external system insofar as it is related through this to the local community as a part of the bank's environment. Or, from the community point of view, we are interested in the bank as a subsystem of the community, and we are interested in those aspects of the behavior of the bank that are "brought into" the bank from the surrounding community, and those aspects of the behavior of the bank that are "put out" by the bank, affecting other units and systems of the community. Such input and output of community subsystems will be analyzed later in terms of the major locality-relevant functions.

But another type of relationship complicates the bank's picture, for we have said that the bank has several branches in other communities. Are we interested in the behavior related to this extra-community system? (Note that this is a crucial question, for the "great change" has operated to make this type of situation more and more prevalent among community-based units.) Here again, our answer can best be given in terms of input and output in relation to the community as a system. We recognize that as a result of its system of branches, the bank may take particular courses of action that in turn will have an impact on other systems in the local community. Some of the bank's behavior, at least, will be related not exclusively to its operation within the local community, but to the needs of the entire bank as a social system, which includes, say, fifteen branches in other communities. Such actions are the output of the bank system, coming into the community as input. We are definitely interested in this type of input into the community system. We recognize that the local bank is a member of two systems, the community system and its own extracommunity system. That is a fact of life, one that is increasingly typical of community units.

Likewise, the local bank may receive input from other units in the community, which in turn will affect the whole aggregate of branches as a social system. Thus, economic conditions in our community caused, let us say, by the decision of a major employer to move elsewhere, may affect the local bank in a way that will constitute input into the branch-bank system as the local bank adapts to its own local community environment. Thus, in the case of community units that are at the same time units of extracommunity systems, we are interested in their input-output exchange with other units (schools, families, churches, stores, governmental offices) of the community system. This input-output relationship is affected by the unit's tie to an extracommunity system, a relationship explored in some depth in chapters 8 and 9.

What are the tasks that the community performs as a social system?   Let us begin negatively. The tasks are not those performed by its constituent units for their subsystem members, or as parts of extracommunity systems; they are those that can be performed only by the local systemic interrelationship of these units. The tasks of the community system are the provision of the locality-relevant functions already mentioned: production-distribution-consumption,   **159**

socialization, social control, social participation, and mutual support. We have noted that for symbiotic and other reasons the performance of these functions is widely arranged through a geographical clustering of the subsystems involved.

Conceivably, each extracommunity system might operate through local units with no clustering relationship to the local units of other systems and without any tendency for service areas to coincide. Similarly, other tasks might be performed by purely local units that again bear little geographical or systemic relationship to each other or to the local units of larger systems. This is simply an abstract way of depicting a type of social organization for the performance of the five specified tasks that does not use the community as a local system. In such an abstract situation we could readily say that the construct "community" is superfluous, corresponding to nothing in reality, and could dispense with the term once and for all. But here the hard facts are against us. The performance of the locality-relevant functions does involve social units and systems (whether or not integrally connected with extracommunity systems) that show at least to some degree the various systemic qualities under consideration.

By what means is the structured relationship among the interacting units of a community maintained? If the various subsystems of the community actually can be found to display a systemic relationship to each other, what sustains this relationship? What provides, particularly in the case of units that are parts of extracommunity systems, that behavior which meets the demands of those systems can also be amenable, at least in part, to adaptation to the behavior of other local subsystems?

We have already noted that communities do not characteristically have a formally organized structure like that of a bank or a school. Their subsystems may have, but they do not. What, then, holds them together?

Kaufman described strong communities as those that "have actions locally oriented across the gamut of human interests, and these actions are coordinated through various associations and are integrated through a common ideology. On the other hand, many localities have at one time had many actions locally oriented and now have only a few, if any."[27]

Landecker has presented a useful fourfold paradigm of "integration," particularly applicable to the community: *Cultural* integration is consistency among cultural standards, varying from extreme

27. Harold F. Kaufman, "Toward an Interactional Conception of Community," *Social Forces* 38, no. 1 (October 1959): 14.

consistency to extreme inconsistency. *Normative* integration is agreement between cultural standards and the behavior of individuals, varying from high conformity to high violation of cultural standards. *Communicative* integration involves an exchange of meanings, or communication, varying from a high degree of intercommunication to prevalence of barriers to communication within the group. *Functional* integration involves the degree to which the functions of members of the group constitute mutual services, varying from extreme inderdependence to extreme self-sufficiency.[28]

Let us look one step beyond this helpful set of concepts to some of the instruments, as it were, through which such integration is developed and sustained on the local basis. Related to all of them is the web of symbiotic relationships supporting sustenance and characterized by division of labor and exchange of goods and services. Units like factories and stores, although especially instituted for production and exchange, share these functions with other units such as families, schools, and churches and participate with them in a "market system" which has important integrating functions. Other aspects of the community's integrative or horizontal pattern merit brief mention here:

First, there are the local political and governmental systems. These provide mechanisms for reflecting and expressing the wishes of various groups within the community on matters within the purview of local government. While imperfect, they nevertheless present means of limiting the extremes of specialized interests and containing them within an overall framework that permits other units to survive and maintain themselves.

Second, there is the local press. The press affords a means of communication that cuts across the specialized interests of the sub-systems and presents an interpretation of these sometimes conflicting interests, an interpretation that purports, at least, to represent the "broad community viewpoint."

Third, we can consider those organizations specifically instituted to effect a horizontal integration of community-based systems. Perhaps the best example is the community council or citizens' council often to be found in smaller cities and villages and the specialized coordinating groups, such as welfare councils, councils of churches, and similar groups in larger cities.

Fourth, there are special units that make no attempt at a broad coordination but do, however, perform important integrating functions within a limited sphere of interest, bringing people of otherwise diverse interests together functionally. Here would be included

28. Werner S. Landecker, "Types of Integration and their Measurement," *American Journal of Sociology*, vol. 56, no. 4 (January 1951).

churches, schools, recreational associations, and so on. Sprott asserted that "it is in the development of sectional [specialized] organizations, each catering for special interests of all the inhabitants, irrespective of status, that we may see, not the disintegration of social life, but its enhancement."[29]

Fifth, Hiller has pointed out that the family itself performs an integrative function. "Thus, when members of a family are employed in different firms or occupy unlike positions of honor in the community, the family members tend to reconcile or to mitigate the contradictions in their roles and to bring them into harmony with norms which operate within the family. Somewhat similar processes may take place in other institutional groups."[30]

In addition to the integrative function performed by more or less formal units in the community, there are the informal groupings of the community that also exercise such a role. Among the most important of these are the social class structure, the power structure, and the informal network of neighboring and informal association. This network is important in several ways. First, it provides a grapevine system of communication, which tends to fill in any gaps left by the formal communications system; second, it involves friendly association among people in various specialized interest groups; third, it is an important channel through which public opinion is formed. This public opinion operates, among other things, to maintain a rough adjustment or reconciliation of the various conflicting interests represented by vertically oriented groups.[31]

Can an external and an internal pattern of activities be differentiated in the community? You will recall that the external pattern has to do with those aspects of the system related to its survival in its environment and the tasks that it must perform in order to assure this survival, while the internal pattern is not dictated by the environment but is based on sentiment, is more spontaneous, and is not formally structured. It is very difficult to locate a community structure corresponding to the external pattern, except the structure of the community's constituent units, which is a different matter.

On the side of the internal pattern, the going is not quite so rough, for certainly the "environment" brings people together on

29. W. J. H. Sprott, *Human Groups* (Harmondsworth, Eng.: Penguin Books, 1958), p. 88.

30. E. T. Hiller, "The Community as a Social Group," *American Sociological Review* 6, no. 2 (April 1941): 200. Hiller's article is one of the basic documents to be considered by anyone seriously concerned with a theory of the community.

31. The material in several of the above paragraphs is adapted from Roland L. Warren, "Community Patterns and Community Development," *Merrill-Palmer Quarterly,* vol. 7, no. 4 (October 1961).

the level of the locality, and in the course of the performing of local-ity-relevant tasks, sentiments arise and interaction takes place which is an elaboration on the locality-relevant tasks, and elaboration that is spontaneous and not dictated by the environment.

Let us summarize this by saying that the problem of finding in the community as a social system the analogues of the internal and external patterns found in small groups and organizations as social systems is a sticky one, although there is at least some indication of an affinity. And let us consider for a moment the possibility that our inability to find a clear external and internal pattern in the commu-nity need not necessarily negate the community's systemic properties but may merely indicate that as we shift over to the community, this particular type of analysis is not as appropriate or helpful as it has proved to be for other types of social system. (Perhaps, on the other hand, some other student of the community will make a contribution by developing the implications of external-internal pattern analysis on the community level in a more adequate fashion.)

The System's Vertical and Horizontal Patterns

A type of analysis that seems much more applicable and useful to me than the external-internal concepts in the consideration of commu-nities as social systems is one that distinguishes between a commu-nity's vertical pattern and its horizontal pattern. In describing this distinction, we shall consider the final question that we posed about the extent to which communities could be treated as social systems: *What is the relation of community social-system units to other social systems?*

As a start, let us remind ourselves that community subsystems are often, though not always, parts of social systems that extend beyond the community. Examples are chain stores, branch banks, branch offices or plants of a national company, and local offices of state or federal governmental agencies. Still other community units, like churches, schools, and local government, stand in a definite though less clearly defined relationship to extracommunity systems. We shall define a community's *vertical* pattern as the structural and functional relation of its various social units and subsystems to extra-community systems. The term *vertical* is used to reflect the fact that such relationships often involve different hierarchical levels within the extracommunity system's structure of authority and power. The relationships are typically those of a system unit to the system's head-quarters, although several intervening levels may occur. Thus, our community's bank was also the central office for a whole system of branches located in other communities. The vertical relationship **163** between the local unit and the other units of the system was downward. Often the relation is upward, from a church to a denominational headquarters, from a local chain store to the district office, from the local branch plant to the national headquarters, from a local health association chapter of the national association.

The term *vertical pattern* is used to indicate that we are not referring primarily to a particular type of unit (though some local units may be clearly more relevant than others) but to a type of relationship shared to a greater or lesser extent by all local units, some very emphatically through clear systemic relationships to extracommunity systems, others less strongly bound in systemic ties to extracommunity systems, others bound not so much to extracommunity social systems as to cultural patterns in the surrounding culture. An example of this last is an individual nuclear family whose systemic kinship ties extending outside the community are minimal, let us assume, but whose structure and function are nevertheless closely related to regional and national culture patterns extending far beyond the community.

At the same time, there is a relationship *across* the many different units and subsystems that operate on the community level. We shall define a community's *horizontal* pattern as the structural and functional relation of its various social units and subsystems to each other. We use the terms vertical *pattern* and horizontal *pattern* to indicate that we are not referring primarily to one type of community unit as opposed to another, but rather to a type of relationship into which all community units come in some of their aspects, a relationship that poses a different set of goals, organizational demands, norms, and so on, in these two contrasting patterns. The term *horizontal* is used to indicate that, roughly speaking, the community units *insofar as they have relevance to the community system* tend to be on approximately the same hierarchical level (a community unit level, as opposed to a state, regional, national, or international level of authority, administration, decision-making, and so on).

The vertical-horizontal distinction corresponds roughly, though not completely, to Homans's distinction between the external and internal systems. As we shall see, the community functions in relation to its environment as it performs tasks that relate it increasingly to the surrounding geographic environment, indeed, to ever larger and larger environments. The specific subsystems performing these functions tend to have strong formal organization dictated by the necessity of getting the job done and also by the patterns laid down by the extracommunity systems of which they may be a part. Thus the vertical pattern tends to be similar to Homans's external system.

164   As the community functions, however, relations spring up that

are based on sentiment and not dictated by the environment. Although these relations correspond to what Homans called the internal system, they are only part of what is meant by the community's horizontal pattern. The other part is the formal organization of the coordination function. The formal aspects of the organization through which the member units of a system are related to each other are placed by Homans in the external system We shall nevertheless consider them part of the horizontal pattern. And here is the crux of the matter: For purposes of community analysis, the division into the relation of local subsystems to extracommunity systems (vertical pattern) and the relation of the subsystems to each other (horizontal pattern) seems more fruitful as a basis for analysis than does the difference between relations dictated by environment or based on spontaneous sentiment, which was the difference Homans singled out for special emphasis in his external-internal distinction.

Turning now to the task-maintenance distinction, we once again find a fruitful analytical tool of great usefulness, but not exactly the same as the vertical-horizontal pattern distinction. The similarity is in the fact that task performance often relates community subsystems to extracommunity systems in a vertical pattern, while maintenance activities have to do more with the relation of different subsystems to each other on the local level. For all practical purposes, the two sets of terms correspond, giving us, incidentally, the opportunity to borrow liberally from theory and hypotheses relating to the task-maintenance dichotomy in our analysis of the community as a system.

They do not correspond precisely, however. An example of lack of correspondence would be a chamber of commerce that carries on a program of improving the appearance of the community's main street. Here is a specific task bringing diverse subsystems together in a common undertaking at the community level. As such, the horizontal pattern, not the vertical pattern, is principally involved. Yet it is a task operation. The vertical pattern is involved, incidentally, in the relationship of the local chamber of commerce to the national Chamber of Commerce.

By and large, however, we can note that task performance by the community's constituent subsystems—schools, churches, factories, voluntary associations—tends to orient them toward extracommunity systems. On the other hand, maintenance functions tend to be carried on across the subsystems of the community, involving the horizontal pattern of relationships among these local units.

We are now in a position to raise and answer a question regarding the manner in which the community as a social system operates to preserve or restore equilibrium. Homans, in a brief but incisive analysis of the disintegration of a New England community, **165**

Hilltown, emphasized the relationship between equilibrium and social control, as noted earlier (see page 19). He wrote:

> What we can see is that interaction, activity, sentiment, and norms in Hilltown, unlike some other groups we have studied, were not working together to maintain the *status quo* or to achieve further integration of the group. Instead the relationships between the elements of behavior were such as to lead, in time, toward the condition Durkheim called *anomie*, a lack of contact between the members of a group, and a loss of control by the group over individual behavior.[32]

Thus, equilibrium involves the community's ability to exercise sufficient social control to achieve adequate conformity to community norms and to minimize change impacts.

It is interesting to note, also, that viewed as a social system, the community does display behavior analogous to the pulsating interchange between instrumental activity, as indicated in goal-attainment and adaptational behavior, and expressive activity, as indicated in integrative and tension-management behavior. One sees this pulsation, described by Parsons and Bales as applying to social-system behavior in the small group, manifesting itself in the community. This occurs as various community units carry on activities, often in relation to extracommunity systems, activities that have the effect of accomplishing certain tasks, such as the development of a new cancer clinic or the organization of a local chapter of a national voluntary association. The performance of such tasks often places a strain on existing relationships among the various community units, and maintenance activities must be performed if a new equilibrium is to be achieved. In a sense, the pulsation is symbolized in the existence of vertically oriented national health associations and the horizontally oriented community welfare councils.

The performance of intrumental functions, largely by the community's vertical pattern, and expressive functions, largely by the horizontal pattern, I described earlier in another work as follows:

> Thus we begin to see the community as a social system which undergoes stresses and strains but whose overall longtime process is one of increasing differentiation of function and structure, and whose chief orientation of interest and association is shifting from the horizontal to the vertical .... We also begin to get a picture of the dynamics of induced community change, in which the problem-area specialist and his vertically-oriented interest group achieve accomplishments which in turn make for greater differentiation of function and also create

32. *Human Group*, p. 367.

tensions within the community. Complementing this function is that of the permissive community organizer with his horizontal focus of interest and his typical leadership functions of tension reduction and coordination among the parts of the system.[33]

Thus, in the question of equilibrium, as in the other questions raised regarding the applicability of system analysis of the community, we find that the community passes muster. We have found the major dimensions of social-system analysis to be applicable to the community in a degree sufficient to give us reassurance that further exploration along these lines is worthwhile. We shall therefore make extensive use of social-system analysis in the remainder of this book.

But before going on, let us consider some of the special characteristics of the community and decide how we shall proceed with them. Looking back now at Moe's three ways in which communities are different from other social systems (see p. 49), we recall observing that the fact that the community is a "system of systems" should give us little difficulty, for so is a formal organization. He also indicated that the community as a social system is implicit in nature as compared with the explicitness of a formal organization. This description is true of a community, but it is also true of a small informal friendship group, such as that described by Whyte in *Street Corner Society.*[34] Such informal groups, although not explicit in the sense of a formal organization, are widely recognized social systems.

Moe's second point, however, is more crucial: The community is not structurally and functionally centralized in the same sense that a formal organization is. This statement is true of communities; it is, of course, also true of small informal groups. In the case of small groups, however, the internal pattern is much more readily discernible and gives a much greater impression of a coherent, identifiable group than that of most communities. We have noted that communities as such do not have formal structures, though their constituent subsystems may have. We have also noted that such community subsystems may be integrally related to extracommunity systems, but that the community itself is not.

33.   Roland L. Warren, "Toward A Reformulation of Community Theory," *Human Organization* 15, no. 2 (Summer 1956): 11, reprinted in *Community Development Review*, vol. 9 (June 1958). See also Roland L. Warren, "Local Autonomy and Community Development," *Autonomous Groups*, vol. 15, no. 102 (Fall and Winter 1959), and "Community Patterns and Community Development," cited in n. 31.

34.   William F. Whyte, *Street Corner Society: The Social Structure of an Italian Slum* (Chicago: University of Chicago Press, 1943).

These are characteristics that we should observe and take due account of as we proceed with our analysis. One additional difficulty remains, the major one yet to be confronted. This is the relative strength of the vertical systemic ties linking community units to extracommunity systems as compared with the relative weakness of the horizontal ties linking local community units with each other. Recognizing the strong relation of the local post office to the United States postal system, acknowledging that its operation and its policies are not determined within the community but are merely implementations of a national system, we are confronted with a choice. We can either say that the post office, not being a community phenomenon, will therefore not be included in our definition of the community system and will be ignored in our analysis; or we can recognize that the post office and numerous other community-based units have stronger ties to extracommunity systems than they do to other units within the community but treat them much as we treat any other community subsystem, in terms of input-output relations with the rest of the community. The local post office, for example, performs certain services related to mail for other community subsystems. It also provides a source of employment in the production-exchange-consumption function; brings money into the community from the federal government in the form of wages and local expenditures for equipment, heat, light, rent; takes money out of the community in the form of postage charges, and so on. We shall follow this course, which is facilitated by our insistence on defining the community in terms of specified locality-relevant functions and on differentiating between input-output relations of the community's subsystems and of the community itself as a social system.

In following this course, preferring to accept and incorporate into our analysis those community subsystems that are strongly related to extracommunity systems, we shall necessarily give more attention to the nature of these extracommunity systems than we otherwise would. Thus, though the task may be more demanding, we shall have come to grips with the problem of the increasing vertical orientation of local community subsystems. In chapter 3 it was pointed out that the "great change" was operating in the direction of strengthening the ties of community subsystems to extracommunity systems and of weakening community coherence and automony. We pointed out elsewhere that this has occurred to such an extent that some students of the community suggest that the term should be completely abandoned. We prefer to paraphrase Mark Twain by saying that the report of the community's death is greatly exaggerated, and to note and to analyze carefully the structural and functional change occurring in American communities as they adapt and change in response to change impacts—particularly the seven aspects of the "great change," which have already been considered in detail.

6 Locality-Relevant Functions and their Allocation

We have defined the community as that combination of systems and units that perform the major functions having locality relevance; and we have identified these functions as the following five: production-distribution-consumption, socialization, social control, social participation, and mutual support. Individuals and systems in the community channel into local accessibility the goods, services, and behavior patterns of the society beyond its borders, and likewise their products, whether material or behavioral, are channeled out from the locality to the larger society. At the same time, there is an interchange of behavior and an exchange of goods and services within the community.

Again and again we have referred to the fact that in this channeling process people and organizations cluster together geographically, and that regional or national products, services, and behavior patterns relate themselves to each other, if only minimally, on a locality basis. Thus, there are not only clusters of people but clusters of organizations that serve them. A special characteristic of communities, as distinguished from other types of social systems, clearly lies in this geographically based functional interrelation of social systems. Partly on the basis of larger cultural and systemic patterns, partly on the basis of local choice, the locality-relevant functions are allocated within the community to one type of operational auspices or another, taking on rather different characteristics in accordance with their differential allocation.

The task of tracing the performance of all the locality-relevant functions at the community level is a formidable one, which, to be complete, would include all community units and all community-relevant activities. Nevertheless, it is of particular importance to examine the relation to each other of various units performing one or another function as well as to trace their respective systemic relationships to extracommunity systems. Some selection is therefore necessary.

We shall adopt a schema that will enable us to probe these relationships in each of the functional fields, but in each case with only one type of local unit, especially selected as appropriate for representing the kinds of relationships prevalent in that functional field. In doing so, it will be not only possible but appropriate to consider units with quite diverse types of organizational structure and relation to the local community. Nevertheless, we shall be able to compare them in their ties to local community people, to similar local units, and to extracommunity systems. Thus, in each of the five functional areas we shall make a systematic analysis of these relationships for at least one "typical" unit. Other types of units can then be compared in the extent to which they resemble these "prototype" units. The advantage will be that by confining our principal analysis to only one typical unit in each functional area, we shall be able to focus our discussion and to analyze systematically, rather than wander in purely descriptive and enumerative fashion over the highly diverse field that is presented. We shall consider each of the locality-relevant functions in turn.

Production-Distribution-Consumption

The first major function of the community is to provide the local organization of individuals and systems that facilitate productive effort and to provide distribution and consumption of what is produced. Since division of labor characterizes American communities, there must likewise be provision for the exchange of goods and services among units in the community. Putting this in its simplest terms, there must, under modern conditions, be opportunity for remunerative work, and goods and services must be locally accessible for purchase.

There are, of course, numerous possibilities for systematizing production. In alternative social systems, economic production may be carried on principally on a family basis, on the basis of a larger kinship group, by ad hoc working or hunting parties, in an organ- **171** ized cooperative effort among members of an organization, and so on. In American communities private industry, taken in a broad sense, is the principal unit of production. Form and Miller's conception of industry is applicable: "Industry is defined here as the local economic institution. It includes all of the business and industries in the locality, and all economic associations, including those of business, unions, and the professions. In addition, it includes interbusiness and interunion associations and specialized positions in these organizations."[1]

The distribution of goods and services may take place in many different ways: through direct allocation to each participant of his or her just share of the product (as in dividing the results of a hunt), through trading of one good or service for another (barter), through reciprocal gifts, and so forth. A high degree of specialization calls for a much greater interdependence among producers for each other's products, and the money and credit system greatly facilitates this process, particularly in American communities, which are characterized by a high degree of such specialization. Thus, individuals can confine their productive endeavors to narrowly specialized tasks (such as bookkeeping or operating a turret lathe) for which they receive money as compensation. With this money they purchase the goods and services they need and that their money will command through access to a small portion of the productive effort of various other people. In a less differentiated society, such as many sections of rural America a century or so ago, an individual might be much less involved in exchange, having produced a much higher proportion of the goods and services that he or she consumes and having produced less for other people and received less from them in return. As noted, the "great change" has intensified specialization, the growth of industrial bureaucracies, and the transfer of functions to the money-tax economy. Consumption patterns are made much more varied by division of labor and the exchange of goods and services, for these processes not only facilitate greater production but also make available a wider range of consumable products.

Specialization and exchange take place not only within communities, however, but among them. The expansion of economic resources available through intercommunity trade was described succinctly by Hawley, using an illustration from preindustrial communities:

> Trade immediately broadens the sustenance base. For example, where community A provides yams grown in its territory to community B for axe heads made from stone found in B's hab-

1. William H. Form and Delbert C. Miller, *Industry, Labor, and Community* (New York: Harper & Brothers, 1960), p. 15.

itat, the resources of A and B are to that extent pooled and each becomes dependent on a larger area. The area added in this way to the original domain of the one community is utilized by that community through the agency of the other community.[2]

Several results of such a process are apparent among American communities. The relative advantages enjoyed by various communities for different types of industrial emphasis lead toward specialization and exchange on an intercommunity basis. Harris's ninefold classification of the principal functions of United States cities has been widely used:

1. Manufacturing city (predominantly manufacturing)
2. Manufacturing city (manufacturing with other characteristics)
3. Retail city
4. Diversified city
5. Wholesale city
6. Transportation city
7. Mining town
8. University town
9. Resort and retirement town[3]

Careful definitions permit objective classification of cities within these types. Form and Miller summed up the classifications that have been made:

> These classifications reveal that one-fourth of the cities over 10,000 population in the United States are manufacturing cities; a little more than one-fifth are either industrial cities or diversified cities in which manufacturing predominates; one-eighth are diversified cities in which retailing predominates; one-sixth are residential cities; and the remaining cities have single functions, for example, mining, transportation, education, resort, or government.[4]

Such economic specialization has been found to leave its imprint on the characteristics of cities. Reiss pointed out that "almost every aspect of a community's structure is related to its basic functions. Reliable differences among the functionally specialized types of communities are found with respect to age and sex structure,

2. Amos H. Hawley, *Human Ecology: A Theory of Community Structure* (New York: Ronald Press, 1960), p. 353.

3. Chauncy D. Harris, "A Functional Classification of Cities in the United States," *Geographical Review*, vol. 33, no. 1 (January 1943). For detailed treatment of the functional classification of cities see Brian J. L. Berry, *City Classification Handbook: Methods and Applications* (New York: John Wiley & Sons, 1971).

4. *Industry, Labor, and Community*, p. 41.

mobility rates, labor force participation, educational attainment, industrial and occupational composition, income and home ownership."[5] Thus, community interdependency is associated with community specialization. It is also associated with the development of regional, national, or international industrial companies with networks of factories and sales outlets in a large number of communities.

Warner and Low described the implications of this development for individual communities with considerable elaboration in their analysis of the shoe industry in Yankee City. They traced the development of the industry from its earliest stages in that city's colonial days to the present and noted many of the aspects of what we have called the "great change":

> Two fundamental changes have been occurring concomitantly, in recent years, in the social organization of Yankee City shoe factories. The first is the expansion of the hierarchy upward, out of Yankee City, through the expansion of individual enterprises and the establishment by them of central offices in distant large cities. The second is the expansion of the structure outward from Yankee City through the growth of manufacturers' associations and labor unions, also with headquarters outside Yankee City and with units in many other shoemaking communities in New England and elsewhere. Both . . . decrease Yankee City's control over its shoe factories by subjecting the factories, or segments of them, to more and more control exerted from outside Yankee City.[6]

The vertical network of economic activity extends outward from community units in many ways, such as the relation of a branch plant to its national company, the relation of local agencies and distributors to nationally advertised producers, the network of wholesaler and jobber relationships, the chain of trade associations and labor unions, the informal connections with state and federal political systems, the various relationships of regulation or subsidy of industry by government, and so on. If one were to seek a prototype most clearly indicative of the relation of local economic units to extracommunity systems, it might well be found in the relationship of a company's local branch plant to the national main office of that company. Yet it must be recognized that other types of vertical connection with extracommunity economic systems exist.

5. Albert J. Reiss, Jr., "Functional Specialization of Cities," in Paul K. Hatt and Albert J. Reiss, Jr., eds., *Cities and Society: The Revised Reader in Urban Sociology* (Glencoe, Ill.: Free Press, 1957), p. 575.

6. W. Lloyd Warner and J. O. Low, *The Social System of the Modern Factory: The Strike: A Social Analysis* (New Haven, Conn.: Yale University Press, 1947), p. 108.

On the other hand, one might ask if there is any identifiable unit that similarly represents the relation of such a local branch plant to other like endeavors within the community at the local level. Here, again, various types of relationships exist, both formal and informal. But the most suitable prototype of this relationship among business establishments at the community level is the local chamber of commerce. This is an organization, in other words, through which formal recognition is given to the common interests of local business enterprises, interests that they share by virtue of their propinquity. In numerous instances the formal organization is actually a chamber of commerce, following organizational lines and regulations laid down by the Chamber of Commerce of the United States of America. In other instances, particularly in smaller communities, somewhat similar organizations of local business interests may exist, but without a formal tie to a national organization.

It is interesting to note that even where the horizontal relationship among business enterprises is formalized in such an organization, the ties of one local business enterprise to another within that organization are much weaker and much more peripheral than are the vertical ties of the respective branch business enterprises to their own particular national companies. Particularly in the case of branch plants, the systemic relation to the national company is strong, highly rationalized, and often under direct, centralized, hierarchical control. Its behavior is much more integrally tied in systemically with the national company than with other locally based enterprises at the community level. Though organizations like the chamber of commerce afford a means of horizontal integration at the community level, they characteristically coordinate these organizations only superficially. The process of rational planning and bureaucratic administration has developed more extensively along vertical lines than along horizontal lines, so far as economic enterprises are concerned. Nevertheless, in the chamber of commerce and similar units one finds the weak beginnings of rational planning and bureaucratic administration along the horizontal dimension.

Risking oversimplification, we can express some characteristics of our "typical unit" of the production-distribution-consumption function in a way that will permit subsequent comparison with other locality-relevant functions.

Major locality-relevant function	Typical community unit	Typical unit of horizontal pattern	Typical superior unit of vertical pattern
Production-distribution-consumption	Company	Chamber of commerce	National corporation

175

While it seems justifiable to delineate the sphere of "industry" as earlier defined to be most representative of the major locality-relevant function of production-distribution-consumption and even to focus more specifically on the business company as a prototype of industry, it would be a mistake to assume that industry, as here considered, accounts for the total community performance of the production-distribution-consumption function. It accounts for only that segment of the total production-distribution-consumption effort that falls roughly within the domain of "private enterprise," whether of individuals or groups, for profit. The profit system and the operation of the open market (with the many restrictions thereon) constitute only one of the channels of the production, exchange, and consumption of goods and services.

Let us take as a simple illustration a swimming pool designed to serve the needs of numerous families. Many such pools are operated under commercial auspices and are thus part of what is ordinarily conceived as the "profit" system. Essentially the same function can be performed through public auspices, however, in which case the profit system is not directly involved, but instead an operation of government. On the other hand, many pools are operated by private membership associations, thus involving a rather different set of relationships. We shall explore the implications of some of these different auspices for the provision of goods and services in chapter 7. Here we simply note that the private profit system, though perhaps the most important means, is not the only means through which the production-distribution-consumption function is performed in American communities.

Socialization

The notion that human beings take on their peculiarly human characteristics as they acquire the social inheritance of a particular cultural group was given great prominence in sociological theory earlier in this century. Such writers as Cooley, Mead, Faris, Park, and Burgess, each in his own way, emphasized that personality is acquired in group contexts, particularly in family groups, and that the abstract dichotomy between individual and society, which had been at the base of much of the earlier social-contract theory, was false and misleading. More recently, efforts by scholars such as Abram Kardiner and Ralph Linton, Margaret Mead, Ruth Benedict, Clyde Kluckhohn, and many others emphasized the close relationship between personality and the culture within which it has developed.

It is on the local level that individuals encounter the culture and social systems of the larger society and are inducted into these systems and acquire the appropriate attitudes and behavior patterns. Looked at from the standpoint of the larger society, it is on the local level that individuals are molded into attitudes and types of behavior through which they become compatible with the society's ways and equipped to carry them on and develop them further. The process through which individuals, through learning, acquire the knowledge, values, and behavior patterns of their society and learn behavior appropriate to the various social roles that their society provides is called *socialization.*

There is a growing recognition that socialization is not simply a process exclusive to childhood and adolescence, but rather a continuing process through which the individual maintains relationships of reciprocation with others within the framework of the many social roles patterning social behavior. Where this process is not sustained, there is a falling away from culturally sanctioned participation in the ongoing matters of the society (see page 18). In recent years, considerable interest has been expressed in studying the various aspects of the resultant alienation of the individual.

Although the community is not the only system actively involved in the socialization of the individual, it is, as mentioned above, the arena in which the individual is confronted with the particular way in which his or her society structures individual behavior.

The individual family plays a decisive role in the socialization of children. Both psychiatric and social psychological theory assign it a formidable impact upon the growing personality. Likewise, informal friendship and neighborhood groups play an important role, as do church and other more formalized associations. In addition, the media of mass communication, such as radio, television, motion pictures, and comic books and other printed matter, constitute direct channels between the individual child and "mass culture."

Thus, socialization involves the family and other small groups within the community as well as several extracommunity units. At the local level, the public school system has been developed as the social system specifically designed to perform the socialization process on a level corresponding roughly, at least, to the community as defined in this book.

The increasing extent to which the school is specifically singled out as a socializing agent, rather than merely as a means of inculcating certain relatively external knowledges and skills, is itself a manifestation of trends of change considered earlier—particularly specialization and division of labor, bureaucratization, and transfer of functions from the family and informal groupings to profit enterprise and government. The progression is especially marked in the account of Crestwood Heights in chapter 4, the community that was **177** farthest along among the four described there in most aspects of the "great change." Apparently, more and more stress is coming to be placed on the community's specialized educational system for accomplishing the socialization function. At the same time, despite strong residues of sentiment to the contrary, less and less is being expected from the family, the neighborhood, and the church in this process. The difference between El Cerrito and Crestwood Heights in this respect is most dramatic.

Accompanying the transfer of greater responsibility for socialization to the school has been the growing proliferation of specialized personnel within the school to cope in one way or another with this increased responsibility. Thus, not only school psychologists and guidance counselors, but even the less personality-oriented staff members, such as dramatics teachers, athletics coaches, and social studies teachers, all have a strong though often undefined role to play in the socialization of the child. In this contest, it is interesting to note the important linkage role of the parent-teacher association, which in effect brings together in a structured manner the principal functionaries of the two institutions in the community most primarily concerned with socialization: the school and the family.

The ties of the school to the larger society have become increasingly strong and a whole supervisory bureaucracy has grown up to stimulate, supervise, and reward the local school for the adequate performance of various specialized and differentiated functions. In this process, the principal extracommunity unit toward which the school is oriented is undoubtedly the state department of education, with its legally prescribed regulatory, supervisory, and enabling functions. The contemporary scene is replete with examples of the increasing assumption of such functions through the extension of education laws and through the implementation of grant-in-aid programs under which local schools come increasingly under state surveillance.

In the socialization function, as in the production-distribution-consumption function, the decision-making prerogative has increasingly been transferred upward to higher levels of decision-making and outward away from the community. In this instance, as in other aspects of the "great change," such transfer has accompanied the progressive differentiation of functions and bureaucratization of their performance.

But the ties of the school system to the larger society are not exclusively subsumed under the relationship to the state department of education. There are also the ties of school administrators and teachers to various state or national professional associations, through which their behavior on the local scene is influenced toward conformity with norms that exist in the larger society governing the

178

proper performance of their roles, and through which they obtain extracommunity support and reinforcement for the standards and procedures that their respective professional associations advocate.

A different set of ties exists with national publishing companies through which books and periodicals from the wider culture are channeled into the curricular content of the school and with various suppliers of a wide range of teaching aids and supplies that, though representing developments outside the community, are adopted in the local schools. A related set of ties, but one in a different sector of the larger economy, brings films, filmstrips, charts, posters, pamphlets, books, and other material into the schools from state and national voluntary associations, both of the altruistic type, such as national health associations, and of the self-interest type, such as industrial associations and labor unions. In addition to these materials, there are often more or less subtle pressures brought to bear by such national organizations to influence the curricular process so as to incorporate materials favorable to their "cause" into the curriculum as "educational." In a different though related vein, the school system, through its purchase of supplies and equipment, is tied in closely as an important customer in the private profit enterprise sector of the society.

The lack of integration of the various agencies with an important role in the socialization of children is a widely acknowledged problem. There is little or no systematic, rational organization of these various agencies under which their effort might be coordinated with a view toward mutually agreed-upon socialization goals. The socialization functions of these various agencies operating in the community are adapted to their own peculiar exigencies; they do not represent a planned rational division of labor aimed at producing the desired outcomes most efficiently. One need only enumerate some of the principal agencies with important socialization functions—family, neighborhood (where such a social unit exists), peer group of children, church, school, TV and other media of mass communication—to recognize their disparity, their different levels of operation, their differential places in the total social system, their relative systemic independence of each other. At times there are minimal attempts to develop a rational, planned relationship between two or more specific parts of this conglomeration of socializing influences, for example, the parent-teacher association; or the "released-time" method for providing religious instruction under religious auspices during school hours; or attempts by parents' groups to censor criminal, sadistic, and lewd magazines and comic books. But these represent only minimal attempts at integration of socializing agencies, which otherwise almost completely lack any systemic interrelation to each other at the local level.   **179**

On the other hand, among the schools, which we are here considering as the community units typifying the socialization function, a relatively high degree of systemic coordination exists. In the smaller communities there may be only one school whose rationally organized bureaucratic structure provides adequate systemic integration. In other communities, regardless of size or number of schools, the operation of a board of education or its equivalent, with an administrative staff, provides an adequate systemic framework for the school system itself. In the context of systemic analysis, it is interesting to note the common usage of the term *school system,* for here the popular usage corresponds with more precise scientific terminology. Of all the differentiated prototype units (each corresponding to a different locality-relevant function) that are analyzed in this chapter, the school and the municipal government show the highest degree of integration within their respective sectors.

It is important to acknowledge that the locality-relevant functions are characteristically distributed among a number of different auspices and that the typical unit selected here for analysis represents only one. This precaution applies particularly to the school's role in the socialization function. The school system's importance is continually overrated, with the result that schools in American society usually promise more than they can deliver, assume responsibility for larger commitments in socialization than they can discharge, and receive the blame for socialization failures that are far beyond their power to control.

The socialization function can be depicted as follows in the schema that will be used for each of the various locality-relevant functions.

Major locality-relevant function	Typical community unit	Typical unit of horizontal pattern	Typical superior unit of vertical pattern
Socialization	Public school	Board of education	State department of education

Social Control

Social control is the process through which a group influences the behavior of its members toward conformity with its norms. It is an important aspect of the systemic behavior shown by human groupings of various sizes, for a certain modicum of conformity to group-prescribed behavior patterns is necessary for any social system to function as such. A brief analysis of some of the aspects of this process will indicate the locality relevance of the social control function, even though this, like other community functions, is not performed exclusively at the community level.

A distinction has long been made between internal social controls and external social controls. It is between restraints that the individual imposes on his or her own conduct and those imposed by others. If not pressed too far, the distinction is useful for those restraints that the individual affirms are more easily enforceable than those that are imposed on one. The process through which individuals come to develop internal controls is, of course, part of the larger process of socialization, discussed above. During this process, children internalize the norms according to which restraints have been placed on their conduct by others. They then experience these internalized norms as "conscience." Cooley's "looking-glass self" was an early formulation of the process through which individuals come to assess their own anticipated actions according to the imagined judgement that others will make of that conduct.[7] Likewise, Mead formulated his concept of the "generalized other" to help explain how, in a sense, the internalization of controls earlier imposed by others is part of what might be called the individual's self-image.[8]

Closely associated with the individual's internalization of the group's norms is the group's ability to apply meaningful sanctions in order to ensure conformity to the norms. In closely knit groups, of the type that Cooley called "primary," such sanctions customarily take the form of praise and blame, gossip, ridicule, and ostracism. These sanctions are important to the degree that the individuals identify themselves with the group and care about what the group thinks of their conduct and how it acts toward them. It is difficult to draw the line in this regard between internal and external controls, for the strength of the imagined judgement of what the group may think will be influenced by the estimated ability of the group to apply such sanctions as those above.

Such informal sanctions are often called "primary-group controls" because they characterize primary-group behavior. They are thus distinguished from controls on behavior that arise in less intimate secondary groups, where a greater reliance must be placed on rules and regulations and on such formal sanctions as are best exemplified in the law. Beyond such measures are the controls accompanying "mass society," where the personal relationship is

7. Charles H. Cooley, *Human Nature and the Social Order* (New York: Charles Scribner's Sons, 1902), p. 152.

8. George H. Mead, *Mind, Self and Society* (Chicago: University of Chicago Press, 1937), p. 158.

lost, where communication may be predominantly one-way, and where mass media of communication may be employed. Mass campaigns against careless driving or for "mental health education" are examples.

It will be recalled that Homans developed a theory of group process in which the concept of equilibrium and the concept of social control are intimately intertwined (see page 146). Mills, however, pointed out that this type of analysis is pertinent only in a "simple" system, not in a complex one. Viewed as a social system, the community would constitute a complex system in Mills's terms. He maintained that for such complex systems the equilibrium model of control is not adequate.[9]

An alternative to the equilibrium theory of social control was offered by Hollingshead a number of years ago. He noted the purported inadequacies of the social-psychological approach advanced by Cooley and the early formulation of the social control concept that was presented by Ross (who, incidentally, produced the first book on social control as such, in 1901). Ross had approached social control from the standpoint of the restraints that society needed to enforce as social life became more impersonal. Hollingshead, on the other hand, advanced the viewpoint that social control is to be found in the relations among the organized structures and processes of social life. For him,

> the essence of social control lies not so much in the mechanisms society has developed to manipulate behavior in a crisis or in the subtle influences so important in the formation of personality, as it does in a society's organization. . . . Our tentative position is that social control inheres in the more or less common obligatory usages and values which define the relations of one person to another, to things, to ideas, to groups, to classes, and to the society in general. In short, the essence of social control is to be sought in the organization of a people.[10]

Associated with the "great change" there has been a development from custom to contract, from mechanical solidarity to organic solidarity, from Gemeinschaft-like organization to Gesellschaft-like organization (see page 144). These are different ways of expressing much the same phenomenon, a development that,

9. Theodore M. Mills, "Equilibrium and the Processes of Deviance and Control," *American Sociological Review*, vol. 24, no. 5 (October 1959).

10. August B. Hollingshead, "The Concept of Social Control," *American Sociological Review* 6, no. 2 (April 1941): 220.

as far as social control is concerned, represents a gradual decrease in the effectiveness of those controls associated with the small group and the relatively simple undifferentiated community and an increase in need for and development of those controls associated with large groups and more differentiated communities.

In this process of differentiation the state has arisen as a mode of social organization in which certain aspects of the control function are delegated to a specifically differentiated body, which has coercive power over all who reside in its geographic domain. Such coercive power, or ultimate control, is the special characteristic of the state as opposed to other auspices that may otherwise perform parallel or identical functions. Thus, government, to use the more commonly employed term, possesses a control characteristic that differentiates it from other community-based units performing a control function: the power of ultimate coercion. The exercise of this power through the police and court systems is an important and exclusive control prerogative.

Hence, local government can be considered appropriate as the prototype unit at the community level for the performance of the locality-relevant function of social control. But as is the case with socialization, the social-control function is performed by numerous types of units both below and beyond the community level. In fact, the lists are identical: family, neighborhood, peer group of children, church, school, TV, and other media of mass communication.[11] It should also be recognized that local government performs other functions in addition to the social-control function, including fire protection, water supply, street maintenance, and so forth.

The operations of government on the local level are an incisive example of the "great change" and its attendant emphasis on the vertical tie of local community units to extracommunity systems. Shortly we shall examine some of the ties of local government to more inclusive governmental units. Meanwhile, let us note that not all governmental activities in the community are performed by local government. Specifically regarding the social-control function, for example, the control over the activities of local industrial units is overwhelmingly in the hands of extracommunity governmental units.

11. Social-control functions are also exercised, whether deliberately or inadvertently, by agencies of mutual support (see p. 199ff.), such as health and welfare organizations. See Elaine Cumming, *Systems of Social Regulation* (New York: Atherton Press, 1968), p. 10. The importance of social control as a function of welfare programs in general is discussed by Richard A. Cloward and Frances F. Piven in *Regulating the Poor: The Functions of Public Welfare* (New York: Pantheon Books, 1971).

Local municipalities can, after all, only enact laws permitted by state governments. State regulations dealing with workmen's compensation, wages and hours, floating of stocks and bonds, labor-management relations, political activities, the use of natural resources, vehicle licensing, and others add enormously to the list of local regulations. Industry's professional workers (nurses, lawyers, accountants, doctors, etc.) are also regulated by state laws concerning licensing and work conduct. In addition to local and state laws, many federal laws deal with labor-management relations, interstate commerce, monopoly, restraint of trade, international trade, and many other areas. The growing volume of state and federal laws did not mean that local problems became less important. Rather, it meant that the control of economic problems could not be achieved by local governments alone. The problems which state and federal governments were called upon to solve were, indeed, urban problems, and urban politics became state and federal politics.[12]

Not only in control activities, but also in other operations of government on the local level, the role played by local offices of state and federal government branches is becoming increasingly important. The local distribution of effort among federal, state, and municipal units is considered by Grodzins to be more the result of "accidents of history, politics, and place" than of any inherent logic.

The traditionally described three-level American government is in fact telescoped on the community. . . The federal government has built city halls for many cities and has paid for tearing down slums in others. It pays insurance directly to the aged and indirectly provides for the health of new mothers. It draws plans for the best land use for a poor farmer and supplies funds for the construction of a vast manufacturing plant to a multi-million dollar corporation. It constructs schools here and libraries there. It aids one community in drawing up a city plan, supplies a second community with funds to build a sewer, gives a park to a third, and provides expert advice to the police chief of a fourth when the hardware store is robbed. By any standard, federal activities of this sort are as "close" to the citizen as any activities of the states and localities. To deny the local character of federal activities one would be forced to deny the local character of local governments. Closeness to the citizen is an attribute of all American governments. Local is as local does.[13]

12. Form and Miller, *Industry, Labor, and Community,* p. 147.

13. Morton Grodzins, *The American System: A New View of Governments in the United States,* ed. Daniel I. Elazar (Chicago: Rand McNally & Co., 1966).

In light of the above quotation, it would seem that the attempt to abstract from community analysis the behavior of units that are not largely locally controlled would leave us with a will-o'-the-wisp, a construct not corresponding to any reality on the community level and having little utility for analytical purposes.

But the vertical ties involved in local governmental units are not confined to the operation of state and federal units at the local community level, for local government itself has its official sanction from state government; and from this source it derives the rules and regulations according to which it may operate, whether these stem from a specially worded "charter" or from a code of regulations governing municipalities of various sizes and classes. Thus, its operations are regulated by appropriate state governmental agencies, its financial operations are controlled and audited, and the legality of its transactions is reviewed.

In analyzing the vertical ties to state and federal governments, however, it is important to note that these constitute two-way channels, channels not only of downward control but of influence upward on policy making at the state and federal levels. Grodzins listed the manners in which this influence is made effective: "(1) Formal representation in legislative bodies, (2) representation in the constituencies of chief executives (in the states, minor executives, too), (3) representation by organizations of public officers, and (4) representation by private interests that are linked to local causes."[14]

A special type of vertical governmental tie has assumed increasing importance in response to some of the aspects of the "great change." This is the procedure of the grant-in-aid. Through a grant-in-aid, it is possible for a superior governmental unit to encourage an activity on the part of local government by supplying some or all of the funds necessary to finance the local governmental activity. More formally defined, a grant-in-aid is "a payment made by a central to a local authority to defray part of the cost of a service administered by the local authority, usually subject to some conditions set by the central government, which may inspect and partially control the service and, if conditions are not satisfactory, withhold future payments of the grant."[15]

With the funds there inevitably follows some measure of control, if only to assure that the funds are administered for the purposes intended, but often including much more specific regulations

14. *American System*, p. 211.

15. Henry J. Bittermann, *State and Federal Grants-in-Aid* (Chicago: Mentzer, Bush, 1938), p. 5, quoted in *Federal Grants-in-Aid* (Chicago: Council of State Governments, 1949), p. 29.

regarding the performance by the local governmental unit of the function for which the funds were granted. Here again, local autonomy of action must necessarily be curtailed in the process. Nevertheless, Wood maintained that such curtailment is easily exaggerated.

These [grant-in-aid] programs are prepared by politicians who depend on local constituencies and a locally oriented party for support. They are supervised by administrators in an organizational structure that vitiates every principle of effective management in order that local autonomy may not be impaired. At every stage in the development and implementation of these programs, elaborate safeguards—constitutional, procedural and informal—exist to ensure the protection of local interests. When issues in the program arise, they are almost always resolved in favor of the local unit involved. . . The American system of grants-in-aid has many problems. Its separate programs could be far better coordinated than they are; its formulas for allocation could be rationalized; the professional specialists working in each program could be more carefully supervised. But the threat to local autonomy and independence is not a genuine problem; it is a straw man in the political debate.[16]

The grant-in-aid procedure does work to diminish local autonomy in a somewhat different sense, however: the availability of grant-in-aid funds for specifically defined types of activity places extreme pressure on community people to tailor their programs to fit the cloth of the existing state and federal programs, rather than to adapt the existing programs to their own peculiar needs. Especially in the field of health and welfare functions, community facilities are often pressed into institutional patterns that correspond to the existing grant-in-aid channels, when some other type of institutional pattern might be more appropriate.

The importance of this method of determining community programs is increasing as the grant-in-aid system grows in magnitude and as the practice grows of building community services around possible sources of outside funds. It is significant that in Springdale, as indicated in chapter 4, local government had largely abdicated its prerogatives in favor of extragovernmental groups and of programs of the state and federal government. The authors indicated the magnitude of the "state aid" coming into the small village of Springdale:

Eighty percent, or $200,000, of the school budget exclusive of building aid is derived from these various forms of aid. Village

16. Robert C. Wood, *Suburbia: Its People and Their Politics* (Boston: Houghton Mifflin, 1959), pp. 241-42.

government collects approximately $11,000 in real estate and water taxes while it receives approximately $5,000 in direct cash aid from the state plus direct state investments in local facilities such as roads, which do not appear in the village budget. In the general fund of town government, approximately $11,000 out of $13,000 is accounted for by direct state aid. For town highway purposes approximately $8,000 represents local revenue while the state contributes $27,000 in direct cash aid.[17]

The authors maintained that the county in which Springdale is located "receives roughly $20.00 in state aid for every $1.00 which it pays in taxes of all kinds."

The relation of governmental units to one another on the community level is often so tenuous and diffuse that, were they not all governmental units, they would have nothing especially in common; nor do they in aggregate indicate any of the properties of a social system. The local office of the state employment service or of the United States Postal Service simply is not related in any functional way to the municipal government that would distinguish it from nongovernmental units operating within the community. Such offices of state and federal government branches are systemically related, as integral parts, to their respective state or federal departments or agencies. Their sphere of activities, their operating policies, and their specific personnel are determined largely, if not exclusively, on the state and federal level.

On the other hand, some governmental units are more closely related to the locality, particularly in the selection of their personnel but also to a certain extent in the determination of their policies. Such governmental units include the 3,044 counties in the United States.[18] Although counties normally comprise a plurality of communities, some are roughly coextensive with a large metropolitan community; in the case of the larger cities, the metropolitan area includes several counties. In addition, there are 18,517 municipalities (inclusive of "all governmentally active units officially designated as cities, boroughs, villages, or—except for New England, New York, and Wisconsin—towns"), 16,991 townships and towns, 15,781 school districts, and 23,885 special districts. These last include districts set up for such functions as fire protection, soil conservation,

17. Arthur J. Vidich and Joseph Bensman, *Small Town in Mass Society: Class, Power and Religion in a Rural Community,* pp. 200-201. Copyright 1968 by Princeton University Press, Princeton, N. J.

18. These, and subsequent figures in this analysis of types of local government, are taken from U. S. Bureau of the Census, *1972 Census of Governments,* vol. I, *Governments in the United States* (Washington, D.C.: U.S. Government Printing Office, 1972). **187**

drainage, cemeteries, housing, urban water supply, highways, and a number of other special functions. They usually, though not always, have taxing power. These various types of local government often do not coincide in the local geographic area covered. Furthermore, by definition they are relatively independent entities with little systemic relation to each other.

But taking cities as the prototype of municipal government at the community level, the lack of coordination within the various departments and special agencies of city government becomes a problem of vast proportions, and city planning publications are replete with examples of the lack of such coordination. Nevertheless, by contrast with the total governmental effort at the community level, the departmental organization of city government does represent a rationally planned bureaucratic structure designed to order the pertinent activities in a systematic way.

Following our schema for presenting the locality-relevant functions and the community units that most characteristically perform them, we have the following for social control:

Major locality-relevant function	Typical community unit	Typical unit of horizontal pattern	Typical superior unit of vertical pattern
Social control	Municipal government	City council	State government

Municipal government is appropriately chosen as the typical unit exemplifying the exercise of social control at the local level. As already mentioned, it not only has the power to insist on compliance, supported by the law, the police, and the courts but the coercive power to charge people, through taxes, for the performance of its services. Nevertheless, in the case of government particularly, there is danger of mistaking the prototype unit and its functioning for the performance of the aggregate function at the community level. In other words, various agencies in the community contribute to the social-control function, many of them in ways more effective than those of the municipal government.

The social-control function applies not only to individuals but also to groups of various kinds operating within the community. In the schema that we have used to portray certain abstracted relationships of various community units to horizontal and vertical systems, an important control function is exercised over the unit by what we have termed the "typical superior unit of vertical pattern": by the national corporation over the local company, by the state department of education over the local school, by the state government over the municipal government. We shall see that this is also true of the two remaining locality-relevant functions to be considered. At the same time, certain controls, though less effective for reasons we have considered, are applied by the corresponding "typical unit of horizontal pattern": the chamber of commerce, the board of education, and the city council.

Social Participation

An important locality-relevant function is that of affording opportunities for social participation. We need not elaborate here that wherever human beings are found they are found living in groups and associating with one another in different ways. The social psychologists mentioned in the preceding sections made it clear that human beings acquire their distinctly human nature through participation in groups. But the type of association into which the individual comes in daily living is largely determined by the associational structure of the local community. The community, among other things, is the locus for providing opportunities for social participation of various types. As we shall see, communities differ greatly in the pattern of associational activities that they afford.

Perhaps the best way to examine these differences is to consider Cooley's concept of the primary group. It will be recalled that he considered such small, intimate, face-to-face groups as family, play group of children, and neighborhood as primary groups because of their "primary" or fundamental influence on the personality. In the course of time, other sociologists employed the term "secondary group" to apply to groups that were less intimate and more formalized in structure, such as an office staff or a civic improvement association. And as we have just seen, they recognized that the types of social control effective in these different group types, though not mutually exclusive, tended to differ. Such informal controls as gossip and ridicule are highly effective in the primary groups, but the secondary groups tend to rely more heavily on such formal controls as rules and regulations, charters, contracts, clear delineation of formal rights and responsibilities, a just and equitable system of rewards and penalties. The distinction is important both logically and chronologically. The tendency in American communities has been for social participation in secondary groups to grow in importance at the expense of that in primary groups. In chapter 3 we have already noted the increasing impersonalization and bureaucratization of many functions and their transfer from the family and other primary-group auspices to commercial and governmental auspices.

An indication of what might be called the rationalization—in the sense of deliberate planning and organization for particular pur-   **189** poses—of social participation is the tendency for friendly association to take place increasingly within the rubric of business or social concerns. The report from Crestwood Heights summed it up as follows:

> Clubs and associations are, indeed, marked features of life in Crestwood Heights, for both children and adults; here again is evidence of how human relationships in the Heights are, more and more, being channeled into impersonal, highly structured, institutionalized patterns. These particular human relationships, like others, serve a definite purpose. Just as it is becoming less common to take a trip of any length merely "for pleasure" (unless, of course, one is retired) and without some ulterior business or professional motive, it is also less usual for people to meet each other purely on a basis of affection or of liking to be together. Human contacts are now more generally organized around some activity or "cause," preferably one which will also advance or make plain the social standing of the participating individuals.[19]

We have also noted an important tendency for association to take place increasingly on the basis of mutual interest rather than that of mere propinquity. Whether in formal or informal association, people have become more selective in their association, not limiting themselves to association with their immediate neighbors, but increasingly passing by their immediate neighbors in order to be with other people farther away whom they find personally congenial or who share their interests and are fellow members in the union, the club, or the church. There is some indication that individuals in urban areas go comparatively far for personal contacts. For example, in the Los Angeles area, it was found that housewives and other home managers went on the average 4.77 miles from their homes for contacts of a personal nature, but only 2.12 miles for contacts of a commercial nature. Hypothesizing that the commercial contacts were largely secondary and the personal contacts were largely primary, the authors of the study report concluded that "it would seem that primary relations, visiting with friends and relatives, are not a neighborhood phenomenon.[20] Of course, it is hazardous to generalize from the situation that prevails in the Los Angeles area. Nevertheless, a large body of research points to the great proliferation of formal voluntary associations and to the transfer of many functions

19. John R. Seeley, R. Alexander Sim, and Elizabeth W. Loosely, *Crestwood Heights: A Study of the Culture of Suburban Life* (New York: Basic Books, 1956; Toronto: University of Toronto Press, 1956), p. 292 of Basic Books edition.

20. Svend Riemer and John McNamara, "Contact Patterns in the City," *Social Forces* 36, no. 2 (December 1957): 139-40.

from the home and neighborhood and informal groups to such institutions as the school, business, and government.

We are concerned primarily with those modes of association that have particular relevance to the clustering of people and social systems in at least a rudimentary systemic manner related to their propinquity. In focusing on the community-level aspects of association, we shall here only make mention of the important informal network of association based on kinship and informal friendship patterns, the informal but important socioeconomic strata in most communities that tend to channel social participation so as to encourage association among those on the same social level and discourage it among those on different social levels, or the informal but important structuring of association in terms of the exercise of power in community decision-making. (These last two will be discussed further in chapter 9.)

We turn instead to a consideration of the formal organizations that provide ready-made structures of social participation, the so-called voluntary associations. As indicated above, participation in such groups has become more important as in the process of the "great change" they have acquired functions that were provided earlier by informal groupings of a more nearly primary nature. A simple outline will show the great proliferation of different types of such formal associations existing on the local level:[21]

Economic groups
Service clubs
Chamber of commerce
Vocational groups
    Unions
    Retail merchants association
    Farmers association
    Boards of banks,
        corporations
    Professional associations

Government groups
Political party organizations
Good government leagues
Patriotic and veterans
    associations
Taxpayers associations

Planning groups
Neighborhood planning
    associations

Community planning
    associations
Community councils

Housing groups
Real estate associations
Housing associations

Education groups
Better schools groups
Parent-teacher organizations
Adult education groups

Fraternal groups
Nationality group fraternal
    associations
Other fraternities, lodges, secret
    societies

Recreation groups
Athletic teams
Athletic clubs

---

21. From Roland L. Warren, *Studying Your Community* (New York: Russell Sage Foundation, 1955), pp. 287-88, paperback (New York: Free Press, 1965).

Hobby clubs
Social enjoyment groups

Religious groups
Churches and synagogues
Groups associated with
churches and synagogues
Primarily religious (Bible
study groups, worship
groups)
Other (clubs, teams, social
groups)

Cultural groups
Concert societies
Study and forum groups
Art societies
Dramatic groups
Literary societies

Welfare groups
Charitable organizations
Boards of social agencies
Welfare or humane associations

Groups for children and youth
Child welfare organizations

Big brother movement
Police athletic league
Youth organizations

Health groups
General community health
groups
Groups on specific diseases
(cancer society, heart society,
etc.)
Safety council

Intergroup relations groups
General groups
Groups serving one particular
minority

**Community organization
groups**
Chests
Councils
Coordinating committees
Federations of clubs
Other intergroup agencies or
organizations

While many of these groups, such as hobby clubs, fraternities, churches, and unions, serve primarily the recreational, religious, or economic interests of their own members, they also have an interest in the determination of community affairs as an additional aspect. And different groups are clearly organized with the express purpose of pursuing some area of interest or concern on behalf of others in the community.

It is to these last organizations, of course, that people refer when they mention the peculiar American penchant for voluntary citizen participation in community affairs. Tocqueville's widely quoted observation, over a century old, is still extremely pertinent: "Wherever, at the head of some new undertaking, you see the government in France, or a man of rank in England, in the United States you will be sure to find an association."[22] Sower and his associates put the matter equally strongly: "The belief in voluntary community action for the welfare of the community may be the characteristic which more than any other single feature dis-

22. Alexis de Tocqueville, *Democracy in America* (New York: Oxford University Press, 1947), p. 319.

tinguishes the American community from communities in other cultures.[23]

There is a wide range of literature on the characteristics of people in relation to their participation in voluntary organizations of various types.[24] Generally speaking, the studies show that people of high socioeconomic status participate in voluntary organizations more than those of low status, and the degree of participation appears to follow a continuum from one extreme to the other. Such studies, which often exclude church membership, indicate a rough generalization that perhaps as many as half of the people are not active members of any voluntary association whatsoever.

One study by the National Opinion Research Center found a direct relationship between the percentage of American adults who belong to one or more organizations and their income level, educational level, level of living, occupation, and home ownership status. On all these characteristics, the lower status groups showed the greatest percentage of people who belonged to no organization and the fewest who belonged to one or two or more. But people on successively higher levels on all these variables showed a larger percentage of membership.[25] Other studies support these findings. One of the characteristics of the lowest status groups in Springdale was that they did not participate in the ongoing organized activities of the community.

23. Christopher Sower et al., *Community Involvement: The Webs of Formal and Informal Ties that Make for Action* (Glencoe, Ill.: Free Press, 1957), p. 27.

24. See, for example, Mirra Komarovsky, "The Voluntary Associations of Urban Dwellers," *American Sociological Review*, vol. 11, (December 1946); Floyd Dotson, "Patterns of Voluntary Association Among Urban Working-Class Families," *American Sociological Review*, vol. 16, (October 1951); Ronald Freedman and Morris Axelrod, "Who Belongs to What in a Great Metropolis?" *Adult Leadership*, vol. 1 (November 1952); Harold F. Kaufman, *Participation in Organized Activities in Selected Kentucky Localities*, Kentucky Agricultural Experiment Station Bulletin 528 (Lexington 1949); Wendell Bell and Maryanne T. Force, "Urban Neighborhood Types and Participation in Formal Associations," *American Sociological Review*, vol. 21, no. 1 (February 1956); John M. Foskett, "The Influence of Social Participation on Community Programs and Activities," in Marvin B. Sussman, ed., *Community Structure and Analysis* (New York: Thomas Y. Crowell 1959); and Charles R. Wright and Herbert H. Hyman, "Voluntary Association Memberships of American Adults: Evidence from National Sample Surveys," *American Sociological Review*, vol. 23, no. 3 (June 1958). *The Journal of Voluntary Action Research*, published by the Association of Voluntary Action Scholars at Boston College, Massachusetts, has, since 1969, published articles relevant to voluntary organizations and their activities. See also a later study by Herbert H. Hyman and Charles R. Wright, "Trends in Voluntary Association Membership of American Adults: Replication Based on Secondary Analysis of National Sample Surveys," *The American Sociological Review*, vol. 36, no. 2 (April 1971).

25. Cited in Wright and Hyman, *Trends in Voluntary Association Membership*, 1971, p. 289.

Why do some people participate more than others in various types of voluntary associations? Looking at the question from the standpoint of a rationale, an outline of plausible motives, Ross suggested that people may participate because they hold such participation as a positive value and "we should seek to encourage participation"; because they believe it contributes to the individual's "mental health" to be active in voluntary organizations; in order to strengthen some worthwhile "cause" for which one is working, and in order to study problems and take concerted action.[26]

But another way of answering this question would be to study what social and psychological characteristics distinguish the high participators from the low. Arnold Rose found, for example, that among migrants to the Minneapolis area, those who reported many friends and some or many organizational affiliations had "more optimistic attitudes, greater satisfaction with their lives, and more confidence in society than groups reporting fewer friends and organizational affiliations."[27] Other studies have shown rather consistent support for the hypothesis that participation is related to interest in public issues and a belief that effective citizen action makes a difference, while nonparticipation is an aspect of alienation, of separation from the ongoing activities of the community, and of anomie.[28]

Much of this activity in voluntary groups involves the performance by secondary groups of still another function, that of mutual support, to be taken up in the following section. There we shall see that many mutual support activities formerly carried on under primary-group auspices have with the "great change" come to be performed more and more by secondary groups. So let us reserve the treatment of this type of voluntary association in the field of community health and welfare for that section.

Many discussions of voluntary participation fail to differentiate between self-serving groups and community-serving groups.

26. Murray G. Ross, "Community Participation," *International Review of Community Development*, no. 5, *Theories and Values*, 1960, p. 116.

27. Arnold M. Rose, "Attitudinal Correlates of Social Participation," *Social Forces* 37, no. 3 (March 1959): 206.

28. See, for example, such early studies as chap. 16 of W. Lloyd Warner and Paul S. Lunt, *The Social Life of a Modern Community* (New Haven, Conn.: Yale University Press, 1941); August B. Hollingshead and Frederick C. Redlich, *Social Class and Mental Illness: A Community Study* (New York: John Wiley & Sons, 1958), pp. 127ff.; Wright and Hyman, *Voluntary Association Memberships*, 1958; and Genevieve Knupfer, "Portrait of the Underdog," *Public Opinion Quarterly*, vol. 12 (Spring 1947). For recent treatments of factors influencing participation in neighborhood activities, see Donald I. Warren, *Black Neighborhoods: An Assessment of Community Power* (Ann Arbor: University of Michigan, 1975) and Milton Kotler's earlier volume, *Neighborhood Government: The Local Foundations of Political Life* (New York: Bobbs-Merrill Co., 1969).

Similarly, they often neglect church participation, relegating this activity to a separate "religious" category and not treating religious organizations as one type, perhaps the most numerous and important, of voluntary association. We shall take the opposite tack. We need, in any event, to select a particular kind of voluntary association as a typical unit for purposes of analyzing its vertical and horizontal orientations. Certainly we are justified in selecting the church as the voluntary association that typically has the greatest number of members in the community and that addresses itself to an important sector of one's social living. Choosing the church as our typical unit of the locality-relevant function of voluntary participation need neither add to nor detract from any theological assertions regarding its special status as a religious institution. Being neither competent in theological matters nor having a particular interest in them in the present context, we can simply ignore them in this treatment, which concerns itself with social participation in the community.

For purposes of convenience, let us follow common usage and refer to any organized unit of worshipers as a church, to the organization of churches of the same religious beliefs and customs as a denomination, and to the organization of the same general theological origin and body of scriptures as a faith. "Churches" thus includes synagogues, as well as such nonecclesiastical bodies as the individual Meetings of the Society of Friends. Denominations include not only the multitude of Protestant denominations but also Greek Orthodox and Roman Catholic bodies. Major faiths would then refer to Christianity, Judaism, and so on.

Let us begin by noting that more Americans are members of churches than any other type of voluntary association, approximately 62 percent of the population in 1974,[29] and let us note also that church membership has been growing over the past century in the United States.

Church Membership as a Percentage of Population

1850	16%	1950	57%
1870	18%	1960	64%
1890	22%	1970	63%
1910	43%	1974	62%
1930	47%		

29. U. S. Bureau of the Census, *Statistical Abstract of the United States: 1976*, 97th ed. (Washington, D.C.: U. S. Government Printing Office, 1976), p. 47. The source for these figures is the *Yearbook of American and Canadian Churches, 1976*.

Looking at historic development from another standpoint, it is interesting to note that the increasing proliferation of religious denominations in the United States is a product of the Protestant Reformation, whose relationship to the "great change" (particularly to increasing specialization and differentiation of interests and associations) is somewhat less direct than some of the other developments we have been considering. Its impact, nonetheless, is analogous in that it provides avenues of participation involving local people differentially in vertical organizations that extend beyond their community. On the basis of membership and participation in one church rather than another, community people are separated from each other in an important aspect of their social participation, as they participate in one or another of the 223 religious denominations having churches in American communities.[30]

The nature of the relation of the individual church unit to local community people varies greatly by denomination. Generally speaking, Protestant churches are much more autonomous, as individual units, than are Roman Catholic churches, among which hierarchical control is pronounced. Nevertheless, there is great variation among Protestant denominations, with Baptists and Congregationalists exercising considerable local autonomy at the individual church level, while Episcopalians and Methodists show much greater control by extracommunity denominational hierarchies. The typical structure of Protestant churches provides for a paid minister who is the administrative and spiritual leader, responsible to a local church board of trustees or deacons, which in turn is elected by the church membership. Generally, boards of deacons are concerned with the spiritual aspects of the church's activities, while the trustees are responsible for the temporal aspects. There is usually provision for both lay and clerical representation from local churches at the regional and national levels of the denominational organization.

The local church at the community level is the scene of the interplay of two somewhat diverse sets of forces. On the one hand are the official doctrines and policies of the denomination, channeled into the local church through denominational meetings, publications, pronouncements, and through the clergy. On the other hand are the local religious sentiments and traditions as they interact with other aspects of organized activities. These local influences are brought to bear on the minister and on the denominational body through public opinion, through whatever degree

30. U. S. Bureau of the Census, *Statistical Abstract, 1976,* p. 234.

of local control exists over the selection and retention of the minister, through the channeling of various financial contributions to the denomination, through representation on denominational boards, through the operation of the community's power structure, and so on. Neither the extracommunity controls nor the local controls are ever entirely absent, but their relative weight varies greatly by denomination.

Following our analytical scheme, it is not difficult to find the typical unit of the horizontal pattern in the form of a local council of churches. This organization is specifically established to promote collaboration among the churches of the local community, which nevertheless retain their individual denominational ties. Thus, the collaboration is on matters that the various denominations wish to pursue in common on the local level but does not necessarily involve agreement on specific doctrine or organizational unification. As was the case with the chambers of commerce, these local councils are usually, though not invariably, affiliated with a national organization, the National Council of the Churches of Christ in the United States of America. Roman Catholic churches do not participate in this organization. In some instances, councils of churches include Jewish congregations, but to include them is difficult, though not impossible, in those councils affiliated with the National Council, since many of the activities promoted by the National Council are of a pronounced Christian nature. This interplay of forces between the attempt of churches representing various religious faiths to collaborate on the community level and the barriers that are presented by their extracommunity denominational or major faith hierarchies is an interesting example of horizontal and vertical relationships.

In any case, the local councils of churches are admittedly and deliberately weak in the sense that they do not seek organizational unification. Rather, they confine themselves to collaboration on occasional "joint services" and other activities that represent only a modicum of coordination. We can thus summarize by saying that the local council of churches, as the typical unit of the horizontal pattern, shows some degree of formalization and bureaucratization of the relationships among churches at the local level, but that its effectiveness is extremely modest. By no means does it approach in systemic importance the tie that most churches have to their extracommunity denominational bodies.

It is an interesting paradox that while literal belief in the church doctrines, which distinguish one denomination from another, has been steadily declining during recent decades, denominational administrative bureaucracies have grown not only in number and volume but in the extent of their functions. On the local level this growth is reflected in the fact that while differences in belief become less important as distinctions separating the local churches, the organizational tie of the churches to their respective denominational boards becomes stronger.

It has already been mentioned that the strength of the vertical tie, particularly as it is reflected in a smaller or larger degree of autonomy exercised by the local church unit over its activities, varies greatly from one denomination to another. Among Protestant denominations, the Baptists have been noted for the strong degree to which they have emphasized the autonomy of individuals in their beliefs and of the local church in its operations. For this reason they have been fundamentally opposed to the development of a denominational hierarchy, which would encroach upon the autonomy of the individual church unit. It is thus especially significant to note that in the American Baptist Convention, one of a number of Baptist denominations, an administrative bureaucracy similar in many respects to those of government and business has grown up with inexorable persistence. Harrison, who studied and analyz d this growth, pointed out the number of adaptations in type of leadership and in interpretation of policy that had to be made in order to accommodate this growth while still retaining the doctrine of local autonomy and as much of its reality as seemed feasible.[31]

The experience of the American Baptist Convention is not surprising, in light of the analysis of the "great change" in chapter 3. It signals, as an extreme case, the growth of denominational bureaucracies in other denominations as well, denominations whose doctrinal opposition to such ecclesiastical bureaucracies was not as strong. Through various degrees of official control over the selection and training of clergy, over the organized liturgical activities of the church, and over its ancillary activities and organizations; through printed doctrinal publications, periodicals, and devotional and program materials of various types; through visitations; and through the ordinary routine of giving "service" to local churches that need help in finding clergy, in conducting worship services, in organizing various religious activities, in conducting civic programs, in recruiting membership, planning budgets, and in myriad other ways, the denominational body performs vital functions without which many local churches could not survive. The denominational body obviously is the appropriate unit to designate as the principal unit of the vertical pattern, and we can

31. Paul M. Harrison, *Authority and Power in the Free Church Tradition: A Social Case Study of the American Baptist Convention* (Princeton: Princeton University Press, 1959).

thus portray churches in our analytical schema as prototypes of social participation as follows:

Major locality-relevant function	Typical community unit	Typical unit of horizontal pattern	Typical superior unit of vertical pattern
Social participation	Church	Council of churches	Denominational body

Mutual Support

Durkheim pointed out that the division of labor created greater interdependence and occasioned a type of symbiotic interrelationship that he charactertized as organic solidarity.[32] Kropotkin likewise emphasized the important function of cooperation, both in animal and human societies, and in a somewhat similar vein turned to the intricate network of interdependence in industrial societies as a dramatic instance of cooperation in modern societies.[33] Kropotkin's "mutual aid" thus is substantially similar to the organic solidarity of Durkheim: a type of interdependence in interaction that is often designated as "symbiotic."

The above concept is allied to, but not identical with, the concept of mutual support employed in this book, for by the mutual-support function we do not mean the continuous relations of symbiotic interdependence, which have been stressed throughout the preceding discourse. Rather, we refer to the type of help that is proffered in those instances where individual and family crises present needs that are not otherwise satisfied in the usual pattern of organized social behavior. Examples are illness, economic need, and problems of family functioning. Illness may keep a parent from taking care of the children and performing other needed family functions. Inability of the wage-earner to work, either through disability or unemployment, may present problems of economic maintenance. Marital discord or difficulty in the performance of socialization and social-control functions may turn the family to outside sources of help. In such cases, where does the family turn?

If we try to answer this question through time, we observe important differences associated with the "great change." Generally, there has been a tendency for the family to turn more and more to

32. Emile Durkheim, *The Division of Labor in Society,* trans. John A. Spaulding and George Simpson (Glencoe, Ill.: Free Press, 1951).

33. Peter Kropotkin, *Mutual Aid: A Factor in Evolution* (New York: Doubleday, Page, 1902).

other units for help and to go beyond kin, neighbors, and the church to specialized agencies set up to offer such help as a principal function. Thus, the locality-relevant function of mutual support, which might be roughly characterized as "providing help in time of trouble," has given rise to a large and complex battery of social units offering one kind of aid or another to individuals and families needing special help beyond their own resources. The assumption of this function increasingly by formally organized special agencies and decreasingly by family, kin, and neighborhood constitutes a large development associated with several aspects of the "great change."

The assumption of the mutual support function by various types of social units does not change its basic relevance to the immediate locality of the individual or family. In American communities it usually involves either personal services that must be offered in a local, face-to-face relationship or money that must be disbursed in order to be available for local use. The organizational network for performing these functions includes both voluntary and public agencies in the "health and welfare" field.

Although the mutual support function is largely performed by voluntary and public agencies, some parts, at least, remain in the less formalized units such as kinship groups and neighborhoods. The persisting importance of these kinship and friendship networks has only recently been fully acknowledged.[34] Still other parts are performed by private enterprise, as illustrated by commercial health insurance. It is interesting to note that health insurance is provided under public tax-supported auspices, under commercial auspices, and under voluntary association auspices. Other types of social insurance, such as workmen's compensation, retirement insurance, and unemployment insurance, may likewise be provided under different types of auspices.

Still another specialized channel of mutual support functions lies in a host of pseudoscientific cult practitioners and quacks offering a wide variety of "services" to the unwary person in times of trouble. An interesting account of how these sources operate was given by Steiner some years ago.[35] Another study reported the local druggist and bartender as performing counseling services for families in various types of trouble and in many instances being preferred to the more formal social agencies.[36] An extensive study in a

34. For a discussion of recent literature about such mutual-support networks, see Martin D. Lowenthal, "The Social Economy of Working Class Communities," in Gary Gappert and Harold Rose, eds., *The Social Economy of Cities*, UAAR, vol. 9 (Beverly Hills, California: Sage Publications, 1975).

35. Lee R. Steiner, *Where Do People Take Their Troubles?* (Boston: Houghton Mifflin, 1945).

36. Earl L. Koos, *Families in Trouble* (New York: King's Crown Press, 1946).

deteriorating urban neighborhood asked respondents to indicate from a list which sources they would utilize for help in times of personal trouble:

> For help with personal problems three sources of help accounted for 76.6 percent of the first choices: clergymen first, relatives second, and lawyers or doctors third. Social agencies were mentioned as first choices by only 6.5 percent of the respondents, but as second choices this percentage was 15.4. . . . Relatives are important sources of aid for both financial and personal difficulties. . . . More than 80 percent of the heads of household say they would use the agencies mentioned, if they had a personal problem with which they thought the agency could help.[37]

Generally speaking, the mutual support function is formally centralized in the field of "social welfare" services. A definitive assessment of the social welfare field in the United States used the following five characteristics as differentiae:

1. Formal organization
2. Social sponsorship and accountability
3. Absence of profit motive as dominant program purpose
4. Functional generalization: integrative, rather than segmental, view of human needs
5. Direct focus on human consumption needs[38]

The developing field of social welfare embodies many of the aspects of the "great change." As social welfare functions are assumed by public agencies, they give rise to highly bureaucratized types of administrative structures, with carefully defined laws and administrative regulations governing their performance, with carefully defined authority and responsibility at various levels of the administrative hierarchy, with standardization of administrative procedures, and so on. They are usually supported by tax moneys (except in the case of the contributory social insurances).

Stein observes that "in addition to the large public welfare agencies, the voluntary agencies and institutions in which the social work function is based tend increasingly to be large, departmentalized, with a hierarchical form of organization, formal policies and regulations, and so on, conforming to the classic Weberian concep-

---

37. Marvin B. Sussman and R. Clyde White, *Hough, Cleveland, Ohio: A Study of Social Life and Change* (Cleveland: The Press of Western Reserve University, 1959), pp. 91-92.

38. Harold L. Wilensky and Charles N. Lebeaux, *Industrial Society and Social Welfare: The Impact of Industrialization on the Supply and Organization of Social Welfare Services in the United States* (New York: Russell Sage Foundation, 1958), p. 146.

tion of bureaucratic structure."[39] Bureaucratization of the voluntary agencies through which welfare services are provided is illustrated by the typical casework setting involving the relation of caseworker to supervisor, of supervisor to administrative structure, and of administrative structure to a policy-making board of directors.

Bureaucratic organization and impersonalization also increasingly characterize private philanthropic support of nongovernmental agencies:

> [Since the Colonial Period] philanthropy has itself undergone a number of revolutions. Its major source of income is rapidly becoming the corporation instead of the individual. "Planned" routines of giving—payroll deduction and year round campaign—succeed impulse giving; and the beneficiary becomes ever more remote in space and vividness from the donor. . . . The collection plate or the beggar's extended hand—or its written equivalent, the "subscription list"— is succeeded by a virtual private tax with social penalties not only for the miserly who do not give at all but for the non-conformists who wish to give otherwise or to some other cause. An industry—fundraising—and a profession—the fundraiser—are developed and elaborated to pressure and persuade, to organize giving and mould opinion, to wage a "campaign," regular, relentless, and, as far as possible, irresistible.[40]

In modern social welfare a high degree of division of labor is apparent in the proliferation of specialized agencies. Family casework agencies, medical rehabilitation programs, public welfare departments, probation departments, mental health clinics, social service departments in hospitals, public health and visiting nursing services, employment offices, vocational retraining facilities—these are but a small selection from a voluminous list of special agencies serving one or another specialized type of individual or family needs. Many of these needs have themselves arisen out of the special circumstances of the "great change."

The division of labor is also apparent in the multiplication of different occupations designed to perform some special type of service. The social caseworker, the occupational therapist, the visiting nurse, the probation worker, the family counselor, the psychiatric social worker, the agency "homemaker"—all these represent specialized occupations designed to afford a mutual support function that

39. Herman D. Stein, "Organization Theory—Implications for Administration Research," in Leonard S. Kogan, ed., *Social Science Theory and Social Work Research* (New York: National Association of Social Workers, 1960), p. 84.

40. John R. Seeley et al., *Community Chest: A Case Study in Philanthropy* (Toronto: University of Toronto Press, 1957), p. 396.

was formerly performed largely by less specialized propinquity groups.

The development of professionalization within such service occupations is widely operative, being characterized by functional specificity, emotional or affective neutrality, impartiality, and the ideal of service. Parsons has analyzed these characteristics as applied to the medical profession, and Wilensky and Lebeaux have applied a similar type of analysis to the social work profession.[41]

Certain value changes associated with the "great change" are particularly relevant to the development of the social agencies as specialized performers of the mutual support function. One of these is the gradual acceptance of governmental activity as a positive value in an increasing number of fields. This development hardly needs further comment. The change from a moral to a causal interpretation of human behavior has likewise been closely associated with the rise of various welfare services and with such developments as the tendency to decrease the considerable stigma still associated with utilizing them and the extension of various services beyond the "needy" to the entire population. Likewise, the shift in community approach to social problems from that of "moral reform" to that of "planning" is well illustrated in the development of community welfare councils as highly organized, relatively routinized structures for assessing and confronting community needs in the health and welfare field.

The principal local units for the performance of social welfare services associated with the function of mutual support are the various voluntary social agencies and health associations and the public, tax-supported agencies. In some states, the administration of the public welfare agencies is a local function, while in others it is a state function, with branch offices of the state department operating on the local level. In either case there is a close connection of most public agencies in the welfare field with state and federal government, through the grant-in-aid aspects of the federal Social Security program and through various matching fund arrangements provided by individual states for such endeavors as delinquency prevention, mental health services, and so on. In many of the larger communities there are local offices of specialized federal services as well, which deal directly with the individual, bypassing the state government. Examples are the federal Social Security offices, dealing with Old Age and Survivors Insurance, and the Veterans Administration, dealing directly with individual veterans in a wide variety of services.

41. See Talcott Parsons, *The Social System* (Glencoe, Ill.: Free Press, 1951), and Wilensky and Lebeaux, *Industrial Society*, pp. 298ff.

Thus, although local municipal responsibility and commitment in public welfare date back at least to the Elizabethan Poor Laws in England, the local public agencies in the welfare field are largely stimulated and supported by state and federal government.

Whatever the variations, however, public welfare services conceived and financed locally are comparatively scarce. It is true that cities, counties, towns, and townships are the scene on which all welfare programs reach the family; local offices of OASI, vocational rehabilitation, unemployment insurance, and the Veterans Administration dot the country. But these are not local doings. In fact, the closer one gets to the local level of government the less one finds welfare consciousness, and the lower grow welfare standards.[42]

Local agencies that are branches of state or federal governments have little direct relation to the locality from the control standpoint and thus resemble other state and federal governmental activities whose relation to the local community was considered in an earlier section. Agencies of local municipalities, on the other hand, are subject to local control through the voting process and may be more or less directly sensitive to local needs and wishes as well as to local political party influences.

The other major type of welfare agency serving locality-relevant mutual support functions is the voluntary agency or association. As mentioned earlier, the voluntary agency typically is structured with a board of trustees or its equivalent, in which legal policy-making authority resides and which engages a professional administrative and service staff that in turn offers services to individuals in the community in accordance with the established policies of the agency. It has been observed that agency boards, consisting of upper-class people, employ middle-class professional workers to offer services to citizens of the lower socioeconomic groups. Like all sweeping generalizations, this one needs qualification. In the first place, there is more overlapping than this pat set of categories would imply. Further, the trend seems to be both for an extension of board membership to include middle-class members and for an extension of agency services to broader segments of the community, not just the lower socioeconomic groups. Perhaps more important, many social agencies have been criticized precisely because they have failed to reach the groups with the lowest incomes.

Voluntary health and welfare agencies make extensive use of volunteer citizens not only as board members but also in other

42. Wilensky and Lebeaux, *Industrial Society*, p. 153.

capacities, such as soliciting gifts or assisting professional staff in various activities of the organization. Obviously, these volunteers constitute an important link between the private agency and the local community, regardless of whether or not the agency is a relatively autonomous unit, such as a voluntary nonsectarian family service agency, or a health association, such as the Red Cross.

We have already considered some aspects of voluntary citizen participation in various organizations. In the preceding section such participation was considered under the social participation function. Although obviously there are numerous "reasons" and numerous levels of analysis of the reasons why people participate in voluntary agency activities, there is considerable indication that their participation—not only in self-interest organizations but also in health and welfare agency activities—is closely tied to their postion in the local community. This is true not only of agency board membership, with its components both of noblesse oblige and of power structure control over an important aspect of community life, but also in the manner in which volunteers come to participate in the more menial tasks of the health and welfare agencies.

In a health survey in a midwestern county, some 700 interviewers participated on a voluntary basis and completed approximately 10,000 lengthy interviews. But how closely was this remarkable participation tied in with a special interest in health and a special knowledge of the survey and belief in its potential for community improvement? The research team that investigated the survey process concluded that "the personnel for the execution of the survey was obtained through feelings of obligation to relationships which already existed among members of local communities and which were usually personal." Further, when asked "How did you happen to take part in the survey?" 36 percent indicated feelings of responsibility toward friends, 9 percent toward an individual because of his or her position, 19 percent to an organization, and 37 percent to the community. Only 4 percent indicated an interest in health in this connection.[43]

Likewise, the friendships and other formal and informal relations among local people were found to play an important role in "joining up" with the National Foundation. "The most frequent trigger event was the occasion of being asked to join by a friend; 52 percent of all Volunteers joined the Foundation in response to an invitation extended by someone whom they knew personally. Another 20 percent were asked to join by some other member of the community; 18 percent were asked to join by an organizational or occupational colleague; and 10 percent volunteered on their own initiative.[44]

Thus the tie of social agencies to the locality through volunteer participation is based not exclusively on the special interests of the volunteers but also on the position of these volunteers in the formal and informal structure of organizations and groups in the community. Volunteers form an important tie between the local community and the voluntary agencies, many of which are closely tied in with national organizations. In its rosiest colors, perhaps, the relationship has been portrayed by Donnison:

> The Red Cross is a local branch of a world-wide movement; yet its swimming and water-safety programme could not be better suited to local needs; its blood donor service and its record of achievement in times of crisis have given it an important place in local affections, and its work is done by local people who know the community and often play an active part in other local organizations. These are the links that matter.[45]

In the field of health and welfare services, one type of agency is especially suited to illustrate the combination of horizontal and vertical ties that characterize local units in the various locality-relevant functions. This is the voluntary health association, as represented by local units of such national organizations as the American National Red Cross, the American Cancer Society, the National Foundation, the National Tuberculosis and Respiratory Disease Association, and the American Heart Association. Although their provisions for local units vary somewhat, they are sufficiently similar to constitute an important coherent pattern, which we shall call the "local health association," using it as our typical unit for the specialized performance of the mutual support function.

In choosing the voluntary health association as the local unit for analysis, we are deliberately selecting a type of unit that has stronger extracommunity ties than do some of the other possible types of local units, such as the voluntary, nonsectarian, family service agency. The latter type of agency is usually not a branch of a larger organization that charters and controls it but an independent community-based agency that may be loosely affiliated with similar agencies in other communities as a member of the Family Service Association of America, a national standard-setting agency offering various services to its member agencies and serving as an important

44. David L. Sills, *The Volunteers: Means and Ends in a National Organization* (Glencoe, Ill.: The Free Press, 1957), p. 102.

45. D. V. Donnison, *Welfare Services in a Canadian Community: A Study of Brockville, Ontario* (Toronto: University of Toronto Press, 1958), p. 156.

spokesman for the family service field. Such local agencies are also related to larger extracommunity systems through the membership of their professional personnel in the National Association of Social Workers and through their participation in their various professional subcultures.

The problem of establishing and maintaining some degree of functional coordination among health and welfare agencies operating on the local scene is a difficult one. In a highly sympathetic review of welfare services in a Canadian town of approximately 14,000 people Donnison concluded:

> Brockville's public services are marked by an emphasis upon the provision of money, equipment and material help, and a lack of trained full-time workers, by a generous support of "good causes" rather than a broad examination of human needs, by a vigorous growth of independent schemes with little coordination of their efforts.[46]

The principal type of organization through which the horizontal relationship among health and welfare agencies is formalized on the locality level is the community welfare council. Originally called a council of social agencies, this type of coordinating agency arose to establish certain cooperative relationships among the health and welfare agencies of the community, to provide them with certain joint services, and to develop new, broadly based programs that did not come completely within the purview of any single agency. For several decades they were made up of formal representation from the various agencies, usually including each agency's director and a leading board member or officer. More recently they have broadened their base of membership in line with the purpose of representing the community rather than merely the social agencies, and they have come to be called by a number of different names, such as community planning councils and councils of community services. Community chests, on the other hand, are joint fund-raising agencies, and united funds are like community chests but include the participation of at least one of the national health associations. Generally speaking, the national health associations stay out of the joint fund-raising organizations but often participate in the community welfare councils. For this reason, as well as the primary emphasis upon community planning and coordination of services, the council is the appropriate unit to serve as our typical unit of the horizontal pattern.

But the usual relation of the local unit of the voluntary health association to a community welfare council is extremely weak and functionally less significant than its strong relationship to the

46. *Welfare Services*, p. 161.

national organization, a relationship in which a state organization may play an intermediate role. While each national organization permits some local autonomy with regard to certain activities, it nevertheless has a nationally determined policy and set of regulations and procedures that its chartered locals are obligated to follow. Its degree of control over the local branches or chapters is exercised in a number of informal and formal ways: through providing leadership in program development to combat the particular disease or health problem that is its target, through field services, through published materials, through periodic regional and national meetings, and through a host of other methods. A local unit that does not meet its obligations can be disfranchised as an official branch of the national organization, and it can be barred from using the fund-raising device of the national organization. In a few instances, local units have been willing to face just this fateful prospect, but most do not even consider it a potential avenue of future action.

It should be understood that local units of national health associations are usually developed by field staff from the state or national organization with the definite intent of being chartered by it and becoming integrated into its program. In the case of the National Foundation, for example, "Chapters do not have policy-making functions, since their legal status is that of administrative units of the national organization." Sills concluded that this strong central control through a "corporate-type structure" is of great importance:

> It has also been demonstrated that the Foundation's capacity to solve or circumvent the two most pervasive problems of voluntary associations—maintaining membership interest and preserving organizational goals—is directly related to its corporate-type structure. Moreover, the major operational programs of the Foundation have been shown to be dependent upon a corporate-type structure for their proper functioning.[47]

The elimination of infantile paralysis, toward which the National Foundation in its earlier form successfully strove, involved many different activities, some of which are appropriate for the local county or community level, others of which are not. It would have been ridiculous, for example, for the search for a polio vaccine to have involved special research units in each of the local chapters. On the other hand, certain other functions are appropriate for local-level activity, including not only certain services but also fund raising.

 47. Sills, *The Volunteers*, pp. 213, 212.

Thus it is appropriate that funds and organizational effort regarding a problem present in the local community should support in part at least a national-level organization that can carry on those aspects of the program relevant to that level. Yet this support involves relegating control over such local chapters in large part to a national organization. Although national policies may be determined through local representation, each community's voice becomes merged with that of numerous others, thus having only a minimal effect on the total outcome. Much of the recent controversy surrounding the role of the voluntary health associations at the community and national levels was based on a lack of clear analysis of the types of function appropriate to the locality level as opposed to the types appropriate to the state or national level and a lack of careful assessment of structure and fund-raising activities in light of the appropriate levels of function.

Meanwhile, though, let us note that the conflict at the community level between the branches of national voluntary health associations on the one hand and the community chests and united funds on the other represented a clear dramatization of points of tension between vertical and horizontal patterns of organization among community units. The health associations represent systems extending beyond the community, systems that exert a great degree of control over the behavior of their local chapters. Two aspects of this control are central to the controversy. One is the strong policy directives orienting the program and activities of the local chapter toward nationally determined procedures (which may hinder their collaborating with other local agencies on more broadly based common efforts in such areas as chronic illness, the aged, and so on); the other is the policy of insisting on independent fund-raising campaigns and in some instances forbidding their chapters to participate in united funds.

On the other hand, community chests and united funds, as well as the community welfare planning councils, which are often organizationally attached to them and usually financially dependent on them, emphasize the locally based interests, the horizontal pattern of organization among separate units at the community level, both in fund raising and in joint planning and programing. The conflict dramatizes the clash of these two sets of forces in American communities, sets of forces that we have seen in earlier sections to be in operation in connection with the other major types of locality-relevant functions as well.

The development of community welfare councils with professional staff and a national organization to give service, represent their interests, and so on, is an important example of the attempt to give structure to the effort to exercise some degree of coordination **209** among the diverse units operating in a particular locality-relevant function. Some degree of functional collaboration has been achieved more noticeably by the family agencies and other locally based agencies than by the voluntary health agencies. Over thirty years ago a famous and highly controverted report on such agencies asserted:

> In no community so far as we have discovered have the separate voluntary health agencies been reorganized into a single all-inclusive organization. On the grounds of logic, necessity, efficiency, personnel and financing, we can no longer justify the separate existence of the specialized agency in the majority of cases.[48]

It contrasted this situation unfavorably with the official health departments:

> In retrospect, the development of comprehensive activities in health departments now appears quite natural and reasonable. It would have been preposterous to set up a separate and distinct—and "independent"—department with a separate board as each new activity became necessary.[49]

Sower and his associates, however, took a gloomy view of the prospects for such horizontal planning among health agencies, at least insofar as the experience of their county with a health council was concerned:

> The survey participants in the local communities did not perceive an overall function of health planning. They did, however, recognize particular kinds of health problems. It is understandable, and at the same time predictable, that the citizens of the county would show more interest in particularized health organizations, such as those concerned with polio, tuberculosis, etc., than in the efforts of a county health co-ordinating council.[50]

And it is the experience all over the United States that local units of national health associations do find it difficult, though not impossible, to pursue their primary interest in a specific disease field or area and at the same time join with other health and welfare agencies in effective programs that cut across the lines of the specific interests of the various agencies. Broad community programs in con-

48. Selskar M. Gunn and Philip S. Platt, *Voluntary Health Agencies: An Interpretive Study* (New York: Ronald Press, 1945), p. 65. For the finding of a later study, see *Voluntary Health and Welfare Agencies in the United States* (New York: Schoolmasters' Press, 1961).

49. Gunn and Platt, *Voluntary Health Agencies*, p. 60.

50. *Community Involvement*, p. 269.

nection with "chronic illness" or "the aged" have offered bases for such outstanding cooperation on the local level as in Niagara Falls, New York, where a strong horizontally oriented study-action program was undertaken among the various health and welfare agencies.[51] Federal legislation dealing with health-service coordination and with programs for the aged has stimulated councils in those fields. Such councils have experienced difficulty in bringing about the desired level of coordination.[52].

Thus, we can schematize the relations of the typical units in the performance of the mutual-support function as follows:

Major locality-relevant function	Typical community unit	Typical unit of horizontal pattern	Typical superior unit of vertical pattern
Mutual support	Voluntary health association	Community welfare council	National health association

We have now completed the tasks of this chapter: to describe the major locality-relevant functions in terms of which the community as a social system has been defined, to examine some of the ways in which each function is performed on the locality level, to identify a type of local unit that can be considered "typical," to examine that unit's ties to the locality, to examine its relations to other analogous units performing within the same functional area on the locality level, and to examine its relations to extracommunity systems.

In each instance, it has been emphasized that not all the relevant units have been explored, but that at least the most important ones have been considered. We have thus been able to investigate several aspects of structure and function in the five different functional areas of American communities. The skeleton framework that has been used can now be put together as shown in Figure 6-1.

These, then, are the locality-relevant functions that it is the community's task to provide. As indicated in chapter 5, there are two

51. See "The Changing Pattern of Illness: A Problem for the Patient, the Professions and the Public," *Viewpoint*, no. 6 (Spring 1960), published by State Charities Aid Association, New York.

52. Recent treatments of health councils and other relations among health service organizations have further elaborated on the intrinsic problems of community health care delivery. See Eliot Freidson, *Professional Dominance: The Social Structure of Medical Care* (Chicago: Aldine Press, 1970); Robert R. Alford, *Health Care Politics: Ideological and Interest Group Barriers to Reform* (Chicago: University of Chicago Press, 1974); and both publications of the Health Policy Advocacy Center: Barbara Ehrenreich and John Ehrenreich, eds. *The American Health Empire* (New York: Random House, 1971); and David Kotelchuck, ed., *Prognosis Negative: Crisis in the Health Care System* (New York: Random House, 1976).

Figure 6-1. Schematic Analysis Of Major Locality-Relevant Functions

Major locality-relevant function	Typical community unit	Typical unit of horizontal pattern	Typical superior unit of vertical pattern
Production-distribution-consumption	Company	Chamber of commerce	National corporation
Socialization	Public school	Board of education	State department of education
Social control	Municipal government	City council	State government
Social participation	Church	Council of churches	Denominational body
Mutual support	Voluntary health association	Community welfare council	National health association

fundamental dimensions to the community as there are to any social system: task performance and system maintenance. The performance of the locality-relevant functions tends to relate the community's constituent units to extracommunity systems. The maintenance of the community as a system, however, involves the relation of these units to each other. These two types of relationships will be considered in chapters 8 and 9. But before considering them in detail, it will be well to examine some of the important differences associated with the choice of local auspices under which these respective functions are performed.

Alternative Auspices for the Performance of Locality-Relevant Functions

7

We have seen that the performance of locality-relevant functions is distributed among different sets of auspices. Although we selected in the preceding chapter a unit that was "typical" for the performance of a particular type of function, we noted that other kinds of units also performed that function.

What are the consequences for the community when a function is relegated to one particular type of auspices rather than another? A quotation from the first Middletown study will illustrate some of the possibilities in one area of functioning:

> Middletown has developed four kinds of institutional devices to deal with this recurrent overwhelming of certain of its members: (1) person-to-person individual giving; (2) giving through voluntary groups such as churches, clubs, lodges, and labor unions, which do not exist primarily or exclusively for this purpose, but which give a semi-personal assistance to the "unfortunate"; (3) giving through voluntarily supported, semi-public social service organizations existing solely to alleviate the condition of the "needy"; (4) giving, through elected or appointed representatives of the entire group, funds raised from the entire group through taxes.[1]

1. Robert S. Lynd and Helen Merrell Lynd, *Middletown: A Study in Modern American Culture* (New York: Harcourt, Brace, 1929), p. 459.

In other words, by the year 1929, Middletown had developed a number of different auspices for performing a part of the mutual-support function. In this chapter we shall attempt to consider systematically the alternative ways available for the performance of this and other functions. The question is important for several reasons:

1. The relegation of a function to one type of auspices or another places it under a vastly different set of conditions regarding its financial support, the locus of decision-making, the body with ultimate responsibility, and the type of control that can be exercised by the community over the performing body.

2. Rapid and important changes are taking place in the pattern of allocation of functions in American communities, an analysis of which helps in understanding the structural and functional aspects of the transformation of American communities, which we have termed the "great change."

3. For ideological reasons, and also because the allocation of a function to one type of auspices rather than another has important practical implications at the community level, the transfer of functions has in many instances engendered serious community conflict.

Food and shelter must be made available, there must be work opportunities, children must be educated, some degree of conformity to custom or law must be maintained, there must be provision for satisfactory associational experiences, and there must be help in time of sickness or want. All of these needs are appropriate for the locality level. But how are they to be provided? Actually, there are a number of different possibilities.

1. First, of course, people may as *individuals or families* "do things for themselves." Actually, there is not a single item among those mentioned in the preceding paragraph (which are simply re-statements of the community-relevant functions examined in the preceding chapter) that it is not appropriate, at least in part, for the individual family to provide. At the same time all of these functional areas involve types of activity that most families under modern American conditions are unable to provide completely, and their provision by other auspices is therefore necessitated.

2. A brief look at these functions will indicate, however, that a somewhat different type of grouping often has an important role in their provision, for in connection with any of these functions, people may group themselves together beyond the confines of the individual family, either on an intermittent basis or as a matter of specific *ad hoc informal organization.* Perhaps the most important grouping in this category has traditionally been the neighborhood, consisting of a group of individuals or families who live in proximity to each other

and who actually carry on such activities as borrowing and lending (of tools, labor, or a cup of sugar), visiting, leisure-time activities, or help in time of trouble. Examples of such groups in operation are a number of farmers working together at harvest, the provision by neighbors of temporary shelter if a house is destroyed by fire or storm, taking care of a family's children if the mother is sick, and so on. As mentioned in chapter 3, recent developments and recent research have brought to the foreground the existence of informal networks within and across neighborhoods, which are based on kinship or friendship and are important sources of mutual help and support.

3. A third alternative is to arrange for the performance of some of these functions through a *formally organized association*. Many of the nineteenth-century utopian communities were of this nature, performing most locality-relevant functions in a formally organized way. Other examples are consumers' cooperatives, housing cooperatives, production cooperatives, voluntary agencies in health and welfare, clubs and associations of various types, private schools, and so on.

4. A fourth kind of alternative is the performance of the function by an *individual or group for financial gain*, whether in the form of wages, fees, prices, or interest. This category includes such activities as selling in stores, fee-for-service health care by physicians, services by trades people of various types, working for wages or salaries, and so on.

5. A fifth kind of alternative is the performance of the function by an *official governmental body*. This alternative needs little elaboration, except perhaps to note the extensive governmental activity in such fields as public health, public assistance, public education, public recreation, and so on.

Communities seldom have occasion to approach in a rational and systematic fashion the question of just what use will be made of each of these five auspices in the performance of individual functions. Rather, choices on specific matters occasionally present themselves, as when a municipality determines whether to provide a public utility through government or through a private company or when a community welfare council deliberates on whether a certain type of voluntary or public agency should be established.

Nevertheless, although different patterns of allocation are seldom the result of community-wide planning, there is considerable variation among communities in the patterns of allocation. Even more important, there is much greater potential variability among these choices than is found in most American communities. Apparently, decisions on specific choices are often made in an atmosphere of controversy and without a clear understanding of the **215** implications of a community's allocation pattern. For this reason, a clear typology of alternatives is desirable as a basis for examining the implications of performing any individual function through one set of auspices or another and also as a basis for analysis of the total pattern of a community's allocation of functions. We shall therefore examine the five types of auspices listed above in relation to a number of different attributes: their source of financial support, the locus of decision-making, the formal body with ultimate responsibility, and the provision for community control over their activities.

Financial Support of Locality-Relevant Functions

Characteristic of the first two alternative auspices (we shall call them "families" and "ad hoc groups" for short) is the relative lack of need for financial support. By their very nature, they are largely outside the money-price system, operating principally through other exchange media such as borrowing and lending, reciprocal help, exchange of labor, gift giving, performing of services, offering of hospitality, and so on. Exchange is governed largely by custom and involves in each case a system of reciprocal obligations, which, like other norms, may involve sanctions if violated. Of course, the family as a unit must gain economic sustenance, which under today's conditions customarily involves income production through entry into the money-price system, through the salaries, fees, profits, or other income of its individual members. Significantly, so-called subsistence farming involves an almost complete separation from the exchange provided through the money-price system. Needless to say, the division of labor, along with other aspects of the "great change," has brought more and more functions into the money-price system and has resulted in the depletion of the number of subsistence farms.

Voluntary associations, our third type of auspices, have varied means of obtaining financial support in the performance of the many functions that involve them in the money-price system. We can delineate three rather distinct types of provision for support. First, various membership associations raise part or all of the money they need through dues. Second, agencies of various types raise part or all of their money through gifts, whether for current expenditures, capital improvement, or income-producing endowment. Third, some agencies, notably private nonprofit schools and hospitals, raise part or all of their money through fees, including fees for service, tuition fees, hospital charges, and so forth. Another source of income is government grants. One could perhaps summarize by saying that financial support for voluntary nonprofit associations comes through money voluntarily paid to them for what they do, either for the donor or for others, by individuals, organizations, or government.

Business companies, on the other hand, receive their financial support through prices charged for commodities or through fees for services. They, too, may have "income-producing endowment" in the form of investments. Included under the concept of business companies should be all economic units producing for a profit, including farmers, self-employed professionals, commission sales persons, trades people, and so on. With the exception of endowment, income comes principally through payments made voluntarily for the purpose of receiving a commodity or service.

Government's chief financial support comes from taxes, which, by contrast with the financial support of other auspices, are mandatory, not voluntary. Obviously, the basis upon which taxes are collected has important implications for the distribution of costs of governmental services among various groups in the population. In addition to taxes, payments in the form of fees are also common, either for special services or for commodities or utilities. And in many cases the income of a governmental unit comes in part through grants-in-aid from superior units.

Thus, although there is some overlapping, the five types of auspices differ from each other significantly in the manner in which they are financially supported.

Formal Locus of Decision-Making

We have maintained that the relegation of a particular function to one type of auspices or another may have important implications for the community. One of these is the question of how, where, and by whom important decisions of policy are made in the different types of auspices.

Abstractly, democratic philosophy calls for decisions to be made by those who will be affected by them. Yet several considerations immediately complicate this pat suggestion. The first is the need for *delegation*. Practical necessity calls for some decisions to be made by people who on one basis or another have been especially designated to make them. Associated with delegation is the question of *relevance*. Some types of decision, especially those requiring special knowledge (of architecture, engineering, medicine, finance, and so on) are appropriately confined to individuals or bodies with special qualifications. Another complication has to do with *prerogative*. Obviously, some people have greater claim to a voice in the decisions of a particular unit than do others. But on what basis? If we are speaking of a business company, what voice should its employed per- **217** sonnel have and in what policy decisions? What about its stockholders? Its customers? The citizens of the community?

Dahl and Lindblom made a significant attempt to investigate some of the considerations underlying an examination of such questions. Though not directed specifically to the community level, their fourfold typology of "central sociopolitical processes" is most provocative. One such important process is the *price system* as a control and calculation mechanism. "But the circumstances in which the price system is an appropriate process for rational social action in the politico-economic area—in short, for economizing—can be stated only if the alternatives to it are well understood." They specify *hierarchy, polyarchy,* and *bargaining* as the three alternatives to the price system:

> Processes for calculation and control are in large part processes involving relations of leaders and non-leaders, whether these leaders be goverment officials or businessmen. Hierarchy is a process in which leaders control non-leaders. One of its most familiar forms is bureaucracy, and everyone recognizes how critical the functioning of bureaucracy is to rational politico-economic action. Polyarchy is a process, sometimes called democracy, in which non-leaders control leaders. The possibilities of economizing are obviously tied up with the effectiveness of this process. Bargaining is a process in which leaders control each other. The American system of checks and balances is a bargaining process; so also is political control through the great pressure groups—business, labor, and agriculture. In a price system all these relations among leaders and non-leaders are found, but in a particular form.[2]

These various types of control are relevant to the different auspices through which locality-relevant functions are performed in American communities.

In each type of arrangement to perform locality-relevant functions, we may ask what form is taken by the decision-making structure. The possibilities within the family are numerous, varying along one dimension from strong matriarchal control to strong patriarchal control, for example. Burgess pointed out that in the Chicago of a generation ago, at least, the locus of decision-making varied according to family location in one or another of the concentric zones that constituted the ecological structure of the city (see chapter 2). Matricentric families prevailed in the suburban zone, equalitarian families in the apartment house zone, patricentric families in the working-

2. Robert A. Dahl and Charles E. Lindblom, *Politics, Economics, and Welfare: Planning and Politico-Economic Systems Resolved into Basic Social Processes* (New York: Harper & Brothers, 1953), pp. 22, 23.

men's zone, and emancipated families in the rooming house zone. Each had its characteristic pattern for decision-making.[3]

It is interesting to note that extended family groups in a number of societies perform many functions that under a more *Gesellschaft*-like social organization are performed by formal voluntary associations, business, and government.

Of the five types of auspices, the neighborhood has perhaps the least to offer by way of formal structure. Yet numerous studies have indicated that decision-making power is not distributed evenly among neighborhood people, but rather that an informal leadership structure can usually be delineated, a structure through which neighborhood decisions are made.

By contrast, the decision-making locus in the three remaining types of auspices is usually formally prescribed and fairly definite. In the voluntary association, formal decision-making authority lies in a board of trustees. Such boards show considerable variation along a number of dimensions. They may be self-perpetuating, having within themselves the complete determination of their future membership, or they may be elected by and responsible to a larger membership body. They may have relatively narrow powers because the major decision-making powers lie in a superior board outside the community, or they may have rather broad or even exclusive powers to determine local policies.

There is considerable evidence to support the general statement that in American communities the boards of voluntary associations consist predominantly of upper- and upper-middle-class people, and of people who have important positions in the industrial or governmental hierarchy or of people who "speak for" or "represent" them.[4] This statement would seem to apply whether one is referring to the boards of voluntary hospitals, those of voluntary health and welfare agencies, or those of private schools and colleges.

The locus of policy decision-making in business establishments is more diversified, particularly as applied to individual entrepre-

---

3. Ernest W. Burgess and Harvey J. Locke, *The Family: From Institution to Companionship*, 2nd ed. (New York: American Book, 1953), pp. 100-24.

4. See "The X Family: A Pattern of Business-Class Control," in Robert S. Lynd and Helen Merrell Lynd, *Middletown in Transition: A Study in Cultural Conflicts* (New York: Harcourt, Brace, 1937); W. Lloyd Warner and Paul S. Lunt, *The Social Life of a Modern Community* (New Haven, Conn.: Yale University Press, 1941); Floyd Hunter, *Community Power Structure: A Study of Decision Makers* (Chapel Hill: University of North Carolina Press, 1953); Christopher Sower et al., *Community Involvement: The Webs of Formal and Informal Ties that Make for Action* (Glencoe, Ill.: Free Press, 1957); and John R. Seeley et al., *Community Chest: A Case Study in Philanthropy* (Toronto: University of Toronto Press, 1957).

neurs and partnerships. The corporation form, on the other hand, is widely prevalent and is similar to voluntary associations in that policy-making power resides in a board of directors (by whatever name it is called). In the case of the business corporation, however, in form at least, such boards do not have self-perpetuating powers: the holders of the voting shares of stock or those to whom these holders have given their proxies select the members. Local units also resemble the voluntary nonprofit corporation in their possible structural or personal ties with corporations that are located elsewhere and that do not draw an appreciable measure of their board membership from the local community. Significantly, board members are elected by voting shareholders, not by customers and not by employees (as in the case of the *Mitbestimmung* in German heavy industry).

Finally, the various governmental branches to which locality-relevant functions are relegated come under different types of decision-making authority. Typically, basic policy is determined by a legislative body, stipulated within the charter of a quasi-governmental "authority," handed down in the form of implementing rules and regulations by a superior governmental authority or vested in some special board, which resembles that of the profit or nonprofit corporation. Examples of this last are the special youth boards and community mental health boards in the counties or cities of several states. Even in these cases, however, major policy matters are determined basically by a legislature, and even more minor matters of program implementation may be dependent on legislative approval through the legislature's function of approving budgets or allocating funds.

Ultimate Authority

In the previous section we saw that the policy decision-making locus may be in a board or some other body through delegation. Let us consider these various forms of auspices from the standpoint of the delegator, that is to say, the body of people who presumably exercise the ultimate authority over the policies of the unit, which authority they may delegate but do not necessarily renounce.

Significantly, the distinction between ultimate authority and decision-making locus is not appropriate to the *Gemeinschaft*-like units of the family and neighborhood. With the voluntary association, business enterprise, and government unit, however, there is a clear distinction between ultimate authority and decision-making locus.

The voluntary association, as a generic form, includes various types of ultimate authority. In the case of a school or college, the board itself constitutes the ultimate authority, in this respect resembling the family and neighborhood forms. In nonprofit corporations having a "membership," the members usually are the ultimate authority, with the officers and boards acting as their delegates. In social service agencies, the board may likewise be the ultimate authority although some agencies recognize a group of "members" made up of interested supporters and financial contributors who elect the board and delegate power to it. In a cooperative, those who are served by the unit also constitute the unit's ultimate authority. Thus, a consumers' cooperative is owned by its customer-members whose ownership is signified by shareholding, and a somewhat similar arrangement characterizes producers' cooperatives, housing cooperatives, and other forms.

Business enterprises make no distinction between decision-making locus and ultimate authority in the case of individual entrepreneurs. Partnerships vary in this respect, with different possible decision-making authority being vested in different types of partners. Profit corporations have a clear delineation between board members as the locus of policy-making decisions and voting shareholders as the ultimate authority.

Community Controls

What kinds of control can be exercised by the community over these various types of auspices? So far, we have been discussing various aspects of the behavior of these units from the standpoint of their internal structure as social systems. It will be recalled that social systems are structural organizations of the interaction of units, which endure through time. In the process, they adapt to impacts from the environment in such a way as to accommodate the impact and preserve the system with a minimum of modification. We have been considering some of the structural characteristics of different kinds of social systems as these are related to their adaptive procedures. We turn now to the types of impact that their community environment can have to modify their behavior along lines that are consonant with the goals of the community as a more inclusive social system.

This attempted impact is a social-control problem. We defined social control as the process according to which a group influences the behavior of its members toward conformity with group norms. In this instance we are considering the community's exercise of social control over the various types of social organization that we have described. In the preceding chapter we chose government as the "typical unit" for the exercise of the social-control function, specifically because it had the power of coercive control over all persons **221** within its geographic domain. Nevertheless, it was emphasized that other types of units may exercise various kinds of social control.

When we examine community controls over member units, government has obvious relevance through its coercive powers. Yet the control functions of government over local community units are often exercised by state and federal rather than by local governmental bodies. Thus, much of the family law in the United States is state, not municipal, law. Similarly, as pointed out in the preceding chapter, regulation of industry is largely in the hands of state and federal bodies, although some local control is retained by the municipality. Voluntary institutions such as schools and colleges and other nonprofit corporations are chartered by state, rather than local, government. The state welfare department, by whatever name it goes, typically licenses or in other ways recognizes various health and welfare agencies and exercises a general supervision over their activities in accordance with state laws. Religious organizations, as well, come under state laws and are granted corporate status by the respective states. Similarly, local governments themselves are given their legal recognition by the state and must operate within the provisions of their special charters or of the municipal code applying to their class of municipality.

Nevertheless, the behavior of various types of social units is also controlled to a certain extent by local government, and its ordinances that apply to individuals apply likewise to various types of social organization.

But social control takes a thousand forms, particularly in its informal aspects, including the pressure of public opinion, the influence of gossip, praise and blame, and so on. These informal pressures, along with custom and local norms, operate directly on the decision-making of individuals as family or neighborhood members, along with the more formal controls operating through the law. In the case of formal voluntary associations, business enterprises, and governmental bodies, however, there are additional formal methods through which community control is exercised.

To the extent that a voluntary association depends upon gifts, whether for capital expenditure or for current operating expenditures, control can be exercised through making or withholding or rechanneling gifts by community members. It is little wonder that this all-important control channel over the existence of voluntary social agencies and health associations should be a focus of community controversy, for whoever controls their pattern of contributions controls their fate.

Another type of control over voluntary associations is through patronage. For example, a community can destroy a local private

school through individual parent decisions to send children elsewhere. A new agency may endure or fail on the basis of the referral behavior of the relevant professional people who can control the flow of clients or patients to its doors. In a somewhat similar vein, a local membership association may be destroyed through the lack of members.

At this point, we are close to the most important avenue of control over business enterprise: customer behavior. The aggregate of individual decisions to purchase or not to purchase a particular product or service may have life-or-death significance for a business. And through customer willingness to purchase for this price but no higher or at this grade of quality but no lower are made the day-to-day policies of local businesses that must sell goods or services in the local market.

Obviously, this control factor does not operate where the local business establishment is not dependent on the local community for customers. Nevertheless, it is dependent on the local community for its labor supply, without which it cannot operate, and by individuals choosing to work elsewhere or not to work, a great degree of control over the business's fate is exercised. For these reasons, it is hardly surprising that the *boycott,* through which individual "market" decisions to purchase or not to purchase are "administered" as group decisions involving large numbers of people, and the *strike,* through which individual "market" decisions to work or not to work are likewise "administered" as large group decisions, are recognized as powerful procedures associated with the public interest and are brought under various types of regulative control through government.

Similarly, government as a type of auspices for the possible performance of locality-relevant functions is subject to a special type of control: voter behavior. The difference between the two popular expressions "You can't fight City Hall" and "Throw the rascals out" is perhaps a measure of the possible range of effectiveness of the vote as an instrument of control over local government. And understandably, the sensitiveness or insensitiveness of various governmental officials and bodies to the popular vote is a constant topic of contention, based on various weightings of delegation, relevance, and prerogative. The utilization of local government as an acceptable performer of locality-relevant functions is in this respect bounded by the two poles expressed popularly by the concept of "entrenched bureaucracy" and that of "political influence."

Recognizing that there is considerable variability, it may nevertheless be helpful to summarize the main points of the exposition so far in the paradigm given in Figure 7-1.

Thus, it is apparent that the decision as to which auspices shall perform a locality-relevant function is one with important **223**

Figure 7-1. Schematic analysis of auspices for the performance of locality-relevant functions

Type of auspices	Source of funds	Formal locus of decision-making	Ultimate authority	Principal community controls
Individuals or families	Member earnings	Variable	Variable	Custom, primary controls, law
Neighborhood & ad hoc groups	No funds needed	No formal locus	No formal locus	Custom, primary controls, law
Voluntary association	Gifts, fees, dues	Board of trustees	Board, membership	Gift patterns
Business company	Sales, fees	Board of directors	Voting shareholders	Market
Government	Taxes	Legislature, board	Voters	Voting

consequences for the community. The foregoing analysis provides us with a method for considering the appropriateness of one type of allocation as against another for any particular function. It also permits an analysis of changes in allocation through time, an analysis that makes clearer the implications of the "great change" as described in chapter 3, particularly that aspect that has to do with the transfer of functions from the family and ad hoc groups to voluntary associations, business, and government.

Effectiveness and Relevance of Community Controls

The types of controls that communities can exercise over different types of auspices vary in their effectiveness and in their relevance to the function involved. In this section we shall consider their effectiveness. By *effectiveness* is meant the extent to which an impact on the behavior of the unit can be made by the community through its control mechanisms; that is, What impacts on any particular auspices can the community, as its surrounding environment, make in order that the equilibrium-maintaining adaptive behavior of the auspices as a system will bring its behavior more closely in accord with community norms?

The family   In the case of the individual family, there are a number of ways through which such social control is exercised by the community. These correspond to four of the locality-relevant functions. They are typified in the school, the church, the social

224

service agency, and the law. Each of these, by performing its own appropriate function, contributes in its own way to the control function. Thus, the church provides an associational function with strong social-control overtones. The school performs a socialization function, which assists especially in the development of controls that arise from the "internalization" of community norms. The social service agency performs a mutual-support function with strong overtones of influencing behavior toward conformity through a casework process. And the law is that aspect of government that codifies the ultimate coercive social-control authority. These controls, as well as such primary-group controls as gossip, praise and blame, and ostracism, appear to constitute strong pressures toward family conformity to community norms. Yet the community controls operating on the family are diversely distributed, and a practical indication of their ineffectiveness in the case of numerous families is indicated by such conditions as marital conflict, divorce, inadequate child care, and juvenile delinquency.

Neighborhood and ad hoc groups They are formed for special occasions, insofar as they have no formal organization, are controlled largely through the informal controls operating on their individual members. As they acquire formal organization, on the other hand, with the emergence of a neighborhood council or other specific form, they become formal voluntary associations.

Business enterprise Before analyzing the effectiveness of community controls on voluntary associations, there may be some heuristic value in first considering the effectiveness of the community controls on business enterprise. It will be recalled that the principal control mechanism here is the "market." Let us recognize at the outset that other control mechanisms, especially government control through law, are also operative in numerous instances. Even though this last statement is true, and even though the market under modern conditions is in many respects an imperfect control mechanism, the aggregate of individual choices to buy or not to buy at a certain price and quality is an important control medium over the behavior of productive enterprises. Paul and Percival Goodman summed it up succinctly: "Everybody who has a penny can influence society by his choice, and everybody has, in principle, a penny."[5]

The theory of Adam Smith in his *Wealth of Nations* is particularly relevant at this point, for in that great work Smith systematically described how, under certain specified conditions, including

---

a lack of government restraint over economic enterprise, the mechanism of the free market would operate so as to influence economic production to conform with consumer norms, principally through assuring that such behavior would produce the greatest profits. As the Rotarians have summed it up in their optimistic motto: He profits most who serves the best.

The economic literature is replete with documentation to the effect that the basic preconditions that Adam Smith laid down seldom apply in the modern world and that hence various factors operate to vitiate the perfect operation of this control mechanism. Under modern conditions, the measures taken by large-scale enterprise to adjust to market conditions may be highly unsatisfactory to a particular community, yet the types of control that that community can bring to bear may be highly ineffective. How a company can make a profit through selling a product at competitive prices while making other adjustments that are extremely painful to many groups in the community is illustrated by the following letter written to the president of a large steel company many years ago:

May 2, 1949

Dear Sir:

Your annual report for 1948 was called to my attention. In my spare moments, today, I have been giving your 1902-1948 record some cursory study. Frankly, Sir, it has me sick at heart. I happen to believe in the free enterprise system, and not in the purest sense either. I can stand the idea of monopoly and of monopoly competition (imperfect competition, if you prefer). In other words, I abhor the idea of a planned economy. However, I just cannot imagine that the operations of the ——— Steel Company could be considered to be regulated in the public interest by price mechanism. Please consider:

a. In your 47 year history you have found 17 different occasions to lay off workers. On 11 occasions you saw fit to rehire and on 19 occasions you hired new workers.

b. You found 12 occasions to reduce weekly earnings—more than once every four years.

c. You found 16 occasions to reduce your purchases from others.

d. You saw fit to operate your plant at LESS THAN 80 per cent of its capacity in 22 different years.

e. You found 8 occasions to reduce common stockholders' dividends and 9 years in which to give them nothing.

f. You found 19 occasions to reduce "steel products shipped" below the year previous.

g. You saw fit to take a loss in only four years and in not one of these years did you operate at more than 36.4 per cent of capacity.

How can people live their lives when you pass on so much trouble and absorb so little? By the way, the above items are only illustrative.

"At all times it (——— Steel) seeks to further the proper functioning of the whole American economy...." This appeared over your signature. Further you believe, I understand, in the responsibilities of management in the American economy.

Honestly now, Mr. ———, you know and I know that the picture presented above does not show management accepting responsibility that the American public will deem adequate. Indeed, until I analyzed your historical record I would never have believed such a picture of management irresponsibility was possible. Further, whether such a picture is ever presented publicly or not, people are going to feel the real results in their living. Free enterprise can never live in a democracy with such pressures buffeting people.

Please do not forget that the national economic planners have a ready solution—complete with charts and diagrams, also promises. They know all about how to make this world utopia, and they are not bashful about saying so.

I hope you will not misunderstand me, but just what do you have to offer as a solution to the problems your record shows your organization to have caused?

Sincerely,

P.S. Please no "ya ta ta" about impersonal market functioning of the forces of supply and demand. I understand the mechanism of the economy; I would like to find a way to make it work to the satisfaction of the people who, in the last analysis, judge it.[6]

The letter illustrates well a number of basic considerations. The first is that while control over profit enterprise is exercised through the market, the control is over the company's ability to make a profit, and thus it can be expected to make only those types of adaptation that enhance or preserve its profit position. As indicated, if this adaptation means higher prices, or lower productivity, or larger unemployment, the measure will nevertheless be taken in the interest of profits. It is only through responses that endanger profits that market controls by the community become effective. As mentioned earlier, one of the most effective of these responses is the boycott, an "administered" control that is carefully regulated by law, and—on the side of the labor market—the strike.

Another point illustrated is that often the potential control exercised by any single community is virtually meaningless. Thus, the decision of a community not to purchase steel for its new school building from a particular company would not be expected to influence the company's policies. The organized decision of many communities might have such an effect, but this control method is not often exercised. The reason is that there is an alternative method of control where many communities are involved, a type of control not implemented through the market: governmental regulaion. This method has been used more in recent decades as people see more and more that the market is inadequate for providing the necessary controls over industrial behavior.

Controls other than the market are also employed when profit enterprise is seen to go against community norms in other than economic ways. For example, the lively dispute over the quality of television programs indicates the possibility of governmental intervention when the purely commercial goals of selling advertising space and thus operating at a profit lead to program content that is considered inadequate or deleterious in quality. Here, clearly, the question is raised of the relevance of the profit motive as the chief operating control in television programing. Other examples abound. We have now moved into the question of *relevance*, rather than that of effectiveness. This important aspect of control mechanisms deserves direct attention.

The question of *relevance* is: How relevant is the type of control mechanism to the performance of any particular type of auspices? In connection with private profit enterprise, the question is as follows: How relevant are the profit motive and the operation of the market to the performance of the particular function under consideration? The answer to this question is largely a matter of history, of values, of cultural differences. It is entirely possible to provide opportunities for worship and for religious association under commercial auspices, but this approach is shunned in the United States, except at the fringe where the production of religious trinkets and motion-picture "spectaculars" on religious subjects provides a marginal area that is highly controverted. Likewise, formal education is perfectly amenable to commercial

228

auspices but is largely restricted to those of government and voluntary nonprofit associations.

Many of the great arenas in which controversies rage over the relevance of one set of auspices or another are extracommunity arenas. The resolution of the conflicts that take place on the state and national scene inevitably affects communities, but individual communities have little control over their resolution, even within their own specific geographical confines. The locus of choice is elsewhere.

Nevertheless, insofar as the choice between performing a function through private business enterprise and performing it through other auspices does arise at the community level, it becomes largely a question of whether the effort to maximize profits should be considered the principal or exclusive channel through which community controls are brought to bear.

Voluntary nonprofit associations　An alternative to private profit enterprise is the voluntary nonprofit association, as exemplified in the voluntary social welfare agency. It is characteristic of such agencies that their funds come principally through gifts and that these gifts are usually for services rendered to people other than the donors. What control, then, do the people of a community have over such voluntary agencies through their gifts? Let us again examine the question from the standpoint of effectiveness and relevance.

Theoretically, at least, the community exercises powerful control in that in most instances a withholding of its gift giving would mean the demise of the unit. On what basis would such control be exercised? Presumably, insofar as it was brought under rational control it would be administered on the following bases: (1) the extent to which the functions that the agency performs actually are given high value by community people, and (2) the efficiency with which the agency was actually performing its announced functions. Actually, most of the announced functions of social agencies are given a relatively high degree of approval and positive value by the people of American communities. But the extent to which these agencies actually perform these functions is somewhat difficult for community people to ascertain, and the efficiency with which they do so is even more difficult to determine.

For this reason, gift-giving patterns are influenced more by the emotional appeal of the "cause" for which the agency is working or the purpose that it is presumably serving than by the efficiency with which the agencies perform their function. Thus, we approach the question of relevance, but let us delay considering it for a few moments. Efficiency is a matter of the economical employment of means to accomplish stated ends. The machine is most efficient that **229** utilizes the least energy to accomplish a given task. The device is most economically efficient that utilizes the least labor and capital to accomplish a given task. Two things are important: the accomplishment of the task and the efficiency of the auspices. On both of these points the facts for intelligent decisions about voluntary social agencies are usually not available.

The analysis of purpose and efficiency in social service agencies by a British observer has equal cogence for the American scene:

> The structure of society, then, and of segments of society, operates to maintain a humane institution in existence once it is established . . . . Social institutions that are intended to supply recurrent human needs have a peculiar toughness that appears to defy dissolution. *For them to be viable it is not, in fact, necessary for them to be efficient . . . .*

> At this point it is sufficient to note that *it is not merely unnecessary for a humane institution to be efficient for it to remain in existence. It is not even necessary for its personnel to have any clear idea what it is for.*[7]

One institutionalized answer to this problem is the development of community chests and united funds for purposes not only of joint fund raising but also for applying some degree of rational, intermediate control between the donor and the many voluntary agencies of the community. In effect this measure substitutes administered control for that exercised by the supply and demand of voluntary agencies and gifts in the "free market." The complex issues involved in its effectiveness and relevance were given extensive analysis by Seeley and his associates. Only three of the many points they raised will be considered here. The first is that actually the united fund exercises much less rational control over the allocation of gifts through its budgeting system than might be apparent. For:

> We have seen no evidence that the money "will go where it is most needed." Indeed, we have met no one willing to say in advance, and in the abstract or the concrete, where it is "most needed." What seems to occur under most federations, at best, is a freezing of the disequalities or accidents of money- and power-distribution that happen to obtain at the time that federation takes place. The claim that a United Fund can allocate funds to all agencies on a more equitable, rational, and useful basis is thus somewhat dubious.[8]

7. Peter Nokes, "Purpose and Efficiency in Humane Social Institutions," *Human Relations* 13, no. 2 (May 1960): 144-45. Italics in original.

8. John R. Seeley et al., *Community Chest: A Case Study in Philanthropy* (Toronto: University of Toronto Press, 1957), pp. 359-60.

The second is the possibility that the chest may acquire strong controls in its own right and control givers rather than serve their interests. The question is

> whether the Chest ought fundamentally to conceive of itself in relation to the community as an occupying army, levying what it needs while provoking as little rebellion as possible, or whether it ought to conceive itself more on the model of an instrumentality of local desire, registering rather than manipulating public opinion, expressing local forces rather than molding them.[9]

The third point has interesting relevance to our consideration of the varying characteristics of different auspices for the performance of locality-relevant functions. Seeley and his colleagues reported in an Epilogue:

> We have been so often and so forcibly struck—as we have reported—with the confusion of thought, the seeming disorder of procedure, the maladaptation of means to ends, the sudden tacks and turns of policy—like the behaviour of children "arbitrarily" dropping one game for another—within an organization governed primarily by top-notch business people, and the contrast between this and the vocational life of the businessman has been so sharp, that we have been driven to ask at least two more reflective questions: The first question is: "Is this contrast accidental, and if not, what purpose does it serve?" The second is: "*Can* such an organization be otherwise operated?"[10]

This observation is particularly relevant to our analysis of alternnative auspies. In the first plce, the behavior of business people in policy-making positions on profit-making boards may be markedly different from the behavior of these same people on the board of such a nonprofit association as a community chest. This variation suggests that the behavior of individuals in analogous positions in different auspices may be a fruitful line for such analysis as we have given other variables in the preceding pages.

In the second place, here is a type of group that is designed to apply the principle of rational-bureaucratic organization to a pattern of gift giving and gift distribution that otherwise would be left to the free operation of the "gift market." But the authors observed in the above quotation that it does not work out that way. Why do essentially the same people operate rationally and efficiently within one type of auspices but not within another?

---

9. Seeley et al., *Community Chest*, p. 401.

10. Seeley et al., *Community Chest*, p. 435. **231**

The authors answered this question by offering the hypothesis that activity on such an agency board offers people in business "a kind of *relief* to their everyday occupations in much the same manner as play serves as a relief from work." Their business participation is characterized by such things as "an unusual amount of attention to detail, foresight, tolerance of the 'human factor,' self-control," and so on, while participation in welfare agencies permits "innovation, invention, freewheeling imagination . . . , the elaboration of plans without any proximate check on their success or responsibility for their failure, and, in general, generous allowance for spontaneity, color, romance and even, upon occasion, some permissible clowning."[11]

Perhaps an alternative explanation, on a somewhat different level, might be offered in terms of the characteristics of community units, described in the previous chapter, of being strongly organized systemically along the vertical axis of task performance and relation to extracommunity systems, but weakly organized along the horizontal axis of their relation to other units of the same or of different types within the community. The community chest is an attempt to impose a rational-bureaucratic coordination *across* community agencies, to coordinate activities whose strongest orientation is toward task accomplishment within their own segmentalized field of activities. We shall examine the reasons for the relative strength of the vertical orientation of community units and the relative weakness of their horizontal orientation in the next two chapters. It will be recalled that the "great change" included a movement in the direction of making this discrepancy greater with time. Thus, the need for adaptive measures in order to "correct" these centrifugal forces through setting up a deliberate, planned coordinating system becomes increasingly pressing if the minimal systemic relationship among units on the local level is to be maintained—if a community as an identifiable social system is to exist at all. But the attempt to "plan" and "administer" such coordination through deliberate rational effort involves great difficulties. Such attempts will be examined in detail in chapter 10.

Returning to the matter of effectiveness of the gift-giving pattern as a community control over voluntary service agencies, we have noted its potential effectiveness but have also indicated the difficulty of acquiring an adequate basis on which to judge whether or not the agency is actually performing its announced functions and whether it is performing them efficiently. The result of this difficulty is a tendency for gift giving to be based almost exclusively on such extraneous factors as the pressure of friends, neighbors, or other individ-

11. Seeley et al., *Community Chest*, pp. 435-36.

uals or groups in extracting money from the individual for one cause or another and the emotional appeal of these respective causes.

But one might ask whether a method of community control that is based largely on emotional appeal and ignorance of what the donee agencies are actually doing is sufficiently *relevant* to be satisfactory. Is the ability of an agency to extract gifts directly from donors or through the budgeting procedures of the community chest a relevant mechanism for control by the community over its voluntary agencies?

Related to this question is a growing development of research activities that are making it increasingly possible to assess the extent to which agencies are actually performing their purported functions. Such research focuses essentially on two questions: first, Does the agency actually reach the clientele at whom it is supposedly aimed? For example, does the "delinquency-prevention" recreational program actually reach those groups of children with the highest delinquency potential? The second question is somewhat more difficult to answer but is equally important: What impact does the agency have on the clientele it reaches?; that is, Does its program have any measurable positive effect that can justly be attributed to the program rather than to extraneous factors?

Such research is highly important, for it provides, in a way, an analogue to the operation of the "free market" on individual entrepreneurs in the profit system. If they are sufficiently inefficient, or if the functions they perform do not have high enough value in the eyes of potential customers, they may be forced out of business. Without careful evaluational research, however, the agency's response in the analogous situation may simply be "Give us more money, for the problem is even greater than we thought!"

Government A still different set of conditions applies where locality-relevant functions are performed by government. Let us consider some aspects of the effectiveness and relevance of the vote as a method for exerting community controls over this type of auspices. The effectiveness of the vote as a control mechanism, particularly in local government, would appear to be high, for if the elected officials do not carry out the wishes of local people, they can be replaced through the ballot. Two factors complicate this ready solution. The first is appointive positions, and the second is bureaucracy.

The use of the vote as a control mechanism over the various agencies of government is complicated by the fact that local government engages in many different types of activities, yet individual voters are not able to vote approval or disapproval on each of these **233** activities. They simply vote on their estimation of the aggregate performance of the regime as it compares with what they consider might be the performance of the rival candidates. Thus, the vote does not allow individuals to discriminate between those aspects of an elected official's activities of which they approve and those of which they disapprove. It is "all or nothing" for the individual candidate.

Closely related to this "global" nature of the voters' approval or disapproval is the fact that many of the officials of local government may be appointed rather than elected. And since the vote can register approval or disapproval of such appointments only as part of the aggregate performance of the incumbent official, little discrimination is provided for the voter to indicate a reaction to any particular appointed official. Thus, although the vote may constitute a potentially effective channel of community control over local government, its discriminating ability is low. It is an all-or-none type of control. Largely for this reason, lobbies have arisen as methods of "administering" the expression of opinion by various interest groups on specific issues.

A related question is the extent to which it is deemed wise to place local governmental activities under the direct decision-making power of the electorate. While such a course enhances the discriminatory potential of the vote as a control instrument, it raises grave questions of relevance. Should the electorate determine through direct vote teachers' salaries, whether or not to fluoridate the water, or what kind of architectural design shall be used in the operating room of the municipal hospital? Certainly, experience with fluoridation plebiscites has indicated that where such technical matters are opened to direct decision by the electorate, the issue comes to be determined on a relatively low level of rationality and a high level of emotionalism. In any case, the broad extension of decision-making to the direct vote of the electorate would make a shambles of local government and prevent the development of long-range policies with any degree of consistency.

On the other hand, it is one of the problems of contemporary civilization that delegated governmental authority, through appointed bureaucracies, can become extremely insensitive to the wishes of the electorate, even to the extent of defeating or debilitating the efforts of newly elected officials who presumably have a "mandate" to change things. For the understandable attempt to keep administrative and technical matters free of the waxing and waning of political party fortunes by immunizing such governmental positions from the effects of the vote has tended to give these positions a large measure of autonomy. Theoretically, new legislation is capable of changing important policies and programs as well as the structure of government departments and special agencies, but such changes seldom reduce the basic problem.

What Selznick wrote about bureaucracy is not necessarily confined to bureaucracies of the governmental type, but it certainly applies to them:

> Running an organization, as a specialized and essential activity, generates problems which have no necessary (and often an opposed) relationship to the professed or "original" goals of the organization. The day-to-day behavior of the group becomes centered around specific problems and proximate goals which have primarily an internal relevance. Then, since these activities come to consume an increasing proportion of the time and thoughts of the participants, they are—from the point of view of actual behavior—*substituted* for the professed goals.[12]

Another type of control operating on appointed administrators or technical experts in the governmental bureaucratic structure is that exerted by their professional groups, with which they may identify more strongly than with the local community. This statement would seem to apply rather broadly, whether one thinks of school or college teachers, city managers, engineers, city planners, or others. One might hypothesize that the degree of professionalization of a particular office is a measure of the degree to which the incumbent may be controlled by such extracommunity professional reference groups. In any case, such control to the extent that it exists, coupled with the control over the bureaucrat's behavior caused by the necessity of keeping the organization in operation, regardless of its goal performance, constitutes a limiting factor on the ability of community people to control local governmental departments and agencies through the exercise of the vote.

But aside from the effectiveness of the vote, what is its relevance? How appropriate is the use of the vote as a means of controlling the activities of local government?

The answer to this question would seem to lie in the area of the relationship between the vote-getting ability of the individual candidate or the political party and his or her ability to carry out legislative policy-making or execute administrational activities in a manner satisfactory to the electorate. The relationship would logically seem a close one and the means of control highly relevant. The situation is somewhat clouded, however, by the fact that other relatively extraneous factors are known to play a minor or major role in

12. Philip Selznick, "An Approach to a Theory of Bureaucracy," *American Sociological Review* 8, no. 1 (February 1943): 48.

235

voting behavior. These include the "stickiness" caused by habitual "straight-ticket" voters who voluntarily renounce their potential for using the vote to register their appraisal of the quality of the elected officials (though they may still influence this quality in the primaries); the popularity and "appeal" of one particular candidate aside from the issues involved—individual "charisma"; the reflected glory or disrepute of the candidates with whom an individual is associated on the party ticket; and the effects of "personal influence" of one's friends and acquaintances upon one's voting behavior, aside from the logic of the issues involved.[13]

Essentially, as suggested earlier, both the effectiveness and the relevance of voting as a means of controlling governmental departments or agencies in their performance of locality-relevant functions are limited on the one hand by the extreme of close sensitivity to popular control, which often means vulnerability of largely nonpolitical issues to political party manipulation, and on the other by the extreme of relative immunity from the exigencies of political elections, which often means the development of a relatively autonomous bureaucracy, which may be highly insensitive to local wishes.

Some Implications

Thus, each type of auspices has its own type of amenability to local controls, and each of these, in turn, involves its own set of advantages and disadvantages. It is somewhat surprising that so little deliberate attention has been given by students of the community to the comparative merits of these various auspices for the allocation of different types of locality-relevant functions.[14]

There is no adequate body of systematic studies and conceptualization in the matter of alternative auspices. As a result, considerable confusion is often caused in local appraisals by the application of types of evaluative measures to the performance of one set of auspices that are appropriate only to a different set. Perhaps the most frequent instance of this misapplication of evaluative criteria is the use of a profit-and-loss type of reckoning in activities for which this is largely inappropriate.

The jibe of the scoffing neighbor who asks the home gardener, "If you counted in your labor, do you know how much these tomatoes would cost you a pound?" illustrates this type of anomaly when

13. See Elihu Katz and Paul F. Lazarsfeld, *Personal Influence: The Part Played by People in the Flow of Mass Communications* (Glencoe, Ill.: Free Press, 1955).

14. There are some exceptions, however. See, for example, Ray H. Elling and Sandor Halebsky, "Organizational Differentiation and Support: A Conceptual Framework," *Administrative Science Quarterly*, vol. 6, no. 2 (September 1961).

it is applied on the level of the family. For on the one hand, there are other satisfactions to be gained from home gardening than simply that of a thrifty disposition of time, resources, and labor. As the home gardener would undoubtedly reply, "They taste better." This would be a way of pointing out that exercise, pride in having "grown one's own," and a number of other satisfactions are to be reckoned in. Should one reckon in the hours spent as part of the "cost" of growing the tomatoes? Yes, if one is trying to compare alternative labor costs; no, if one looks at it as a leisure-time pursuit.

Yet it is apparent that do-it-yourself activities of the family, like various neighborhood activities, have an economic aspect that in one sense brings them into the "market" picture and makes them comparable to similar activities performed under different auspices. The neighbors who cleared and graded an empty lot for a ball field could have hired a construction company to do it. Perhaps the most important aspect of this alternative is that had they done so, they could have estimated fairly carefully how much it would cost, and they could have found a market in which different contractors would bid competitively.

Thus, many activities lend themselves to a type of market analysis, even though this analysis does not fit the entire operation. Likewise, government offices and voluntary associations must keep accounts, disburse funds, hire personnel, make purchases, and in other ways act as part of the market system. Yet their very functions are almost by definition those that someone has decided, no matter how deliberately or unconsciously, are more appropriately performed by these rather than by profit auspices. Presumably, the rationale for such decisions lies in the assumption that these functions have other aspects that should be included and that might be inappropriate or even neglected if performed for a profit. As a result, cost figures, while in part relevant, are not in themselves the most important consideration. This point has been made with regard to mental hospitals:

> But our hospitals use up money rather than make a profit, and it is as absurd for us to evaluate our efforts in dollars as it would be for a reducing salon to evaluate itself in terms of tons of flesh dissipated during the year instead of in terms of profit.

> In evaluating a mental hospital from the point of view of the larger society, we must measure how well it keeps people who have been deviant away from the rest of society. We must gauge the value of the hospital in terms of how much it assists the society to function efficiently. But from the point of view of people in the hospital, evaluation is in terms of how to bring about growth and change in patients. This is of interest to the

237

community because we are a humanitarian people, but it is not a serious matter like keeping the deviant isolated.

Because we are in a business dominated society, the community is likely to evaluate the hospital in terms of the cost of patient care. Unfortunately, this doesn't measure either of the integrating functions that the hospital plays—protecting society and treating patients.[15]

Turning to still another type of auspices, it is interesting to note that the consumer cooperative movement is founded on the assumption that consumer outlets should provide other functions than solely the selling of consumer goods for a profit. The educational and associational values of retail outlets are given special emphasis in this type of voluntary auspices, as is the principle that profits should be distributed to customers, and that customers, through share-holding, should have a voice in policy-making.

In still a different field, that of certain public health educational, demonstrational, and research activities, most American communities have opted to allot a considerable role to voluntary health associations in the performance of these functions. On the other hand, public health officials in Germany, while somewhat impressed by this extensive voluntary activity in American communities, raised the question with the author of whether it would be much more efficient and much more economical to have these functions performed exclusively by the tax-supported governmental health departments. The question raises an important alternative. The decision, if rational, must lie in carefully formulating what the objectives are and then choosing that set of auspices that most closely approximates them.

But enough has been said to indicate that:

1. Various types of functions can be performed by different types of community auspices.

2. According to which auspices performs them, source of funds, formal locus of decision-making, ultimate authority, and community controls over the performance of the function will differ.

3. In the absence of other clearly defined and measurable criteria, the ability to make a profit or the ability to perform a function at low financial cost tends to become the sole criterion for evaluating the efficiency of the operation, regardless of which auspices performs the function.

15. John Cumming, "Values and Evaluative Research," in *Social Research in Health and Welfare Agencies: Proceedings of An Invitational Conference on "Social Research in the Development of Health and Welfare Agency Programs"* (New York: State Charities Aid Association, 1961).

4. Thus, community controls over the performance of locality-relevant functions are made difficult by the absence of adequate standards of evaluation or by the application of profit or cost criteria to functions where such criteria are not relevant.

5. The rational relegation of functions to various alternative community auspices depends on the further development of methods of analyzing the implications of such relegation.

8 The Community's Vertical Pattern: Ties to the Larger Society and Culture

In preceding chapters we emphasized the increasing importance of the relation of American communities to the larger society surrounding them. We saw that such ties are multiplying and strengthening to the extent that it is questionable whether the ties of community units to each other on the local level are sufficiently strong and meaningful for them to constitute a localized social system called the community. Chapter 5, which dealt with the extent to which the community could properly be considered a significant social system, also showed that local units have two rather distinct types of systemic ties: the relationships through which they are oriented to the larger society beyond the community constitute the community's vertical pattern, and those that local units share with each other on the local level constitute the community's horizontal pattern.

In the present and following chapters we direct ourselves to an analysis of these vertical and horizontal patterns. In the process, particularly in this chapter, we shall be taking on a major and somewhat ambitious analytical task. We shall try to develop a set of analytical tools with which we can explore the relations of what seem, at least, to be extremely diverse local units to their respective extracommunity systems. Can we in essentially the same manner relate such diverse local units as supermarkets, branch banks, branch factories, labor unions, churches, schools, voluntary associations, and local offices of state or federal governmental units to their respective extracommunity systems? Different as such local units may be, are they sufficiently similar in their respective extracommunity systemic ties so that it is possible to describe and analyze these ties with the same set of concepts? Is there, in other words, a discernible set of relationships to extracommunity systems that is sufficiently general to be called a pattern, that which we have alluded to as the community's vertical pattern of organization?

This chapter answers these questions in the affirmative and attempts to provide such a set of analytical concepts and to apply it to these extracommunity ties. It would be better if there were more analytical material available in the literature of the community to build on, but unfortunately, the growing recognition of the importance of extracommunity ties has not been accompanied by a commensurate development of research on the nature of such ties or of conceptual tools for analyzing them. As a result, the exploration of the relationship between community and larger society has been largely confined to two extremely simple and inadequate models.

The first model considers each community, along with other similar communities, as part of a larger geographic unit. Often, this larger unit is considered as somehow representing a larger community, to which the other smaller communities are ancillary and in many respects subordinate and dependent. Such a model gives rudimentary recognition to the fact that cultural areas extend beyond communities and that many communities are related to other larger communities in specific ways.

The second model is slightly more complex. It is an extension of the model given above, but with greater specification of the kinds of dependency and subordination that relate the smaller community to the larger, more complex one. It not only specifies the types of service for which the small community is dependent on the larger one, but it recognizes a number of different levels of such dependency, according to the size and complexity of the larger community involved in the relationship. Examples of such types of specific relationships are the relation of retailers to wholesale establishments in a larger community, the relation of physicians to local hospitals and of local hospitals to regional health centers, and so on. Thus, this second model has the advantage of specifying the nature of the dependent relationship of the smaller community to the larger one. Actually, the relationship is one not so much of unilateral dependence as of symbiotic interdependence between the smaller communities and the larger one, but the ways in which the larger community depends on the smaller ones are not usually given an equal emphasis.

241

What both these models have in common is the implicit assumption that the larger society is somehow extraneous to the community and that the community is related to the larger society through its relationship to a larger community whose service area includes the community in question. This assumption ignores the basic fact that aside from communities there is no "larger society." We cannot therefore logically treat the "larger society" as if it were an extracommunity phenomenon, even though it may be largely independent of any particular community.

Hence, although it has been recognized that every community is a part of the larger society, it has not been equally emphasized that the larger society is a part of every community. This statement is more than a play on words. A clear recognition of the way institutions of the larger society are "built into" every community and behavior patterns of the larger society are enacted in every community will make possible a somewhat different model of the relationship of community to larger society. It makes possible a realization that the larger society need not be "related" by the investigator to the local community, for it is already there. It is there in local cultural patterns, such as family living norms and behavior patterns that are local embodiments or enactments of parts of the culture of the larger society; and it is there in the form of social systems, such as churches, businesses, and governmental units, which are intimately related in a systemic manner to larger social systems that extend across numerous communities. Redfield, an astute observer of community phenomena in less complex societies, was specifically aware of the presence of the larger society even in his relatively simple Maya village:

> I recall the presence in Chan Kom of a school established for the people through decisions and policies with which the people had little to do. I recall the organization of villagers, brought about by townsmen, expected to vote the straight Revolutionary party ticket. I still wonder how to express, in words or perhaps in a diagram, the criminal hearing I observed in the village on an occasion when certain Indians were charged with killing cattle that had broken into their cornfields. Local people conducted the hearing, but a messenger had been sent off to tell the authorities of the city of the event, and while the investigation was taking place in the village the local officers who conducted it kept discussing among themselves what would be the attitude and action of the official from the city on the matters that they were at that moment concerned with. I cannot forget the long efforts of the Chan Kom villagers to persuade the national government to give them formal title to their communal lands, or the endless discussions over the merits of the school or about the trustworthiness of those strange people, the

American archeologists, who were doing something mysterious in the ruined stone buildings of the ancients. All these things are a part of the life of such a little community. They happen right in the village, yet they are somehow outside of it. How shall we deal with the relative outsideness of these things that happen in the village?[1]

Vertical and Horizontal Patterns

At this point, our analysis of the systemic aspects of American communities may provide us with a set of useful conceptual tools. In that analysis, the concepts of vertical pattern and horizontal pattern were developed. A community's vertical pattern was defined as the structural and functional relation of its various social units and subsystems to extracommunity systems. Its horizontal pattern was defined as the structural and functional relation of the community's various social units and subsystems to each other. These terms were then shown to be related to, but not identical with, Homans's concepts of the external and internal systems and to the task functions and maintenance functions (or instrumental and expressive functions) of small-group theory. It may now be helpful to relate them to a distinction made by Redfield in considering the problem he posed in the above quotation. Later in his analysis, Redfield observed:

> I prefer to begin with this statement: "In every isolated little community there is civilization; in every city there is the folk society . . . ." For in Chan Kom or Middletown, the early and primitive society and the secular, civilized, urbanized society that might be fully conceived or defined, are both present in important degree and in an interpenetration that demands analysis . . . .

> But if we think of Plainville or Middletown as an interpenetration of two opposite kinds of living, thinking, and feeling, as analyzable, as if we saw in Plainville or Middletown first an isolated, homogeneous, sacred, and personal community of kinsmen, and then as if we saw in it the heterogeneous, secular, and impersonal community that we find approximated in cities, we will find ourselves defining the community not in terms of space but in terms of a position relative to two kinds of human collective living, as just this local and particular arrangement of aspects of the one in relation to aspects of the other.[2]

1. Robert Redfield, *The Little Community: Viewpoints for the Study of a Human Whole*, pp. 129-30. Copyright 1955 by The University of Chicago Press, Chicago, Ill.
2. *Little Community*, pp. 146, 147.

Here, again, there is a rough correspondence between the vertical pattern and Redfield's urban component of community living, between the horizontal pattern and Redfield's folk component. Redfield's distinction fortunately permits us to recognize that a community does not consist of a number of units, some of which can be classified as vertical and some as horizontal, but rather that each of a community's units typically has both vertical and horizontal aspects. It is true that some types of unit have a stronger vertical component (the branch plant of a national manufacturing company) and that others have a stronger horizontal component (a community welfare council). It may likewise be true that some individuals (Merton's "cosmopolitan influentials") are more strongly oriented vertically in their community participation, while other individuals ("local influentials") are more strongly oriented horizontally.[3] But the attempt to identify a community's vertical units and its horizontal units is misleading. It is not the units that constitute the vertical or horizontal pattern; it is the vertical or horizontal aspects of the units—their relation, respectively, to extracommunity systems and to each other—that constitute it.

Thus, we can say that the clubs, unions, businesses, governmental units, churches, and other institutions of the local community have two sets of relationships, which can be separately analyzed and whose characteristics are rather different. As we shall see, these two orders of relationships not only permeate community institutions but also characterize the established social roles within the community's organizational structure.

Most models of the community's relation to a larger region consider communities as units, relating them in their entirety to other communities in the region. Whether or not this type of analysis was adequate for preindustrial communities, it offers little help in analyzing contemporary American communities, for the relatively differentiated parts that constitute the contemporary American community are related increasingly to the outside world not so much as parts of the local community but as parts of a specialized extracommunity system to which they belong. Putting this another way, the important contemporary link between the community and the outside world is not an undifferentiated link between the community as such and other communities of the surrounding region, but it is the link between the highly differentiated parts of the community and their respective extracommunity systems. These systemic links relate

3. See Robert K. Merton, "Patterns of Influence: A Study of Interpersonal Influence and of Communications Behavior in a Local Community," in Paul F. Lazarsfeld and Frank N. Stanton, *Communications Research 1948-1949* (New York: Harper & Brothers, 1949).

the different parts of the community to many extracommunity units covering widely divergent geographic regions and often with widely diverse location of system headquarters.

What gives this highly varied pattern of extracommunity relationships particular cogency are two related facts. One is that, generally speaking, these vertical ties are stronger than the horizontal ties among units of any single community. The second fact is that the "great change" continuously operates to strengthen these vertical ties and to establish new ties between community units and extracommunity systems.

An important characteristic of the vertical pattern is the rational, planned, bureaucratically structured nature of the extracommunity ties. The ties between supermarket and regional headquarters, between branch plant and national office, between school and state education department, between municipal government and state government, between the local office and the main office of a state or federal governmental unit, between voluntary association and state or national headquarters, between union local and union national, between church and denominational board—such ties are clearly defined through contract, charter, legislation, or administrative promulgations. They are structured along bureaucratic administrative lines, and the relation of the local unit to the extracommunity system is usually clearly prescribed in terms of the overall objectives and operating procedures of that system. The particular form of the relationship to the larger system is not left to chance: in Sumner's terms not "crescive" but "enacted." Consequently, the local community unit is an integral part of a rationally ordered, bureaucratically administered extracommunity system. Having said this, let us acknowledge that this description is not absolute, but relative, and that some types of extracommunity systemic ties are less deliberate, less planned, and less bureaucratic than others. Nevertheless, by contrast with the horizontal ties *among* diverse local community units, the vertical ties are toward the planned, rational, bureaucratic extreme.

Thus, the "great change" brings with it a situation in which increasingly differentiated community units are coming to be related more integrally to extracommunity systems in ways that set up quite different norms, behavior patterns, and role expectations than those involved in the interrelation of these diverse units on the local level. Their interrelation on the local level, the community's horizontal pattern, is characterized not so much by bureaucratic structure and administration as by the symbiotic relationships associated with their geographic propinquity, not so much by "administered" decisions within a rationally organized structure as by the "market" decisions of individual units operating on the community level. Under these circumstances, a useful function is performed by the informal "power structures," within which mutual convergences of interest among community-based units can be recognized and points of possible friction can be worked out with some sense of their local relevance. These and other aspects of the community's horizontal pattern will be considered in the following chapter.

There is a clear, though not perfect, correspondence between the community's vertical pattern and the performance of task functions and the horizontal pattern and the performance of maintenance functions. It will be recalled that both types of functions are essential to a social system, the one having to do with getting the things done that have to be done in order for the system to survive, the other having to do with maintaining the system itself as a viable entity.

Locality-relevant task functions were considered extensively in chapter 6. A review of these functions will indicate their strong vertical relevance, for the matter of economic production, distribution, and consumption and the performance of the various tasks associated with socialization, social control, social participation, and mutual support all involve working through such units as business companies, schools, governments, churches, and voluntary associations, usually with strong ties to extracommunity systems of which they are an integral part. In all these types of institutions the function of the headquarters "field staff" or its counterpart is characteristically that of working with the respective local units in a relationship within which the local units are encouraged or admonished or coerced to adapt themselves structurally and functionally to the tasks whose performance is the goal of the larger system. This relationship may vary from autocratic and coercive to democratic and permissive. No matter which, it is part of the role expectations of the field staff that they will be able to show a reasonable measure of success in achieving the conformity of the local unit to the purposes and procedural patterns of the larger system, again whether this is a church, a school, a welfare department, a voluntary association, a supermarket, a union, a factory, or some other unit.

At the same time, there is a growing appreciation among widely varied types of extracommunity systems that the relationship of the local unit to the rest of the local community is important. The development of community relations departments and community relations consultants in various fields is indicative of the stress placed on local community relationships by extracommunity systems of different types.

Yet anyone familiar with the field and with community consultants in health, welfare, industrial, religious, or other areas will agree that these large systems, on their part, are caught up in the same dilemma as the local community units: The values, goals, norms, and behavior patterns of the vertical pattern and of the horizontal pattern do not coincide, and where they differ, a decision must be made of which to follow. Many individuals in linkage positions are caught up in this dilemma, and we shall consider such positions shortly. Most extracommunity systems of which I am aware have resolved this problem in some combination of the following two ways (both of which opt in favor of the extracommunity system): Either the community-focused interest and activity are fairly deliberately a "public relations" attempt to achieve good will in the community while still keeping the local unit's program closely related to national program goals or the community consultant staff find themselves a rather diffuse and peripheral part of the national system, occasionally able to accomplish a minor program accommodation but seldom having a strong voice in the administrative bureaucracy, which is, in contrast, deliberately and rationally task-oriented in terms of the larger system's objectives.

Structural Relationships

Now that we have concluded a preliminary analysis of the community's vertical pattern of social organization, we turn to an analysis of some of the specific aspects of the relationship of community units to extracommunity systems.[4]

Local units often have different structural relationships to their respective extracommunity systems, and one may note several dimensions on which such structural differences range. Typically, the larger system consists of several units, located in various communities. One dimension of the relationship has to do with the *geographic area* within or for which the local unit is supposed to perform its function. A local church or chain store has its service or trade area, as does the local school. On the other hand, a local warehouse may provide service to the system's retail units in a number of different communities; a local plant may provide the total supply of its particular product for the national manufacturing company.

A second dimension of the relationship has to do with *flow of authority*, whether to or from the local unit. Authority, in the Weberian sense of power exercised in the name of an institution,[5] is usually fairly easy to ascertain on the basis of charter, contract, legis-

---

4. An unpublished doctoral thesis by Yitzchak Brick explores some important dimensions of the vertical patterns of relationships. See Yitzchak Brick, "The Relation of Vertical Ties to Community Competence," unpublished Ph.D. thesis, Brandeis University (Waltham, Mass., 1975).

5. See *From Max Weber: Essays in Sociology*, trans. and ed. H. H. Gerth and C. Wright Mills (New York: Oxford University Press, 1946), pp. 294-95.

lation, or promulgation. The exercise of power that is not legitimated in the formal institutional structure is more difficult to investigate, however. Let us therefore confine ourselves at present to the exercise of formal, legitimated authority, and the direction of its flow.

There are two relatively simple models of the flow of authority among units of a system in which one or more of the units stands in a special coordinative relationship to the others. The first involves the flow of authority downward from the geographically or functionally more inclusive unit. Such downward flow is illustrated by the authority of a bishop with respect to the individual churches included in the many communities of his diocese, or the authority of a national corporation whose branch offices are not decentralized administratively.

In smaller communities the extracommunity ties of community units will usually be those of subordination to the policies and administrative procedures of the regional or national "headquarters" unit. In larger communities, the likelihood increases that in the case of at least some of the extracommunity systems the central, authoritative unit will be located within the community, with ties of authority running downward to the subordinate units of other communities. In such circumstances, one might assume that the specific community that includes the "headquarters" unit would have control over the various units in other communities. Such an assumption is not warranted, however, for the important relationship is not from community to community but from system unit to system unit. Large bureaucratic organizations constitute social systems with their own identity and with decision-making apparatus that may have little relevance to any specific community, even including the community where their headquarters may happen to be located.

The second model is one in which authority flows upward to the central office from relatively autonomous units organized in a type of loose federation. In such systems the tie of a local unit to the extracommunity system does not involve formal subordination to the regional or national system. The relationship is ideally one of receiving service from a central office, rather than of being subordinate to it. Examples of this type of system are the organization of the Baptists and the Quakers, with their strong emphasis on the autonomy of the local worshipping unit; or certain consumers' cooperative organizations, whose regional wholesale functions provide an optional service to the locals and are under the control of the locals; or individual community chests or united funds, which are virtually autonomous but receive various services and program aids from their national organization.

248

Two considerations, however, blur this easy distinction between the models in the flow of authority. The first is that where several units are involved in basic policy determination, no single unit can retain complete control over the headquarters' policies. In this situation, the fact that control over a system lies in the hands of various local units does not assure or even permit control to lie exclusively in the hands of each specific local unit. Thus, even where local units are the ultimate source of authority, control over the system's policies by any single community is usually impossible. Nevertheless, some extracommunity systems permit the specific local unit to have virtual control at least over its own activities, and it may be free to accept or reject the proposed policies or program suggestions of the system's headquarters.

We have already alluded to the second consideration. Power over the local unit may be exercised not only as the legitimated authority inherent in the express nature of the unit's relationship to the system headquarters but also in ways for which there is no express institutional authorization, as in the situation that Harrison reported in his study of the American Baptist Convention:

> The Baptist denominational executives are given responsibility and limited power, but no legitimate authority. In order to overcome the lack of official status, they seek more power and when they are successful in this enterprise they seek authority. Relatively speaking, it has not been difficult for them to acquire the power necessary for the achievement of their assigned tasks. This has been accomplished by means of an unanticipated formation of an informal system of inter-personal and inter-group relations which bypasses the formal rules of order .... It is this system of informal power as contrasted with the system of formal authority which plays a necessarily prominent role in Baptist organizational life.[6]

Functions of Local Units and System Headquarters

We turn next to the functions that the local unit and the total extracommunity system are supposed to perform with respect to one another; and since the functions of the total extracommunity system are usually coordinated in a headquarters type of arrangement, we shall focus our analysis on the respective functions of the local unit and of the system's headquarters. Of course, some types of local units but not others might perform several of these functions. Nev-

---

6. Paul M. Harrison, *Authority and Power in the Free Church Tradition: A Social Case Study of the American Baptist Convention*, pp. 62, 70. Copyright 1959 by Princeton University Press, Princeton, N.J.

ertheless, let us see if we can cover the field at least crudely with an economy of types of function.

Beginning with the locally-based unit, we can identify four main types of functions in relation to the system's headquarters.

1. *To Make a Product or Provide a Raw Material That Is Fed into the Extracommunity System.* One immediately thinks of a manufactured product, to be distributed nationally, let us say, by the system's headquarters. This is the principal function of many local manufacturing plants that are branches of large companies. But let us consider this possibility more imaginatively. We could also include in this category the principal function of a military training camp located in ·or near the community, whose relation to its system would be that of processing raw recruits and making them available for distribution by the system headquarters (Department of Defense). Again, the product may be a subpart that is then assembled, along with subparts from other community-based units, into a finished product. Or the local unit may simply gather and ship a raw material such as ore, coal, or wood to other units of the system for further processing.

2. *To Provide a Local Service as a Local Outlet of the Extracommunity System.* Actually, this relationship covers a wide range of extracommunity functional ties. Thus, fraternal organizations, social agencies, community chests, schools, churches, and various local governmental units typically provide some kind of service to local people in relation to an extracommunity system of which they are an integral part. As indicated earlier, they may be relatively autonomous as system units, like the local family service agency in its relation to the Family Service Association of America, or certain types of local churches. At the other extreme, they may have little local autonomy, existing only because they are "chartered" by the system headquarters and being under clearly defined policy and administrative jurisdiction of the headquarters. Examples approaching this extreme are some of the local Protestant and the Roman Catholic churches, the local branches of some of the national health associations, and the local offices of such state and national governmental units as the state health department, the state employment service, and the federal Bureau of Old Age and Survivors Insurance.

3. *To Sell the Products of the System Locally.* This category includes local supermarkets and local distributing outlets of national companies. But it also includes two other types of functions, both vaguely indicated by the purposely ambiguous word *sell.* Perhaps the word *persuasion* better describes one of these functions, for often a function of a local unit is to persuade local people to think or act differently in accordance with the program objectives of the extracommunity system. In this sense, the program has to be "sold," as in the case of education by the local cancer unit for early diagnosis of

cancer or the case of greater civic consciousness by the League of Women Voters.

The other function is "selling" as the concept is extended to include fund raising where at least a share of the local unit's income from it is passed along to the system headquarters. This function applies not only in cases where virtually the sole purpose for the existence of the local unit is fund raising for the system headquarters but also in the case of relatively autonomous, multifunction units such as local united funds or specific types of social agencies that belong to such a federation as the National Federation of Settlements. In the case of such units, however, the fund-contributing function in relation to the system headquarters may be small in comparison with the service functions performed locally.

4. *To Participate in the Extracommunity System's Decision-Making Process.* The typical formal pattern for such participation is provision for representation of local units in the policy-making boards and committees of the extracommunity system. In large national associations with a large membership body, such structured provision for representation is often highly complex, and the sensitivity of the system headquarters to any particular local unit is bounded by the factors of *delegation, relevance, and prerogative* described on pages 217-218. Many types of extracommunity systems do not make explicit provision for such representation of local units in policy-making.

These four functions appear to constitute at least a rough outline under which the functions of local units in their relation to extracommunity systems can be largely if not entirely subsumed. Corresponding to these functions, or, more precisely, systemically related to them, are a set of functions at the other end of the extracommunity tie, those that the system (here treated as the system headquarters) is supposed to perform with respect to its local units. Recognizing, again, that these functions must be interpreted broadly if they are to encompass the great diversity of different types of systems with community-based units and recognizing that the functions are neither mutually exclusive nor ascribable individually to every type of extracommunity system, we can nevertheless subsume most of the functions under four main headings.

1. *To Provide a System Product to System Units for Utilization or Local Distribution by Them.* The product may be a tangible thing such as an automobile or a suite of bedroom furniture; it may be much less tangible, like insurance or advertising; or it may consist of goods or services not ordinarily thought of as industrial or commercial commodities, such as the national bargaining power and procedures of a union national, the lobbying activities of a trade or professional association, or the educational materials provided by a national

organization of social agencies. It is such "products" of the system that local units "sell," receiving in exchange payments, dues, gifts, taxes, and so on.

2. *To Provide Formal Structure, Administrative Direction, and Coordinative and Other Services to the System Units.* Local units that perform similar functions may need only certain minimal coordinative services from the system headquarters. On the other hand, such units may be coordinated under authoritative hierarchical control. Local units performing different functions that are systemically related, typically require considerably more administrative direction from the system headquarters, in order that the interdependent parts of the system may operate smoothly in the performance of the system's tasks.

3. *To Provide Other Services to the System Units.* Depending upon the type of system, these may include providing field staff for consultation on the units' operating procedures, providing training opportunities for employed or volunteer personnel, preparing and distributing instructional literature for the personnel of local units, providing national advertising or other publicity campaigns that will create a favorable climate for the local unit to "sell" the system's products, and so on.

4. *To Provide Services Outside the System.* This function is closely related to the first function of providing a product for distribution. The distinction between these two related functions is between distribution of the service, or "product," by local units and distribution by the system headquarters. Thus, the headquarters may offer a consulting service to nonsystem units, as in the case of a national voluntary agency offering such services to a governmental unit, or may conduct a national publicity campaign designed to educate the public in some broad matter of general welfare, such as health, safety, and so on.

We have thus explored some of the chief aspects of the functional interrelationships of local units and extracommunity systems. In their various combinations, they may constitute a relationship in which broad powers of decision-making are exercised by the local unit or in which, at the other extreme, few such powers are exercised by the local unit. The latter thus constitutes a branch office of the system headquarters. The United States Postal Service and the Department of Defense represent the latter type of situation in respect to the relation of system headquarters to local post offices and military bases, while the former situation is exemplified by the relation of a federation of women's clubs to the diverse local clubs affiliated with it or by the relation of local governmental units to the National League of Cities. Conceived as the extent of autonomy of the local unit, this dimension can be analyzed in more specific terms, such as the local unit's degree of autonomy in establishing its formal structure, in determining its operating policies, in choosing its program areas, in conducting its operating program, in choosing its local officials, whether paid or voluntary or both, in its freedom to accept or reject program proposals from the system headquarters, in its right to terminate its relationship with the system headquarters and still continue performing its functions, and so on.

Relation of Unit Status Roles to Extracommunity Systems

Another major aspect of the community's vertical pattern is the relation of the chief status roles of the local units to the extracommunity systems. The social role concept has received extensive elaboration in the past few decades.[7] For our purposes, a social role can be defined as the pattern of behavior that individuals assume in social interaction, based on their own previous experience and degree of conformity to what they think are the expectations of others.

Gross and his associates made an extensive analysis of definitions of the role concept and found three elements common to most of those that they considered. These elements—social locations, behavior, and expectations[8]—provide a useful set of concepts for our analysis of the roles of local unit officials as these are related to the respective extracommunity systems.

The offices occupied by the variety of local unit officials, whether voluntary or paid, are positions within both the local community social structure and the structure of an extracommunity system of which the local unit is a part. We are concerned here with their positions, or social locations, as they relate to an extracommunity system. Among the broad spectrum of local units, the aspect of *location* in the social structure of an extracommunity system varies all the way from virtual absence of any such location within an identifiable extracommunity system to a position that is an integral part of an extracommunity system.

Of the many possibilities, let us consider on the one hand the president of a local bridge club with no extracommunity affiliation or the owner-operator of a local retail store. Here, the extracom-

---

7. A brief bibliography is given by Edgar F. Borgatta in "Role and Reference Group Theory," in Leonard S. Kogan, ed., *Social Science Theory and Social Work Research* (New York: National Association of Social Workers, 1960).

8. Neal Gross, Ward S. Mason, and Alexander W. McEachern, *Explorations in Role Analysis: Studies of the School Superintendency Role* (New York: John Wiley & Sons, 1958), pp. 11-20.

253

munity systemic tie is minimal or nonexistent. Should the local bridge club affiliate itself with an extracommunity federation of bridge clubs or the local retailer affiliate with local retailers from other communities in a local distributing cooperative, the unit would in each case be involved in a relatively weak type of tie. The positions involved in the tie would involve the retailer's status as a member of the cooperative (or an officer, if he or she should be so elected) and the status of the president or other elected delegate of the local bridge club in the extracommunity federation. At the other extreme would be the local postal employee, who occupies a rigidly defined (civil service) position within the extracommunity system, or the manager of the local supermarket, who also occupies a clearly defined position within the national supermarket chain. In the latter case, the expectations motivating the supermarket manager come largely from outside the community, though local people may have a large influence on day-to-day merchandising decisions through their market behavior.

Consider the person occupying a role in a local unit that simultaneously involves a role in an extracommunity system. The person occupying such a role is at once a part of the extracommunity system, having a corresponding position in its structure and behaving in regard to expectations of the extracommunity system, and also a part of the local community system, having an appropriate position in its structure and behaving in regard to expectations of the local community system. Such linkage roles are sometimes difficult to enact while meeting social expectations from the two different types of systems simultaneously. To the extent that such expectations diverge, it may become impossible to meet them to the satisfaction of both systems.

Equally important, such linkage roles are living embodiments of the extracommunity system within the local community. If they are (in varying degrees) integral parts of an extracommunity system, they are also (in varying degrees) integral parts of the community system. As stated earlier, one need not go outside the community to look for its extracommunity ties. These can be found within its diverse component units, which themselves, as units of the local community system, are also integral units of an extracommunity system. In other words, as stated earlier, communities are not related to the "larger society" as wholes, as entities, as much as they are related to the larger society through their respective diverse community units.

Two observations can be made about the *behavior* of the individuals in such linkage roles. The first is that the behavior expected may be patterned in only a minimal way by the prescriptions of the extracommunity system, leaving considerable initiative to the occupant of the role regarding how to behave in attempting to fulfill the expectations of a person in that position. Or on the other hand that person's behavior may be carefully prescribed with only the narrowest room for individual variation.

The second observation is that even in the most rigidly prescribed roles there is what Linton has called a "range of permissible variation" within which individual differences may be accounted for and consonant with which specific individuals may find the expectations for them somewhat different from the expectations for any other particular individual who might occupy that role within the extracommunity system. What the system might permit one specific individual it might not permit another because of purely personal history, influence, and the expectations that the person has generated by virtue of a specific type of performance in the past.

We have already edged over into the third role element, that of *expectations*. With relation to the extracommunity system, the role expectations of local unit personnel are formulated in terms of the values, goals, and program objectives of that system. In the vertical pattern, these are usually highly task-oriented, directed at performing efficiently the functions that the unit performs with regard to the system. If it makes a product or provides a raw material for the extracommunity system, if it provides a local service as a local outlet of the system, if it sells system products locally, if it provides decision-making participation for the system, then these functions are expected to be performed on the system's terms, not necessarily the terms of the local community. Thus quotas imposed on the local unit by the system headquarters, program goals and procedures, policies, decisions to expand or contract, rules and regulations, organizational plans all constitute expectations of the behavior of the personnel of the local unit. Local unit roles must be filled within limits of tolerated variation, whether or not doing so constitutes behavior acceptable to the local community.

Warner and Low have described forcefully the extent to which the manager of an absentee-controlled shoe factory must meet the expectations of the company *as against* those of the community. There is little need for him to participate in community activities.

He can operate the factory in strict accordance with the orders of the main office more easily, in fact, if he does not take part, either as an individual or as a representative of the factory, in local associational activities. If he does involve the factory in community activities, he involves it and the larger enterprise of which it is a part in community responsibilities and subjects it to community pressure and control. This is precisely what the top officials of the large enterprise do not want. They want the factory to be as free as possible of community pressures so that

255

its operations can be dictated in strict accordance with the profit-making logic.[9]

Thus, the extracommunity system's role expectations may be at variance with those of the horizontal pattern, which will be treated in the following chapter. Positions that simultaneously involve the individual in two different systems constitute linkage roles. In such linkage roles as we are considering, the expectations of the extracommunity system may loom large in relation to the expectations of the local community system, which may be relatively indifferent to the role performance of the local unit official, or the expectations of the local community may loom large in relation to the expectations of the extracommunity system. Presumably, it is in the area where expectations from both systems are relatively large and where the expectations of the systems conflict noticeably, that the individuals in linkage roles find themselves in a "squeeze," or role conflict, and where they find themselves caught up in the maelstrom of heated controversy involved in the simultaneous relationship of their units to two incompatible systems. Should the branch plant move to a community with a cheaper labor supply? Should the school principal institute the new changes being pushed by the state education department but that local people resist? Should the local health association make a greater concession to program or fund-raising demands made upon it by the local community, and can it without getting itself into trouble with state or national headquarters?

System Controls and Unit Controls

The type and degree of control that an extracommunity system can exercise over a local community unit, and vice versa, provides still another aspect of the vertical pattern of the community's social organization. We have already noted that such control is customarily exercised through institutional authority vested in the system headquarters as well as through other types of power. In addition to institutionally legitimated power or authority, Max Weber emphasized specifically the power associated with charismatic leadership and with tradition.[10] But in modern extracommunity systems a still different type of power is exerted by system officials and their surrogates, such as field staff, district supervisors, and so on. This is the power attendant upon the performance of the system's functions in relation to the local units, particularly that of providing services to

9. W. Lloyd Warner and J. O. Low, *The Social System of the Modern Factory: The Strike: A Social Analysis* (New Haven, Conn.: Yale University Press, 1947), pp. 118-19.

10. Gerth and Mills, *From Max Weber*, pp. 295ff.

them. Personnel training programs, special district or national meetings, informational communications, and program suggestions provide not only a service to the local unit but a channel of influence over the local unit, possibly beyond what is specifically authorized in the system's formal structure and basic "charter." Harrison has suggested the term "rational-pragmatic authority" to denote this kind of power.[11]

In addition, there is the influence that comes through personal contact, through the ability of the headquarters representative to give or withhold rewards, such as an extra service beyond what is required, his or her approval, the ability to say a kind word at system headquarters, or through the informal network of reciprocal but tacit obligations often built up between any two parties in addition to the specifically patterned formal relationships that they share.

Similarly, a certain amount of control can be exercised by the local unit over the system headquarters. Even in the most authoritarian systems where authority may flow only downward, considerable informal influence may be exerted by subordinate units, if only through the difficulty that subordinate units may have in implementing the system's policies at the local level. On the other hand, with systems whose authority flow is allegedly only upward from local units, there is seldom a complete control of the policies and procedures of system headquarters by the local units, even in aggregate. This is one of the aspects of large-scale bureaucratic organizations that has been found to hold in widely diverse types of extracommunity systems: the development of a considerable degree of autonomy by the system's employed bureaucracy.

With the above extremes of no control and total control of the system by the local units, a wide variety of different control mechanisms may operate in various degrees, enabling the local to influence the behavior of system headquarters. Such control includes the formally instituted authority that certain types of systems invest in their locals, along with the formal provision in some systems for the representation of locals on policy-making boards. But it also includes a number of informal means of control. In some systems, locals may be able to exert influence through their function of fund raising for the system through the "selling" function. While they may be required to turn this money, or a fixed proportion of it, over to system headquarters, there is sometimes a real possibility that they may refuse to do so or that they will use this issue as a means to coordinate local protest against the headquarters' current policies. This frequently occurs among voluntary associations, including labor unions and churches. In some systems there is the implicit possibility

11. *Authority and Power in the Free Church Tradition*, p. 209.

that one or more local units, if too dissatisfied, may simply withdraw from the system and go it alone or in concert. Although strong sanctions can be brought to bear against the individual unit, depending on the type of system, the possibility that local disgruntlement will lead to a general "secessionist" movement is an underlying fact of life limiting the autonomy of system headquarters vis-à-vis the local units.

An additional type of local influence over system headquarters, discernible in widely varying types of extracommunity systems, is the access of local unit officials, voluntary or paid, or of influential local citizens to the system's power structure. It may be possible for such local citizens to go over the heads of the lower echelons of the system headquarters on behalf of the interests of the local unit.

Access to the system power structure should perhaps be considered simply as one of several types of "politicking" that customarily go on between personnel involved in local and in headquarters units. In a very real sense, even in many highly centralized authoritarian systems, headquarters officials, both policy-making and administrative, must "please" the great bulk of the locals or else trim their sails for heavy seas. After all, extracommunity systems, like other types of social systems, are characterized by a functional interrelationship of parts. They constitute a sort of symbiotic interactional framework. Thus, often, although not necessarily always, it is to the interest of the various parties concerned in the system to play the game of mutual give-and-take that characterizes the fluctuating relationships by which the system accommodates various types of strains placed upon it, strains caused in part, at least, by the simultaneous participation of the local units in the locality-oriented systems constituting local communities.

Grodzins has made a strong case for the influence of local political and governmental units in the political process.

> The correct conclusion to be drawn from consideration of local influence on federal and state programs is not that the local view is controlling. It is rather that the localities are full and powerful participants in the process of decision-making. They are not always and everywhere decisive, but in most programs at most times some group of localities (or single one) exercises a substantial influence.[12]

Unit-System Input-Output Exchange

It may be helpful to examine the types of input-output exchange that local units have with their respective extracommunity systems,

---

12. Morton Grodzins, *The American System: A New View of Governments in the United States* (Chicago: Rand McNally & Co., 1966).

for such relationships constitute both possibilities and limitations of the local units as they are involved with each other in local systemic relationships.

We can begin with the input into the local unit from the extra-community system. What kinds of things, processes, or effects are brought into the community through the extracommunity ties of various community-based units? In a sense, virtually everything that comes into the community does so through the relationship of an individual or unit of the community to some individual or unit outside the community. These relationships typically involve interaction, and many of them are accompanied by the other characteristics that would constitute an extracommunity system.

Other ties by local units to outside units, though interactional, may not involve the local units as an integral part of an extracommunity system. The difference is illustrated by a locally owned and operated store and a local chain store. The locally owned store typically gets most of its retail products through interaction with jobbers, wholesalers, and individual producing companies outside the community. Although it thus interacts with such extracommunity units, it is not involved in formal systemic relationships with them; that is, the interaction does not involve other systemic attributes, such as boundary maintenance, which were discussed as characteristic of social systems in chapter 5. On the other hand, the ties of the chain store to its extracommunity system may involve all those aspects characterizing a social system, including even a formal structure.

From the standpoint of the local unit of an extracommunity system, input from that system may include the following:

1. Capital or operating funds for the operation of the local unit. Examples are the local branch plant of a manufacturing company, a mission church financed largely by the denominational board, a demonstration unit financed by a voluntary health association, an employment bureau financed by the state government.

2. Services to the local unit. Examples are staff services from headquarters to help a unit solve a specific problem; general field supervisory services that may be a resource to local management, whether involving a school, a social agency, or the local office or manufacturing plant of a national company; a local government service of a state government department; and so on.

3. Program objectives and procedures for the unit. What the local unit sets out to do and the methods employed in doing it are included in this type of input. As indicated earlier, systems may vary according to the amount of choice left to local units as to whether or not they will adopt the specific program objectives and procedures proposed by system headquarters.

4. Personnel for the operation of the local unit. Typically, the **259**

higher one goes in the administrative echelons of the local unit, the greater the likelihood that the officials may have been sent into the community by the extracommunity system; the lower in the echelons, the greater the likelihood that the personnel have been recruited from the local labor market.

5. Products or services for distribution within the community. This point has already been covered in terms of functions, on page 251.

6. Looked at from the standpoint of the community, part of the input from the system to the local unit may be the provision of employment opportunities to local community people.

7. Similarly, looked at from the standpoint of the community, the local unit may make business opportunities available for local retailers and suppliers that may be considered an input from the larger system.

8. In still a different vein, the community may receive as input, through the personnel that the local unit imports, certain skills, technical knowledge, and social attitudes. The studies of both Springdale and Crestwood Heights reported in chapter 4 emphasized the important role played by such largely imported professional and managerial people in bringing about social change.

9. Various actions of the local unit as a result of its interaction within the extracommunity system are also fed into the local community as the local unit's output. Expansion or reduction of the unit's labor force is an example.

A similar analysis could be made of the output of the local unit into the extracommunity system, including those outputs that can be identified as more or less direct results of imput into the local unit from the community. Thus, the unit may feed raw materials and subparts into the extracommunity system. It may likewise feed funds into the extracommunity system, funds that it has gathered locally through "selling" the products of the system. Depending on its nature and function, the local unit may have received such funds in the form of money paid for postage stamps or for automobile licenses; taxes collected on income, real estate, or sales; gifts to the community chest or to individual agencies; prices charged for products sold locally, and so on.

Or the local unit may introduce into the system innovations in the form of social inventions or new mechanical processes as other local units of the system adopt a procedure that the local unit has demonstrated to be worthwhile. Again, the local unit may feed "trouble" into the extracommunity system in the form of labor difficulties or of adjustments that must be made to the local economic situation but that affect the total system adversely. As a final example, the local unit feeds back into the system its own adjustments to the policies of the larger system, either in the form of symbiotic adjustments among the system's parts or in the form of expressed reaction, either informal or through the formal channels set up for local unit participation in the policy-making and program development of the system.

Perhaps sufficient examples of types of output have been given to illustrate the point that such input-output relationships are possible to analyze, and although they are numerous and of different types, the principal types and instances can be identified and described.

In chapter 6 it was pointed out that the functions of an extra-community system ordinarily have relevance on a larger level than that of the local community. There the example was given of polio vaccine, the research for which did not have to be duplicated in every community in the country, but whose results, once obtained, could be channeled to the appropriate community organizations and facilities.

Thus, the community unit that collects funds for the larger system may not necessarily be the unit through which the products of the larger system are distributed to the local community. And likewise, the unit that feeds raw materials or processed parts into the larger system is not customarily the distribution unit for the finished part. In another area, the unit that collects taxes for the state government may be quite distinct from the various departments of the state government whose locally based units provide services to the local community.

In many instances, however, the product of the system is actually distributed by the local unit in some direct relationship to the funds that the local unit takes in and passes along, at least in large part, to the system headquarters. Examples of this arrangement are the services that a voluntary health association provides in the local community and on the basis of which, largely, it raises funds within the community. An analogous example is the chain store, which raises "funds" through selling the products of the system. Here there is a close relationship between funds raised and products of the system distributed by the local unit.

In the foregoing analysis of the systemic ties of local units to extracommunity systems, we have considered the relation of the unit's structure and authority situation to the extracommunity system, of the unit's functions to those of the extracommunity system, of the social roles of the unit's officials to the extracommunity system, of the reciprocity of control processes between unit and system, and of the input-output exchange of the unit with the extracommunity system. From what has been presented, one can see that these community units, in their vertical aspects, come under a series   **261** of conditions that are of the utmost importance in the determination of their behavior. These include the preconditions for the establishment and survival and success of the local unit as defined by the system of which it is a part; structural and functional relations of the local unit to the system; the procedures and considerations according to which goals are set and decisions are made; and the measures of survival and success according to which those associated with the local unit will be judged by others in the system.

It has also been pointed out that in this vertical, extracommunity orientation the function that the unit purportedly performs, its manifest function or task, receives primary emphasis. Its relation to other functioning units within the community is given a minimum of attention, and when attended to, generally emphasizes the public relations tasks that must be done in order to permit the unit to perform its assigned functions within the extracommunity system with a minimum of hindrance from the local community.

As we shall see shortly, the horizontal pattern of relationships of such community-based units presents quite a different set of structural interrelationships, of goal determination and decision-making considerations, and of measures of survival and success of the personnel involved.

Relation to the Larger Culture

We have been exploring the systemic ties of community units to the larger society. But what of the ties to the larger culture? The question is not an idle one, for obviously there is something from the larger culture influencing the behavior of local community individuals and units over and above, or different from, their systemic ties to extracommunity systems. Things get done at the local level in certain specific ways because of influences from outside the community that cannot be directly traced to systemic linkages. Let us take a simple example. The local cancer unit takes its particular structure and policies from the fact that the unit is set up as an integral part of an extracommunity system, whose pattern for the establishment of local units must be followed. But in contrast, a women's club may be established that is not an integral part of a formal extracommunity system and whose form and structure are therefore not determined by such a system. Yet the women's club may bear in its major characteristics a striking resemblance to other women's clubs throughout the communities of America (a fact that Helen Hokinson converted into the subject matter for a delightful series of cartoons in *The New Yorker* over a period of years). Obviously, the women's club form of organization is not invented again each time such a group is formed in an American community. Whence, then, comes the remarkable similarity in form of such organizations?

The women's club is a persistent pattern of social organization existing within the American culture, a type of pattern that many sociologists classify as an "institution." It involves a structured way of meeting some need. It is a pattern for behavior that exists even though it may not currently be embodied in a specific organization. People may not have a women's club, but if they want one, they know how to go about organizing one or can readily find somebody who does.

In a sense, the same can be said about a family. Although there is obvious diversity in family behavior patterns, there is still a similarity that would be remarkable were the family not recognized as an institutional form with broadly prescribed roles and behavior patterns, some of which are supported by statutory or common law. Not everyone need establish a family, but if one is about to do so, there is a great deal of guidance available from the institutionally patterned behavior thought appropriate for such a social group in American culture. The pattern is not developed anew in each community. It is not essentially a community phenomenon at all, but a part of the larger culture. Neither, on the other hand, is it extraneous to the community, for it exists in the community as a part of the culture, the patterned ways of behaving, of the people who live there. In this respect, the larger culture, like the larger society, is not something one must tie to by leaving the community. Just as the larger society exists within the community as an aspect of the local units of extra-community systems, so the larger culture exists within the community as the patterned ways of behavior that local people share with other communities of the larger cultural area.

But how do these characteristics of the larger culture come into the local community? Must we content ourselves with a vague notion of a mass culture "out there" beyond the confines of the community, a diffuse, spongelike agglomeration of traits that is also somehow mysteriously discernible at the local community level as well? If we are to be more specific, we shall need to ascertain the means or channels through which cultural traits are diffused to the local community, the type of diffusion, and the relation of this cultural diffusion process to the ties of local units to extracommunity systems.

Market Diffusion: Universals

Let us explore briefly what besides systemic ties is involved in the relation of the community to the larger culture that surrounds and permeates it. The larger culture gets into any particular community **263** almost exclusively through diffusion. Using a set of terms that has already proved useful in other contexts, let us note that such diffusion may be either of the "market" type or of the "administered" type. Although much remains to be learned about the dynamics of the process, it is known that in both preindustrial and industrial cultures many social practices and ways of doing things become diffused over wide areas of the earth, apparently without anyone's deliberate intent to accomplish this. Such unplanned spread of cultural traits and behavior patterns apparently operates in the dissemination of values and value changes, in the spread of accepted ways to confront certain situations and to meet certain needs, and in the spread of many elements of the material culture as well. Thus, much of what happens in remarkably similar fashion in American communities may be accounted for through this unplanned or market type of diffusion.

Ralph Linton has made a lasting impact on cultural analysis with his concepts of cultural universals, specialties, and alternatives. He defined *universals* as "those ideas, habits, and conditioned emotional responses which are common to all sane, adult members of the society."[13] It appears to be precisely in the area of such universals that the market type of cultural diffusion prevails, including such aspects of the culture as language, basic values, and much patterned behavior. Thus, in a real sense, much of what happens in a local community is merely the local enactment of cultural forms that are shared over a much larger geographic area but are distributed through a type of market diffusion. It is extremely difficult to distinguish any particular systemic ties through which these universals are diffused.

Administered Diffusion: Specialties and Alternatives

Other parts of the local community's culture, on the other hand, may be much more specifically related to extracommunity systems. This specific relationship is true of all the examples we have considered of local units with systemic ties to extracommunity systems. The public school, the branch bank, the post office, and the denominational church receive as input from their respective extracommunity systems a variety of new ideas, program objectives and procedures, and material and technical aids to be utilized in accomplishing their objectives. These come both through the tie of the unit to the system and through the tie of the unit's professional personnel or labor force to their respective professional organizations or labor unions.

---

13. Ralph Linton, *The Study of Man*, p. 272. Copyright, 1936, D. Appleton-Century Co., Inc., New York.

Charts, posters, educational pamphlets, journals, filmstrips and motion pictures, conferences, consultations, instructional materials, specifications, new processes, and new equipment are channeled into the local community through such ties. They are also channeled into local units that are not integral parts of formal extracommunity systems. Thus, the private nondenominational school, the locally owned bank, and the locally owned manufacturing plant all maintain interactional (though not completely systemic) ties with extracommunity units and systems that may involve the introduction of new cultural traits into the community.

Two characteristics appear to attend such diffusion. The first is that the diffusion, rather than being of the market type, is overwhelmingly of the administered type. The new objectives, procedures, and equipment are deliberately fed into the local unit from the system of which it is a part or with which it is in contact. Such administered diffusion takes the form of managerial innovations, changed professional standards, personnel training, consultation services, new products, educational material for the general public, sales promotional material, and so on.

The second noteworthy characteristic of such diffusion is that it corresponds roughly to Linton's description of cultural *specialties*. Such specialties are "those elements of culture which are shared by the members of certain socially recognized categories of individuals but which are not shared by the total population."[14] We have already noted, particularly in chapter 3, the increase in division of labor and specialization on the community level as one important aspect of the "great change." We also noted that specialists characteristically share a special subculture and often are organized into professional associations and other specialized interest groups. In chapter 4 their importance in introducing innovations was noted, especially in connection with specialized school personnel, but also to a certain extent with respect to the clergy. In addition, it was observed that such specialists, including managerial personnel, professional practitioners, and educators, may form a category of local residents (though they are more likely than the average residents to be newcomers to the community) predisposed toward welcoming cultural innovations in the community.

Such innovations are customarily introduced through members of a specialist group, as part of the normal exercise of their profession. The school principal wants to introduce a new pupil personnel service; the head surgeon wants to introduce a rehabilitation center; the church pastor wants to introduce a family camping weekend; the city manager wants to introduce an urban renewal pro-

14. *Study of Man*, p. 272.

gram. The point is that such innovations are more likely to be supported by other professional personnel, even though they are not directly concerned vocationally, than they are by most other people.

We can summarize the current discussion by saying that much of what goes on in a local community is an enactment of cultural specialties that have been administratively diffused through the systemic ties of local community units and their personnel.

But there is another type of administered diffusion through which the local community receives cultural innovations. This is the diffusion of traits of the mass culture to various publics in the local community through the mass communication media. Television, radio, motion pictures, and newspapers, magazines, and books are the predominant media of such communication, although other means, such as billboard advertising and the distribution of throwaways and pamphlets, are also part of the process. Such media, even though presumably available to the total population, are customarily geared to and sought out by certain specific publics. Thus, the channeling into the community is not directly to individuals who share membership in the same formal organization, but rather to aggregates of people, generally called "publics," who share common interests. The diffusion of new fashions; of descriptions of new models of automobiles, refrigerators, or cigarettes; the book-of-the-month or cheese-of-the-month; the daily pontifications of nationally known newspaper columnists or the periodic histrionics of television stars— all these come into the community through mass communication media and are given attention or appropriately adopted by members of relatively specific publics.

The diffusion of such cultural traits is obviously highly administered. Interestingly, this type of diffusion of traits from what has been called the "mass culture" through the mass media involves predominantly Linton's third type of cultural traits, the *alternatives.* Alternatives, according to Linton, are traits that "are shared by certain individuals but which are not common to all the members of the society or even to all the members of any one of the socially recognized categories."[15]

Thus, alternatives are neither universally prescribed nor are they the specialized concerns of rationally organized and socially recognized groups. They represent an area of free choice by the individual dictated neither by the demands of the larger culture nor by the demands of his or her specialized group. Here is an area where it is only appropriate to expect all-out advertising, as con-

15. *Study of Man,* p. 273.

trasted with the type of advertising in professional journals that is kept within relatively narrow ethical limits.

Individuals apparently want and need guidance through the maze of possibilities of material possession, taste, and opinion open to them. The desired guidance in the choice of such matters is provided in their own communities through the mass media of communication. People need not choose and appraise rationally all the possible motion pictures or television programs available to them. With the guidance provided by the mass media, they can select those stars whose pictures or programs they most enjoy and thus not have to review the entire gamut.

But the *star system,* so characteristic of the motion-picture public, is not restricted to the broad area of entertainment. It also has its counterpart in the book-of-the-month club where a few "star" literary critics select one's reading. In the realm of current events it may be a small number of "star" columnists who help the reader form an opinion about what the news "really means"; or the name brand, whether of automobile, cigarette, or frozen vegetable, may help individuals select from the otherwise bewildering proliferation of alternatives open to them.

Let us digress one step further to relate the current discussion of the functional relevance of the star system in the diffusion of traits from the mass culture to the increasing bureaucratization and depersonalization that were described as aspects of the "great change." Brand names were not so important when one could consult the local grocer about the quality of the beans. One can hardly consult an automatic vending machine or a television set, and it is only slightly more promising to consult the checkout clerk in a supermarket about which product to buy. That clerk performs only a specialized fragment of the earlier grocer's more diffuse function, and the fragment does not include giving counsel, informed or uninformed, on the relative merits of one product as against another.

Perhaps at this point we can review the procedure with which we have analyzed the community's vertical pattern. We began by asking whether we could develop a set of conceptual tools with which we could examine the relation of a great diversity of local units to their respective extracommunity systems. Although the going was rough in some places and the concepts somewhat rudimentary, we were able to develop an analysis that seemed as appropriate for churches and their denominational ties as for local factories and their ties to national manufacturing companies; as suitable for the relation of voluntary health associations to their "nationals" as for the relation of a local urban renewal program to the federal Urban Renewal Administration. We have not found these relationships to be identical, but we have found the same types of dimensions to apply to them all.

We have found it important, in addition, to recognize that strong interactional ties may exist between local units and various extracommunity units and systems, interactional ties that do not relate the interacting units together as social systems in the sense in which these were described in chapter 5 but that nevertheless play an important role in influencing the behavior of certain local units. We recognized that many of the functions performed by national system headquarters may be provided by extracommunity units or systems of which the local unit is not an integral part but with which the local unit simply has a reciprocal exchange relation.

Finally, we noted a type of outside tie that could be more appropriately described as a cultural rather than a societal tie. It gave recognition to the fact that most of the patterned behavior on the local level is not *sui generis*, a product of the local community exclusively, but rather is enacted in the local community in some relationship to what is believed and cherished and expected and performed in a multitude of other communities in American society. We found that the dynamics of this process involved ties of the type considered earlier in the chapter, but that it was helpful to make a distinction between market and administered diffusion and to note that the process of diffusion of universals, specialties, and alternatives was somewhat different, particularly in relation to the systemic ties considered earlier.

Thus we have attempted a comprehensive analytical framework, weak and spotty as it may be in some of the details, designed to describe and "account for " the kinds of things that go on within American communities but involve important relationships to the larger society. These relationships we have found to be not that of a general total community to a spongelike mass culture or larger society, but specifically describable and specifically differentiable in terms of different systemic and cultural ties.

In aggregate, we have found the vertical pattern to present a set of relationships and a set of conditions that are not only describable but also clearly distinguishable—even though they may involve the same local units—from the horizontal relationships to which we turn in the next chapter.

The Community's Horizontal Patterns: 9
Relation of Local Units to Each Other

The strong ties linking many local units to extracommunity systems and orienting them structurally and functionally toward them form the basis for an important question to which the present chapter is addressed: With such a strong vertical pattern, how do the community units relate to each other on the local level in anything approaching a systemic manner? Put more simply, What holds the whole thing together on the local level?

The question is of great practical and theoretical importance. Theoretically, the answer will enable us to consider the apprehension shared by a number of specialists in community studies as to whether there is really any basis for using the concept of community to denote locality groups in American society. Might it not be better simply to study the various social organizations with their local units, which we have been calling extracommunity systems, much as was done in the preceding chapter?

Practically, the question has implications for many types of local action. Exactly what is involved in a "community relations" program of a national company, and why is it important? If national associations are to gear their programs more flexibly to suit the needs of the local community, what is meant here by *community*? And what is meant by the word *community* in the term *community development*? What is the community that is being developed? **269**

In chapter 5 the question was raised of whether and to what extent it is possible to identify a community (defined as that combination of social units and systems that perform the major social functions having locality relevance) as a social system with the attributes there described. It was pointed out that there exist on the locality level identifiable combinations of social units and systems that manifest the characteristics of a social system in varying degrees, but that generally speaking these characteristics, particularly as regards boundary maintenance and the strength of the structural interrelationships, are weak in contrast to other types of social systems. A notable example of stronger, more clearly ascertainable systems are the extracommunity systems treated in the preceding chapter.

Nevertheless, even among the most diverse units, a set of interrelationships does exist based on common locality, for the operation of one type of local unit presupposes the presence and operation of others. If a manufacturing plant needs employees, these employees in turn will need to have access in their daily lives and at the locality level to other types of functions and facilities—for providing food, offering possibilities for voluntary association, providing for the formal and informal enforcement of social norms, training the young, helping out in time of trouble, and so on. In turn, each of the units involved in the performance of these functions presupposes the others.

Despite their strong ties to extracommunity systems, the functioning of such local units characteristically involves at least a minimum of local interaction and sometimes more than a minimum. From the theoretical standpoint, the behavior of these units cannot all be explained without reference to such interaction on the locality level. From the practical standpoint, no local unit, no matter how strongly integrated in an extracommunity system, can function long in complete disregard of the impact that its own behavior makes on other units in the locality. Our present task is to explore and delineate the nature of the relations among units on the locality level. Included in the concept of local operating units are individual persons, insofar as their behavior has locality relevance, as well as combinations of individuals organized into functioning groups, whether formal or informal.

One might well question whether the nature of these relationships among local units does not constitute the "real" community, in the sense of the "community system," in distinction from the relations of local units to their respective extracommunity systems. These latter by definition are not confined to the community but lead us out of the community into systems whose basic operating dynamics are only remotely related to any particular community.

Perhaps the vertical pattern of organization on the locality level is not appropriate to an analysis of the nature of communities as we have defined them.

But this is obviously overstating the case. We have acknowledged, even insisted on, the great influence of extracommunity systems on local units. But we have likewise emphasized that the presence of such highly vertically oriented units at the locality level has relevance to what happens there. No analysis of the local behavior of such units can account for what occurs withour referring to these extracommunity ties. Were this not so, there would be more justification for ignoring them in an analysis of community phenomena. Further, we have maintained that the ties to extracommunity systems are inherent in the structure and function of local units. One need not go "outside" the community to find the larger society. The larger society inheres in the local community in ways enumerated and described in the preceding chapter.

Thus, our conceptual platform for analyzing the ties existing between diverse units at the locality level is as follows: At the locality level, it is possible to locate a structured interaction that displays in minimal degree, at least, the characteristics usually thought of as constituting a social system. The units of such interaction, particularly as they engage in performing the enumerated locality-relevant functions, are often strongly related to extracommunity systems in a whole combination of relationship aspects that we have called the vertical pattern of social organization. These same functioning units, however, interact with each other on the local scene in a somewhat different combination of relationship aspects that we have called the horizontal pattern of social organization. The behavior of local units at the community level consists of the dynamic interplay of these two patterns, an interplay that at one time may bring the vertical relationships into sharp focus and at another time the horizontal relationships. But in this interplay neither type of relationship pattern is ever completely absent. The fluctuation between the two, analyzable in terms of input-output from one pattern to another, and the tendency for the confining pressures of one set of relationships to grow rapidly as the contrary set begins to move beyond a certain point, constitute the equilibrium-maintenance behavior of the community as a social system. Having considered the vertical pattern in the previous chapter, we now turn to the horizontal pattern.

Let us begin by reminding ourselves that although not identical with it the horizontal pattern closely approaches the maintenance function of the task-maintenance dichotomy, The horizontal pattern relates to the formal and informal structures and processes through which the local units maintain a systemic relationship to one another. These include both the "internal system" described by Homans, the **271** "group behavior that is an expression of the sentiments towards one another developed by the members of the group in the course of their life together,"[1] and that part of Homans's "external system" that has to do with the formal organization of relationships among units for task accomplishment as dictated by the conditions of the system's survival in its environment. For those interested in further cross-referencing, the horizontal pattern would correspond to the integrative function and the pattern-maintenance and tension-management function that Parsons subsumed under the internal category.[2] There is also an important sense in which the horizontal pattern corresponds to Redfield's concept of the "folk" society, as opposed to the urban society.

While the vertical pattern, as we have seen, is characterized by such *Gesellschaft*-like qualities as deliberate and rational planning and bureaucratic structure, the horizontal pattern is characterized by sentiment, informality, lack of planning, and diffuse, informal, and ad hoc structuring of an essentially nonbureaucratic nature. The bureaucratization of social organizations that forms an important aspect of the "great change" has had much greater impact on the task-oriented vertical organization of the community's units than it has had on the nature of their relationships to each other.

Nevertheless, some degree of formalization and bureaucratization has become evident in the community's horizontal pattern in the later stages of the "great change." This is apparent in the development of such institutions as the community chest, the community planning council, the chamber of commerce, the federation of churches, and the community development council. All of these represent attempts to structure in a rational and deliberate fashion the relationships of diverse community units to each other. Such rationalized, bureaucratic structures are perhaps best understood as adaptations of the community system to the increasing orientation of units to extracommunity systems. Community coherence, which could earlier be achieved through market behavior involving custom, sentiment, and a high component of primary-group interaction, must now be deliberately "administered" through express provision for its formal channeling. It is thus possible to offset strong centrifugal forces generated by the increase in strength of extracommunity ties and thus maintain the equilibrium of the system. Even so, the formal and rational ties that such organizations

---

1. George C. Homans, *The Human Group* (New York: Harcourt, Brace, 1950), p. 110.

2. Talcott Parsons, "General Theory in Sociology," in Robert K. Merton, Leonard Broom, and Leonard S. Cottrell, Jr. eds., *Sociology Today: Problems and Prospects* (New York: Basic Books, 1959), p. 7.

seek to structure are usually far weaker than the ties of the individual member units to their respective extracommunity systems.

Structural Relationships

The same conceptual tools will be employed to analyze the horizontal pattern of orientation as were used for the vertical pattern.

Geographic area   One aspect of the structural interrelationship of local units is geographic, having to do with the area in relation to which they are operative. We can distinguish an *area that is served* and an *area of local symbiotic dependence*. In the case of any single unit, these two areas may or may not coincide. Consider a local post office. In a small city, this is designed to serve roughly the entire city as a channel for the interchange and for the receipt and shipment of mail. At the same time it is dependent locally on roughly the entire city for its labor force, for fire protection, for transit facilities for its employees to and from work, for schools, banks, law enforcement, street repair, other local services needed by its labor force, and so on. Thus, its area of service and its area of symbiotic interdependence coincide roughly with the boundaries of the local community. Indeed, it is only in the sense of the relative coincidence of a whole series of such service and local dependency areas that one can speak of the boundaries of a community in a spatial sense.

On the other hand, the area of service may be much larger than the area of local symbiotic dependence. As an example, a museum may serve an entire region, a whole country, or in a very possible sense, the whole world. Thus, its geographic service area may be virtually unbounded, but its area of local dependence may be much smaller, constituting the area within which its labor force lives and from which it receives electricity, fuel, protection, and so on.

In early chapters of this book the classical model of a community was considered and found to be largely inapplicable under present conditions. This model, from our present perspective, can be characterized as one in which, for all important local units, the area of service and the area of local symbiotic dependence coincide. It is precisely in this sense that one can best conceptualize the trade-area approach of the early rural sociologists, whether ascertained by the plotting of service area borders for a number of different local village functions and finding them to be largely coincident, or whether ascertained by noticing the direction taken by the ruts in the farmhouse driveway, indicating that "going to town" for whatever purpose always meant the same town for any individual farm family.

While the above analysis of area of service and area of local symbiotic interdependence is highly oversimplified, it serves at least   **273** to highlight the fact of this lack of coincidence and to underscore the importance, however difficult, of recognizing the spatial aspects of both vertical and horizontal patterns of orientation. It is precisely in the area of boundary maintenance in a geographic sense that the systemic aspects of the community are most difficult to discern and describe.

Authority flow   The direction of authority flow constitutes another facet of the structural relationships to be analyzed. We noted that in the vertical pattern authority typically flowed downward from system headquarters to local community units, but that in some instances the balance of authority flow was upward, from autonomous community units to a system headquarters with service functions and little overall authority.

By contrast, the flow of authority among different types of local units on the community level is relatively meager, and where present, specifically delimited. Quite a different set of relationships applies. As was pointed out in chapter 5, there is no ascertainable formal structure of the community as a social system. There is no board of directors, or president, or officers, or members in any formal sense. The closest analogue to them is the formal structure of the local government, which is, of course, highly structured and usually highly bureaucratized. But we need to remind ourselves that the local government is only one of the diverse kinds of systems operating at the local level. It has a strictly delimited sphere as a coordinating agency, and outside this limited sphere of legal authority it is simply one agency among many in the community. Within what formally prescribed administered pattern are the offices and functions of local governmental units coordinated with those of other systems in the community, such as business companies, schools, churches and clubs, voluntary associations and agencies? The answer must be, Within none.

In the absence of such a formal organizational structure, some types of similar or closely related units are organized more or less formally. These were considered in chapter 6, where the chamber of commerce, the board of education, the city council, the council of churches, and the community welfare council were considered as important examples of the organization of related functional units within the community. Of these specific organizations, the ones that are usually most closely organized with a downward flow of authority and carefully prescribed organizational pattern are the municipal government and the public school system. By contrast, the other types of coordinating structure, although formal attempts at administered coordination, are relatively weak both in function and authority, as compared with the individual units that they seek to coordinate. Typically, the authority flow is upward rather than downward, and although they may concern themseives with matters of broad community importance, they are usually matters of peripheral concern to their member units. These individual units, to repeat, are much more directly concerned with their own specific task accomplishment, a concern that relates them more closely to other units in an extracommunity system than to each other on the locality level.

Although the authority of many types of horizontally oriented structures may be weak, such units may be able to exercise other types of power toward conformity with their norms and policies than that of formally constituted authority. Thus, the United Fund may exercise power over the policy of member agencies through its control of the purse strings rather than through any specific authorization of policy-making authority over member agencies. The chamber of commerce may be able to muster various types of pressure to secure the conformity of one of the local businesses; for over and beyond the strong motive of social approval, the underlying reality of dollars-and-cents pressures through the individual disposition of other members of the organization cannot be ignored with impunity by the individual businessman or firm.

Thus, considerable influence can be brought to bear on individual units within the horizontal pattern, even though there is no formally defined authority structure within it. The types of such horizontal control will be discussed later in this chapter. For the present, having examined the authority dimension of the horizontal pattern, let us turn to the functions of units in relation to the larger system within the horizontal pattern and the function of the larger system in relation to the units.

Functions of Local Units and the Community System

While local units are related in the vertical pattern to the extracommunity system, in the horizontal pattern they are related to the community system. Indeed, the community can be considered a social system precisely insofar as it represents a functioning interrelation of local units with identifiable systemic attributes. Let us see, then, whether it is possible to delineate specific types of reciprocal functions performed by local units and by the community as a system. Or, less precisely, What does the unit do for the system, and what does the system do for the unit?

First we shall consider the unit functions in relation to the community system. Is it possible to ascertain and classify such functions into broad categories appropriate for the various types of units involved: businesses, governmental offices, churches, stores, individ-   **275** ual professional and service trades, social agencies, schools, clubs, and so on? Some important unit functions are readily identified.

1. Performing a Locality-Relevant Function. In chapter 1 the community was defined as that combination of systems and units that perform the major social functions having locality relevance. These functions were enumerated as production-distribution-consumption, socialization, social control, social participation, and mutual support, and they were examined in detail in chapter 6. There it was pointed out that such functions were also performed in part by individual families at the one extreme and by extracommunity systems at the other and hence were not exclusive functions of the community. Nevertheless, the provision of such functions through churches, stores, business companies, governmental units, and voluntary associations operating as units in some type of interactional relationship based on propinquity is precisely the area of locality relevance that characterizes the operation of the community as a social system. For analytical purposes, these functions were grouped under the categories enumerated above. On the level of practical, day-to-day living, they take the form of providing food and other things available for sale in local stores, providing professional or other services, teaching youngsters in the schools, providing police protection and other governmental services, providing churches for worship and related activities, providing various other voluntary associations for formal social participation, providing hospitals and social agencies, and so on.

2. Providing Employment and Income. The various functioning units of the community provide a means of productive endeavor through which individuals may have access to what is produced. In most American communities in the later stages of the "great change," this provision is accomplished principally through specialized work for money, which is then used to purchase the things needed. In chapter 7, however, private profit enterprise was only one of the five auspices analyzed for the accomplishment of production-distribution-consumption. The others were individuals and families, neighborhood and ad hoc groups, voluntary associations, and government. Particularly as these last two auspices and private-profit enterprise become involved in the performance of functions (and they are becoming increasingly involved as an aspect of the "great change"), division of labor and monetary exchange become important. Although one ordinarily thinks of private industry as providing employment and individual income, it must not be overlooked that private industry provides only a part of such employment and that various types of nonprofit units, both governmental and voluntary, are important sources of employment and other income.

276

Community units provide not only sources fo employment; they also provide sources of revenue for other units in the community. Industry and businesses are taxed, as are individuals, on varying bases, thus providing revenue for governmental units. On the other hand, voluntary associations and agencies are not so taxed. Likewise, various units may provide funds for other units through gifts or through fees. The system of gifts-prices-profits-fees-taxes-wages constitutes the means through which the financial basis for individuals and community units is provided and the exchange of functions takes place.

3. Providing a Link Between Various Units and Individuals in the Community and the Culture and Social Systems of the Larger Society Beyond the Community's Borders. This function, although closely related to that of performing one or more community-relevant functions, deserves separate treatment. It will be recalled that the cultural universals apparently become diffused chiefly in an unadministered fashion by word of mouth among individuals. Specialties and alternatives, on the other hand, are introduced into the community principally through the extracommunity systemic ties of the various local units and through the mass media of communication. Thus, various local units provide channels through which innovations are introduced into the culture of the local community. Stores, schools, churches, business companies, individual self-employed professionals and service personnel, government offices and agencies, and voluntary agencies and associations are constantly introducing cultural changes. Some of these changes may involve simply the methods of their own operation. Others may involve new products and new uses for products, new services, new knowledges or ideas or attitudes, and new types of organizational forms affecting not only their own immediate personnel but also becoming broadly disseminated in the community. Mass communication media similarly introduce innovations in the form of facts and arguments to support new attitudes, new products, new fashions, new leisure-time pursuits, new political points of view, and so on. In doing so, they often give support for the actual systemic dissemination of products or procedures carried on by other local units.

But there is an important additional aspect of this linkage function that local units provide for each other locally through their respective vertical ties. They provide a channel through which impacts are brought to bear on the community from various extracommunity systems and impacts from various units of the community are brought to bear on their respective extracommunity systems. It will be recalled that equilibrium maintenance is one of the essential characteristics of social systems. This arises from the very definition of a social system as a structured interaction among various member units that persists through time. Communities, as we have noted, actually do show a certain amount of equilibrium maintenance in the sense that an impact from one of the units in the system will be followed by adaptive behavior on the part of the others. While this process is usually called equilibrium maintenance, the concept does not denote a static view of the community, for the structure of the interaction of the various units of the community is constantly being modified as new impacts are introduced. Indeed, such constant modification is vital for the preservation of the structured interaction of the parts. The point is that, in order for such structured interaction to be maintained at all, it must constantly be modified to accommodate impacts introduced by the various member units.

As an example of the introduction of an impact from an extra-community system, let us take the expansion of a local branch plant of a national manufacturing company. The company's decision to expand its production is channeled into the community in the form of the altered behavior of the local plant. It builds new buildings, hires more people, imports a few executive personnel, pays more taxes, and perhaps starts raising the level of air and water pollution, creates a need for additional sewage facilities and police and fire protection. Depending on the magnitude of these impacts, the interactional structure of the community will communicate these behaviors in the form of different types of impacts on other community units, eliciting various kinds of adaptive behavior, which will be evidenced not only in their actions but also in their modified structure. These impacts are fairly tangible and fairly apparent. Because the net impacts of such expansion are in most cases viewed as highly favorable to other local units, there is considerable community-based agitation in the direction of economic development.

Other examples of the channeling of impacts from extracommunity systems could be given. In some instances they represent fairly clearly the coursing into the community of impacts that are largely advantageous and highly welcome. In others, they are generally considered to be disadvantageous. Most such impacts contain various proportions of advantages and disadvantages, and the same type of impact may affect two community units differently. The decision, for example, of the branch plant to reduce production drastically will be felt by local retailers in the form of less purchasing but by the local employment insurance office as a mass of new applications for unemployment insurance payments.

But the link that a local unit provides between various different local units and its own extracommunity system is a two-way channel. Impacts move not only from the extracommunity system through the local unit to other community units; they also move from other units on the local community scene through the specific local unit to its extracommunity system. Thus, in the preceding example, the local church may respond to its slackened income caused by the unemployment of its members by reducing its contribution to its denominational board, and its extracommunity system receives an impact channeled through it from other units in its local community.

From its standpoint, the local community can be seen as the field in which units interact with each other on the local scene, maintaining a continuous but constantly changing pattern of interaction with each other and at the same time responding to, and making impacts on, their respective extracommunity systems.

We have examined the principal functions of local units in relation to each other within a structure of interaction called the community. We have tried to answer the question: What does the unit do for the community system? We now turn to the opposite aspect of the relationship: What does the community system do for the local unit? In a sense, we are asking at this point: What benefits devolve to the local unit by virtue of the fact that it is related on the local scene to a number of diverse units in a patterned structure of interaction? We can delineate two principal functions, each vital to the local unit and its extracommunity system, that the community system performs:

1. *Providing a Market for the Local Unit.* In actuality, two somewhat different markets are provided within the community system. One is the market for disposing of the product of the unit. The most obvious example is customers for a supermarket, but of course equally pertinent to this type of analysis are recipients of unemployment checks, potential new members for a local denominational church, and users of streets, public utilities, and governmental services of various types. The other type of market provided by the community system is a labor market: a source of people to help develop what the unit produces, be it education, protection, opportunity for recreation, or industrial products.

For some types of local unit, the consumer market is of principal relevance; for other types, the labor market. Let us explore these relationships briefly. Once more, in attempting to explore similar systemic characteristics even in systems with highly dissimilar functions, we can identify three different types of local units from the standpoint of the functions of production and distribution of goods or services. And once more, although these concepts are customarily used with exclusive reference to the private profit sector of the economy, we shall use them more generally to apply to all types of units providing locality-relevant functions. Whether they are stores, fac- **279** tories, voluntary associations, or schools, they can all be classified by using the same typology.

First, there are those units that are primarily engaged in producing goods or services to be distributed in a larger area than the local community. Factories are an obvious example, but so is a university of national orientation (as distinguished from a "community college") as is a federal tax collection office. Units of this type are only minimally concerned with the immediate community as a market for finished products. They are concerned much more vitally with the local community as a source of labor. In the case of the university, the recruitment of its productive labor force (faculty) may be national, however, rather than local. This situation represents simply a somewhat extreme example of what we noted in an earlier chapter: that in nationally oriented organizations the higher the echelons, the greater the percentage of personnel recruited from outside the community. Nevertheless, maintenance personnel, secretarial help, and numerous other categories of labor must be recruited locally. In other types of organizations a much greater proportion of the productive labor force may be recruited locally.

Second, there are local units primarily engaged in distributing locally the products of an extracommunity system. For these units, such labor is employed not for purposes of producing a product for the extracommunity system so much as for distributing products of the system that have been produced elsewhere. The obvious example of this type of unit is a local supermarket or the local distributing agency of a national manufacturing company (such as the sales agency for a specific automobile or specific insurance company). In such cases, many more community people are involved as consumers of the system's product than as producers or distributors of it.

Third, and perhaps more numerous than either of the above extremes, are the units with various combinations of production and distribution functions. They depend on the local community in a major way both as a source of labor for producing and distributing the system's products and as a source of consumers for these products. Various departments of the municipal government provide excellent examples of this mixed type.

The appropriateness of the specific community for the unit in the above different situations is apparent when one considers the relationship between industrial plant location and an available labor supply on the one hand and industrial location and proximity to a consumer market on the other. But these dimensions are also applicable to the most varied types of local units, not merely to units of industrial production.

2. Providing Locality-Relevant Functions Necessary for the Unit's Continued Operation. Simply stated, such units as schools, churches, factories, governmental offices, stores, and the rest not only provide a locality-relevant function but also depend on each other's locality-relevant functions for their own survival as individual units; that is, such units are symbiotically interrelated at the locality level. This, it will be recalled, is the inescapable fact that continues to make analysis on the locality level relevant and important, even though the "great change" represents a heightened operation of extracommunity ties. Thus, although the symbiotic interdependence of local units on each other seems so obvious as to be boring, its obviousness does not detract from its importance, for it is precisely this interdependence of school and church and work place and local government that produces and sustains the clustering of people in living areas where the functions of a whole array of such units may be made accessible locally and continuously to all.

From the standpoint of the existence and functioning of any of the local units, there is the need for police and fire protection, for transportation and communication facilities, perhaps for a local consumer market, certainly at least in part for a local labor supply. But in addition, insofar as the local availability of a consumer market or a labor market looms large in the unit's operations, the needed clustering of people in turn necessitates immediate local daily access to a wide range of locality-relevant functions. There must be schools, churches, employment opportunities, governmental services, opportunities for formal and informal association, and so on.

Thus the community system provides the setting within which the local unit can perform its functions and maintain itself as a viable entity.

Relation of Unit Status Roles to the Community System

City manager and bureau of sanitation worker, school principal and classroom teacher, factory manager and unskilled worker—all involve status roles in local units, which are integral parts both of the vertical pattern and of the horizontal pattern. In the preceding chapter their relation to the vertical pattern was considered in terms of social location, behavior, and social expectations. In this chapter we shall consider these same elements of such status-roles but in relation to the horizontal pattern. Our frame of reference will be that of other individuals and units in the locality that are not necessarily parts of the same extracommunity system, for this is the scope of the horizontal pattern: across the various units at the locality level, rather than toward the specific extracommunity system of which the individual local unit is a part.

Various *locations* within local units are not as clearly defined **281** with respect to each other within the horizontal pattern as they are in the vertical pattern. Positions at different levels of authority and prestige are clearly delineated in the vertical pattern and often are visually depicted through organization charts. But positions are less clearly related to one another either in a functional way or in terms of authority across the various local units. Thus, various positions within the churches are not clearly related to various positions within the governmental structure, or within the voluntary associations, or within the business organizations. Relations of subordination-superordination, authority, prestige, responsibility are not clearly defined in any formal way among the positions of these various systems. This is simply another aspect of the fact that extracommunity systems are more bureaucratically organized than is the community as a social system.

Yet the relationships of prestige and of power, if not of authority, are far from randomly distributed among positions in diverse units in the horizontal pattern. Numerous community studies have indicated that in terms of some measure of general social status certain positions in local units have reasonably definite status implications. Further, such formal positions have been found in power structure analysis to be associated with the exercise of power in the community. This power is related to the ability to get things done rather than to authorized power within a clearly defined bureaucratic structure. Thus, position of whatever type in the various local units carries implications of prestige and power in relation to the horizontal pattern. While such implications are perhaps more important in connection with the relations of top administrators or policy-makers to the pattern of local power distribution, they are also applicable to positions lower in the unit structure echelons, as illustrated by the circumstance that unskilled workers in Company A may have higher local status than their counterparts in Company B because of the differential prestige of the two companies.

In another respect, position in the vertical and horizontal patterns can be illustrated by the "big fish in the little pond" situation. What this condition illustrates is simply that the position of personnel manager in Company A's local factory may involve one set of status relationships with regard to Company A's national structure and a different set of status relationships with regard to the community in which the factory is located. Barber has commented on this relationship as follows:

> No less than elsewhere, in modern, highly differentiated industrial societies a man's local position may be somewhat higher than his position in the class structure of the whole society. And, contrariwise, though perhaps more seldom, a big fish

may not be recognized for what he is in a small pond. A prophet may be without honor in his own country. A Nobel Prize winner may be esteemed much more highly in the international world of science than he is in the small suburban village in which he lives. The local community and the national society are not identical; nor are the structures of their stratification systems.[3]

Behavior appropriate to one's status-role in a local unit involves different aspects of position and of role expectation in relation to the vertical and horizontal systems. In the example above, the Nobel Prize winner's occupational role may have little relevance on the locality level, while that of the local banker may have great relevance and involve high status. In a different context, the status relations might be reversed.

In considering status-roles in the two patterns of orientation, it is interesting to explore the relevance of the task-maintenance polarity. Generally, while task and maintenance, instrumental and expressive, "rational" and "sentimental" forms of behavior are relevant to the vertical and the horizontal patterns, the vertical pattern makes more specific demands regarding task, instrumental, and rational aspects of behavior, while the horizontal tends to emphasize the maintenance, expressive, and sentimental aspects. This is a difference in degree rather than in kind, and we should not carry the contrast too far. Nevertheless, it is interesting to note the extent to which Seeley and his associates observed this contrast in the behavior of businessmen in their own units and in the community chest, an organization that tends to relate the interests of many divergent units to each other across unit boundaries (see page 231).

In another vein, much behavior in local units can be viewed as an attempt to reconcile the different, sometimes conflicting, demands of the vertical and horizontal pattern. We shall return to the linkage role concept a little later in this connection. Here we shall note a type of behavior particularly characteristic of the strains of the two sets of demands and particularly relevant to the horizontal pattern. If the vertical pattern is characterized by "following the rules," the horizontal is characterized by "making exceptions," by being "human" rather than merely impartial, by personal relationships rather than categorical. The device of the quietly ignored rule, the convenient exception, the "special concession" is a means through which strains caused by rigidly impartial bureaucratic systems can be eased, even though, as indicated in chapter 3 (see page 70), this type of behavior is typically at the risk of the individual

3. Bernard Barber, *Social Stratification: A Comparative Analysis of Structure and Process* (New York: Harcourt, Brace, 1957), p. 95.

official. It is particularly appropriate to the local unit official who is faced with living in the locality while meeting the expectations of an extracommunity system.

As in all status-roles, those in community units involve a range of "permissible variations," and individual enactors of the roles will vary from each other in personality and "style." Just as role behavior in relation to the vertical pattern shows such individual variations, so it does also in relation to the horizontal pattern. Thus, the Methodist minister used to play Santa Claus every year at the YMCA party, be extremely active in the mental health association, and be a jovial leader in the local Rotary Club; his successor may do none of these, but may behave rather differently with respect to local organizational participation and may have a somewhat different personal role relationship.[4] Presumably such individual differences in personal role enactment are of great importance in relation to the horizontal pattern.

A different set of *expectations* inheres in the horizontal pattern than in the vertical. Although the two may overlap, the values, goals, and objectives of the locality may impose a different set of demands from those of the extracommunity system. Two illustrations, which are highly prevalent in the present decade, are that of the factory manager faced with a decision to curtail production and lay off a large number of employees and the executive secretary of a local health association, confronting local pressures toward federated fund raising and extracommunity prohibitions against it. In each case, there is a conflict between the demands of the horizontal pattern (be "human," be a "good citizen of your local community," adapt to local needs) and those of the vertical pattern (get the job done, behave in a way that will further the goals of the extracommunity system, follow the rules).

Another aspect of role expectations is the extent to which a specific position in a particular local unit may carry with it more or less specific local expectations on the behavior of the incumbent in relation to other units. Thus, the factory manager, the school superintendent, or the clergyman may be expected to belong to a specific political party or be of a specific religion. In addition, certain types of civic participation not specifically derivable from his or her formal position may nevertheless be strongly expected. It may not be expected that the new Methodist minister will follow his predecessor as Santa Claus, mental health zealot, and jovial Rotary mixer (though some slight consternation or at least disappointment may be caused in each case if he does not), but it may nevertheless be

4. See Roland L. Warren, "Cultural, Personal, and Situational Roles," *Sociology and Social Research*, vol. 34, no. 2 (November-December 1949).

strongly expected that he will engage in some type of equivalent participation in community organizations. By the same token, incumbents of particular positions may find tacit membership in local power cliques readily available and waiting for them, simply because of the positions they occupy although there is no formally structured guarantee of this. Their unit-roles may involve such expectations, but their individual behavior within those positions may be such as to preclude this particular type of clique membership.

Actually, individual communities show considerable variation in the extent to which they expect certain types of civic participation from local company officials. Persons in the field of industrial community relations report some degree of bewilderment at finding some communities expecting, for example, that the executives of one of their branch factories will take an active role in community affairs and finding other communities resenting such participation as an attempt to "run the whole community." By the same token, different national companies have different policies that either encourage, ignore, or discourage the participation of their branch executives in different types of community participation. Frequently, for example, "civic" participation is encouraged but "political" activity is discouraged. More recently, though, there has been an overall movement by many large industrial companies to encourage the participation of their local personnel in political activities as well.

Another aspect of role expectations of the horizontal pattern is the development of a set of informal reciprocal obligations that grow up in the interaction of people on the local level. On one level, this may be a kind of neighborly exchange among those who reside close to each other. On a different level, it may involve an exchange of favors among various types of leaders in the same community. As an example, a particular leader may be able to get slightly better treatment than usual for a friend with someone in a different community unit on the basis that the relationship might some day be the other way around and that the official asking the special consideration might be expected to reciprocate. Such expectations arising out of informal association and reciprocation constitute a component of the social expectations of the horizontal pattern.

In connection with the informal expectations of the horizontal pattern, a family of the occupant of a local unit position, particularly a leadership position, often constitutes a channel through which certain generalized expectations are brought to bear with pressure. Thus, the wife of the minister, of the agency executive, of the company official, or of the governmental official may communicate (with pressure) a certain selection of the many possible kinds of expectations that might at least be appropriate for such an official, depend- **285** ing on the wife's own specific emotional and organizational ties, interests, and loyalties.

In responding to the numerous expectations of the local system, only some of which can be met to the satisfaction of all concerned, and especially in responding to the conflicting expectations of the vertical and horizontal patterns, the individual often finds it impossible to satisfy all expectations. On what basis does one choose?

The question is much too complex to explore fully here, but one or two comments are appropriate to our discussion. The question is largely one of the manner in which disparate values, goals, and objectives of the vertical and horizontal patterns are internalized in the individual's own value system. One would suspect that a highly relevant factor would be the extent to which individuals see themselves as organization men or as community men. It might be expected to be related to whether they see themselves as permanent members of that specific community or as transients residing there only during a particular stage of their occupational careers. It certainly is related to the question of which groups constitute important reference groups for the individual.

Warner and Low made a clear distinction between the management of the absentee-owned factory in Yankee City and that of the locally owned independent factory. They described the managers and supervisory personnel of the locally owned factory:

> They are thus involved in the general social life of the community, belonging to various associations, clubs, and other organizations. . . . Part of the motivation that determines their business behavior is the desire that fellow townsmen regard them as upright and fair business men who treat their employees properly. Such desires frequently militate against their acting strictly in accordance with the profit-making logic; business advantages are sometimes sacrificed because the manager (or owner) places greater value on community prestige than he does on increasing factory earning by some means which would endanger that prestige.[5]

Another facet of the problem of conflicting role expectations is the ability of individuals to endure a certain degree of discrepancy in the goals they pursue, a certain degree of disjunction in the behavior they engage in, without being plagued by excessive guilt feelings. In this connection, the individuals in many community unit status-roles are excellent subjects for the study of dissonance.

5. W. Lloyd Warner and J. O. Low, *The Social System of the Modern Factory: The Strike: A Social Analysis* (New Haven, Conn.: Yale University Press, 1947), p. 118.

Yet it is perhaps easy to exaggerate the difficulties of the individual who must face conflicting role demands. Politicians, for example, thrive on their ability to make resolutions of difficult conflicting demands that will fit the situation appropriately, not so that all parties will necessarily be fully satisfied but at least so that an accommodation can take place. Like the politician, other occupants of status-roles who find themselves facing conflicting demands of vertical and horizontal patterns may derive some small comfort from the fact that they are usually not expected to satisfy completely all expectations; rather, they are expected within each pattern to make a suitably acceptable resolution of the conflict, granted that the conflict does exist and that some accommodation is necessary. Few societies place individuals in customary role situations where the conflicting demands are fateful, where decisions cannot be avoided, and where the conflicts are irreconcilable. But where such situations occur, they can be the substance of high tragedy. Linton pointed out the specific use of such situations in Greek tragedy.

Community System Controls on Local Units

When we explored the systemic aspects of the community in chapter 5, it was necessary to point out that many of them were weak, particularly the aspects of boundary maintenance and identification of a strong internal pattern. Any social system must provide ways for assuring that interaction of units will take place in accordance with the system's norms, norms that are closely related to the maintenance of the system as a structure of interaction. We defined social control as the process through which a group influences the behavior of its members toward conformity with group norms, and we considered Homans's analysis, which tied social control to the system's process of equilibrium maintenance. In a situation of equilibrium and effective control, "any small change in one of the elements will be followed by changes in the other elements tending to reduce the amount of that change."[6] Homans pointed out that departures from the system's norms constitute such changes and will be followed by behavior designed to reduce the departure. The departure, however, need not necessarily be a departure from the norms, but only from the individual's customary degree of conformity to the norms.[7]

If the interaction of various diverse units with each other on the local scene operates as a social system, we shall expect to find means through which the behavior of the individual units is

6. *Human Group*, pp. 303-4.

7. *Human Group*, p. 299.

influenced in the direction of conformity to group norms. Let us consider some of the different channels through which such control is exercised.

Government   In chapter 6 we described government as the principal unit for the exercise of social control, since in government is lodged ultimate coercive power over the individuals within its geographic boundaries. Nevertheless, we noted that the authority vested in local government is small compared to that of state and federal governments. Most ot the laws and enforcement authorities in the industrial, religious, health and welfare, associational, and educational fields are state-level authorities; industrial regulation is an exception having strong controls at the federal level.

Nevertheless, local government exercises controls through ordinances governing the individual behavior of unit members—through zoning ordinances, health codes, building codes, and so on. Beyond these rather minimal controls over local community units, however, local government exercises surprisingly little control, and we must look elsewhere to find effective limits to the behavior of local community units such as churches, businesses, organizations, and the rest.

Coordinating units   Another formal channel through which controls from other local units are brought to bear on any particular community unit is the series of local organizations of units in approximately the same functional areas. In chapter 6 the typical coordinating units of the horizontal pattern were found to be the chamber of commerce, the board of education, the city council, the council of churches, and the community welfare council. Other analogous coordinating units are to be found at the local level, but the ones selected were representative respectively of the broad areas of community-relevant functions around which the analysis in this book is organized.

While the city council and board of education have authoritative control in their respective purviews, the chamber of commerce, federation of churches, and welfare council represent much looser types of organization with a net upward flow of authority from relatively autonomous units. These looser types of federation thus have little authority but may exercise considerable power through various means, including the informal controls of praise and blame exercised by peers, the channeling of favors, and, in the case of the welfare council's frequent connection with the community chest or united fund, through their influence on the unit's income. In each sector, professional or occupational norms are operative, and a certain degree of conformity to these norms is necessary for the approval of one's peers. Such organizations thus provide a part of the horizontal pattern of controls through which the behavior of community units is influenced by the ties that they have on the locality level.

Civic associations   Another source of local influence on various types of units consists of a variety of formal civic associations of a "nonpartisan" nature. These include taxpayers' associations, civic improvement associations, Leagues of Women Voters, and a host of organizations whose emphasis is on civic improvement, "clean government," or community development. Their influence is exercised through their special knowledge, through their effect on public opinion, through their access to power figures, and through their ability to conduct "campaigns" for various civic purposes. While in any particular local unit's action that has broad community implications their influence may not be decisive, their presence is often an important factor in the evaluation of alternatives by a local unit, be it a labor union, a government office, or a business company.

Community power structure   Perhaps the most important instrument for bringing to bear local community considerations on specific community units that experience strong pressures from extracommunity systems is the community power structure. It is not usually possible to find a single power structure with equal control over all aspects of community life. Nevertheless, all studies to date support the general existence of concentrations of power over decision-making in every segment of community life, and they report various degrees of overlapping among these different concentrations of power in specific groups of people.

To the extent that there is interaction among individuals in positions of power in different segments of community life, this interaction constitutes a channel through which conflicting interests become resolved or at least accommodated. The power structure may constitute the most important channel through which influence from various segments of community life can be applied to any particular unit so that the action of the unit will be related as satisfactorily as possible to the interests of a wide variety of the diverse units of the community. Thus, the interests of the broad community can be brought to bear on any unit that might otherwise be inclined to act largely in the rubric of its own exclusive area of goals and objectives or its vertical tie to an extracommunity system.

Market behavior   A much more diffuse control over various community units is exercised through the individual "market" reaction of community people as they appraise the behavior of the unit in question. It is this type of individual reaction that is often involved in an individual unit's concern for "public opinion." Units that depend on the community for a market may be especially sensitive to such diffuse, unorganized reactions, and especially sensitive to public opinion in this sense. Its relevance for units that seek to sell products or to solicit contributions or that depend on votes among community people is obvious. But even among units appearing to have less direct reason for being sensitive to such diffuse public opinion, the dimension is seldom completely absent.

In this connection, the existence of networks of informal association has special relevance, for they provide an intervening variable between those who would influence individual opinion and the individuals they seek to influence. Such informal group behavior may determine both whether or not individuals "receive the message" and whether or not they receive it favorably or unfavorably.

Such market behavior, involving decisions to buy or, in the labor market, decisions to work, may be vital to the existence of the local unit. We have already noted that the deliberate transformation of these decisions from a market context to an administered context involves the boycott and strike, both of which are surrounded by stringent governmental regulations. And interestingly, these methods of achieving administered decisions, along with political activity that seeks to "administer" the voting decisions, in each case relate individuals in the community to strong extracommunity systems: religious organizations (in the case of censoring), labor unions, and political parties.

Communications media   The community press, radio, and television constitute a focus of control to which many local units are sensitive as they pursue their own task-oriented goals. The influence of the press is perhaps greater, comparatively, than it would be if the two broadcasting media exercised a more deliberate editorial policy with regard to the news of local community events and issues. It has often been acknowledged that the press, in taking a community view of local events, must stand in some relation of accommodation with the business interests of the community. The flow of advertising primarily from business establishments further predisposes the publishers favorably toward this segment of the community. A further limitation has been the "abdication," in many instances, of a vigorous local editorial policy in favor of using nationally syndicated columnists and cartoonists. Nevertheless, the local press, along with television broadcasting, does afford a forum for the airing of local issues, usually from a broader viewpoint than that of any particular segment of the community. As such, it provides a means through which the disruptive effects of the task-oriented activities of individual community units may be countered in a process that is tangibly related to the equilibrium-maintenance function of the system.[8]

Extracommunity systems Lastly, an effective type of control can be exercised in the interest of the horizontal pattern by activating the appropriate extracommunity system. Hunter found that "there are certain individuals in Regional City who . . . act as liaison persons between the local community and the national groups who set policy, and they are influential in doing so."[9] Such people in key linkage positions often have access to the larger extracommunity system of which local units are a part. Even in the small village, these direct lines to "higher-ups" in the extracommunity system may be present. In Springdale there was a powerful check on local units to limit their behavior in keeping with the interests of other parts of the local community.

> Jones as a farm leader can organize pressures on the 4-H agent's superiors in the agricultural college and on his county board of trustees. Jones, Flint and Lee, until the latter left the Baptist church, can go above the organizational head of the ministers, In school politics, Jones and Flint operating in concert can appeal to the state's regional educational supervisor and can informally approach professors in schools of education who are personally and professionally important to the principal. These processes tend to assure that the roles of religious, educational and 4-H leaders do not overbalance community life, and that the individuals who are the technical leaders of these agencies do not infringe on the general community and the general leaders of the community.[10]

Thus, a series of controls operates to limit the behavior of community units in accordance with at least a minimum of consideration for the interests of other units in different segments of the community's life.

8. In a study of Stuttgart, Germany, a city of over 600,000 population, the press's function in this respect was found to be relatively great, particularly because of the weakness of other parts of the horizontal pattern. Thus, "the press was found to represent more actively, to more people, and in connection with more aspects of Stuttgart life than any other agency except perhaps the city government, the horizontal interests of the Stuttgart community as a community." Roland L. Warren, "Citizen Participation in Community Affairs in Stuttgart, Germany," *Social Forces* 36, no. 4 (May 1958): 326. For extensive treatment of the local press in the American community, see Morris Janowitz, *The Community Press in an Urban Setting* (Glencoe, Ill.: Free Press, 1952).

9. Floyd Hunter, *Community Power Structure: A Study of Decision Makers* (Chapel Hill: University of North Carolina Press, 1953), p. 169.

10. Arthur J. Vidich and Joseph Bensman, *Small Town in Mass Society: Class, Power and Religion in a Rural Community*, pp. 269-70. Copyright 1958 by Princeton University Press, Princeton, N.J.

Local Unit Controls on the Community System

In its turn, the individual unit finds at its disposal various means through which it can influence the local community toward conformity with its wishes or toward resisting conforming to the needs of other units when such conformity would jeopardize the fulfillment of its own needs.

In many instances, the unit has the backing of a state or national organization in pursuing its goals and developing its operations in the community. This backing is important in at least three respects. First, it lends support to the local unit in following policies that may not be satisfactory to other community units. The unit is not alone but is recognized as an established part of an extracommunity system that may have great prestige and power. The church thus rests on a strong denominational organization; the local army post represents a powerful force from the national scene; the voluntary agency has the backing of its national organization; the local union is a member of the AFL-CIO; the local plant bears the seal of a powerful, nationally known corporation.

Another way in which this tie to an an extracommunity system strengthens the unit vis-a-vis the horizontal pattern occurs when the unit's policy is determined elsewhere and therefore its basic charter or law does not permit it to make the concessions to local policy for which it may be experiencing pressure through the horizontal pattern. Thus, Sills reports that National Foundation chapters do not make policies but are in the legal status of administrative units of the national organization.[11] In somewhat parallel fashion, the superintendent of schools may simply remind local people that a particular action is prescribed by the state's education law and leaves no alternative. Likewise, the plant manager may report that the decision to retrench was not his, but made at national headquarters, thus permitting him to resist pressure from the horizontal pattern. Or the union may strike the local plant as part of an industry-wide operation, with no possibility of local review. All these examples represent restrictions on the autonomy of the local unit by the extracommunity system. The point is that they represent at the same time a support of the local unit in its resistance to local pressures.

A third implication of extracommunity ties for the horizontal pattern is the access of the local unit to system headquarters as a means of exerting pressure on the local community. A telephone call from the governor's office may help the local unit of the state government get its way in an imminent decision involving various seg-

11. David L. Sills, *The Volunteers: Means and Ends in a National Organization* (Glencoe, Ill.: Free Press, 1957), p. 213.

ments of the community. The threat of blacklisting by the American Association of University Professors may strengthen the hand of local faculty against community pressures to limit academic freedom. Indication from the national office that a favorable decision in local taxing policy will dispose the company toward expanding its operations in the local community may be effective in bringing other segments of the community into line with the local plant's wishes. The visit of a top executive from the extracommunity system may likewise give to the local the support of the "presence" of the national at a particularly crucial point in community controversy.

A somewhat different source of control over the horizontal pattern by the individual unit might be considered as the "underlying threat to withdraw." This threat implies a loss to the community if the situation becomes so unsatisfactory for the local unit or for its extracommunity system that drastic action is required. Examples of diverse implementations of this control mechanism are the canceling of the charter of a local cancer unit of the American Cancer Society; the withholding of state or federal matching funds from a local welfare department; the withholding of state aid from the local school system; the decision to move the local branch plant away from the community. Although all of these examples have actually taken place on one occasion or another, their principal effect is to influence local behavior by strengthening the hand (through, to a certain extent, tying it) of the local, through constituting a threat of unwelcome action whose impact will reach out through the horizontal pattern unless the local unit is permitted to operate with at least the minimum amount of acceptability from its own standpoint.

An important means through which individual units influence the horizontal pattern is through the positions that their leaders occupy in that pattern. The plant manager is on the board of the community chest; the Red Cross executive is in an important policy-making position in the community welfare council; the labor leader, the church official, and the school superintendent are usually well ensconced in the organizational pattern of the community. Through such positions, individuals can exercise some influence on community action. In taking part in policy-making, they can attempt to influence decisions in a direction acceptable or advantageous to their own units.

In their associations with other influential unit leaders of the community, both through formal offices and in informal association related to such offices, the unit leaders also have access to other individuals of influence. Since numerous studies indicate that a large share of decision-making takes place informally among leadership groups who then implement their decisions through the community's formal organizational structure, this ready access to other **293** influential people is an important means through which unit leaders can guard the interests of their units and promote those community actions that will favor them.

Thus, through various means, the local unit interacts with other units in the horizontal pattern in relationships of reciprocal controls.

Unit-Community Input-Output Exchange

The relation of local units to the horizontal pattern can be further explored by considering their input-output exchange. What kind of function, service, or impact does the unit feed into the horizontal pattern, and what kind is fed into the unit from the horizontal pattern?

We begin with the input that the local unit receives from the horizontal pattern. This input includes:

1. The services that constitute the "production" of the other units in the locality. Many such services are directly or indirectly necessary for the unit to survive and to perform its own operations. Thus, not only transportation, fuel supply, highway maintenance, fire protection, and police protection are provided the unit but also the various other services and functions—churches, schools, and so on—that must be available for the unit's labor force.

2. A variety of services more specifically related to the actual operation of the unit. A school needs to be able to purchase books and equipment, to have special traffic protection at certain times. A manufacturing plant may require local commercial services such as banking, insurance, legal assistance, suppliers, shippers, jobbers, and the like. These services must be fed into the operation as a regular part of its procedure.

3. A labor force. While there are instances of a unit bringing virtually its entire labor force with it, the bulk of the labor force of most types of units must be recruited locally. For this reason, the labor market is an important factor in plant location.

4. Capital and operating funds. As considered in earlier chapters, such funds may come in the form of prices for sales, fees for services, taxes, investments, gifts, interest, and so on, depending on the nature of the unit and its auspices.

5. Cultural traits from the locality. This type of input, though seldom "rationalized" or even anticipated, nevertheless is fed into the unit both through its labor force and through its interaction with other units and individuals in the locality. Local customs regarding working hours or other working conditions; local attitudes toward the type of unit involved; local values regarding the worth of what the unit is providing by way of a function; local conflicts between

class or ethnic subcultures—all may find their way into the classroom, into the agency board, onto the factory floor, into the government bureau, into the church.

6. Social pressures of various types. These may be communicated informally through the informal power structure and at times through formal associations. Such varied pressures may include: contributing to local philanthropies or political parties, conforming to local practice regarding legal holidays, foregoing the possibility of hiring another unit's laid-off workers, conforming to certain pressures of the churches, retaining idle workers rather than laying them off, and so on. These examples apply specifically to a factory. Some of these, and many others, would apply to a newspaper, a school, a public library, the post office, or a voluntary association.

7. Good will. This is closely related to the preceding type of input. It is perhaps more a condition governing other inputs than an input itself. In any event, it is important. A local unit enjoying the good will of other units in the horizontal pattern may find its various other types of input quite different than if it did not enjoy such a degree of good will. Worker attitudes and productivity, cooperation of local municipal services, backing and support from the community's influential people and organizations, a sympathetic ear at city hall, a good press—all of these, if not themselves input, at least affect the quality of the input from the indicated sources.

8. Impacts caused by the action of other units. Reduction in the police force may necessitate increasing the staff of night watchmen. Layoffs at the plant will affect the bank's deposits, the church's collections, and the retailer's sales.

Thus, regardless of the type of unit, it will receive inputs of various types from other units in the locality: inputs that are a deliberate part of its operating needs, inadvertent inputs from the adaptive adjustments made by other local units, inputs involving the attitudes and behavior of those it employs or with whom it deals.

In like manner, the local unit has an output to the other diverse units of the locality. Let us consider this output, which the other units of the horizontal pattern receive as input from it. The list of items is similar, since one unit's output is reflected in another unit's input. Thus, each unit may do the following: perform some combination of locality-relevant functions; provide employment for its labor force; channel funds into the community; introduce cultural traits into the community, either deliberately as in a school or voluntary health association or inadvertently; exert social pressures on other units in its own interest; behave with a large or small measure of "good will"; and through its own adaptive behavior inadvertently cause impacts to which other locality-based units must adjust.

Thus, from the above standpoint, the horizontal pattern can be seen as a "field" within which the various units are constantly exercising adaptive behavior as they seek to pursue their goals and perform their functions while making the necessary adaptive changes—in relation to their vertical systems and to the horizontal pattern of interrelations—that enable them to persist as viable units (equilibrium maintenance).

Two important studies from the community literature offer a dramatic illustration of the contrast in the vertical and horizontal patterns of orientation of local community units. One of them, Sills' study of the National Foundation (formerly the National Foundation for Infantile Paralysis) exemplifies the extracommunity system and the local unit's vertical ties to it.[12] The other, the study of the Indianapolis Community Chest by Seeley and his associates, affords an intensive analysis of a particular means for attempting to organize in a rational, systematic, bureaucratic way the horizontal relationships among diverse local units in a particular field of local activities: that of health and welfare agencies.[13]

Although neither book is primarily concerned with contrasting the horizontal and vertical patterns of orientation, their aggregate effect is to provide an excellent example of the contrast. Seeley and his associates, for example, made much of the contrast between the relative success and efficient organization of the local Red Cross chapter and the extremely diffuse and ill-defined organizational structure and operational procedures of the chest.

> The most striking contrast in the planning and organization of the two campaigns is in the clear, fixed ranks and the established methods and traditions of campaigning in the Red Cross . . . and the more obscure levels in the Chest hierarchy and the constant improvisation of campaign pattern. The first pattern leads to the comfortable feeling of tradition, to clarity about status at any one time, to inter-year comparability. . . . The (Red Cross's) stable relations from year to year provide sharp contrast with the Chest situation of continuous change of pattern. The latter results in relations so muddied that no one knows from year to year what are the proper protocols for even the most basic relations, for example, those between the lay campaign manager and the professional staff and sub-staff.[14]

12. *Volunteers.*

13. John R. Seeley et al., *Community Chest: A Case Study in Philanthropy* (Toronto: University of Toronto Press, 1957).

296   14. *Community Chest*, pp. 419-20.

In terms of the present analysis, the importance of the contrast is not that of a successful Red Cross chapter and an unsuccessful chest in a particular city, nor is it that of national health associations and local federated fund-raising units in general. The importance is even more generalized. It is that of the implications of the "great change": of the strengthening of unit ties to their respective extra-community systems and the corresponding weakening of their ties to each other at the local level. The contrast illustrates the increasing difficulty of attaining viable horizontal coordination among units during a time when extracommunity systems are becoming increasingly rationalized and bureaucratized. The difficulties faced by such attempts at horizontal rationalization and bureaucratization as chests and united funds, councils of churches, local chambers of commerce, and community welfare councils are underscored by the success that Sills reported for the National Foundation. Sills claimed that the National Foundation was singularly successful in avoiding the major pitfalls of large organizations: maintaining membership interest and preserving organizational goals. He attributed this success largely to the corporate structure of the Foundation, a structure that outdoes other national organizations in centralizing policy-making authority.

> In contrast to the situation which prevails in many national organizations, the Foundation's local program is quite standardized throughout the country. The patient care program differs from county to county more in magnitude than it does in content, and the broad outlines of the March of Dimes are established by National Headquarters and followed, with local variations, in most communities. All local organizations are subject to the same rules and regulations, and are in direct contact with National Headquarters through one of its employees—the State Representative.[15]

Thus, once again we are drawn to the importance of the contrast in the nature of the relationship of local units to each other and to their respective vertical systems. The weakness of bureaucratic structures for patterning their relationship to each other in rational fashion will be referred to once more in chapter 10, where an analysis is made of community action episodes and community development.

Community and Society: Three Instances

Having concluded our analysis of horizontal and vertical patterns, there may be some value in stepping back a moment and consider-

15. *Volunteers*, p. 214.

ing an important theoretical question that runs through the literature of community studies. The question relates to the levels of social phenomena having relevance to the local community. Many books on the community, for instance, include chapters on family life, economic activity, educational activities, religious activities, and so on. Often this material differs so little from the general institutional approach used for describing American society in general that one looks almost in vain for the community relevance. Why should such material be considered in community studies and in more generalized texts on the community as a social form? How much of patterned behavior is of the community and how much is of the larger society? It seems difficult to conceive how such a question can be avoided.

The reader will recall that where this question has been raised in the present work, the theoretical orientation has been, substantially, that American society is not something inherently different from the community but that the patterned behavior of American society finds its embodiment, indeed its only embodiment, in communities. Nevertheless, for any particular community, this patterned behavior, which is American society, not only permeates the community but extends far beyond it and involves other loci (communities and extracommunity systems) than the particular community under consideration. Yet, while each community may embody or "enact" the institutions of the larger American society, it would be exaggerated and fallacious to consider each community as merely the end of the line for a congeries of extracommunity systems: as a mere passive concentration of activities directed exclusively from elsewhere with its units only puppets on a stage whose only special reality is geographic, puppets whose actions are completely accountable through tracing the strings manipulated by extracommunity systems, The community is not a quasi-reality without any claim to existence *sui generis.*

Since the overwhelming importance of extracommunity systems and of patterned behavior from the surrounding culture has been stressed throughout the present analysis, it may be helpful to take a brief look at three distinct modes of local interaction—social stratification, level of economic activity, and intergroup relations—and their local and extracommunity components.

The vast literature on social stratification leaves little doubt that socioeconomic status has important extracommunity aspects. The various studies of the prestige of various occupations, for example, exhibit considerable uniformity in their ascription of high status to such occupations as college president, bank president, and physician at one end of the scale and unskilled laborer at the other. Occupation, considered as an important status determinant by most students of the subject, is obviously closely related to attitudes that are not community-bound but extend across the broad sweep of American society, regardless of community.

What is true of comparative occupational prestige is also true of many of the cultural characteristics associated with different socioeconomic status positions. The amount of formal education, tastes and practices in literature and entertainment, types of formal and informal association, and tastes in clothing and home furnishing have all been shown to vary with socioeconomic status in a manner that is most readily understood as relating to the larger society and its culture more relevantly than to the local community. In a wide variety of cultural traits the banker and the physician and the college president in California resemble their counterparts in New York much more closely than they resemble the automobile mechanic, the drill-press operator, and the office clerk in California. A related fac- tor is that people of a particular socioeconomic status level who move into a different locality characteristically seek out and to a large extent are sought out by people in the new locality of approxi- mately the same socioeconomic status and pattern of living.

Yet it is apparent that Warner and his associates were correct in their assertion that "class varies from community to commu- nity."[16] Such variation is noticeable in the extent of the range of socioeconomic status differences within specific communities. Such differences have been found to be relatively small in some studies, relatively great in others. In some communities, entire class divisions may be missing at one end or another of the spectrum, such as the lack of lower socioeconomic status groups in some suburban commu- nities. Thus, communities differ not only in what might be called status span but also in the proportion of the population in the dif- ferent status levels.

Barber made a distinction between family status, local-commu- nity status, and social class position, pointing out that the three do not necessarily coincide. In discussing local-community status, he asserted:

But where local community and larger society diverge, as they certainly do in modern industrial society, and as they do also even in many of the non-industrial societies we know about, individuals and families will be evaluated by two different stan- dards, one for the contributions made to the local community, a second for contributions to the larger society. Each of these two collectivities has problems and functions of its own, and

16. W. Lloyd Warner, Marchia Meeker, and Kenneth Eells, *Social Class in America: A Manual of Procedure for the Measurement of Social Status* (Chicago: Science Research Associates, 1949), p. 23.

each values individuals and families in the light of its own special needs.[17]

Some of the relevant differences have already been considered in the present chapter in connection with the consideration of status-roles in relation to the horizontal pattern.

From a somewhat different standpoint, although the two are related, social class in the larger society and in the local community cannot be assumed to be the same. As Hatt pointed out:

> Theoretical problems which immediately rise from such an assumption of the identity of the local community with the national life are that modern industrial society is characterized by, among other things, regional specialization, local differentiation, impersonality and mobility. These are factors which cannot by definition exist on the level of the local community. To this extent, Jonesville *cannot* be taken as America. Any satisfactory theoretical conception of stratification in the mass society must, therefore, allow not only for its local impact, but also for its significance in the patterns of the larger society.[18]

It seems apparent that many of the considerations above are related to the present analysis of the horizontal and vertical patterns of organization of local units. In the one context, the individual is judged from the standpoint of his or her status as it is related to the various units of the local community in their relationship to each other, with the social expectations and values that inhere in this context. In the other context, one's status is viewed from the standpoint of one's relation to extracommunity systems, one's position in the larger society beyond the community's border. Anyone who has felt the differential context of being considered at one and the same time, or in a fluctuating continuity, as a neighbor and as an expert, as a local organization member and as a member of a national association, will perhaps readily grasp this polarity of status relevance, with its change in status as the context shifts from one pattern to the other.

A somewhat analogous relationship is apparent in the community's level of economic activity. Thus, while in a sense economic activity in the larger society can be thought of as the aggregate of the activities of its various communities, it is apparent that for any par-

17. Bernard Barber, "Family Status, Local-Community Status, and Social Stratification: Three Types of Social Ranking," *Pacific Sociological Review*, 4, no. 1 (Spring 1961): 8.

18. Paul K. Hatt, "Stratification in the Mass Society," *American Sociological Review*, 15, no. 2 (April 1950): 218.

ticular community most of the crucial factors to which its various economic units must adjust are beyond the control of that community.

Changes in these factors penetrate the community in many ways. They take the form of changes in demand for the products of various local producers; changes in the state or federal tax structure; changes in federal policy with respect to crop support prices or acreage controls; changes in rediscount rates; fluctuations in the national stock market; the introduction of new products in competition with local products; national union wage settlements and other contract agreements; changes in the national or state minimum wage. Such changes, whether of the market or administered type, introduce environmental impacts to which local units must adapt. These adaptations take numerous forms, such as changes in the level of factory or agricultural production, changes in local interest rates, individual decisions to change investment patterns, individual decisions regarding purchases of homes, appliances, and other products, company decisions to take on or lay off workers, or decisions of governmental units regarding public works.

In turn, such adaptations become, themselves, factors in the environment of other local units, to which they make their own specific adjustments. Thus, one unit's adjustment becomes another unit's impact from the environment.

In the process, impacts are not only carried into the community from extracommunity systems but they are transmitted outward to other units of extracommunity systems.

Yet in this process, although their units experience somewhat similar impacts and engage in somewhat similar adaptive behavior, communities vary from each other in ways that cannot be accounted for completely by the exigencies of the "national business picture." Different types of entrepreneurial units are sensitive to certain types of development but not to others. Some may be affected favorably by an impact that means virtual disaster to others. Thus, according to the differential constitution of their entrepreneurial units, communities show considerable variation in the manner in which their local economic activity is related at any particular time to the national level of activity.

Economic activity at the local community level may also be affected by specific events or decisions that, though minimal in the total economic picture, may be crucial on the local scene. Here, perhaps the most striking example is the decision of a company to pull up and move away or the decision of another company to locate a large plant in a community. Likewise, the discovery of new natural resources such as oil or ore, the invention of new processes for using already available resources, or the depletion of resources all have a **301** local community impact that may cause the level of economic activity in the community to depart drastically from the national trend.

Thus, American communities present the interesting polarity of local initiative and conditions contrasted with the fluctuating national and international scene. On the one hand there are the urban renewal programs, the newly developed industrial parks, the organized economic development corporations, the "Shop in Mainville" campaigns, the worries about the decline of this or that industry on which the local community depends, the search for new industries. On the other are the broad sweeps of economic activity, which bear communities differentially but inexorably, now up on one wave of high economic activity, now down into the generally shared trough of recession. Like small boats on great surges of waves, they may be able to achieve tangible advantages or disadvantages in comparison to other communities. But as one looks at the larger picture of national fluctuations in economic activity, the portion of their economic fate that lies within their own hands in any "administered" sense seems on the whole to be increasingly small.

A similar polarity can be seen in a still different type of social behavior, that of intergroup relations. Let us consider, specifically, relations between blacks and whites. It is not difficult to discover aspects of the behavior involving the two groups in any particular community that are a part of the larger social situation. Prejudice is more than a local matter based on unique experiences in the locality. To a very great extent, it is part of the larger culture, operating throughout the land though modified by regional differences. Discrimination in employment, in housing, and in educational opportunity is found in communities throughout America.

Yet one need only think of the different initial approach to public school integration in Little Rock, Arkansas, Atlanta, Georgia, and Boston, Massachusetts, to underscore the vast difference in behavior subject to fluctuation on a local basis. Thus it is interesting to look at wide national or regional developments as they come into differential impact according to the unique characteristics of the individual community. Basic misunderstandings, strong prejudices, dissatisfactions, fears, hostilities, desires for some type of accommodation, and attitudes of mutual respect and understanding exist in various admixtures in each individual community. Against this differential background, there is, on the one hand, the gradual national change toward reduction of discrimination in employment, in civil rights, in housing, and so on, a change along the many dimensions of which various communities have made their own individual and particular changes. On a different level are the specific waves of impact, which, as they encounter the individual situation in these diverse communities, receive differential responses. Such impacts as the Supreme Court decision integrating the public schools, or the sit-in demonstrations, or the ghetto riots of the late sixties and early seventies find their differential embodiment as they become enacted upon the local scene of one community after another, each responding in ways related to its own special circumstances as well as to the broad ground swell of change that these waves represent. The relation between the local aspects of social stratification, level of economic activity, and intergroup relations is discussed again in chapter 11 in connection with the treatment of crescive and purposive change.

In this chapter and the preceding one we have attempted to analyze, using essentially the same conceptual framework, the horizontal and the vertical patterns of orientation of community units and to explore their interrelations. In the next chapter, we turn to community action and community development in their relation to these contrasting patterns of organization.

10 Community Action and Community Development

Consider the following brief accounts of community action: In a midwestern county of some 65,000 people, there was a movement for a county health self-survey. The people who developed the plan were a hospital superintendent, the director of the county health department, the county agricultural agent, an extension health specialist working for the state government, and various professionals who were organized into a health council. A primary objective was health education, but it was also believed that the facts gathered would be of help in health planning. The approval of various groups such as the medical association and the county board of supervisors was obtained for the project. Over fifty people were engaged to recruit interviewers throughout the county to administer the schedule of questions that the group had developed. In all, over 700 people acted as interviewers and entered 10,000 of the homes of the county to fill out the schedules.

The organizational effort involved in such a county-wide survey was extremely great. Different plans for recruiting interviewers were utilized in the various communities of the county. The health council, which had been extremely weak at the inception of the survey, became vigorously active, and the activity intensified as the survey progressed. Activity and attendance at council meetings during the time of the analysis of the data and preparation of the report were particularly intense. When the report was prepared, it was presented at a banquet meeting attended by fifty persons.

This was the last action of the health council. The newly elected president called a regular meeting, and no one attended. Further, although many facts had been gained, little action resulted, and they had little influence on county planning or on individual health behavior. . . .[1]

> Recently [Charles Homer] got the idea that Regional City should be the national headquarters for an International Trade Council. He called in some of us, (the inner crowd), and he talked briefly about his idea. . . . We got right down to the problem, that is, how to get this Council. We all think it is a good idea right around the circle. There are six of us in the meeting.
>
> All of us are assigned tasks to carry out. Moster is to draw up the papers of incorporation. He is the lawyer. I have a group of friends that I will carry along. Everyone else has a group of friends he will do the same with. These fellows are what you might call followers.
>
> We decide we need to raise $65,000 to put this thing over. We could raise that amount within our own crowd, but eventually this thing is going to be a community proposition, so we decide to bring the other crowds in on the deal. We decide to have a meeting at the Grandview Club with select members of other crowds.
>
> When we meet at the Club at dinner with the other crowds, Mr. Homer makes a brief talk; again, he does not need to talk long. He ends his talk by saying he believes in his proposition enough that he is willing to put $10,000 of his own money into it for the first year. He sits down. You can see some of the other crowds getting their heads together, and the Growers Bank crowd, not to be outdone, offers a like amount plus a guarantee that they will go along with the project for three years. Others throw in $5,000 to $10,000, until—I'd say within thirty or forty minutes—we have pledges of the money we need. In three hours the whole thing is settled, including the time for eating! . . .
>
> There is one detail I left out, and it is an important one. We went into that meeting with a board of directors picked. The constitution was all written, and the man who was to head the council as executive was named—a fellow by the name of Lon-

---

1. For a full account of this action, studied by a team of social scientists, see Christopher Sower et al., *Community Involvement: The Webs of Formal and Informal Ties that Make for Action* (Glencoe, Ill.: Free Press, 1957).

ney Dewberry, a third-string man, a fellow who will take advice. . . .

The public doesn't know anything about the project until it reaches the stage I've been talking about. After the matter is financially sound, then we go to the newspapers and say there is a proposal for consideration. Of course it is not news to a lot of people by then, but the Chamber committees and other civic organizations are brought in on the idea. They all think it's a good idea. They help to get the Council located and established. That's about all there is to it. . . .[2]

In the prairie town of Blackfoot, Canada, a team headed by a sociologist and a psychiatrist attempted an intensive educational campaign to change attitudes toward mental illness. The educational campaign was waged intensively among the 1,500 people of this community for a period of some six months by a number of different staff personnel. The chief principles that it attempted to convey were that behavior is caused and is therefore understandable and subject to change, that there is a continuum between normality and abnormality, and that there is a wider variety of normal behavior than is generally realized. It was explained that the team's interest was in learning what the citizens thought about mental illness and the mentally ill.

The initial approach was to a local store owner who was an old acquaintance of one of the research team. The team moved outward using names of community leaders supplied by this contact. The owner of the local weekly newspaper promised to cooperate and during the course of the campaign gave excellent coverage to mental health activities. The mayor's approval was gained. A questionnaire and group of interviews to be used to take a "before" measure were explained in the press and created incidental community interest. Interviewers were greeted with hospitality.

The team worked with a recently organized parent-teacher association scheduling a winter series of programs. A radio program was sponsored by the PTA and administered by the project. The PTA also sponsored a "film festival" of mental health films. A speaker was provided through the project for the local teachers convention.

Advertising space was purchased in the local newspaper to announce various meetings and to editorialize on various project radio programs. Pamphlets on mental health topics were distributed

2. Floyd Hunter, *Community Power Structure: A Study of Decision Makers* (Chapel Hill: University of North Carolina Press, 1953), pp. 173-74.

in various ways. Extra books on mental health were made available at the local library. A study group was formed and conducted various discussions about human behavior under the leadership of a psychiatrist. A mental health film was shown to the civil servants' association. A young parents' group held six meetings at which films and talks on the personality of the small child were presented and discussed. The board of trade requested a talk on the psychiatric services of the province. A group from the local Canadian Legion branch were taken to visit a veterans group in a ward of a large mental hospital some seventy-five miles away.

Somewhat more than half of the community people were aware of the educational program. Intensive contacts (over 20 each) were made with about 40 adults. Some 160 adults attended an extensive series of meetings, and nearly 400 people attended between 1 and 5 meetings. In addition, an unknown number of people heard the radio programs and saw the newspaper accounts.

Carefully prepared interviews and questionnaires at the end of the intensive campaign indicated roughly that the total amount learned was practically zero. Perhaps even more significantly, the interviewers were greeted with open hostility. Several people did not want to cooperate in the interviews, and it was suggested that the sooner the project leave the community the better. . . .[3]

> Example B is a small village of recent settlers in Israel, a village in which there was a fairly rigid power structure with three families serving as the traditional leaders of the sixty families who constituted the village. The government social worker assigned to work with these people (and several villages) moved slowly and carefully. It was soon apparent to her that the leaders of the village were more concerned with their own gain than with the welfare of their people, that while their leadership was tolerated and accepted as inevitable, they were neither liked nor trusted by the people, and that much of the apathy which characterized the life of the village could be attributed to these facts. Nevertheless, the traditional way of getting action in the village was through these leaders, and if the government was to secure cooperation from the village in raising certain crops and getting the village established on a self-supporting basis, it seemed apparent that they would have to work with and through these leaders. The worker, herself, felt she could not be part of this inequitable power structure. Gradually as she became acquainted with the people she was able to discover persons who were liked, respected, and trusted by the villagers.

3. For a full account of this effort see Elaine Cumming and John Cumming, *Closed Ranks: An Experiment in Mental Health Education* (Cambridge, Mass.: Harvard University Press, 1957).

Without neglecting the formal leaders, she gradually spread her area of consultation on welfare needs to include the informal leaders, and she eventually held several meetings at which both formal and informal leaders were present. These latter, silent at first, soon learned with the support of the social worker to speak at meetings. A much more realistic picture of village needs and resources was developed. The formal leaders, feeling their power slipping, fought the movement that included consultation with informal leaders. This the worker tried to handle in long private discussions with the formal leaders, but as the power moved more and more into the hands of the villagers, two of the formal leaders left the village, while the third formal leader adjusted to the situation and became an accepted leader in the new village organization. This latter took the form of a council elected by all the villagers each year; three years after its initiation, it was making a good deal of progress both in terms of developing community life and in terms of material (mainly agricultural) gain.[4]

Community Action Models

These four examples indicate the bewildering breadth and scope of community action: action initiated locally and action stimulated by an external agent, successful actions and unsuccessful actions, actions with clearly defined objectives and others without them, those with broad community participation and those with narrow community participation, formally organized action channels and informally organized action channels, action within the existing power system and action to change the power system, action with preconceived goals and action with emerging goals.

Is it possible to devise a model that will contain any given community action but also permit us to locate various aspects of the action along certain relevant dimensions? Various attempts have been made to do so, and we shall consider some of them briefly in a moment. The values are obvious: "Any classification, no matter how crude," wrote Homans, "provided only that it is used regularly, forces us to take up one thing at a time and consider systematically the relations of that thing to others. This is one of the roads that leads to generalization."[5] Perhaps more than this cannot be asked at this stage in development of our theory about communities. We do not want to outrun our data. As Wilbert E. Moore wrote, "Much of

---

4. Murray G. Ross, *Community Organization: Theory and Principles* (New York: Harper & Brothers, 1955), pp. 55–56.

5. George C. Homans, *The Human Group* (New York: Harcourt, Brace, 1950), pp. 44-45.

what passes for theory . . . consists of conceptual schemes, methodology, and constructed analytical models or typologies. . . . A betting man would be better advised to rely on established relationships among variables than on ways of thinking about variables that might some time be reduced to observation."[6]

It is helpful to distinguish community action episodes, as considered here, from other social processes occurring in the community. In addition to the seven aspects of the "great change," which were given extensive treatment in chapter 3, there are a number of dynamic processes, which may be continuous or intermittent and that themselves do not constitute change but may have various relationships to it. These include the basic social processes, such as cooperation, competition, and conflict, and the ecological processes of centralization-decentralization, invasion, succession, symbiosis, and segregation. Other processes, such as socialization and social control, have already been considered as major locality-relevant functions, the local provision and allocation of which is the main function of the community as a social system.

These processes are more or less continuous. By contrast, community actions of the type we are considering are episodes. They have their beginnings and their endings. They are initiated to accomplish some purpose; they involve a process of organization and task performance in the direction of accomplishing the purpose, which in the process may be modified; then with the resolution of their effort the action subsides and the episode is finished. An understanding of such community action episodes is important for several reasons:

1. It helps to delineate the structure of the community. Students of the power structure, for example, are coming to appreciate the importance of power as it is exercised in community action rather than merely as a reputational ascription.

2. It helps in understanding the community in its dynamic aspects, rather than in its relatively static structure, as has long been customary. In a sense, a community is what it does, and much of what it does can be grasped by studying episodes of action.

3. It helps in understanding better the role of change agents with respect to their objectives in such fields as public health, social welfare, mental health, and industrial development.

Most attempts at community action models are relatively naive theoretically. They simply seek to carry the action through a number of stages, noting the different focus of attention and different social relationships that prevail during these successive stages. Among such

6. "The Whole State of Sociology," *American Sociological Review* 24, no. 5 (October 1959): 716-17.

309

models are those by Green and Mayo and by Kaufman considered in chapter 2 (see page 38). The analysis given to each stage in these action models often contains more analytical sophistication than their mere enumeration indicates.

Paul A. Miller's analysis of the decision-making process is perhaps even more closely tied in with a theory of the action process, particularly as he relates the various stages to the four interrelated concepts of position, authority, property, and influence. Similarly, Delbert C. Miller has developed a method for prediction of issue outcome that focuses on (1) the critically activated parts of the institutional power structure; (2) power arrangement of the community power complex; and (3) solidarity of the top influentials. Roberts has developed a model of community decision-making and has attempted to relate a considerable amount of social-psychological theory to it.[7]

All these are attempts to develop models for analyzing various kinds of community action. They are not concerned with influencing the process but with analyzing it. One of the most sophisticated and most useful models so far available for such analysis was that developed over a period of years at Michigan State University and tested both in Miller's study of community action to secure new hospitals and in the study by Sower and others of the county self-survey in health, summarized briefly at the beginning of this chapter. This model affords a thorough analysis of the process in terms of the following stages: convergence of interest, establishment of an initiating set, legitimation of sponsorship, establishment of an execution set and mobilization of community resources, and fulfillment of "charter." The Michigan group emphasized that a process such as the county health self-survey "may be viewed as the operation of a unique social system or quasi-system. . . . Thus, the social system that comes into being in the 'self-survey' is itself a social structure, even though temporary, which is activated and de-activated within the framework of already existing structures."[8]

As opposed to these analytical models, a whole series of clinical models have been developed designed not so much to facilitate analysis as to guide practice. They have arisen out of the field of community organization as a social work process, out of the field of

7. Paul A. Miller, "The Process of Decision-Making within the Context of Community Organization," *Rural Sociology*, vol. 17, no. 2 (June 1952); Delbert C. Miller, "The Prediction of Issue Outcome in Community Decision-Making," *Research Studies of the State College of Washington*, vol. 25, no. 2 (June 1957); Beryl J. Roberts, "Decision-Making: An Illustration of Theory Building," *Health Education Monographs*, no. 9, 1960.

8. John B. Holland, Kenneth E. Tiedke, and Paul A. Miller, "A Theoretical Model for Health Action," *Rural Sociology* 22, no. 2 (June 1957): 150.

community development, and out of the field of community consultation. In these fields value commitments accompany certain of the prescribed stages of the model. Ross's definition of community organization provides the outline of an action model, but of the clinical type: "Community organization is a process by which a community identifies its needs or objectives, orders (or ranks) them, develops the confidence and will to work at them, finds the resources (internal and/or external) to deal with them, takes action in respect to them, and in so doing extends and develops cooperative and collaborative attitudes and practices in the community."[9]

A definition somewhat similar to Ross's is used by the International Cooperation Administration to describe the community development process:

> A process of social action in which the people of a community organize themselves for planning and action; define their common and individual needs and problems; make group and individual plans to meet their needs and solve their problems, execute these plans with a maximum of reliance upon community resources; and supplement these resources when necessary with services and material from governmental and nongovernmental agencies outside the community."[10]

Lippitt and his associates made a much more elaborate attempt to conceptualize the process of planned social change, especially in relation to a change agent who is attempting to induce such change. The effort is especially to be commended for its bold attempt to consider in the same conceptual framework the relation of the change agent to what the authors called the "client system," regardless of whether the client system is an individual, a face-to-face group, an organization, or a community. Interestingly, their conceptualization is weakest, and they present the fewest cases where the client system is a community. Their phases of planned change are:

Phase 1: The client system discovers the need for help, sometimes with stimulation by the change agent.

Phase 2: The helping relationship is established and defined.

---

9. *Community Organization*, p. 40. The definition has been slightly shortened in this quotation. Ross, incidentally, has made a valuable contribution by clearly distinguishing what he calls the "planning" aspect from what he calls the "integration" aspect of the community organization process.

10. "The Community Development Guidelines of the International Cooperation Administration," *Community Development Review*, no. 3 (December 1956), p. 3.

Phase 3: The change problem is identified and clarified.

Phase 4: Alternative possibilities for change are examined; change goals or intentions are established.

Phase 5: Change efforts in the "reality situation" are attempted.

Phase 6: Change is generalized and stabilized.

Phase 7: The helping relationship ends or a different type of continuing relationship is defined.[11]

Two comments are perhaps appropriate. The first is that a community as a client system differs from an individual, a small group, or an organization in ways that present difficulties to the change agent. The individual and small group are small enough to be confronted as a unit. The organization is often too large to enter into a direct face-to-face relation with all its parts, but its formal structure is highly explicit and formally, at least, there is little difficulty in locating the appropriate members of the structure with whom to deal. The community is likewise large, typically too large to confront all the members, but it lacks the formally organized structure of an organization. I do not mean to say that the change agent working with the individual as a unit and the group worker do not have analogous problems of understanding the complexity of intra- and interpersonal structure and processes or that the agent working with the organization does not have a similar problem of relating himself only to the appropriate people in the formal organization. But in the case of the community, these problems are multiplied by the complexity of parts combined with absence of formal structure.

Lippitt and his associates analyze community action under the general rubric of a change process deliberately instituted with the help of an outside agent in order to modify the structure and functioning of the client system. Further, the client system is presumed already to exist in clearly recognizable fashion and the entire action sequence is directed toward changing this preexisting system. In contrast, the Michigan State model of community action conceives of the action system as an ad hoc system comprising not the community but rather a special system within the community that arises out of a task to be performed and may very well dissolve after the task performance has taken place.

11. Ronald Lippitt, Jeanne Watson, and Bruce Westley, *The Dynamics of Planned Change: A Comparative Study of Principles and Techniques* (New York: Harcourt, Brace, 1958), p. 123.

Community Action as the
Behavior of a Social System

The value of analyzing community action as the behavior of a special social system should be apparent from the analysis developed in this book, for our thesis has been that associated with the "great change" there has been a strengthening of the vertical pattern and a weakening of the horizontal pattern. Thus, while the specific community units customarily have well-established, rationally developed procedures for accomplishing their tasks, there are few established patterns for collaborating across the diverse units of the community. In chapter 6 we considered some of these collaborative media, such as the chamber of commerce, the board of education, the city council, the council of churches, and the community welfare council. Each is a framework for collaboration among organization units in similar types of activity. These groups vary in effectiveness but are seldom as strong as the vertical systems that they attempt to coordinate. Some types of action involve units from different types of activity, however, and here there is usually less by way of a formal, routinized method of procedure. Such actions, involving participation from a number of diverse community units in ways not customarily employed, are clearly within the concept of community action. Almost by definition, they call for the establishment of a special action system within the community. The community itself, however, seldom acts as a totality.

The special action systems involved in the community action episodes engage in both task-performance and in system-maintenance behavior. Each type of behavior is subject to analysis in terms of a sequence of stages. In the following analysis, we shall be focusing on the development of the action system. Unfortunately, it is not possible to reduce both the system-maintenance and the task phases to a close sequence of paired stages, as will shortly be apparent.

Turning briefly to the four illustrations of community action at the beginning of this chapter, we can discern the special action system in each case. In the health survey, a special organization of volunteers had to be created by the nucleus of most interested officials who were working within the framework of the health council. In Regional City, Charles Homer worked through his own crowd to involve the power structure in planning and financing the International Trade Council, and it was then merely a matter of enlisting various organizations to support the idea and present it favorably to the public. In Blackfoot, the action system consisted of the mental health project staff in various cooperative relationships to various groups in the community. Apparently, no viable indigenous action system was developed. In Israel, the village worker consulted with **313** various individuals and evolved an action system, which in a sense included a transformed power structure. Of the four cases, this was apparently the only one in which the action system left any noticeable impact on the basic structure of the community as a social system.

These four instances of community actions are certainly diverse cases as far as the action system is concerned. A series of questions concerning such action systems suggests itself from the description of social systems given in chapter 5.

Of what units is the action system comprised?

To what extent is the action system distinguished from its surrounding environment? What is the nature of its relationship to other social systems?

What is the nature of the structured interaction—both formal and informal—of the units of the system, units being either individuals or subsystems?

What are the tasks that the system performs?

By what means is the structured relationship among the interacting units of the system maintained or transformed?

Charles Homer and his International Trade Council in Regional City can serve as an example. As soon as one asks the first question—Of what units is the action system comprised?—it becomes apparent that there were at least four different action systems involved successively: Homer's crowd, the several crowds that constituted the financial power structure, the associations and press, and the entire community. For the moment let us consider only Homer's crowd as the action system: it was composed of just a few individuals—a top leader and several of his associates. It had boundaries in that many informants in Regional City could tell you who belonged to Homer's crowd and who did not. Chiefly through its leader, it was related to other crowds on a high level of community decision-making. Each of its members, in turn, appeared to have a string of associates with whom he was linked in relations of reciprocal obligation and whose aid could be enlisted for executing various phases of a task such as the one involved. Through Charles Homer's prestige and influence and his relations of reciprocal obligation to leaders of other similar crowds, they were able to activate the top leadership of the community.

Though it had clear boundaries, Homer's crowd was not a formally organized system. It had neither officers nor charter nor membership dues nor formal provision for selecting leaders nor a formally specified procedure for reaching conclusions. Yet it is important to note that it had *informal* provision for all of these functions. The member units in this case were clearly individuals rather than organizations. Hunter told us that such crowds were held

314

together by similar interests and resulting common sentiments. From the standpoint of the larger community, these crowds performed the function of policy-making and action initiation. They constituted channels of information and opinion up to the top leaders and of policy decision and execution down through the various crowd members, with their respective followers at lower levels in the power hierarchy.

In the present instance, the "task" involved was to establish an International Trade Council under circumstances that would assure its support and success from the relevant groups. Hence, the immediate task was to draw up a complete plan, activate the other crowds through the established pattern of a luncheon at one of the clubs, present the plan, and enlist their financial support as well as their approval of the structure of the new council and the person who was to direct it. Beyond this were the associations and the "general public."

By what means did the structural relationship of the action system (Homer's crowd) become transformed into a different and enlarged action system? Note that this transformation was accomplished simply by activating already existing channels of mutual action, linkages between the top crowds, linkages to various followers of members of Homer's own crowd. The larger system of top leadership, which Homer's crowd activated, already existed as an informal social system, had well-established channels for proceeding in cases like this, and had well-established relationships of mutual obligation among crowds. This larger system of top leadership crowds thus existed as an informal network of relationships sustained in informal day-to-day contacts among various of its members and presumably in the more personal dyadic and triadic relationships that might be involved in individual business, social, and community episodes. In addition, it became activated on an ad hoc or episodic basis when some appropriate community action must be decided upon and set into operation.

In like manner, any of the other community action cases we considered can be examined as an action system—superficially, as above, or in much greater depth—using the outline of questions suggested.

The succession of different forms and boundaries that the action system took in Regional City is not at all atypical. In the midwestern health self-survey, there was also a small group of initiators, in this instance working within a formal organization, the health council. There was the expanded group, which reached its point of greatest size as 700 interviewers were activated by the 50 subsidiary leaders who recruited them in the various sections of the county. Later, the action system contracted to the health council, and after **315** the council's dissolution, could be found only in a residue of informal channels of reciprocal obligation among the professional leaders of the county who were involved.

In Blackfoot, Canada, the mental health education team came from outside the community and entered at various stages into more or less transitory ad hoc relationships with such organizations as the parent-teachers association; but as the action proceeded, the most relevant action system was always the professional team, which in a sense did not make any enduring impact on the action systems of the community or develop an indigenous one to carry out its assigned tasks.

In the Israeli community, the social worker decided deliberately to reject the possibility of working in relation to the existing three-family power structure and went about developing a diffuse relationship, which gradually evolved into a transformed power structure for the community, including a formally organized community council.

A Five-Stage Model

In all the above cases, the action system went through various stages of structure and process. Yet these cases appear to differ from each other greatly in the type of system and type of successive system stages involved. Can they all be gathered under the same conceptual roof?

Such a model will be suggested here. It is far from adequate, but at least it will be a start. Perhaps one can accommodate the various dynamic aspects of the development and change of community action systems using a fivefold pattern: (1) initial systemic environment; (2) inception of the action system; (3) expansion of the action system; (4) operation of the expanded action system; and (5) transformation of the action system.

1. Initial systemic environment. In system analysis it is helpful to consider the initial systemic environment in which the action system emerges. Here we are concerned with the community and the various social systems that constitute it. In what ways can a new community action system be related to the existing systemic organization of the community? There are two principal focuses for investigation:

a. What condition of operation of the existing system (involving dysfunctions, "felt needs," problems, equilibrium-disequilibrium, opportunities for positive community gains) creates a favorable situation for the inception of the particular community action system?

b. What systemic patterns for community action already exist in the community to which the community action system may be related in some functional way?

The many theorists who follow the general orientation of Kurt Lewin tend to view the action system as arising from some type of trouble or dysfunction in which the client system (in this case the community system) finds itself. Being clinically oriented, they tend to examine the relationships between a change agent and the troubled system in a process through which the change agent helps the system to reconstitute itself more adequately.

Sower and his associates, on the other hand, view the initial systemic environment from the standpoint of a convergence of interest in exploring a possible community action that arises, for whatever reason, among various community people or systems and leads to the inception of an ad hoc community action system: in their terminology, the establishment of an initiating set.

The Lewinian approach, looking at the inception of the action system as being rooted in some problem condition of the existing systemic environment, though useful in many cases, is not always applicable. Certainly, many community actions, such as that initiated by Charles Homer, are better described as arising from a community situation in which an opportunity for positive action and advantage is envisaged, rather than the correction of some deficiency of the existing system.

A related question is the previous experience of the community in accomplishing specific actions. In some instances the condition out of which the action emerges is that of an active community with well-established channels for episodic horizontal action, which in a sense "enjoys" doing such things much as an athlete enjoys using his body in vigorous undertakings. The attitude here might be: "Well, we got that one going. What's next, boys?" At the other extreme, perhaps, are those communities that have grave deficiencies precisely because they do not have established horizontal patterns for episodic action. They do not know how to cooperate, how to get things done, except within the vertically oriented systemic units such as specific churches, business establishments, schools, government departments, and the like. In such communities the action may arise specifically to develop channels of cooperation, to strengthen the horizontal system. Much current thinking about the relative stress given to task and maintenance in any particular community action could be clarified considerably by viewing the systemic context out of which the community action arises, particularly its horizontal pattern.

2. Inception of the Action System. A series of factors is involved in the inception of the action system. The first concerns its locus within the existing systemic environment. It may originate with a particular formal organization, such as a chamber of commerce or welfare council, or even a church or PTA. Or, more likely, it may originate with a smaller formal committee or informal clique of people within such an organization. On the other hand, it may originate within the informal structure of the community, in a clique of friends. Likewise, the action system may arise principally on the initiative of local people or principally under the stimulation of an outside agent. In the four examples given earlier, two were primarily local in their initial inception, two were stimulated by external agents.

In any case, an important question is the relation of the newly instituted action system to those other systems in the community that the action system must eventually involve in various ways in order for the action to be accomplished. As an example, such diverse community actions as instituting a cancer education campaign, gaining community approval for fluoridating the water supply, and raising funds for a new hospital, although all related to the health field, might call for different types of relationships between the action system and various power groups in the community. Pertinent factors in this relationship would be the linkages that the members of the action system at this stage have to various individuals and organizations in the community, both formally and informally.

The principal task of the action system at the inception stage is to define the accomplishment that is to result from the community action and to determine which elements of the community must be involved in order to assure this accomplishment.

3. Expansion of the Action System. Characteristically, in order to achieve its purposes there must be an expansion of the action system, for almost by definition, the type of action that any particular initial action system is capable of accomplishing unaided is not a community action.

The principal question to ask in the expansion stage is, For what purpose are additional individuals or groups to be brought into the action system? The different possibilities are numerous. This important point is often left vague. Certainly, one set of alternatives is that they are brought in to support or sustain or help carry out the necessary functions of the action system itself, as it proceeds toward the accomplishment of its specific objective. Thus, local community leaders were involved in the action system in the Michigan county in order to secure and supervise interviewers who would go from house to house. Or they are brought in to support or sustain the ultimate achievement toward which the action system is working, so that once the new clinic is acquired, the medical profession will support it through its referral practices; once the health self-survey is completed, its recommendations will be carried out; once the new

International Trade Council is established, it will be supported by local business interests. Parenthetically, it is interesting to note the appropriateness of the informant's remark in the Charles Homer case: "We decide we need to raise $65,000 to put this thing over. We could raise that amount within our own crowd, but eventually this thing is going to be a community proposition, so we decide to bring the other crowds in on the deal."

The direction and flow of expansion may be determined by the functions to be performed by the new members of the expanded system. They may be needed for planning the task aspects of the community action. They may be needed for executing the various tasks that have been accepted as part of the operational plan of the action. They may be included in order to constitute linkages or channels of communication to various groups whose cooperation or support, in one fashion or another, may be needed at this stage or later. They may be introduced into the action system for the prestige and sanction that they can lend to it. They may be brought in only so that their cooperation with the end product of the action will be assured (for example, so that they will use the new community center once it is built).

In considering these different functions that are to be performed by component parts of the expanded action system, it is helpful to consider what type or form of action will ultimately be desired or necessary by way of approval or support and from which groups in the community. For example, the action target may be to change individual behavior (taking a full course of polio shots or behaving differently toward the mentally ill). It may be voting, as in the case of a school bond issue or a fluoridation referendum. It may be the contribution of funds, as in the case of a drive for a new hospital or the establishment of a new voluntary agency. It may be participation in new patterns of community decision-making, as in the Israel example.

The initial action system is thus expanded according to what is expected from different individuals or groups in the community either in the operational stage of the action system or later on.

4. Operation of the Expanded Action System. One might more readily name this phase the task-accomplishment stage of the action system, however, the action system operates in all its phases and it would therefore be a mistake to denote this phase of greatest size of the action system by a term that indicates that this is the principal accomplishment phase. In the Charles Homer case, most of the important work was done before the action system was expanded beyond the small group of top crowds and before the chamber of commerce, various other organizations, or the press were called in. **319**

On the other hand, this extended period of operation of the system as enlarged to its fullest dimensions may actually constitute the task-accomplishment phase, as in the Michigan health self-survey, or as in the stage of solicitation in a hospital building campaign.

Thus often, though not invariably, this phase includes the carrying out of an extensive operation involving a large number of people or groups. It may actually constitute the stage in which the community action, as such, gets done, as, for example, in a community clean-up campaign. It may be that the principal activity is the development of a set of plans for something that is yet to come, like a new organization. It may be a phase in which activity is mainly directed at gaining broad acceptance for a new idea, as occurred when fluoridation was introduced. Or it may involve principally the attempt to change individual attitudes and behavior among a large number of people in the community, as in a mental health education campaign. Much of the activity at this stage will depend on the nature of the desired fate of the action system in relation to any additional system or task accomplishment that it sets up.

5. *Transformation of the Action System.* As the ad hoc community action ends, the action system may have various fates. It may have arisen to accomplish some task, like conducting a health self-survey, and then dissolve. It may have arisen to accomplish a task involving the setting up of a future action system, like the organization of a health council, and then dissolve. It may have arisen to become transformed into a future action system, like a group of top community leaders working to institute a community college and in effect constituting the first board of trustees of the college. Or the action system may have been more diffuse, involving simply the restructuring of the informal aspects of the total community, building up stronger horizontal ties through the diffuse relationship of a change agent working with community members to help them function more effectively together in a widely diverse set of contexts.

In any case, we are concerned here with the systemic residue of the community action. What is left from the action, systemically, after the action episode is terminated? An important dimension is the formal or informal nature of the systemic relations that remain. A new organization has been established, which can take other community action in the future, or a set of informal relations has been established or strengthened, which may likewise facilitate future action. Incidentally, although the health council failed after the Michigan health self-survey, Sower and his associates reported that strong informal ties of association and reciprocal obligation and of possible future collaborative action had been developed among the principal professional leaders involved, and that through these

320

informal channels, future county health actions might be facilitated.

Community actions can thus be viewed as action systems developing from their inception to their dissolution or transformation, in relation to the action task that they have been instituted to accomplish. We have traced this development emphasizing the action systems rather than the tasks themselves, since this procedure seems to get close to the dynamics of the process. One might have started with the task accomplishment process, or the planning process, as Ross calls it.

As a model of the task accomplishment process, we shall use an outline of five stages: (1) awareness of problem or goal; (2) gathering facts; (3) seeking possible solutions; (4) choosing a course of action; and (5) implementation. We shall not analyze these stages in detail but merely emphasize that they constitute a useful framework, not an absolute set of inexorable stages of task accomplishment.

These five task stages do not correspond precisely to the five stages in the development of the action system. Particularly in the phase of expansion of the action system, it is apparent that steps 2, 3, and 4 of the task process—gathering facts, seeking possible solutions, and choosing a course of action—may already have been accomplished, may be going on during the action system's expansion, or may not really go on until after the expansion phase.

In the case of the county health self-survey, the expansion of the action system preceded the fact-gathering stage. In the International Trade Council case, the expansion of the action system took place only after the facts had been gathered, possible solutions sought, and courses of action carefully laid out to the last detail. This great disparity is, of course, related to the many possible purposes involved in the expansion of the action system. Thus, though both the system and the task action begin at phase 1 and proceed generally through to phase 5, they do not do so in neat, joint, invariable sequence.

Perhaps this is the appropriate place to mention that both the action system and the task-accomplishment process may have subphases that in themselves constitute small cycles that may undergo one or more of the stages of the larger process.

The present analysis suggests an important analytical consideration in studying any community action system: the delineation of the manner in which the task-accomplishment phases are related to the stages of development of the special action system.

Some Comments on the Model

Let us relate a number of pertinent considerations to the preceding analysis. The first question has to do with the relative importance of **321** task accomplishment as against horizontal pattern development in any given community action. How much stress is placed by the participants on the tangible objective of the action, such as a set of survey findings, or a new trade council, or a desired amount of mental health education, or the introduction of new agricultural methods? And how much relative emphasis, on the other hand, is placed on developing the ability of groups within the community to work together in ways that cut horizontally across the special interests of the various task-oriented units? Among our four illustrations, the first three quite clearly favored task accomplishment, while the Israel project emphasized the development or strengthening of the horizontal pattern. We shall return to this question shortly in connection with community development as a process.

The second question is closely related: How does the task goal emerge? Does it emerge late in the development of the action system, as the fruit of a long process of gathering facts and seeking possible solutions? Or has the action system really been developed only to implement a prior decision about the nature of the task problem and the proper solution to be applied? There are instances of both in the examples cited.

There is another aspect to this question of how the task goal emerges, having to do with its relation to the vertical pattern. In many instances community action is instituted by an association or other group that is attempting, as it were, to apply a predesigned "package," often from the next higher level of an extracommunity system. It may be a voluntary health association, attempting to involve large segments of the community in some activity that is a current part of the national association's program goals. It may be a health official attempting to gain acceptance in the community for the organization of a county health department, under fairly precise specifications and fairly heavy pressure from the state health department. The important point here is that it is a type of task outcome that is indicated by the program goals of an extracommunity system of which some local unit is a part. At the other extreme, of course, it may be a task objective that has developed out of the local situation and out of the decision-making process of local people as they examine their problems and opportunities.

A third consideration is also related: At what point, if at all, does a change agent intervene in a professional capacity in the community action? He or she may, of course, be responsible for the inception of the action system. This was clearly the case both in the Blackfoot mental health education campaign and in the Israeli village. On the other hand, the professional change agent's role may be much less decisive in the action, and the action system may be quite independent of his or her participation. It may utilize a consultant merely to get technical information on details, rather than to be a major impetus in the decision-making process. The excellent model of the consultant's role in planned social change developed by Lippitt and his associates confines itself largely to those situations in which the consultant is to play a major part in the reorganization of the client system. In many instances, the intervening change agent is an "expert" or a "consultant" or a "field worker" brought into relation with the action system by a community unit that has initiated the action because of its relation to the program of its extracommunity system. In any case, the close relationship of a consultant to a special part of the action system is particularly significant, especially where the consultant's role is a decisive one.

A fourth question has to do with the relation between task accomplishment and the maintenance of the action system. Such dichotomies as task versus maintenance and instrumental activities versus expressive activities are widely familiar and merit comment in the present context. Task accomplishment is sometimes disruptive, and there is considerable indication that the pulsation between instrumental and expressive phases, noted by Bales in the abstract situation of the laboratory, applies to community action systems in the field as well. It is important also to note that tangible task accomplishment is often itself one of the strongest forces contributing to the maintenance of the system. The group that sees that it is getting somewhere may be more willing to put up with and contain the disequilibria that task accomplishment often creates.

Whether or not persons and groups are willing to support the action at any particular stage of development depends only partially on who the members of the action system are and what their relationship and the action system's relationship are to other social systems in the community. It depends also on the acceptability of the action objectives and of the task steps that are being taken to work toward these objectives. While this acceptability obviously relates to basic community values, the *way* in which it is related in terms of acceptability-unacceptability will depend both on the characteristics of the action system and on its task goals and accomplishments.

A final question relates the discussion even more closely to the matter of values. It has to do with the posture of the action system toward the established power system (or systems) of the community. As the findings of power-structure studies become transformed into guiding principles for various professional change agents in health and welfare, they usually take such forms as, "Don't buck the power structure," "Get the power structure on your side, or at least neutralize it if that is impossible," and so on.

Tumin, on the other hand, pointed out that "most problems facing communities arise from the very nature of their social struc- **323** ture and culture patterning, and are to be seen as the natural pathologies of those systems. Any genuine solution to such problems therefore is likely to involve some considerable re-shuffling of the *status quo.*"[12] And, of course, the Israel example in this chapter is an excellent illustration of a change agent deliberately deciding to do the exact opposite of "working with the existing power structure." Thus, it is important to note the deliberate or inadvertent position of the action system regarding the existing community power situation.

Community Development as a Process

So far, we have been considering community action as individual episodes, community *actions,* that activate the horizontal pattern for the period of the action episode, bringing together in a specific action system units of the community that are not otherwise so related.

Another type of activity also concerns itself with the community's horizontal pattern, but its emphasis is on strengthening the horizontal pattern itself, rather than on achieving the ad hoc objectives for which episodic community action takes place. This type of activity has been called *community development,* although other terms, such as *community planning* and *community organization,* are closely related. From this standpoint, community development is distinguished by its emphasis on the long run, and its primary attention to strengthening the horizontal pattern. Further, it represents a deliberate attempt to "administer" a program of strengthening the horizontal pattern, rather than leaving it to the operation of the interactional "market."

There has been considerable ambiguity in the use of the term *community development.* Sanders pointed out in a helpful analysis that the term can be considered to denote a process, a method, a program, and a social movement.[13] Often, confusion results when these possible meanings are not clarified.

Another source of ambiguity lies in the possible relations of community development to community organization and community planning. A third source of difficulty has centered on the frequent application of the term to largely preindustrial communities, with the associated idea that it has to do with a rapid and controlled

12. Melvin M. Tumin, "Some Social Requirements for Effective Community Development," Background Paper, Conference on Community Development and National Change, sponsored by the Center for International Studies, Endicott House, December 13-15, 1957. Published in *Community Development Review,* no. 11 (December 1958), p. 23.

13. Irwin T. Sanders, *The Community: An Introduction to a Social System* (New York: Ronald Press Co., 1958), pp. 407-8.

industrialization of such communities. A final source of difficulty has centered on the question of whether the goals of the process are specific task objectives—water purification, water fluoridation, delinquency prevention, economic development—or the change in the interrelationships among local people.

The above difficulties are partly semantic, stemming from the fact that different people use the term *community development* in different senses, any of which might be acceptable if carefully defined and delineated but none of which has reached general acceptance and invariant usage.

Community development   We shall define community development as *a deliberate and sustained attempt to strengthen the horizontal pattern of a community.* This definition conceives community development as a process, not as a method for reaching certain extraneous objectives, such as a new playground or an industrial development corporation. It is not a program emphasizing a set of specific activities. It is not a social movement, consisting of a program with emotionally dynamic overtones. Although these are all possible and plausible, though different, meanings, as Sanders suggested, we prefer to describe these meanings in other terms and to reserve the term *community development* for the process indicated above, a process that Sanders described as

> change from a condition where one or two people or a small elite within or without the local community make a decision for the rest of the people to a condition where people *themselves* make these decisions about matters of common concern; from a state of minimum to one of maximum cooperation; from a condition where few participate to one where many participate; from a condition where all resources and specialists come from outside to one where local people make the most of their own resources, etc.[14]

Community development is not confined to activities with preindustrial countries, nor is it necessarily concerned solely or even primarily with industrial development. The term is coming to be used increasingly in the United States and Canada to denote activities that have the strengthening of the horizontal pattern as an important focus. Much of what is considered community development abroad would not fall within the present definition, for the activities involved frequently do not aim primarily at strengthening the horizontal pattern of the local community but at accomplishing some specific objective such as changing methods of agriculture,

14. *Community*, pp. 407-8.   **325**

improving the industrial base, improving sanitation, increasing literacy, and so on.[15]

What relation do community organization and community planning have to community development conceived as a deliberate and sustained attempt to strengthen the community's horizontal pattern? According to Dunham, community organization for social welfare is "the process of bringing about and maintaining adjustment between social welfare needs and social welfare resources in a geographical area or a functional field."[16] Ross's definition was given earlier (see page 311). In Sanders' distinction, community organization in social work represents a *method* for getting things done in the community.

Community organization   The term *community organization* has been developed in America largely within the health, welfare, and recreational field to describe, among other things, a method for reaching certain objectives that are beyond the scope of any single agency. There has been considerable controversy within and around the social work field as to whether community organization is an exclusively social work process, as some maintain, or whether it is a process that can be applied equally by other professions, such as community planners, agricultural agents, adult education specialists, and so on. In one frequent usage it is limited to the field in which social workers primarily operate and is identified with "generic" social work process. Obviously, this is much more restrictive as to field of operations than the definition of community development that we are considering.

As already mentioned, there has been a more or less historical distinction, somewhat adventitious, between *community development,* as applied principally o preindustrial communities, and *community organization,* as the term is used in Western communities, especially in the United States and Canada. The term *community development* is often used in relation to activities in preindustrial, largely rural, communities, customarily including a "global" scope of activities, such as education, industry, housing, health, welfare, and government, and usually involving a major role of the national government in initiating the program. "Community organization," on the other hand, is customarily employed to describe activities in industrial, largely urban communities, customarily restricted to the health and

15. For a fresh review of the community development field see Lee J. Cary, ed., *Community Development as a Process* (Columbia: University of Missouri Press, 1970).

16. Arthur Dunham, "What is the Job of the Community Organization Worker?" *Proceedings of the National Conference of Social Work* (New York: Columbia University Press, 1949), p. 162.

welfare field and involving a major role for local voluntary organizations and agencies rather than the national government.

But these matters, though important, say more about the scope and setting than about the process. Much the same process may be employed in both settings, as indicated by the striking parallelism of Ross's definition of community organization and the definition of community development used by the United States International Cooperation Administration (see page 311). Thus, as far as process is concerned, there is little difference between *community development* and *community organization* as the terms are customarily used. The difference is in the kinds of settings and tasks and personnel with which they have been associated.

Community planning   The term *community planning* has often been used with relation to community activities. Let us consider the two principal activities denoted by this term and then relate them to community development. The first activity is that associated with the terms *city planning* and *town planning*. Governmental or quasi-governmental boards and occasionally voluntary associations conduct a specific type of activity that focuses upon the physical aspects of the community and for whose implementation certain methods are available such as surveys, official maps, community plans, zoning, and building codes. But it is also employed to denote the whole area of concern for the physical aspects of communities as these relate to community living patterns, ranging from Ebenezer Howard's influential book *Garden Cities of To-morrow* and the Goodmans' *Communitas* to such current studies as the monumental New York Metropolitan Region Study and, in another vein, *The Death and Life of Great American Cities*.[17] In its narrower meaning associated with the activities of planning boards, the term has little relationship to community development, although it should be noted that there is a continuous ferment within, or at least on the periphery of, the planning profession that agitates for a broader conception of planning and looks toward more consideration being given the social aspects of planning, as related both to the task objectives of planning and to the process through which plans are formulated and decisions reached.

The second major use of the term *community planning* concerns the process of going about achieving certain specific objectives of broad community interest. Ross, for example, specified that commu-

17. See Ebenezer Howard, *Garden Cities of To-morrow* (London: Faber and Faber, Ltd., 1945), originally published in 1898; Paul and Percival Goodman, *Communitas: Ways of Livelihood and Means of Life*, 2nd ed. (New York: Vintage, 1960); and Jane Jacobs, *The Death and Life of Great American Cities* (New York: Random House, 1961). The several volumes of the New York Metropolitan Region Study are published by Harvard University Press.

nity organization has two aspects: community integration and planning. The latter involves "the process of locating and defining a
problem (or set of problems), exploring the nature and scope of the
problem, considering various solutions to it, selecting what appears
to be a feasible solution, and taking action in respect to the solution
chosen."[18] It can readily be seen that we are dealing here with the
task aspects of community action rather than the process or "integra
tion" aspects.

It will be recalled that in considering community action a dis
tinction was made between social system phases and task phases.
They were associated with each other but clearly distinguishable,
being related in different ways in different community actions. Community actions were analyzed in terms of the ad hoc action systems
that developed to carry them out, rather than in terms of the task
phases. In community development, likewise, there is perhaps an
advantage in emphasizing the social system side rather than the task
accomplishment or "planning" side. But the social system involved in
community development is the total community's horizontal pattern,
while the social system involved in community action was the specific
ad hoc action system. As in the case of community action, this
approach is believed to be fruitful because it directs attention to the
dynamics of the social interrelationships involved rather than to the
substantive question of how a particular task is attempted and the
extent to which it is accomplished.

Community Development and the "Great Change"

But there is an additional, more theoretically important reason for
emphasizing the changes in the horizontal pattern, rather than specific task accomplishment, in defining and delineating community
development. Throughout this book, it has been stressed that the
"great change" in its various aspects considered in chapter 3
operates to strengthen the vertical ties of community units to extracommunity systems, to make less viable the horizontal ties based on
propinquity of community units to each other, and to remove from
the local community many types of decisions about what will take
place on the local scene. The older, largely informal ties that held
community units in an effective functional interrelationship are no
longer found adequate. As a result, various deliberate attempts are
made to achieve at least the minimum necessary functional interrelationship, which formerly existed largely without special attention
being given it. The individual behavior of the "market" no longer

18. *Community Organization*, p. 51.

suffices for the coordination of community units, and thus such coordination must be at least partially "administered."

For the administered maintenance and strengthening of strong horizontal ties, a number of types of unit have been developed. We considered many of them in chapters 6 and 7. While such units were developing, there emerged, particularly in connection with the councils of social agencies and other activities oriented toward social work, a professional rationale as to the process through which such coordination should be achieved. In social work there already existed a process theory for casework with the individual, based on client assent, permissiveness, and the caseworker as an enabler rather than a "leader," with a strong emphasis on confronting the client's current difficulties in a way that would better prepare him or her to face other difficulties more effectively in the future. Thus, it was hardly surprising that as social workers gradually became aware of and deliberately developed a community organization function, they looked upon casework, group work, and community organization as all constituting the same "generic" process, only slightly modified to accommodate the respectively different settings in which it was employed. Thus, community organization as practiced by social workers has been more deliberately aware of an emphasis on process as well as task than has been the case with some of the other settings in which coordination of local units has been attempted, for example, city planning, chamber of commerce activity, and so on.

A comparable awareness of the importance of helping communities become more effective by helping strengthen their horizontal pattern has been apparent in the growing field of community development as represented by the community development institutes or divisions of state universities and agricultural colleges. As distinguished from the social workers, practitioners in such institutions have tended to deal more with the smaller communities and to take as their client the whole community rather than such functional parts of it as the "the welfare community."[19] They also have considered their field of possible operations to be global, in the sense of including not only social services but government, education, industrial development, physical planning, and recreation in their scope of activities. But they, like the social workers, and like many of those active in "community development" in relation to preindustrial communities abroad, have been specifically aware of the importance of the goal of strengthening the horizontal pattern and of the process through which specific task goals are achieved.

Nevertheless, practitioners in all three fields report continuous frustration in trying to emphasize the strengthening of local unit ties

---

19. See Ross, *Community Organization*, p. 41.

to each other, rather than placing emphasis on the specific task goal that a particular community action episode may seek to achieve.

Tumin has described the issue clearly, referring to "the competing claims and demands of two major purposes which often cross."

> The first of these emphasizes, predominantly, the need for improvement of the material conditions of life, and measures its success in terms of certain technological gains, or by some indices of economic growth, with only secondary interest in community participation.
>
> The second emphasizes predominantly the need for the development of concern for problem solving and a spirit of self-reliance in communities which have typically depended on others for the solution of their problems.
>
> It is pointless to aver solemnly that these two goals constitute equal priority aims of any good student of community development. That goes without saying. The salient fact which must be confronted is that *sharp strains and incompatibilities in programs arise with almost monotonous regularity out of the conflict of the different priorities which are given to these two purposes.*[20]

Is the specific action goal—the new swimming pool, the new clinic, the successful fluoridation referendum—the primary matter, with educational and cooperative activities among community units chiefly a method for accomplishing this task? Or is the strengthening of the horizontal pattern the primary matter, with the specific selection of one task or another of lesser importance? The alternatives seem academic, since both are so obviously involved in many community action episodes and development programs. But unfortunately the two goals do not coincide so as to obviate the necessity of choice between them when actual action episodes are involved.

Frequently the methods that would ultimately strengthen the horizontal pattern must be abandoned if the specific task objective is to be accomplished. Broadly based decision-making must be replaced by decision-making by a few, who then "sell" the task objective to others. Education and discussion and individual decision-making based on a full understanding of the facts and a thorough interchange of opinions must be renounced in favor of getting influential individuals and groups behind the task objective, using political, economic, and social "pressure," and employing propagandistic methods of persuasion rather than educational methods of presenting facts impartially and encouraging discussion. The process of

20. "Some Social Requirements for Effective Community Development," pp. 3-4. Italics added.

330

encouraging people to make their own decisions about what is good for them thus gives way to the process of convincing them of what a change agent or a small group of "leaders" thinks is good for them.

Thus a kind of reverse "goal displacement" takes place. In bureaucratic theory, goal displacement is the process through which bureaucratic leaders divert their energy and that of the bureaucratic system toward strengthening the system itself, rather than accomplishing the functions that the system was set up to accomplish. "As a result of this process, the actual activities of the organization become centered around the proper functioning of organization procedures, rather than upon the achievement of the initial goals."[21] Or decisions are made that will make the top bureaucratic positions more attractive and satisfactory rather than on the basis of accomplishing the system's announced functions.

This type of goal displacement characterizes established, task-oriented bureaucracies. But in community development activities where the goal is the strengthening of the community's horizontal pattern through the development or strengthening of specific action systems in a series of community action episodes, the goal priority is reversed. The strengthening of the horizontal pattern itself becomes the highest goal, with task accomplishment subsidiary to it. Yet the organizational goal becomes displaced as the task accomplishment usurps it. This reverse goal displacement should not be surprising when we recall that community development, like community action episodes through which it takes place, involves an activation of the horizontal pattern of the community in ways in which it is not customarily activated. (If it were, the "community development" would not be necessary.) Thus, the community, as a social system, has not been made to pay the price of bureaucratic goal displacement largely because it has not received the values that bureaucratic organization affords. When it attempts to achieve these values through a rational, administered approach to creating or restoring a strong horizontal pattern in a deliberately "administered" fashion, this goal is easily displaced by the more immediate task goal of the action episode involved—be that a new school bond issue, a community center, the attraction of a new industry, an urban renewal program, or whatever.

21. David L. Sills, *The Volunteers: Means and Ends in a National Organization* (Glencoe, Ill.: Free Press, 1957), p. 62. Sills asserted that the preserving of organizational goals, along with the maintaining of membership interest, constitute "the two most pervasive problems of voluntary associations" (p. 212). For other discussions of goal-displacement, see Robert K. Merton, "Bureaucratic Structure and Personality," *Social Forces*, vol. 18, no. 4 (May 1940), and Philip Selznick, "An Approach to a Theory of Bureaucracy," *American Sociological Review*, vol. 8, no. 1 (February 1943).

The problems involved in "administering" a strengthening of the horizontal pattern are interesting and complex. For example, the "administering" of a strengthening of informal ties among people and groups is almost a contradiction in terms. What was formerly spontaneous neighboring now becomes the formal activities of a neighborhood association. What was formerly accomplished by personal contacts now becomes administered as a formal contract, charter, or "interagency agreement."

Shifting focus somewhat, various practitioners report that "people just don't want to be 'coordinated.' " In context, this statement often means that although individual citizens and community units do not want to build up a coordinating structure just for the sake of achieving some vague objective of "coordination," they may well be induced to enter into coordinated activity around specific tasks, such as an urban renewal program, providing needed services for the chronically ill, combating juvenile delinquency, raising voluntary contributions, and so on. But notice that here, again, the task is given hegemony, and in the clinches it can be expected to prevail.

Sower and his associates gave considerable attention to seeking the reasons for the dying out of the health council whose strengthening was one of the objectives of the health self-survey that they studied. They pointed out that the council's members were really representatives of other organizations whose goals commanded a greater loyalty. They pointed out that there are real value conflicts involved in the planning function, with deep-seated American predispositions against delegation of overall planning authority to any specific group. But in seeking for explanatory hypotheses, they suggested:

> One possible hypothesis is that there is almost no way to justify and legitimize a council type of organization in the structure of the average American community. Basic to any organization is that it must have some legitimate reason for existence, it must be justifiable. Churches, for instance, save souls, maintain moral standards, and generally do good; schools educate children; lodges provide insurance and meeting places for their members; athletic clubs provide recreation and keep down waistlines.[22]

It is interesting to notice the specific way in which these examples relate to the locality-relevant functions discussed in chapter 6. These are obviously specific task functions. A little later in their discussion, Sower and his associates observed that one might expect the citizens to take greater interest in specific health organizations than

22. *Community Involvement*, p. 266.

in a coordinating council. They emphasized, quite understandably, the factor of "conflicts with deep-set beliefs in individualism and fears of overall planning bodies."[23]

But in a sense, they proved too much. All the explanations they gave would make it equally unlikely that community welfare councils could exist and flourish. And yet they do. The issues involved are important and relevant. Among other functions that the earlier councils of social agencies performed was that of providing a series of common services to the member agencies. Thus, over and beyond the coordination and joint action functions, the councils offered their member agencies a tangible service as one of the benefits of membership and participation. A notable instance of such common services was the maintenance of a social service exchange, a central registry of the agencies with which individuals and families have been in contact. Through such common services, the agencies received something more than the satisfaction of a vague aspiration toward "coordination," strengthening the community," or, in our terms, strengthening the horizontal pattern.

Significantly, the social service exchange became highly rationalized and bureaucratized in its function. It was thoroughly task-oriented, in the sense of existing in order to provide a specific tangible service to the member agencies. Its operations could therefore be rationalized and systematized. The performance of such tangible, task-oriented services gave the councils a reason for being, over and beyond their more diffuse "coordinating" goals. They were able to form themselves as organizations, establish a strong national service organization, and regularize their own procedures. The councils represent one of the few and best examples of attempts to bureaucratize along horizontal lines. As suggested above, they were enabled to do so largely because they emphasized task almost to the exclusion of process in at least some of their operations, their common services to member organizations. With this basis of coherence, they were able to develop relatively regularized procedures for activating the horizontal structure of the community, particularly in the health and welfare field.

In relation to this analysis, it is also significant that, as the above occurred, it was possible for the councils to shift their emphasis from a relatively static, and to a certain extent, relatively ineffective, divisional structure to a situation in which it was possible to organize in relatively systematic fashion special ad hoc units to accomplish specific program objectives. They thus, in effect, were able to coordinate not in the name of coordination but with considerable flexibility for specific tasks that are attractive as program

23. *Community Involvement*, p. 269.

goals: housing, chronic illness, multiproblem families, juvenile delinquency. Underlying the flexibility, however, is a bureaucratized
organization and an explicit, though empirically based professional
rationale.

Bureaucratization *across* community units has also been notably
achieved in connection with a related task in the health and welfare
field, that of fund raising. The community chests and united funds
represent an attempt at systematic organization and administering of
gift giving as a basis of support of the voluntary agencies of the
community and, in the case of united funds, of the national health
associations as well. Compared to the national organizations, the
community-based chests and united funds may be less well organized and less effective, as Seeley and his associates found in their
study. Nevertheless, the highly bureaucratized nature of chests and
funds is apparent. They represent, in our terms, an attempt to
"administer" gift giving to voluntary associations, an activity previously left largely to the gift "market" (see page 230). It is interesting that here, too, we find an almost complete shift from community
development, conceived as a process of strengthening the horizontal
pattern, to emphasis on accomplishing the task of extracting funds.
Thus, as noted in chapter 7, Seeley's group asked "whether the
Chest ought fundamentally to conceive itself more on the model of
an instrumentality of local desire, registering rather than manipulat-
ing public opinion, expressing local forces rather than molding
them."[24] Here, again, is goal displacement, in this instance toward
strengthening the bureaucratic procedures in order to accomplish
the task; but there is the additional implication that the task may be
displaced from that of serving the community to that of manipulat-
ing the community in the interests of fund raising. These investigators therefore raised the question: *"Is the paramount objective of the
Chest* (or ought it to be) *the extraction of money from the public or the
organizing of that public into a community,* united in virtue of its shared
endeavor to provide for certain health and welfare activities?"[25] No
more apt illustration could be given of the problem of goal displacement from that of community development in the sense of strengthening the horizontal pattern to that of task accomplishment.

To recognize the existence of this type of goal displacement
and to find its roots in the association of task orientation with the
vertical rather than the horizontal pattern of the community is
obviously not to deny a task component to community development
activities. Quite the reverse, it is rather to affirm the great pressure

24. John R. Seeley et al., *Community Chest: A Case Study in Philanthropy* (Toronto:
University of Toronto Press, 1957), p. 401.

25. *Community Chest,* p. 401. Italics in original.

from the task aspects to preempt the process itself, even where the initial emphasis is deliberately on process.

Is it not possible, however, to approach community development from the standpoint of task? Is it not possible deliberately to emphasize the task aspects from the outset but nevertheless give considerable attention to the process as well, that is, to seeing that the community's horizontal pattern is strengthened through the joint effort to accomplish the task? This question is being raised increasingly by field personnel and local officials of various largely vertically oriented extracommunity systems. It reflects a growing awareness on the part of public health personnel, education officials, voluntary health agencies, and national industrial corporations of the relations between their respective operations and other parts of local communities in which their units are found.

Many of the task activities of such vertical systems are thought of as themselves constituting community development. Such activities as setting up clinics, attracting a new industry to the community, fluoridating the water supply, or floating a new school bond issue are understandably included in a broader concept of community development than that used here. They certainly are included in the definition of community development by T. R. Batten, an expert on that concept: "an action taken by any agency and primarily designed to benefit the community."[26] But the accomplishment of such tasks as those listed above does not necessarily strengthen the community's horizontal pattern. Indeed, it often weakens it, both because in so many instances it involves goal setting and major initiative for action being removed from the locality to a "system headquarters" and because on the local scene, in the zeal for the accomplishment of the task, procedures that would strengthen community coherence are replaced by procedures more deliberately oriented to achieving the task goals.[27]

Even in task-oriented ventures, however, different degrees of emphasis may be given to the subsidiary goal of strengthening the horizontal pattern of the community. Tasks such as the above may be accomplished and leave the community's horizontal pattern stronger as a result, or weaker. Much depends, of course, on the methods employed in the task effort.

An important shortcoming of the foregoing analysis is the fact that in attempting to delineate task and process for analytical purposes, it has been made to seem like an either-or situation. While it

26. T. R. Batten, *Communities and their Development: An Introductory Study with Special Reference to the Tropics* (London: Oxford University Press, 1957), p. 2.

27. See Roland L. Warren, "Group Autonomy and Community Development," *Autonomous Groups*, vol. 15, nos. 1 and 2 (Autumn and Winter 1959-60).

may be either-or when we ask the question, "In the clinches, which takes ascendancy?" this is far from denying that task and process aspects are involved in all community action episodes and in all community development activities. The two are inseparable except in abstract analysis. The question is solely which shall be given top priority and how we shall define the community development process. By considering it a process through which the horizontal pattern is deliberately strengthened, it is possible to avoid the misconception of equating community development with task accomplishment.

Taylor, in considering community development in local villages as part of a national development program, emphasized the importance of the role of local self-help groups. "Unless and until such self-perpetuating groups are developed, communities as such have not developed no matter how many things have been done for them."[28]

We can summarize, then, by saying that community development is an administered process of strengthening the community's horizontal pattern. It usually consists of one or a series of successive action episodes in which specific task goals are sought. In the process, even though strengthening the horizontal structure is deliberately given the major emphasis, there is a strong tendency for the task goals to usurp the process, changing the goal of the activity and the procedures involved to the major emphasis of accomplishing the task. In community action sequences where the task is given principal emphasis from the outset, it may nevertheless be possible to utilize procedures that will strengthen rather than weaken the community's horizontal structure. But the predominance of the task goal implies that the horizontal structure will be strengthened only if this strengthening does not interfere with task accomplishment—and it often does.[29]

Prospects for Community Development

The foregoing analysis may seem somewhat austere. What indications are there that are favorable to the possibilities for success of deliberate efforts to strengthen the horizontal pattern of American communities?

First, there is the underlying reality of the propinquity of the multitude of diverse units that constitute the community. Although

28. Carl C. Taylor, "Community Development Programs and Methods," *Community Development Review*, no. 3 (December 1956), p. 35.

29. A newly critical and analytical literature is developing on the goals and functions of community development. See p. 386 for some current references.

mere propinquity does not assure strong functional interrelations among people or units occupying the same local area, the propinquity in this case is accompanied by extreme symbiotic interdependence. To perform adequately in their respective extracommunity systems, the units must come into relationship with each other in certain specific functional exchanges, as indicated in chapters 6 and 9. Their individual interest in this symbiotic exchange constitutes an assurance that, if they can help it, they will not permit the community situation to deteriorate to the extent that their own symbiotic needs are threatened without looking toward cooperating with others with whom they can take joint action.

In this connection it should be recalled that just as there are constant pressures toward isolating the local units from each other as they become more systematically entwined in their respective extracommunity systems, so there is a contrary tendency. This is the tendency, noted in chapter 5, for categorical relationships to become personal, for people, in other words, to want to step out from behind their fragmented, bureaucratic masks as unit officials and confront each other as whole persons. The attempt engulfs them in role conflicts such as those described in chapters 8 and 9, but few will remain content not to at least try.

There is not only the personal inclination, not always followed, to treat others as whole people rather than as occupants of unit positions; there is also the presence of strong cultural values giving high lip service, at least, to cooperative, neighborly concern. There may not be a cracker barrel and a potbellied stove in the new supermarket, but these have not been erased as symbols of a neighborly intercourse, which many people today desperately seek to regain. If many people seek to regain the value by, in effect, installing cracker barrels and potbellied stoves in supermarkets, or by grouping highrise subsidized housing units around a New England-type common, or by holding cookouts in suburban backyards, at least these are indications that people seek a bridge across the narrow confines of rigid organizational differentiations.

Part of the reason why some of the efforts toward reaching across the vertical barriers seem pathetically ineffective is the lack of social inventions that will more adequately replace horizontal relations of the market type with those of the administered type. Service clubs, chambers of commerce, housing authorities, community welfare councils, planning boards, neighborhood associations, settlement houses, and neighborhood centers all represent attempted solutions to this problem. There is, in sum, a ferment of development in American communities toward finding new ways of deliberately organizing a kind of functional cooperation that can no longer be left to the vagaries of the market. **337**

Along with new ways of organization there has arisen a convergence of interest in community development among a large number of practitioners in one or another institutional setting. These include agricultural agents, adult educators, public health educators, community relations personnel in industry, city planners, community organization specialists in social work, social group workers, community development workers in preindustrial areas, and a growing number of practitioners in community development divisions of universities. Practitioners in these diverse institutional settings are coming to develop a common body of experience and, to a certain extent, a common body of practice theory. As a social worker, Witte has observed, "I could not help but wonder why I found personnel from a wide range of occupational fields working so successfully in what one might easily conclude is a distinctively social work bailiwick? It occurred to me that we, as American social workers, sometimes tend to regard as our own, certain basic tenets of democracy in which our practice is rooted."[30] Likewise, di Franco, comparing community development with extension education, concluded that "in comparing principles there is no difference of any consequence on the overall approach when both are basically concerned with helping people help themselves."[31]

The growth of interdisciplinary conferences on the subject of community development is another indication of this professional convergence. In 1960 the National Training Laboratories instituted an annual Community Leadership Training Laboratory at Bethel, Maine, to which was added two years later a similar laboratory in the intermountain region. The wide variety of local, state, and national organizations represented among the participants in these laboratories gave strong indication of the growth of community development as a focus of great interest for a variety of practitioners.

The current activity in the area of community development indicates that the field has some of the characteristics of a social movement. Sanders described this aspect of community development as "a cause to which people become committed. . . . It is dedicated to progress, a philosophic and not a scientific concept. . . . CD as a movement tends to become institutionalized, building up its own organizational structure, accepted procedures and professional stan-

30. Ernest F. Witte, "Community Development in India, Iran, Egypt and the Gold Coast," in *Community Organization in Social Work: Its Practice in Old and New Settings* (New York: Council on Social Work Education, 1956), p. 67.

31. Joseph di Franco, "Differences between Extension Education and Community Development," *Community Development Review* 4, no. 1 (March 1959): 24. This was originally published as Comparative Extension Publication No. 5 (Ithaca, New York: State College of Agriculture, Cornell University, October 1958).

dards."[32] Thus, more than a process as we have defined it, a whole complex of organizations and activities based more or less clearly on the goal of strengthening communities, particularly in their horizontal aspects, has arisen as a social movement, giving the effort sustained support.

Finally, there is growing indication of a bridging of the wide gap that has so long existed between the practice theory of community practitioners in various fields and the behavorial sciences. One of the reasons why a good body of behavioral science theory on community development is not available is that there is a lack of good theory on the community itself as a particular form of human organization. In the absence of such theory, a type of clinical approach, largely empirically based but not tested in any rigorous way, has arisen to provide "principles" of procedure for the practitioner. These principles consist of empirically derived statements about cause and effect, with an admixture of value admonitions—statements, in other words, much more appropriate to community development as a social movement than as a scientifically investigable process.

This purely pragmatic approach has not contributed significantly to a scientific body of theory regarding the community from which specific practice applications could be derived in any rigorous way. Perhaps the analogy to chemistry and alchemy is not altogether inappropriate. The alchemists were in search of solutions to very important problems, such as the extension of human life span and the transmutation of metals. They were not opposed to learning from experience. Quite the opposite was true: they were fervent in their desire to learn what new experience someone else a thousand miles away might have had in finding something effective. But their experience was not rigorously guided by the systematic principles of scientific investigation, and hence specious relationships became the basis for faulty generalization. Further, they had no scientific framework of theory within which to order observations that they made in a process that would thus gradually improve theory itself. As a result, they sought to accomplish things that were virtually impossible; they used methods gained in experience whose efficacy was spurious; and they were unable to make knowledge add up in a meaningful way. Only gradually did there arise a body of scientific theory, based on factual investigations by people whose primary motive was curiosity rather than miracles. Scientific chemistry never found the philosopher's stone, but in its place grew a body of scientific knowledge, closely related to systematic hypothesis testing, which permitted engineering accomplishments that would have been considered miraculous by the alchemists.

32. *Community*, pp. 401-8.

In the field of community action there has been a parallel development. Here, too, important problems present themselves. Practitioners are also willing and anxious to benefit by experience, curious to learn about some new technique that someone has found to be successful a thousand miles away but similarly devoid of a systematic methodology for learning from experience in a way that will assure valid rather than specious generalizations about relationships and devoid of a body of abstract theory within which new knowledge can be meaningfully related and that can itself be modified to accommodate new findings that the older formulation was not adequate to encompass.

Two developments indicate that perhaps a beginning is being made toward the construction of a sound body of knowledge concerning the community and the extent to which community phenomena can be brought under a degree of deliberate control. One is the increasing attention being given in recent years to the realization of the relative lack of systematic community theory and the inadequacy of such theoretical formulations as exist.[33] The next decades may see far-reaching reorganizations in community theory caused not only by the rapid changes that are transforming the nature of communities, but also by the mature reexamination of some of the naive conceptions of the community as a social phenomenon, which have characterized much previous investigation.

The other development is an increasing awareness on the part of community practitioners of the need for a more adequate framework within which to orient their practice. They are looking increasingly to the behavioral scientists to help them. There is still the danger that what the behavioral scientists are really being asked for is a philosopher's stone in the form of a bundle of techniques that will help the practitioners accomplish the tasks they set themselves. But such techniques, unrelated to sound theory, are nevertheless a type of community alchemy, a kind of substitute for systematic investigation within a carefully thought-out theoretical framework on the basis of which sound propositions can be made—and tested. There is no other way to scientifically valid knowledge.

---

33. Jessie Bernard's *The Sociology of Community* (Glenview, Ill.: Scott, Foresman & Co., 1973) gives a highly sophisticated critique of contemporary community theory.

The Great Change— 11
Adaptation and Revolt

Reflections on a Troubled Decade

Ralf Dahrendorf wrote a challenging book about the development of American sociology in its relationship to American society in general. It was a creative attempt to move back and forth between the characteristics of American society as these emerged in historical development and the characteristics of American sociology, which purported to describe American society but at the same time bore the indelible characteristics of the society in which it emerged. As such, Dahrendorf's book was inevitably a *tour de force,* and a brilliant one.[1]

The decade that ended in the early seventies presents a fascinating subject for similar treatment, for in that decade social action within communities and social theory about communities came into close relationship. In this close relationship, social action appeared to be the prime mover with social theory being forced by the pressure of events to catch up. It might have been otherwise. Social theory about communities might conceivably have reached the stage where its implications were seen to be crucial for current history and where

1. Ralf Dahrendorf, *Die Angewandte Aufklärung: Gesellschaft und Soziologie in Amerika* (Munich: R Piper & Co., 1963).

various groups and organizations might have converged to apply in history some of the understandings that theory had provided.

But the impetus for change came not from a theory of action and social change such as Marxism or Maoism, although these and other theories of purposive change had their strong adherents. Rather, the impetus, "typically American," was a pragmatic one. It was found in the changing fates of different groups of people in American society, and more important, in the changing perceptions of these fates. Poverty emerged as a problem of great national salience, not because there was more of it than formerly but because various groups of people were beginning to look at it in a different way. Civil rights and the whole question of racial and other types of injustice in various parts of the American social structure came to be heated issues, not because the situation was any worse than earlier but because people—various people representing different groupings—were coming to think differently about these issues. Likewise, the disquieting notion that somehow American society had lost its course, had drifted away from the high aspirations it once held, had become overcommercialized, overdirected, overmilitarized, overmaterialistic, grew in the course of the decade and became associated with a whole generation in revolt. And again, this movement of youth, even though it was precipitated by a disastrous foreign war, was not directed at conditions that were new. Rather, it was directed at conditions that, though fairly old and rather deeply grounded in American society, were coming to be looked upon in a new way.

There occurred in the communities of America, large and small, a series of dramas that appear kaleidoscopic and even chaotic in their juxtaposition. There was the burgeoning of federal programs, the series of crises over urban transportation in various cities, the increasing problems of pollution, the increasing financial strains on the cities' inadequate tax bases, the exodus of whites to the suburbs and the influx of blacks to the inner cities, and the repetition of this process on a smaller scale in satellite cities. There were the ghetto riots and the emergence of various forms of social protest relatively undeveloped in the preceding decade; there was the increasing attention given to the social problems of the cities both at City Hall and in Washington; there was, of course, the whole issue of school desegregation. The series of federal programs designed to help localities cope, in one way or another, with their growing problems culminated, at decade's end, in three programs, which gained wide currency and support: Model Cities, new towns, and revenue sharing.

The above inventory includes only one selection from the broad panoply of events and issues in American communities. Others might be chosen with equal claim to representativeness. Any such list indicates a bewildering complexity, a complexity that it may be helpful to analyze in relation to the conceptual framework of the foregoing chapters in this book.

Most of the major issues and events mentioned above relate in various ways to a small number of summary, and therefore somewhat abstract, propositions:

1. People were reacting in one way or another to the "inevitable" effects of the "great change," taking the position with more or less deliberation that the "great change" is, after all, a social product and can be influenced through social intervention.

2. The importance of the vertical dimension of community organization grew greatly, most notably in the increasing role of the federal government in the affairs of the cities.

3. There were both intellectual confusion and heated agitation regarding the relation of "natural" change to "purposive" change and the extent to which social change is to be considered a natural phenomenon that takes its course largely independently of the wishes and actions of individual social actors or the extent to which social change can be guided, and the appropriate methods through which this guiding can be done.

4. There was a growing inclination to look at communities as abstractions and to pay more attention to the various components that make them up. Claims to represent the "public interest" were met with increasing skepticism. A plurality of diverse and sometimes conflicting interests was recognized as the norm, with the consequence that processes of contention and theories of conflict grew in importance.

These somewhat broad and abstract propositions provide a convenient outline for an analysis of the way in which the social developments of the past decade reflect back upon community theory.

Response to the "Great Change"

It will be recalled that the "great change" is simply a general term to denote a series of interrelated developments constituting the mainstream of change in American society as well as in other parts of the world. These changes can be conveniently subsumed under the following headings:

1. Division of labor
2. Differentiation of interests and association
3. Increasing systemic relationships to the larger society
4. Bureaucratization and impersonalization
5. Transfer of functions to profit enterprise and government
6. Urbanization and suburbanization
7. Changing values

Quite obviously, these changes arise through human behavior, and are presumably open to modification through deliberate human intent. Yet in our time they are so visible and so important that they seem to march with a fateful inexorability, constituting almost "forces of nature" to which people must, in all practicality, adjust.

In earlier chapters we have noted a number of ways in which adjustments are made to the "great change." In the discussion of suburbanization, it was suggested that some aspects of suburban life, particularly the commuter suburbs, can be seen as a reaction to the "great change" and that, in a sense, the commuter suburbs constitute "the small town's last stand." In the preceding chapter it was noted that community organization and community development could be interpreted as "administered" attempts to bring about coordination among community units under circumstances of increasing diversification and fragmentation where custom, face-to-face relationships, and informal adaptation could no longer be relied upon to effect that coordination.

The dynamics of both diversification and fragmentation in recent years constitute a large part of the current concern with the viability of communities, large and small, but especially of the larger cities. Recent population changes have been dominated by the growth of the metropolitan population, as indicated by the population of Standard Metropolitan Statistical Areas, of which cities of 50,000 or more are usually the core area. The number of SMSA's increased from 212 to 243 in the decade from 1960 to 1970. More recent figures show an increase to 264 SMSA's by 1974. The total population of the United States increased by 13.3 percent during the decade ending in 1970, from 179,323,175 to 203,211,926. The percentage of people living in metropolitan areas increased from 63 percent in 1960 to 68.6 percent in 1970 and 72.8 percent by 1974.[2]

But the increase in metropolitan area population was not distributed evenly between the central cities and the rest of their surrounding metropolitan areas. The central cities increased by 4.7 percent in population during the decade from 1960 to 1970. At the same time, however, the metropolitan population outside the central cities was increasing at more than five times that rate, or 25.6 percent. The trend continued in milder form from 1970 to 1973 with the population within the central cities actually declining by 0.3 percent while the population within the SMSA's but outside the central cities grew by 1.6 percent.[3] It is this vast growth in metropolitan

2. U. S. Bureau of the Census, *Statistical Abstract of the United States: 1976*, 97th ed. (Washington, D.C.: U.S. Government Printing Office, 1976).

3. *Statistical Abstract of the United States: 1976.*

population outside the central cities that is referred to by such terms as *suburbanization, growth of the urban fringe areas,* and *growth of the suburbs.*

A number of aspects of the process of increasing suburbanization have gained particular attention in recent years. First, it is important to note that the suburbs occur largely as products of the market for land, homes, and amenities as individual families seek a place to live and as individual business concerns determine a suitable location for their operations. Because of a number of circumstances, more and more of them choose the suburbs rather than the central cities. Suburbanization is largely the resultant, then, of an aggregate of individual decisions in the "market." The growth of suburban population is then more the result of individual decision-making than of any social policy commitment by government to stimulate suburban growth. And yet, even this apparently "uncontrolled" and undirected development was not completely independent of governmental policy. The program of the Housing and Home Finance Agency in guaranteeing home mortgage insurance is believed to have had the side effect of stimulating suburban growth at the expense of housing in the inner cities. It is difficult if not impossible to untangle the skein of "purpose" and "drift" in social change. This question will be considered further in a later section.

An important and fateful aspect of the suburbanization process in recent years has been its ethnic selectivity. There has been a widespread exodus of whites from the central cities to the suburbs, accounting for the tremendous suburban growth described above. The white population of Chicago declined by over a half million (18.6 percent) between 1960 and 1970. During the same period, Detroit's white population declined by 29.2 percent, St. Louis's dropped by 31.6 percent, Newark's by 36.7 percent. During the same decade many blacks moved to the suburbs, but the proportion was generally small and in some cases the proportion of blacks in the fringe areas actually declined because of the influx of still larger proportions of whites.

At the same time the black populations of the central cities grew massively. By 1970 four of the larger central cities had populations that were over half black. These were Washington, where the black population reached 71.1 percent by 1970, Atlanta, Newark, and Gary. Detroit, St. Louis, Baltimore, New Orleans, Wilmington, Birmingham, and Richmond all had black populations of 40 percent or more.[4] The metropolitan areas outside the central cities are burgeoning, maintaining (with certain exceptions) about the same low

---

4. These figures are from U.S. Census press release CB71-22, U.S. Department of Commerce (February 10, 1971).

proportions of black population, but the central cities, though declining in overall population, are growing markedly in their black populations.

Historians remind us that cities have been the traditional point of reception for migrants both from other countries and from rural areas in the United States and that the great influx of blacks into American cities represents a continuation of this trend as well as a continuation or reappearance of problems that attended earlier newcomers to the cities: low wages, comparatively high unemployment, poor housing, discrimination by police, poor quality public schools, high crime rates, high rates of contagious diseases and those caused by diet, among others.

At the same time, many social observers, including historians, point to important differences in degree or kind between the situation confronting blacks and the one that confronted earlier newcomers to the cities. Earlier, it is pointed out, there was a much larger demand for unskilled labor and an easier route up through the ranks to managerial positions. The reform movement in municipal administration has had several effects, but one side effect of the elimination of much of the "graft" and "corruption" of the older type political machines has been the removal of an important social force sensitive to the needs and wishes of a disadvantaged population. Perhaps most important among the many differences is the fact of color and of discrimination on the basis of color—institutional racism, in the current vocabulary—which becomes a self-reinforcing basis for excluding blacks from opportunities that were more readily available to other types of migrants.

An important implication of the growth in black population in the larger cities (and of other ethnic minority groups such as Chicanos and Puerto Ricans) is that as the ethnic group population increases, the disproportionately small representation of ethnic group members in positions of power and authority in the institutional structure becomes more noticeable. Their underrepresentation in governmental offices, in positions of industrial power, and in the professional and policy-making structure of the voluntary sector becomes an important issue, with attendant frustration and rage at the "liberal" position of many whites that there should be "no discrimination" but that there should likewise be no "lowering of standards," that "opportunities are open for qualified blacks," and the like.

Another important implication is the possible effect on national urban policy[5] of the increasing "blackness" of the inner

5. Daniel P. Moynihan, *Toward A National Urban Policy* (New York: Basic Books, 1970).

cities. Will a society that is not yet free of strong components of racism be as willing to focus effort and funds on improving living conditions in cities that are largely black as it would be if this were not the case? It is difficult to predict the answer, except to venture that the question will not be answerable in terms of a simple yes or no, but rather in a most varied and complex fashion.

The growth of the suburbs and the flourishing of the metropolitan areas presents an ever-growing need to cope with the fact that the metropolitan areas, though they consist of tangled webs of interconnectedness and interdependency, do not typically constitute governmental jurisdictions. Rather, they are comprised of numerous jurisdictional areas standing in various relationships to each other[6] and sharing problems of mutual relationship, which can only be solved through joint effort but for which there is no metropolitan government as a basis for addressing them and having at its disposal funds for dealing with them. The need for metropolitan government would seem to be more pronounced than ever; yet the outlook for the spread of metropolitan government as such is not a particularly optimistic one. Efforts to institute metropolitan area governments have met with great resistance in the United States and have failed to win widespread support in the population.[7] Notable among the few successes in establishing some limited form of metropolitan government have been Toronto, Miami, and Nashville.[8]

Perhaps the most important reason for the failure of the metropolitan government movement to catch on has been that suburbanites live where they do because they prefer it to city living and they do not care to see their lives or their tax structures, school systems, and public amenities blended with those of the cities. Oliver Williams and his associates made an intensive study of governments in the Philadelphia area and concluded that territorial differentiation is desired as is suburban government autonomy.

The fact that older industrial centers may, in the process of social segregation, end up with indigent populations for whom

---

6. The 1972 *Census of Governments* reported a total of 22,185 local governments within the 264 U.S. Standard Metropolitan Statistical Areas, an average of 84 local governments per metropolitan area. U.S. Bureau of the Census, *Census of Governments*, 1972, vol. 1 (Washington, D.C.: U.S. Government Printing Office, 1972).

7. Scott Greer, *Metropolitics: A Study of Political Culture* (New York: John Wiley & Sons, 1963).

8. Harold Kaplan, *Urban Political Systems: A Functional Analysis of Metro Toronto* (New York: Columbia University Press, 1967); Edward Sofen, *The Miami Metropolitan Experiment: A Metropolitan Action Study*, rev. ed. (Garden City: Doubleday & Co., 1966); and Brett W. Hawkins, *Nashville Metro: The Politics of City-County Consolidation* (Nashville: Vanderbilt University Press, 1966).

they cannot provide is, if of any interest to Main Line residents, The fact that older industrial centers may, in the process of social segregation, end up with indigent populations for whom they cannot provide is, if of any interest to Main Line residents, perhaps welcomed by them. The very existence of inequities testifies to the success of specialization. Redistributions of resources and services are the most difficult area in which to achieve metropolitan agreement, in part because they are closely related to social inequalities.[9]

They pointed out that special districts, separate area-wide jurisdiction, and other mechanisms are used to perform those functions that are necessary to maintain the system of metropolitan spatial differentiation, including such facilities as rapid transit, water, and sewage, but without setting up a general metropolitan government. Through their existence special districts thus reduce the pressure for metropolitan government by removing the most pressing reasons for it. In addition, state and federal governments effect a partial redistribution of funds available to local governments through taxes and grant-in-aid programs.

The issue of metropolitan government is further complicated by the different ways different groups have related it to the growth of black minorities in the central cities. It may be favored by those who believe that inner city facilities such as housing and schooling can only be made adequate through expanding the city to include the suburbs in metropolitan government; it may also be favored, however, by those whites who feel that metropolitan government affords a mechanism through which whites may remain in the majority in determining the affairs of the inner city, even if the majority population there is black. On the other hand, metropolitan government is opposed by still other groups for the reverse reasons.

While suburbanization can be considered an adaptation to the "great change" that is made largely at the individual level of families and firms determining their individual locations, a related adaptation, but on the level of more deliberate national policy, is the development of new towns. The New Communities Act of 1968 contained provisions to encourage the development of new towns by offering certain inducements for the financing of private development efforts. Even before that a number of such new towns were in various phases of development. We need not treat them exhaus-

9. Oliver P. Williams et al., *Suburban Differences and Metropolitan Policies: A Philadelphia Story* (Philadelphia: University of Pennsylvania Press, 1965), p. 304.

tively,[10] but it is interesting to note that they constitute a particular type of adaptation to conditions of the "great change." Varied goals are prescribed for them, including reducing the uncontrolled growth of existing cities, providing balanced, planned physical and social activities, providing means for encouraging the development of Gemeinschaft-like sentiments, reducing the commuting problem, stimulating regional development, providing a more desirable mix of social classes and ethnic groups, and so on.

Two aspects of new towns are particularly relevant to our present discussion. First, unlike communes, which will be discussed presently, the new towns characteristically do not represent a rejection of the "great change" but constitute a type of adaptation to it, a means of presumably reaping as many advantages from it as possible while avoiding some of its attendant disadvantages. Second, they represent a further embodiment and reinforcement of the "great change" in that, instead of communities growing naturally, they are administered as the result of deliberate intent.

Another notable example of adaptation to the "great change" is afforded by the various activities and special programs designed to bring coordinated effort to the problems of the cities, problems which, themselves, were by-products of the "great change." These efforts to administer or "concert" community decision-making, to mobilize efforts, to coordinate endeavor, have put city governments squarely in the field of social planning.

If the movement of individual families and firms to the suburbs can be considered adjustment to the "great change," certain other recent developments in community living can be considered not as adaptations to the "great change," but as a revolt against certain aspects of it. Two forms of this revolt are particularly pertinent to the changing conditions in American communities: the revolt of the poor and the revolt of the youth. The first produced the neighborhood control movement. The youth revolt was more basic in that it constituted a more thorough rejection of prevalent social values and social structures and called for a transformation in values and in forms of living. Both were perceived as and, in fact, were threats to the existing social structure in the cities.

Let us consider first the more moderate threat, the movement for neighborhood control. The threat, though it was seen as revoluntionary, was relatively modest, so modest, in fact, that it should

10. See William Alonzo, "The Mirage of New Towns," *The Public Interest,* no. 19 (Spring 1970); James A. Clapp, *New Towns and Urban Policy* (New York: Dunellen Publishing Co., 1971); Richard O. Brooks, *New Towns and Communal Values: A Case Study of Columbia, Maryland* (New York: Praeger Publishing Co., 1974); and Raymond J. Burby, III et al., *New Communities U.S.A.* (Lexington, Mass.: Lexington Books, 1976).

349

perhaps be considered as adaptive to the "great change" rather than a revolt against it. The one merges into the other, of course, and it is senseless to make the distinction in absolute fashion. Yet, although it might be argued that neighborhood control was an adaptive device through which existing social institutions could remain viable and persist under conditions of the present stage of the "great change," the movement was characterized by a considerable degree of hostility to the existing institutional structure in American communities and hence had many of the aspects of revolt. In addition, it was a movement that was generally resisted by the existing institutional structure.

The "great change" had brought spatial differentiation and segregation, the growth and complexity of government offices, the expanding role of federal government and national industrial companies, the complex administrative structures of large governmental and nongovernmental organizations. It also had created the reliance on impersonal organizations for functions formerly performed by family or neighbors, the development of sophisticated data-gathering processes, the onset of computers, the disappearance of the local ward boss, the tendency to consolidate schools into larger and larger units, and many other related developments.

The movement for *neighborhood control* came as a revolt against this impersonal organizational superstructure, a sense that one had little control over the institutions governing one's life, a sense that decisions were made by remote, faceless and heartless people, a sense that nobody really cares what this all means to individuals at the level where they encounter it.

Several strands were woven into the neighborhood control movement. In the first place there was a growing realization within many organizations, both governmental and nongovernmental, that centralized administration became increasingly dysfunctional as growth continued and that therefore some degree of *administrative decentralization* should be pursued. Social agencies, health services, and many of the activities of city government might be more effectively administered through units that were closer physically to the various sections of the city they served.

A second strand supporting the neighborhood control movement was the more generalized movement toward *local control,* which in recent years has made itself apparent on various governmental levels. Examples are the increase in the regional office prerogatives of federal agencies vis-à-vis Washington headquarters and the growing interest in "block grants," which provide a method for enabling cities or states to have greater latitude in the way they spend federal monies.

A third strand had much less support from existing organizations and was more explicitly directed against them. This was the movement for *participatory democracy*. It is interesting that this movement toward drastic changes in decision-making processes was shared both by the Black Power movement and by the student movement. It consisted of the general principle that everyone affected by a decision should share in making it and the corollary that decisions should be made by direct democracy rather than by representative democracy.

A fourth strand was that of *black power* itself, the conviction by blacks (also Puerto Ricans, Chicanos, and native Americans) that they must organize and through organization gain greater power over the institutions governing their lives.

The neighborhood control movement constituted, as it were, a massive and deliberate rebuttal to those who accepted the inevitability of the "great change" and saw neighborhoods as no longer viable entities for decision-making. It constituted, at various levels of awareness, explicitness and theoretical sophistication, a deliberate attempt to intervene in the process of social change and reverse a trend that had earlier been accepted as more or less inevitable. Although it is too early to assess the long-term effects of this movement, its short-term effects were quite noticeable in the struggles for control within such federal programs as the antipoverty program and the Model Cities program. The movement toward neighborhood corporations embodies the idea of setting up structures for neighborhood control of various aspects of housing, industrial, and other facilities. The "little City Halls," the local multiservice centers, the neighborhood health councils, and the local tenants associations all indicate the growth in salience of neighborhoods, the deliberate decision to make the neighborhood important.[11] The movement constitutes an interesting example of the extent to which people can, through deliberate decision and effort, intervene in ongoing social changes, large and small, to alter them. This theme runs through the present chapter.[12]

---

11. Alan A. Altshuler, *Community Control: The Black Demand for Participation in Large American Cities* (New York: Pegasus, 1970); James V. Cunningham, *The Resurgent Neighborhood* (Notre Dame, Ind.: Fides Publishers, Inc., 1965); Suzanne Keller, *The Urban Neighborhood: A Sociological Perspective* (New York: Random House, 1968); Milton Kotler, *Neighborhood Government: The Local Foundations of Political Life* (Indianapolis and New York: Bobbs-Merrill Company, 1969); and Hans B. C. Spiegel, ed., *Citizen Participation in Urban Development, Vol. II-Cases and Programs* (Washington, D.C.: NTL Institute for Applied Behavioral Science, 1969).

12. For various treatments of the complexities of community control, see chapters 28, 29, 40, and 42 of Roland L. Warren, ed., *New Perspectives on the American Community* (Chicago: Rand McNally & Co., 1977).

Other types of response—in part adaptation, in part revolt—can be found in the variety of temporary experiential groups such as encounter groups, sensitivity training groups, and related attempts to acknowledge and then in part overcome the alleged impersonality of human encounters in industrial society in the more advanced stages of the "great change." These represent attempts, deliberate attempts, to achieve what can be thought of as Gemeinschaft-like relationships based on the whole personality instead of the fragmented encounters that an increasingly impersonal and "dehumanized" institutional structure otherwise provides. In a less emphatic way the entire group dynamics movement and the human relations movement in industry can be considered deliberate attempts to restore, *within* the circumstances of the "great change," a more personalized and humanized pattern of social relationships.

A much more revolutionary response to the "great change" is represented by the youth revolt. This is more than merely a negative response to certain aspects of the "great change," for it constitutes a rejection of the entire institutional structure of American society and the value system upon which it is based. This is a somewhat strong statement, and we must acknowledge the amorphousness of what is here being examined, the various shades of belief and disbelief and of acceptance and rejection that its adherents embody. Like all social movements, it has various strands: some are fairly well marked areas of agreement but there are also many areas in which there is a wide spectrum of opinion. Yet, to repeat, we are interested here in those aspects of the youth revolt which challenge the value base of the institutional structure of American society. We do not need to examine the many facets of this challenge. In the next chapter we shall encounter it again in connection with the assessment of different strategies for bringing about change at the community level. Here we are concerned with the relation of this youth revolt to the "great change," especially its implications for community living.

The youth revolt is especially important at the community level in that it has developed a whole series of "alternative institutions" which in effect constitute a different way of life, a modest but significant set of alternatives to existing community institutions. Most of them show rather rapid changes in form and function. Some of them are extremely tenuous. Some may last; others may be but passing flashes of development on today's scene, perhaps to be replaced tomorrow by still other similar developments.[13]

13. Bernard Jones, "Communes as Alternative Institutions," University of Colorado. Mimeographed paper presented at 1970 meetings of the Society for the Study of Social Problems (August 19, 1970). The periodical *Doing It!*, published by the Urban Alternatives Group, prints articles on various aspects of alternative institutions. Also, Vocations for Social Change, based in Cambridge, Mass., provides assistance to those attempting to create alternative work places and lifestyles.

Among these alternative institutions of the youth revolt, the most directly relevant are the communes: a variety of individual attempts to set up communal groups varying in size from a household of young people to a group of two or three hundred attempting to live a relatively self-sufficient existence, characterized by the attempt to develop "authentic" social relationships, unsullied by formal authority, by bureaucratic structures, by pecuniary motivation, by "gadgetry," and so on. There is great variety among such groups[14] and we need not catalogue them. For our purposes it is important to note that they are deliberate attempts to restructure the totality of community living, obviously involving a radical rejection of the various aspects of the "great change."

While communes represent attempts to restructure the totality of community life, certain other developments in the youth revolt are directed more specifically to certain segments or functions. Thus, if we take as an outline the locality-relevant functions elucidated in chapter 6, we find certain small groups setting up productive enterprises on a small scale, including clothing, nature food, and handicraft stores. We often find principles of cooperative sharing of whatever one of the group has been able to acquire through exchange, labor in the "establishment," or in a parcel from back home in Scarsdale. Underground newspapers of various types constitute for some a source of livelihood as well as a means of expression and communication. In many places, "free schools" have been set up as alternatives to the educational institutions of the rejected society. They deliberately minimize such "great change" phenomena as point-credit systems, complex authority structures, "credentialism," and sophisticated technical aids such as "teaching machines." Social control functions are much less formal, though quite obviously there are strong norms associated with the rejection of "middle-class values" and the affirmation of "humanistic values." Social participation functions are provided not only by informal association and by mass gatherings such as rock festivals, but also by work in the various alternative institutions themselves: in the underground press, in the commune, in the free school, and in other settings where shared values become the focus of joint effort. Mutual support is apparent in the practice of "sharing" and in the crash pads.

Such fragments of an alternative institutional structure hardly add up to viable communities, and it is difficult to see how the more than 200 million people of the United States, for example, could be

---

14. Rosabeth Moss Kanter, *Commitment and Community* (Cambridge, Mass.: Harvard University Press, 1972). See also, Marguerite Bouvard, *The Intentional Community Movement: Building a New Moral World* (Port Washington, N.Y.: Kennikat Press, 1975).

kept alive in communes such as those developed by the youth revolt or in cities and villages constructed from the scattering of alternative institutions so far developed. The long-range impact of such developments is highly uncertain; it is hard, though not impossible, to imagine that they will pass out of the picture in a decade or so, only to be looked back on as aspects of "the bizarre seventies." In any case, they constitute a truly revolutionary rejection not only of the "great change" but of the major components of the American institutional structure.

Federal Programs

As was pointed out in chapters 3 and 10 and in the preceding section, the adaptations that are made by individuals or by larger organizations in response to various aspects of the "great change" in turn constitute parts of the social reality to which people must respond and a reinforcing component of what we are designating as the "great change." This is particularly noticeable in the gradual development of intense federal involvement in the affairs of local communities, primarily cities, a development that has become extremely marked in recent years. The growth of cities, itself a part of the "great change," had brought with it a number of interrelated problems (see pp. 13-20), which are an integral part of the national society and which therefore cannot be "solved" or prevented in any individual city—problems, moreover, that the cities had neither the resources nor the will to confront in aggressive fashion.

Increased federal participation in the affairs of the cities can be considered a response to this situation; but such increased federal participation, in turn, constituted a further development in the direction of strengthening the vertical pattern of community orientation, so that, for example, much of what happened in a particular city depended on decisions made in a Congressional appropriations committee, in the Bureau of the Budget, or in one of the departments or special agencies of the federal government. Likewise, the tendency of vertically oriented activities and structures to fragment local community efforts became noticeable in the proliferation of individual federal (and, in part, state) grant-in-aid programs, so that a definite response to this situation was in turn made through devising certain programs designed to "pull together" the various fragmented activities around particular problems or constellations of problems in the cities. This "pulling together," or "coordination," was in turn a compensating effort to strengthen the horizontal pattern of orientation among community units, threatened by this and other aspects of the "great change." But as noted in chapter 10, such

354

coordination takes place not as the result of "natural" ecological forces, or of informal contacts, or of common procedures based on custom but is rather an "administered" type of coordination, itself contributing to the proliferation of formal organizations and specialized efforts and constituting a minor contribution to the process of bureaucratization.

We need not trace the vagaries of all the complex developments in grant-in-aid programs in recent years. As early as 1963, Charles I. Schottland pointed to over a hundred separate federal programs relating to the general welfare of local communities, and indicated that "if we are to make sense out of these, we must find some new ways of coordinating and planning to encompass these many programs."[15]

Even as he spoke, there was developing the first of a succession of programs designed to bring about such coordination, to concentrate various resources, including federal grant-in-aid funds, on specific problems or geographic areas of the cities with the hope that joint effort could produce more favorable impact than the fragmented efforts of numerous independent programs.

Interestingly enough, the first national program in this series was financed by nongovernmental auspices through concerted efforts involving not only the pertinent agencies but the citizens as well. It was the "grey areas program" of the Ford Foundation, which developed from an initial grant in 1960 into a series of grants for city-wide efforts to improve slum conditions with particular emphasis on youth problems and programs.

The President's Committee on Juvenile Delinquency and Youth Crime was established in 1961 to coordinate efforts at the federal level and to stimulate and help finance joint efforts at the local level.[16]

The Economic Opportunities Act was passed by Congress in 1964. It contained several different components, of which undoubtedly the most widely publicized was the Community Action Program. This required that local agencies be established to plan measures for the elimination of poverty and consign programs to various other agencies that were part of the overall plan.

Federal funds for the Community Action Program came through the Office of Economic Opportunities, an independent federal agency. The most notable aspect of this program was the magnitude of the funding made available for this relatively comprehensive

15. Charles I. Schottland, "Federal Planning for Health and Welfare," in *The Social Welfare Forum* (New York: Columbia University Press, 1963), p. 116.

16. Peter Marris and Martin Rein, *Dilemmas of Social Reform: Poverty and Community Action in the United States* (New York: Atherton Press, 1967).

effort. Thus, the local Community Action Agencies (as they were called) were given a fund of resources with which not only to finance new programs focussed on the needs of the poor and on removing the inequalities in opportunity that the poor confront but also to stimulate the existing agencies to become more sensitive to the needs of the poor and to devote a larger portion of their efforts to these needs.

Before this bold new program had had a chance to prove itself one way or another, it became embroiled in a series of controversies, the main two concerns being the expense of the program and the implementation of the provision for "maximum feasible participation of residents of the areas and members of the groups served." In addition, it was recognized that even this relatively broad program was not structured to coordinate the efforts, programs, and organizations enough to face the complex, interwoven problems of the cities, especially of people in slum areas.

Thus, only two years after the Economic Opportunities legislation, there came a more complex, deliberately more comprehensive program, the Model Cities program, instituted by the Demonstration Cities and Metropolitan Development Act of 1966. The act was based on the premise that urban slum problems are interrelated and to make an impact on them there would have to be a comprehensive program sufficiently concentrated to make a noticeable difference on the people affected. Therefore, it was designed for application not to the entire city or metropolitan area but to a specific disadvantaged neighborhood of the city, which was not to exceed one-tenth of the population of the city as a whole. In contrast to the Economic Opportunities program, whose local Community Action Agencies could either be governmental bodies under the jurisdiction of the city government or nongovernmental organizations, the City Demonstration Agencies of the Model Cities program were required to be responsible to the municipal government. But in addition, "widespread citizen participation in the program" was prescribed in the legislation.

An indication of the comprehensiveness of the program's scope is given in the wording of the legislation itself:

> To plan, develop, and carry out locally prepared and scheduled comprehensive city demonstration programs containing new and imaginative proposals to rebuild or revitalize large slum and blighted areas; to expand housing, job, and income opportunities; to reduce dependence on welfare payments; to improve educational facilities and programs; to combat disease and ill health; to reduce the incidence of crime and delinquency; to enhance recreational and cultural opportunities; to establish better access between homes and jobs; and generally

to improve living conditions for the people who live in such areas; and to accomplish these objectives through the most effective and economical concentration and coordination of Federal, State, and local public and private efforts to improve the quality of urban life.[17]

Financial inducements were provided as a means of attracting cities to engage in the planning and programming activities called for by the program, and 150 cities were admitted to the program.

The sequence of federal measures described briefly in this section constituted only one small part of the total federal effort to develop new programs during these years. These programs comprised the major attempts by the federal government to encourage local communities to coordinate their fragmented efforts to solve their own problems including those efforts that were federally stimulated through grant-in-aid programs.[18]

Several trends are discernible in the nature of federal efforts to influence and help local communities in recent years:

Trend toward comprehensiveness　In the foregoing sequence of programs you can discern a steadily developing trend to address problems in larger and larger contexts and to recognize that one-shot efforts in fragmented fields will not produce adequate results. Since the ramifications of the problems of the elderly, or juvenile delinquency, or housing, or unemployment, or mental illness, or physical deterioration of neighborhoods are all broad, the solution of each calls for efforts that cut across many fields. Increasing recognition has been given to the overlapping and interrelationship of these problems and has produced an awareness that any effort to solve any of them must be comprehensive. By the same token, since the problems do overlap and often do involve the same agencies and the same programs, coordination is needed in order to address them. The Model Cities program represented a broadening of all previous efforts to attain such coordination.

Trend toward local control　The movement toward administrative decentralization has already been mentioned. The Economic Opportunities Program left considerable leeway to individual localities as to what types of Community Action programs they would develop as

17. Demonstration Cities and Metropolitan Development Act of 1966, Public Law 89-754, Title I, Sec. 101.

18. In an article at the time, Gilbert Steiner indicated that the Model Cities program was an attempt by the federal government to pass on to the localities the task of coordination of federal programs, a task that the federal government itself had been unable to accomplish either in Wahsington or at the regional levels.

long as they remained within the guidelines prescribed by the Office of Economic Opportunities. The Model Cities program was a deliberate extension of this movement. Among other things, it provided for up to 80 percent reimbursement, called supplemental funds based on the total local funds advanced for the local share of federal grant-in-aid programs. These supplemental funds were available for programs designed to meet local needs, and the programs did not have to conform to the narrow requirements of any specific grant-in-aid program.

From the outset this aspect of the Model Cities program was considered by many to be a "foot in the door" to "block grants" or "shared revenue." That is, it would constitute a precedent for turning over sums of money to cities for their use according to their own local disposition and their own local needs without the confining restrictions placed on specific grant-in-aid funds and without the cumbersome and costly procedures of close review and supervision by federal agencies. It would at the same time develop a body of experience in the cities for the administration of such block grants. The Model Cities program allowed considerable local initiative and local formulation of problems and programs while in its early stages providing for heavy surveillance and review by federal and regional offices of the Model Cities Administration. After a few years, these restrictions were drastically modified and experiments were undertaken in a few cities to give increasing self-determination to the local City Demonstration Agency.[19]

Trend toward "rationality"   As the federal effort has grown and as individual city governments have taken more responsibility largely as a result of such federal stimulus but also because of the growing magnitude of city problems, there has been an obvious effort made to apply rational planning methods and to make use of social science findings. This tendency toward "rationality" arose from several sources. One was the increasing involvement of planners from the city planning profession in social problems. They were accustomed to sophisticated, often quantitative techniques for coping with the physical problems of the cities and sought similar techniques to cope with the social problems. At the same time, system analysis, welfare economics, cost-benefit analysis, planned program budgeting systems, and other techniques for dealing with complex, interrelated problems were being introduced into the social planning

19.   For an extensive analysis of the issues and problems with the Model Cities programs see Roland L. Warren, Stephen M. Rose, and Ann F. Burgunder, *The Structure of Urban Reform: Community Decision Organizations in Stability and Change* (Lexington, Mass.: D.C. Heath-Lexington Books, 1974), and Bernard J. Frieden and Marshall Kaplan, *The Politics of Neglect: Urban Aid from Model Cities to Revenue Sharing* (Cambridge, Mass.: M.I.T. Press, 1975).

and social administration field. They provided a set of calculation techniques that had proved of value in defense and aerospace industries, and it was believed they could be adapted to the field of social problems. At the same time, it was coming to be recognized that individual "programs" which were thought of as solutions to various social problems often engendered side effects that were self-defeating and that operated deleteriously on still other programs and problems.[20] As a former mayor of Boston put it, "Intuition and humanitarian impulses when dealing with complex areas such as a city can be relied upon to produce the wrong answer far more often than not." He spoke of the development of computer simulation models to test in advance the effects of proposed policies. "Such analysis will be very helpful in bringing some semblance of order in the management of complex social systems."[21]

Trend toward citizen participation   The growth in attention to "citizen participation" in various programs addressed to social problems has been quite evident in recent years and has constituted a source of great controversy. Three rationales seem to support it.

First is the employment of citizen participation as a means of gaining acceptance for various programs. Notably in urban renewal and highway construction programs, but also in other programs as well, citizens' groups have often opposed programs of the state or city government, sometimes quite successfully. Thus, participation in the development of such programs has been a means of gaining citizen support and reducing overt opposition.[22]

Second, the social problems of the cities have often been thought to be caused, in part at least, by deficient attitudes or behavior on the part of the individual citizens; hence it was concluded that any program to overcome poverty must improve these attitudes and give hope, reduce alienation, build up confidence in the possibility of self-improvement, engender civic spirit, and the like. Citizen participation has been seen as a means for doing this.

Third, the neighborhood control movement described earlier has demanded citizen participation as a means for affording citizens

20. Daniel P. Moynihan, "Policy vs. Program in the '70's," *The Public Interest*, no. 20 (Summer 1970).

21. *The Boston Globe* (November 30, 1970).

22. It does not always have such effects. There is considerable indication that in many circumstances programs such as urban renewal, school desegregation, and fluoridation are more likely to encounter opposition if there is widespread participation. James Q. Wilson, "Planning and Politics: Citizen Participation in Urban Renewal," *Journal of the American Institute of Planners*, vol. 29, no. 4 (November 1963); Robert L. Crain, Elihu Katz, and Donald B. Rosenthal, *The Politics of Community Conflict: The Fluoridation Decision* (New York: Bobbs-Merrill Company, 1969); and Robert L. Crain, *The Politics of School Desegregation* (Chicago: Aldine Publishing Co., 1968).   **359**

their just share of control over the institutions that govern their lives.[23] According to this latter point of view, much poverty is inherent in the structure and operation of the American institutional order and not attributable to the deficiency of individuals who are victimized by this structure. Consequently, nothing substantial can be done about poverty without changing the institutional structure and reallocating power, and this must involve a larger share in decision-making on the part of the poor themselves.[24]

There are several important theoretical issues involved in these trends, as well as certain incompatibilities among them. They will be addressed in chapter 12.

In concluding this section on federal programs, it is well to consider the larger context in which these programs have emerged. One way of looking at this larger context is to recognize that with the "great change" it becomes increasingly difficult to address the problems faced at the community level through action taken solely at the community level. This point was made briefly in chapter 1. Federal programs such as those discussed above are designed both to stimulate local community organizations to address these problems and to afford financial and in part technical resources to help them do so. They thus constitute *national programs* for addressing problems *at the local level*.

But must not some of these problems, or some of their aspects, at least, be addressed on levels more inclusive than the local community level? Three sectors or areas in which local phenomena and national phenomena mix but are not identical were discussed in chapter 9. There it was pointed out that social stratification, the level of economic activity, and intergroup relations involve both local and extralocal components.

The relationship is difficult to specify in all its details. As is most obvious in the case of level of economic activity, there are cer-

23. Expressions such as "their just share of control over the institutions that govern their lives" are used occasionally in this and the following chapter to convey not only the meaning but also the subjective feeling with which these matters are discussed by their advocates.

24. For a selection of informative writings and viewpoints on what are here called citizen involvement and citizen action, see Ralph M. Kramer, *Participation of the Poor: Comparative Community Case Studies in the War on Poverty* (Englewood Cliffs, N.J.: Prentice-Hall, Inc., 1969); Daniel Patrick Moynihan, *Maximum Feasible Misunderstanding: Community Action in the War on Poverty* (New York: Free Press, 1969, 1970); Stephen M Rose, *The Betrayal of the Poor: The Transformation of Community Action* (Cambridge, Mass.: Schenkman Publishing Co., 1972); Norman I. Fainstein and Susan S. Fainstein, *Urban Political Movements: The Search for Power by Minority Groups in American Cities* (Englewood Cliffs, N.J.: Prentice-Hall, Inc., 1974). The three volumes edited by Hans B. C. Spiegel give a series of analyses of various aspects of citizen participation during this period: *Citizen Participation in Urban Development*, vol. 1: *Concepts and Issues;* vol. 2 *Cases and Programs;* vol. 3: *Decentralization* (Fairfax, Va.: National Resources Corporation, NTL, 1968, 1969, 1974). See also the special issue of *Public Administration Review,* vol. 32 (September 1972).

tain actions that can be taken at the local level, and the federal government may develop programs to stimulate such local action. But aspects of these problems remain that transcend the local level and cannot be encompassed by programs based on the national aggregation of efforts made at the local level. Regardless of what any individual community or group of communities may be encouraged to do to increase the level of local economic activity, there still remain large components based on concerted action or inaction at the federal level. As an example, federal fiscal policy has great effect on local economic activity and indeed may outweigh in its effects the measures taken at the local level to stimulate economic activity.

It is slowly coming to be realized that action at the federal level is important for a wide range of problems, and that such action embraces more than merely stimulating activities and programs at the local level, however important this stimulation may be. American society is not simply the aggregate of what is generated spontaneously and autonomously in the aggregate of local communities but has system properties of its own, which must be confronted at the national level and which present any locality with a set of constraints that limit the effectiveness of local efforts taken alone.

"Crescive" Change and "Purposive" Change in the Community

In what sense can social change trends be taken as "fixed" and in what sense can they be taken as alterable? Is not all change the outcome of the deliberate "intent" of the people involved, acting either individually or collectively? Then in what sense can or should change be taken as "given," and to what extent should change efforts be confined to what is presumably possible and "realistic" within these broader trends?

These abstract questions are important in understanding the rapid changes occurring in American communities today, especially as they are related to the question of "what can be done about" the problems of American communities.

Consider the two major examples given earlier, in relation to the "great change." The neighborhood movement was depicted a few pages ago as constituting a deliberate, self-conscious attempt by people in inner city neighborhoods to oppose and change a "trend." It constitutes a refusal to accept complacently the "inevitable" consequences of the great change, with its increasing bureaucratization, strengthening of vertical ties, taking of decision-making farther away from the locality where people live, and so forth. But the fact that numerous people begin to become concerned about these aspects of the "great change" and begin to take action, in turn, becomes part of **361** the social process, part of the social dynamics of change. Can we say more about this relationship as it affects community change?

Likewise, the youth revolt is a movement that refuses to accept various aspects of the "great change," especially those inhering in the aggregate societal structure (as distinguished from local community structures). It, in turn, becomes part of the historical reality, which is a "given" at the present time.

What aspects of the given social reality at any particular time are really "changeable," and what aspects must for all practical purposes be taken as "given," or "fixed," something we "adjust to" rather than "act upon"? The whole question of anomie and alienation would seem to be related to this question of the extent to which individuals are simply acted upon and the extent to which they are, or feel themselves to be, active in forming the social process.

The distinction, in relation to social change, is often framed in terms of "planned change" vs. "natural change," the natural change being what would happen anyway and the planned change being what occurs when a social actor, individual or group, deliberately intervenes in the situation. But the concept of "natural" change is misleading, for there is no reason to call the changes that some people bring about natural and the changes that others bring about something other than natural. Likewise, not all change that is deliberately brought about is planned in the sense of "rational" planning. Hence, instead of natural change, let us employ Sumner's term *crescive change,* giving it the meaning of change that occurs and will be occurring independent of our own direct intervention[25] and employ the term *purposive change* for the change that a social actor is deliberately seeking to bring about, whether or not such change is planned in the narrower sense.[26]

On the basis of this distinction, it is clear that "social change" programs in American communities, such as those federal programs described above, constitute purposive change programs. It is likewise apparent that what we have been calling the "great change" is simply a name for an interrelated group of crescive changes. In these broad terms, it can likewise be seen that the crescive changes appear to be the "prime movers," as it were, with purposive changes constituting principally adaptations to changes already taking place. It is as

25. William Graham Sumner, *Folkways: A Study of the Sociological Importance of Usages, Manners, Customs, Mores, and Morals* (Boston: Ginn and Company, 1906). Actually the meaning given the term *crescive* by Sumner is slightly different from that employed here, but the term is his.

26. Roland L. Warren, *Types of Purposive Social Change at the Community Level,* Brandeis University Paper in Social Welfare, no. 11 (1965), reprinted in Roland L. Warren, *Truth, Love and Social Change and Other Essays on Community Change* (Chicago: Rand McNally & Company, 1971).

though the "great change" is taking place "anyway," and efforts are made simply to deal with certain effects of the "great change" that are viewed as problematic.

We already noted in chapter 10 that community development is thought of as such an adaptive process, seeking to strengthen the horizontal pattern of the community in response to the trend toward greater orientation of community units to extracommunity systems. It is interesting to note that community development may occur in different contexts with respect to the "great change." In one sense, community development is employed in the so-called developing countries as a means of inducing the "great change," as part of a purposive national plan. In another sense, community development may be employed as a means of coping with aspects of the "great change" that have already been perceived as problems.[27]

As already indicated, the growth in attention to purposive change in American cities today is based on the conviction that crescive change has not led to satisfactory outcomes, and that making living conditions in American cities satisfactory must occur through deliberate attempts to "intervene" in the social process, through deliberate attempts at purposive change.

If communities are made by people, they can be remade or at least altered by people. The "great change," even though it may not be subject to total collective control, may at least be guided. People must therefore control community change, steer it into acceptable channels. So go the assumptions, at least.

Two observations can be made about purposive change efforts at the community level.

The first is that many of the most important changes taking place in American community life have not been subjected to control at the community level or at any other level and a realist must question the extent to which it is possible to control them.

The second is that the changes that are brought about through deliberate intent at the community level are changes of an adaptive type, changes that at best alleviate the side effects of the more basic changes mentioned above.

There is no need to be absolute in the distinction between changes that are subject to purposive intervention at the community level and changes that are not. Nevertheless, the distinction, though often overlooked, is important.

Three of the most important changes tending to shape the structure of American cities in recent years have been the changes in

27. Roland L. Warren "The Context of Community Development," in Lee J. Cary, ed., *Community Development as a Process* (Columbia: University of Missouri Press, 1970). Also included in Warren, *Truth, Love, and Social Change.*

industrial technology, the growth of the suburbs, and the influx of blacks, Chicanos, Puerto Ricans, and other minority groups into the inner cities. The three developments are interrelated.

Changing technology has made it feasible for individual industries to locate away from railroads and waterways and has encouraged their location at the periphery of the city rather than at the city center. At the same time, it has called for different skills, a differently constituted labor force.

Suburban growth has occurred to such an extent that more people living in metropolitan areas live outside central cities than within them. It has resulted from the decisions not of city councils or of federal program administrators but from the aggregate of decisions of individual families and firms, made on an individual basis, to move or not to move to the areas involved.

Likewise, the growth in numbers and in proportions of the total inner city population of blacks, Chicanos, or Puerto Ricans, has carried with it tremendously important implications, many of which stem from the interrelated circumstances of their poverty and their victimization by discrimination. Their growth in numbers in the central cities was largely based on the decisions of individuals and families to move there and was not the result of deliberate social policy at the community, state, or federal level (even though certain policies, such as federal housing policy, had the side effects of contributing to the trend).

These are only examples of the magnitude and importance of changes that occur quite apart from any ability or intent of city governments or other decision-making units to bring them about or discourage them.

Most community change efforts are attempts to adapt to basic changes such as these, which are taken as given. By the same token, such community-level change efforts do not make much of an impact on basic changes such as those just considered but make an impact instead through setting up organized efforts to cope with the effects of such changes or to provide "coordination" for the various organizations that are already on the scene attempting to alleviate one or another aspect of the situation: be it juvenile delinquency, drug addiction, unemployment, school drop-out problems, inadequate housing, poor transportation facilities, or whatever.[28]

A realistic understanding of the level at which change efforts are taking place may prevent exaggerated expectations as to the effectiveness of such change efforts. For all practical purposes, the

28. For a systematic treatment of purposive change efforts at the community level and other levels of society, see Roland L. Warren, *Social Change and Human Purpose: Toward Understanding and Action* (Chicago: Rand McNally & Co., 1977).

ability of communities through purposive change efforts to shape the future structure and process of community living is extremely restricted, as is that of the state and federal government. This is not to say, however, that such leeway as exists is being fully utilized or even wisely utilized.

Nevertheless, the way communities employ their potential ability to affect the shape of future community living is of great importance. In the preceding chapter we have considered community organization and community development as two methods for such change. Here it may be well to note some structural aspects of American communities that help determine the methods through which change is attempted.

In chapter 6 it was noted in connection with the locality-relevant functions that in each case there was a community-level unit that served the function of relating a number of subunits within its purview to each other. Thus, the board of education is charged with the function of developing a system of public schools and distributing them throughout the city in some systematic and deliberate fashion. Likewise, the community welfare council is charged with relating various mutual-support organizations to each other in a systematic and orderly fashion. In chapter 6 the purpose was simply to indicate that such an organization existed corresponding to each of the five locality-relevant functions, and such organizations were contrasted in each case with the corresponding extracommunity system headquarters.

An aspect of these organizations is that they are legitimated to make decisions on behalf of the community within their respective functional sectors of interest. To say that such organizations are *legitimated* to make decisions is merely to indicate that their right to make such decisions is accepted by the various organizations and groupings with an interest in that functional sector. Typically, such right is specified in law, but it need not be as long as all pertinent parties to the functional sector (health, school system, business activity, etc.) acknowledge that right.

The fact that such organizations are found in virtually all American cities is an indication of the structural similarity of American communities. Actually, there are usually many more community decision organizations[29] than those singled out for description in

29. The term was coined by James J. Callahan, Jr., at the time a doctoral candidate at the Florence Heller School, Brandeis University. See Roland L. Warren, "The Interaction of Community Decision Organizations," *Social Service Review*, vol. 41, no. 3 (September 1967), and "The Interorganizational Field as a Focus for Investigation," *Administrative Science Quarterly*, vol. 12, no. 3 (December 1967). Both of these are reprinted in Warren, *Truth, Love, and Social Change;* The behavior of community decision organizations is extensively treated in Warren, Rose, and Burgunder, *Structure of Urban Reform.*

chapter 6. Examples of other organizations fitting this description are housing authorities, urban renewal agencies, antipoverty agencies, health departments, and so on. Such community decision organizations, along with the City Council, are of utmost importance in considering purposive community change, for it is in and through and around such decision organizations that purposive decisions are made at the community level to influence or steer the course of events, the shape of the future, within the limits of their respective jurisdictions. It may be true that certain important decisions affecting the future of the community are made at lunch in the First National Bank building or at the country club by individuals high in the community power hierarchy. But such powerful individuals must in most cases have their wishes or decisions legitimated by the appropriate community decision organization in order for those wishes to be implemented. Hence, such organizations are crucial loci of purposive community change. By the same token, an examination of their respective prerogatives and activities indicates the essentially adaptive nature of the purposive changes that they bring about.

The relation of community decision organizations to the power structure is reciprocal. On the one hand, individuals have inordinate power because of their special access to one or another of these organizations; on the other hand, it is through such organizations that their wishes are legitimated and implemented.

This reciprocal relationship between community decision organizations and the existing power hierarchy sets certain definite constraints on the amount and nature of change that can be expected from such community decision organizations. Roughly, it can be said that they are organized for adaptive changes that serve to maintain the existing allocation of power rather than to change it. Changes that enhance the status of those in positions of inordinately great power, or at least that do not jeopardize their position, may well be accepted and furthered, provided they meet other requirements as well. But changes that threaten the interests of those who control community decision organizations are not likely to be welcomed, and organizations and interests that further them are likely to be combated. This general relationship has been illustrated in the last decade in many community change efforts and especially in the case of the Economic Opportunities program with its local Community Action Agencies and the Model Cities program.[30] These two programs, because of their comprehensiveness and because they attempted to bring about change that in many instances threatened

30. An especially interesting case is given in Sherry Arnstein et al., "Maximum Feasible Manipulation," *City*, vol. 4, no. 3 (October/November 1970), and Michelle Osborn's "Postscript: The Conflict in Context," in the same journal.

the existing power distribution, were resisted and in general their programs were modified in such a way as not to disturb the existing configuration of forces.

As mentioned in connection with the growth of federal programs, an important characteristic of purposive change efforts in recent years has been their provision for citizen participation in the change process. Students of American history are well aware that the notion of citizen participation is not new. Tocqueville pointed out the widespread extent of citizen participation over a century ago,[31] and it has continued and grown to the extent that virtually every governmental operation is accompanied by a citizens' group that performs certain "watchdog" functions.[32] But such participation has been largely by the upper half of the population in socioeconomic status, and positions of leadership and special power have been confined to a group of elites. A relatively clear distinction was maintained between participation by community leaders, by the "right people," and participation by the clientele of health and welfare agencies. People who participated as citizens to whom the respective organizations were accountable in some fashion were generally the more well-to-do elements of the population. In more recent programs a policy-making role by disadvantaged persons who really constitute or represent the clientele of the organizations and programs involved has been acknowledged and activated.

This development is characterized by two aspects. The first is the increasing provision, on the part of existing community decision organizations, for some type of "citizen participation" that extends to disadvantaged groups as well as to elite groups. This provision is especially exemplified in the "maximum feasible participation" of the Economic Opportunities program and in the "widespread citizen participation" of the Model Cities program. It is also characterized by the increasing tendency of direct service agencies of various kinds, including health services, social services, and education, to set up advisory committees consisting of disadvantaged citizens in part or in whole, or to invite a limited number of disadvantaged citizens onto their policy-making boards. The Department of Housing and Urban Development, for example, encourages local housing authorities to include representatives of the tenants in the membership of

31. Alexis de Tocqueville, *Democracy in America* (New York: Oxford University Press, 1947).

32. Nevertheless, many citizen organizations—as well as governmental commissions—have become the allies, rather than the "watchdogs," of the activities they are concerned with. See Theodore Lowi, "The Public Philosophy: Interest-Group Liberalism," *The American Political Science Review*, vol. 61, no. 1 (March 1967); and Charles I. Schottland, "Federal Agencies, National Associations, and the Politics of Welfare," in Roland L. Warren, ed., *Politics and the Ghettos* (New York: Atherton Press, 1969).

the governing commissions of such authorities. And typically, new federal programs addressed to the problems of the cities include some provision for citizen participation.

The provision for citizen participation is usually quite structured and quite controlled, controlled in the sense that the "participation" provides for "a voice" in the decision-making process by disadvantaged groups but explicitly prevents *control* of the decision-making process by such groups. It is believed that through such controlled participation existing organizations will be induced to be more responsive to the needs and wishes of disadvantaged citizens, but always within the constraints of what is permissible and acceptable to a controlling group of decision-makers who represent groups and interests relatively high in socioeconomic status and relatively privileged within the existing institutional structure. Much of the dynamics of community conflict and change in the past decade has reflected this attempt to implement controlled participation.

But there is a source of purposive social change other than the existing community decision organizations. It is represented by what was described a few pages back as the neighborhood movement. The relation between this social movement and the "citizen participation" provided for by various social agencies is an interesting one. The neighborhood movement is a generalized social movement, which, like other social movements, has as its goal a change or reform in the institutional structure. Also, like other social movements, it is furthered by specific organizations but is not completely contained by them. The "citizen participation" component in agency programs can be seen as a response to the neighborhood movement, an attempt to adapt to the neighborhood movement in a way that will accommodate it but at the same time not endanger the vital interests of the agencies involved. At the same time, the provision for citizen participation makes possible a role for neighborhood movement leadership and provides resources and legitimation for that leadership, thus feeding back into the neighborhood movement in a reinforcing way.

Since in their encounters within the citizen participation rubric the social agencies and the neighborhood people have interests that coincide only in part but that also at times conflict, the citizen participation rubric becomes the arena for the resolution of the differing interests of the neighborhood movement and the social agencies. The tension in the relationship can be understood as the interplay of two sets of opposing forces: the attempt by neighborhood people to control the agencies and the attempt by the agencies to control the neighborhood movement. In this interaction, an important question is whether the citizen participation is "meaningful": does it make a difference in the outcome of decision-making, or is it merely perfunctory or ceremonial, without having any noticeable impact on agency policies or programs?[33]

The relationship between citizen participation and the neighborhood movement illustrates the relative nature of the distinction between crescive and purposive change. From the standpoint of the agencies, the neighborhood movement represents a crescive change to which they are adapting in more or less purposive fashion. From the standpoint of the neighborhood residents, the existing agency structures and programs have arisen as a part of crescive change, and the neighborhood movement itself, in which the slum area residents are participating, is part of their purposive reaction to these and other aspects of the "great change."

Another instance of the interrelationship between crescive and purposive change is presented by the development of "new towns." We have already noted that new towns themselves represent an adaptation to the "great change." The new town movement is based on the objective of community growth through purposive change rather than through crescive change. Rather than letting communities arise and grow "like Topsy," the idea is to plan where and when they are to be developed and to guide their development according to certain preconceived objectives. It is hoped that communities will then be developed that are superior to what would be developing crescively without such deliberate, concerted efforts.

But an interesting process takes place in most new towns. They have their beginnings in a formal organization such as a profit or nonprofit corporation or a consortium of different organizations. At the outset, plans are made and early construction occurs within a framework of deliberate control by the developers. As construction takes place and residents are attracted, there is a new element added in setting the planned community's course: the residents themselves. There is often a contest between the developers and the residents, as the residents grow in number and begin to develop interests and wishes and objectives of their own that differ from those of the original developers. As time passes, there is a gradual devolvement of control from the original developers to the generalized community. The new town has metamorphosed from a formal organization to a community, and its future growth and change are determined increasingly by change that is crescive rather than purposive. Eventually, it "blends into the landscape," becoming difficult to distinguish except perhaps for certain remaining physical features from

---

33. Selznick has utilized the terms *substantive participation* and *administrative involvement* to denote this difference between meaningful and ceremonial forms. See Philip Selznick, *TVA and the Grass Roots: A Study in the Sociology of Formal Organization* (New York: Harper Torchbooks, 1966), p. 220.

the surrounding communities. This, roughly, has been the sequence of events in Radburn, New Jersey, in the so-called Greenbelt towns of the 1930s, in Reston, Va., Columbia, Md., and in much of the British experience. It parallels, *mutatis mutandi*, the sequence in many of the nineteenth century Utopian communities, and also the theo-cratic communities of the seventeenth century such as Plymouth Colony, Philadelphia, and Baltimore.

Throughout this process, the relation of the "developers" to succeeding waves of new residents is similar in many respects to those of the agencies to neighborhood residents described above in examining the relationship between "citizen participation" and the neighborhood movement.

It is tempting to look once again at "community development" in the context of the new towns. In a sense, they represent a reversed sequence. For while new towns begin with a formal organi-zation and deliberate, purposive intent and end as relatively undis-tinguishable from crescive communities, the community development effort seeks the reverse of this process. It seeks to con-vert crescive change into purposive change planned at the commu-nity level. As usually applied in small face-to-face communities both in America and abroad, it involves in effect the attempt to convert the community into a formal organization for purposes of concerted decision-making. In communities of more than a few hundred this change becomes difficult, if not impossible, and hence community development efforts attempt the same thing involving people on the more limited neighborhood level; or, on the larger city level, they set up federations that constitute new community decision organizations or new coalitions of existing community decision organizations.[34]

In a different vein, it is interesting to consider the relation between crescive and purposive change in connection with one of the most salient social concerns of recent years, that of poverty. As mentioned earlier, the Economic Opportunities Act was passed in 1964 in order to mount a concerted attempt to eradicate poverty, a definite instance of purposive social change addressed to one of the outstanding problems confronting American communities. Five years later the President's Commission on Income Maintenance Pro-grams reported that "during the 1960s the number of poor persons decreased sharply. From 1960 through 1968, the number of persons in poverty dropped from 39.9 to 25.4 million and the percentage of the population in poverty fell from 22 percent to 13 percent. More

---

34. The contrast between formal organizations and communities has been analyzed by George A. Hillery, Jr., in *Communal Organizations: A Study of Local Societies* (Chicago: University of Chicago Press, 1968), a book that in many respects is the most signifi-cant contribution to community theory to be published in recent years.

recent figures show that since 1968 the number of persons in poverty declined from 25.4 million to 24.3 million in 1974 and increased to 25.9 million in 1975. The percentage of the U.S. population in poverty declined from 13 percent in 1968 to 12 percent in 1974.[35] But even the most sanguine supporters of the Office of Economic Opportunity would hesitate to attribute this diminution in numbers of poor people to the antipoverty program as such. Much had to do with the general rise in the level of economic activity. With this rise, many unemployed and underemployed poor were brought out of poverty through newly available jobs. What role the purposive efforts of the antipoverty program has played in bringing such relatively large numbers of people "out of poverty" is difficult to assess, but a realist must consider the role as minor when contrasted with that of crescive changes, such as the higher level of economic activity over which the antipoverty program had little control.

In this section, a distinction has been made between crescive and purposive social change and some of the implications of this distinction have been explored. We turn now to address the topic of purposive community change in greater depth.

Cooperation and Contest in Purposive Community Change

One of the most important developments of recent years has been a growing deliberate utilization of contest strategies in community change efforts. In chapter 12 we shall treat some theoretical aspects of this shift. At present, let us simply confine ourselves to identifying and describing some salient features of the actual developments that have taken place.

The point of departure is well illustrated in chapter 10. The problem confronting purposive community change is the lack of cohesion of community units with each other and their respective increasing orientation toward extracommunity systems. In order for necessary or desirable changes to occur, there must be purposive efforts to bring these various local units together within the community for decision-making on matters that involve them all. Individual ad hoc community actions and long-term community development processes are the means through which such purposive coordination

---

35. *Poverty Amid Plenty: The American Paradox.* The Report of the President's Commission on Income Maintenance Programs (Washington, D.C.: U.S. Government Printing Office, 1969); and U.S. Bureau of the Census, *Statistical Abstract of the United States, 1975,* 96th ed. (Washington, D.C.: U.S. Government Printing Office, 1975), pp. 399-401.

can be effected. As indicated in this chapter, community decision organizations perform the function of concerting decision-making at the community level in their respective spheres of legitimation. Occasionally special efforts are necessary to concert the efforts of one or more community decision organizations. Through such means, people and organizations can plan and take joint courses of action on the basis of their identifying and pursuing common interests and objectives.

The rough model of the community depicted in the foregoing paragraph is pertinent to many different types of situations. But in recent years there has been a growing awareness that many community matters on which action is needed do not reflect a convergence of interests and wishes on the part of the various interested individuals and groups, but, on the contrary, represent a broad divergence of interests that in many cases seem impervious to reconciliation. Many important issues have come to be perceived as zero-sum games, in game theory terminology, where the extent of one party's gain is the extent of another party's loss. A most obvious example is the controversy concerning the location of major highways through the cities or of urban renewal programs, both of which often entail the forcible condemnation of what usually turns out to be low-income housing.

Another aspect of the realization of the strength of conflicting interests and the difficulty of arriving at voluntarily acceptable change objectives is that often the opposing interests appear to line up with a group of poor on one side of the issue and one or more community decision organizations on the other side: the board of education, the welfare department, the urban renewal agency, or whatever.

Thus there is not only a divergence of interests but often a polarization of interests between "established" agencies and the poor. We have already alluded to two interrelated developments that have provided impetus to this polarization: the neighborhood movement and the student revolt.

Let us consider some underlying characteristics of the increasing awareness of conflicting interests and the consequent modification in viewpoints concerning strategies appropriate for purposive community change.

A first characteristic is a growing impatience with diagnoses of urban social problems that in effect find the "cause" to lie in the deficiency of the people who constitute "the problem." There is a growing conviction on the part of welfare recipients, for example, that they are being unjustly condemned in that their economic dependency is blamed on their own moral or educational or motivational deficiency. Other examples are the allegation that the poor are poor because they "won't work," that juvenile delinquency is attributable to "inadequate parental guidance," that unemployment is attributable to lack of skills or inadequate work habits.

In each case there is an alternative explanation, an explanation that attributes the difficulty to a deficient institutional structure, which produces such individual pathologies just as "naturally" as it produces baseball stars and Fourth of July parades. Dodging, for the moment, the substantive validity of these alternative diagnoses, the social fact is that the "individual deficiency" diagnosis is becoming less palatable to many slum area residents, and as a result of the social movements noted above they have learned to prefer the alternative explanation, which blames the institutional structure.

They have also become disenchanted with the expectation that the existing established agencies of the community, community decision organizations, direct service organizations of various kinds, governmental departments, and the like, can be induced to become more responsive to their wishes by means of a collaborative strategy such as was depicted in chapter 10.

Hence, there is the need for a transfer of power, for the poor to organize themselves and insist on a larger measure of influence and control over the institutions that affect their lives. This point of view is juxtaposed to the agency point of view regarding the "welcoming" of "citizen input" through citizen participation.

Likewise, there is a growing conviction on the part of many of the poor that what is needed is "structural change," that changes must be brought about in all the institutions that affect their lives: not only in social service organizations but in the entire institutional structure involving economic production and sustenance, education, housing, police, justice, public services, and municipal government in general. These aspirations naturally encounter predictable resistance from those who occupy desirable positions within the existing organizational structure.

Another ingredient, more subtle and perhaps more important, is the growing challenge to the legitimacy of the existing organizations. By legitimacy is simply meant the acknowledgement on the part of all pertinent parties of an organization's right to act in its claimed domain. It will be recalled that community decision organizations are defined as organizations legitimated for decision-making on behalf of the community in their respective domains. It is precisely such legitimation that is being questioned by many ethnic-group-oriented and neighborhood-oriented organizations, which claim that the established organizations are part of an unjust, racist social structure, which systematically victimizes the poor. The claim of the community decision organization to speak on behalf of the community is challenged by the angry assertion: "It doesn't speak for us."

By the same token, some of the more militant organizations go much deeper in their social criticism, asserting that the whole social system of "capitalism" is based on a false set of values of aggressiveness, racism, and oppression and that reform will not overcome injustice but that a much more basic revolution in the social structure, social values, and policies is needed.

In considering the above developments it is important that they be taken in a relative rather than in an absolute sense. In the first place, there are many areas where common interests are still believed to exist among various groups in the community and are actively sought. In the second place, there is a whole spectrum of intensity of opinion and feeling regarding each of the characteristics just mentioned. It is easy to exaggerate the extent of adherence to these points of view among the great bulk of residents of the cities, whether from the more dilapidated areas or not. Many slum dwellers are such not particularly concerned with changing the institutional structure as such or even with challenging the legitimacy of existing organizations. Rather, they perceive their problems on the basis of unjust or dishonest or incompetent people who occupy the key positions in such organizations. They do not challenge the system or doubt that it can be made to work justly as long as good people, including a larger proportion of minority group members and slum area residents, occupy an appropriate share of such positions.

What all of the different facets of this breakdown of consensus indicate is a growing diffidence, in whatever terms it is expressed, to accept the notion of a "public interest," a single type of solution to one problem or another that is "best for everyone." Whether or not it is expressed in these terms, there appears to be an acknowledgement that interests differ profoundly and durably and that although reconciliations of "apparent" differences can be found, most such differences are for all practical purposes basic and irreconcilable. The gradual collapse of the notion of a "public interest" in this sense has important practical and theoretical implications whose exploration is the principal focus of chapter 12.

Purposive Community Change and the Single "Public Interest"   12

In this chapter we are concerned with the relationship between individual interests and common interests and the respective implications of assuming a model of community that emphasizes collective or inclusive interests versus assuming a model that emphasizes individual interests. In the previous chapter we noted a significant modification in the *way* change is considered, a modification that places relatively more emphasis on the diverse, often conflicting interests of various groups in the community and relatively less emphasis on the process of change in a situation of mutual agreement where almost everyone recognizes that the ·change is in the "public interest." For purposes of brevity we shall use the term *public interest* to denote the presumed common interests that individuals have in any given proposal for community change.

We may as well distinguish at the outset two somewhat different applications of the term. In one usage the public interest is simply the aggregate of individual interests, the best possible mix of different sets of interests and priorities. From a somewhat different point of view, the public interest is not derivable from a mere summation of individual interests, but rather it is the thing that is best for the collectivity as a collectivity. If we think of the community as an inclusive social system (including as components or subsystems   **375** units that are themselves systems), we can distinguish between the well-being of the inclusive system and the well-being of the individual components, which make it up. In other words, we can look at the well-being of the whole or the aggregate well-being of the parts. The two may or may not be identical. They are both conceptions of a "public interest."

Or, one might take a different focus, paying little attention to the system as a whole and focusing rather on the well-being of some specific subsystem, such as a particular business, association, religious group, or neighborhood within the local community. In doing so one is not concerned with the inclusive interest of the community but with the specific interest of a particular unit.

Purposive Change and the Public Interest

The relation of these somewhat abstract considerations to community change theory is readily apparent. Until a few years ago the underlying assumption of a public interest dominated community change theory. Consider Ross's definition of community organization given in chapter 10: "Community organization is a process by which a community identifies its needs or objectives, orders (or ranks) them, develops the confidence and will to work at them, finds the resources (internal and/or external) to deal with them, takes action in respect to them, and in so doing extends and develops cooperative and collaborative attitudes and practices in the community."[1]

In this definition, the focus is clearly on the well-being of the inclusive system—the community. One is concerned with *its* interests and how *it* identifies them, ranks them, and takes action with respect to them. There is an underlying assumption, which is not so obvious: that this interest of the community as a whole does not in any way conflict with the interests of any of its subsystems. The interests of the total community and of its component parts coincide. Therefore, the problem of purposive change is getting people to understand just why a certain proposal is in the public interest, and getting them motivated to implement the proposal so that the alleged benefits will devolve to the community.

Consider again the model of community action depicted in chapter 10. A few years ago a study was made of 35 episodes of community action taken from accounts given in the literature, varying from two- or three-page descriptions to entire books. In the course of this study it became apparent that in many of these epi-

---

1. Murray G. Ross, *Community Organization: Theory and Principles* (New York: Harper & Bros., 1955), p. 40.

sodes there were two action systems: one attempting to bring about the change and one opposing it.[2] Further, it was found that in action episodes that engendered opposition, different types of change strategies were used and other characteristics of the episodes differed considerably. Obviously, a model of purposive change such as that proposed in chapter 10 would have to be modified in circumstances where the change goal is opposed. Further, such opposition, far from being an occasional, aberrant phenomenon, is typical of many of the most important issues affecting the lives of community people. Where shall the new highway go? Shall local schools be placed under neighborhood control or remain under central control? Shall the water supply be fluoridated? Shall children be bused to promote school desegregation? How strong shall the regulations be regarding air pollution? Which part of town will be demolished to make room for the new hospital or business center?

In such circumstances, purposive change must proceed usually without a full consensus but rather over the overt opposition of parties that claim either that it is not really in the public interest or that what is supposedly in the public interest actually jeopardizes their private interests or both. In such cases it seems more appropriate to consider the action episode as a type of opposition and negotiation than to think of it as a reasoned process of seeking (and finding) what is "best for the community." Nevertheless, most community change theory is based on the often fallacious assumption that there is a public interest and that people can find it and agree on it.

Why do we emphasize change strategies based on the assumption of a common public interest, when in so many cases the actual circumstances prove such an assumption to be irrelevant to the issues involved?

Part of the answer lies in a particular direction given to Western philosophy by Socrates, as Plato describes him. For Socrates the ultimate reality was a set of ideas, which, though they did not exist in the physical world, were even more basic than the physical world. Part of this ideal world was the assumption that the Good is one and that it can be discovered through a particular process of reasoning (the Socratic dialectic); hence, where disagreements appear, it is simply because one or both parties are in error. A patient following of reason will lead the contesting parties to the true conception of the Good, which is the same for everyone. Hence, there can be no informed disagreement on what is in the public interest, nor can there be any discord between what is in the public interest and what

2. Roland L. Warren and Herbert H. Hyman, "Purposive Community Change in Consensus and Dissensus Situations," *Community Mental Health Journal*, vol. 2, no. 4 (Winter 1966).

is in the the interest of individuals who make up the community.[3] Since disagreement, where it occurs, is based on ignorance only, the appropriate change strategy must be one of education through which one or both parties come to discard their erroneous notions and agreement is reached on the one single Good, which can then be collaboratively pursued.

Another part of the answer lies in a trick that system theory plays on us. We begin by noticing certain abiding, structured interaction, and we notice that this structured interaction, or social system, has certain properties. We begin to refer to it as "it" and then make statements about "it." It does certain things, it has a certain boundary, it carries on exchange relations with its environment, and it contains certain subsystems. Soon we begin to think of what will be "good" for it, what lies within its interests, considering it on a level quite distinct from the many different, often conflicting units that make it up. In this process we inadvertently begin to favor what will help the system to function smoothly and on the other hand to look with disfavor on what may disrupt the smooth functioning of the system. Behavior that is in accordance with the system is approved; behavior that threatens the system is often called "deviant" with negative implications.

Another source of the emphasis on the public interest—the assumption that community interest and individual interests will not conflict, and its corollary that collaborative patterns are appropriate and desirable as strategies for community change—lies in the Western penchant toward agreement. In an experiment, Solomon E. Asch found that in comparing two sets of geometric figures, individuals were highly influenced in their judgments by information about judgments of others. They tended to bring their own judgments into conformity with the judgments of others.[4] Social perceptions tend to be influenced by the perceptions of those around us, and the realization that one sees things differently from the rest of one's group is an uneasy one. From the group's standpoint, likewise, the lone dissenter is a cause of uneasiness. The reaction may be: "We haven't tried hard enough to explain it to him," or "She only sees these things selfishly," or "She just objects for the sake of being stubborn," or "The poor fellow is sick." The thought that well-intentioned people will find common answers to similar problems is a strong one. It

3. This notion runs through many of Plato's dialogues, including *The Republic*. It is addressed at length in the *Protagorus*.

4. Solomon E. Asch, "Opinions and Social Pressure," *Scientific American*, vol. 193 (1955). The implications of this experiment, as well as others by Crutchfield and Milgram, are discussed at length by Charles Hampden-Turner in his book *Radical Man: The Process of Psycho-Social Development* (Cambridge, Mass.: Schenkman Publishing Company, 1970).

is bolstered by the fact that on numerous occasions what begins as an initial disagreement ends up with a happy resolution. Mary P. Follett's book, *Creative Experience*, is replete with illustrations of how patience and discussion were able to produce a resolution of what seemed a bitterly controverted problem.[5] If many such bitter disagreements proved to be resolvable, is it not likely that all such disagreements are resolvable through more meaningful dialogue, fuller communication, better knowledge of the facts, trying to understand the other person's point of view, and similar measures?

The above arguments, once identified and examined, appear less than compelling. Yet they do seem to support the otherwise unexplainable commitment to change strategies based on the assumption of the single public interest in situations involving parties with conflicting interests.

As a more tangible basis for the consideration of community change strategies, let us take three types of change agents and the rationales on which their change efforts are based.

Ross's book, cited earlier, is probably the single most important work in the field of community organization as practiced by social workers.[6] In a sense, the definition of community organization quoted from it indicates the heart of the strategy. Different social actors in the community are to come together to ponder what is best for the community and then to go about working toward obtaining it. The professional community organization worker helps the community in this process. Throughout Ross's book it is reiterated that with adequate knowledge, removal or reduction of emotional blockages, and open and constructive interchange, the community will indeed be able to identify the public interest, and various parties to this process will reach agreement as to what that is and be willing to pursue it through the development of an appropriate course of action. In all of this, there is virtually no discussion of opposing interests, of situations where one group's gain may be another group's loss, of how the proponents of a program are to move ahead under the frequent situation where full agreement has not been reached and does not seem reachable. Rather, assuming the existence of an ascertainable public interest, Ross lays out what is essentially a social interaction strategy for finding it. He simply does not

5. Mary P. Follett, *Creative Experience* (New York: Longmans Green, 1924).

6. A series of reports from a special project of the Council on Social Work Education gives a more recent definitive treatment. See Arnold Gurin et al., *Community Organization Curriculum in Graduate Social Work Education: Report and Recommendations* (New York: Council on Social Work Education, 1970), and Robert Perlman and Arnold Gurin, *Community Organization and Social Planning* (New York: John Wiley & Sons, 1972).

address the problem of what to do under circumstances of enduring opposition.

In summary, the public interest that is determined by following Ross's strategy is a public interest based on knowing assent of interested and involved parties. It is right because the right process has been executed to reach it; and, therefore, its implementation is virtually assured. Since there is no hidden opposition, there are no parties waiting with whetted knives to cut it down.

As contrasted with Ross's emphasis on social process in reaching proposals for change, the more conventional method of the city planner provides a different approach. The process through which change proposals are developed is a professional process based on science and an intricate professional technology. There are the plot maps and the overlays and the demographic ratios and the numerous indicators of this and that—a whole paraphernalia of impressive tools with which to solve the technical problems confronting the planner: where the highway will be located, how this particular neighborhood will be zoned for land-use, whether more funds should be invested in mass transportation. City planners' considerations are substantive and technical, rather than processual, and the legitimacy of their proposals comes from the careful and systematic professional analysis with which they have considered them, rather than from the skill with which they have helped people reach agreement in setting up their own objectives. The city planner, too, purports to be developing change goals that are in the public interest, but this claim is supported by the technical aspects of the question rather than by the fact that it is a joint social product. Indeed, the time-worn complaint of the city planner is that politicians and other dicision-makers lack either the wisdom or the courage to enact his or her clearly beneficial proposals.[7]

A third type of change agent is illustrated by public health officers who attempt to introduce new practices into the community. They are usually physicians with special public health training. Their authority to act in certain matters is clearly defined in a public health ordinance, but they may also seek to bring about change through new proposals that are not already part of law. Since the proposals are in the realm of disease prevention, based presumably on the latest bio-medical findings and since they are for a purpose that virtually everyone supports—the prevention of disease—these proposals are usually noncontroversial. The principal problem is to

---

7. An extensive account of the problems of the city planner regarding the implementation of plans derived on a technical basis is given in Alan A. Altshuler, *The City Planning Process: A Political Analysis* (Ithaca: Cornell University Press, 1965).

get enough information to the city council or to the mass of voters so that they will realize the importance of the measures the public health officers advocate and be willing to take appropriate action. In short, their change goals are usually noncontroversial and it is acknowledged that they speak not from selfish interest or from partisan political interest but from scientifically grounded arguments for improving community well-being.

The change strategies just considered differ from each other in several respects. The community organizer emphasizes a process of decision-making and does not purport to contribute in any decisive substantive way to the outcome, leaving that to the people whose interests are involved. The city planner develops a rational solution to the technical-substantive aspects of the problem, hoping that the acceptance and implementation by the authorized decision-makers will follow on their conviction of the soundness of the proposal. The public health officer seeks to introduce practices that public medicine determines will be beneficial for health and engages in a strategy of educating the public to the wisdom of the proposed measures, which are based on the authority of science.

Note that the community organizer does not propose but rather facilitates a process through which proposals are conceived and executed. The city planner and the public health officer make definite substantive proposals based on technologies grounded in the natural sciences. The difference has received great emphasis for two or three decades; that is, should goals be set by the change agent or by the change target?

However, the similarity has been largely overlooked. The similarity lies in the circumstance that they all presuppose a single public interest and presume to represent it. They all presume to assure the "best" solution for the community, based either on the assumed validity of a participative decision-making process or on the technical application of scientific knowledge. Professional change agents do not seek change to further their own selfish interests, or those of some group with which they are affiliated, but they are personally "disinterested," above the battle, nonpartisan, seeking merely to help determine and realize the community's best interests. Even if we are to allow that here and there hardship must be worked on someone in order to achieve what is best for the community—an unsafe building must be condemned, a costly hygienic procedure must be introduced in restaurants, a new agency must be discouraged from forming because it would merely duplicate services already being provided by an existing agency, a group of houses must be demolished to make room for the expansion of the university—nevertheless, the notion that community interests exist and that they should override private interests has deep roots. Even among those who **381** might be placed at a disadvantage, the moral obligation of the larger public interest is acknowledged.

Changes have take place in recent years that have been so drastic as to make the few preceding paragraphs seem naive. It is difficult now to recall that people could argue seriously that these professional representatives of the various community decision organizations were merely acting dispassionately and utterly validly for the community interest. The decade of the sixties changed all that. There has arisen a growing challenge to the assurance that there is a single valid community interest that overrides the interests of parties who might object to any particular proposal. Likewise, there has been a growing disenchantment with the belief that the major community decision organizations represent a single, inclusive community interest as distinguished from the interests of the more powerful and well-to-do. At the same time an impressive array of issues has tended to follow a line of division between such community decision organizations and the poor. Controversies such as the following contribute not only to the notion of the fragmentation of what was earlier accepted to be the single public interest but also to the polarization of interests into two relatively identifiable sets of opposing interests: over urban renewal (bitterly rebuked as "Negro removal"); over fluoridation (where opponents were generally less well-to-do, less well-educated); over antipoverty programs (where the accusation arose that the existing agencies were merely growing rich by absorbing antipoverty budgets into "services" for the poor that were of questioned effectiveness); over the distribution of United Way funds (overwhelmingly to white agencies serving white middle-class people); over police policies; over alleged exploitation of slum tenants by landlords and of slum customers by retail stores; over inordinately high insurance rates in slum areas.

Change Modes That Assume a "Public Interest"

At the same time, and no doubt influenced by the change in perspective on current issues described above, there has been a resurgence of change theories based on conflict rather than collaboration. Different formulations have sought to emphasize one or another aspect of the implications of the more complex situation just described.[8] One can perhaps summarize the principal reformulations by saying that they implicitly or explicitly reject the relevance

---

8. See, for example, Jack Rothman, "An Analysis of Goals and Roles in Community Organization Practice"; Harry Specht, "Disruptive Tactics"; and Roland L. Warren, "Types of Purposive Change at the Community Level"; all of which are reprinted in Ralph M. Kramer and Harry Specht, eds., *Readings in Community Organization Practice* (Englewood Cliffs, N.J.: Prentice-Hall, Inc., 1969).

of the assumption of the single "public interest" and make the corresponding modifications in considering change strategies. More specifically, rather than taking change strategies in the abstract, they consider them in the following ways: in relation to the context in which change is proposed—whether or not the interested parties share basically the same point of view and set of interests; the nature of the change goal—whether it is to get a specific piece of legislation passed, a new service organized, a change in policy of an existing agency, a change in individual attitudes or behavior practices, and the like; the systemic context—who has the power to determine the issue's outcome, whether the people proposing the change have sub-stantial power within existing decision-making mechanisms, and so on.

In this connection, it is helpful to examine change strategies within the context of whether there is general agreement among the parties who have an interest in a proposed change or disagreement To the extent that points of view are similar, a strategy of *collaboration* seems highly appropriate. Thorough discussion may bring out new facets of the problem and assure a more adequate approach to it. A pooling of resources may further the wishes of all parties. It is this situation that Ross assumes in examining community organization strategies.

In a different context, there may be little opposition to a proposed change, but little support either. The principal problem of change agents is gaining that support, which they believe they can gain if only the facts are known and their importance sufficiently understood. Their strategy therefore lies in undertaking a *campaign* of educating the decision-makers to the importance of what is involved and the wisdom of the specific proposals. The city planner and health officer often operate in such a context.

There is definite opposition to the change in an even different context. Further, this opposition does not seem to melt away in response to an educational campaign. If the change goal is to be accomplished, this opposition must be defeated. Thus, a *contest* takes place: for example, whether Candidate A or Candidate B is elected to office, whether a specific piece of legislation is passed or defeated, whether a proposed urban renewal plan is accepted or rejected by the city council, or whether a construction company will or will not employ a specific proportion of minority group workers on its building project.

In these terms, it is interesting to note that in the case of numerous fluoridation controversies, the public health officers initially conceived of the situation as calling for an educational campaign. In many cases, however, vigorous opposition to the fluoridation proposal developed, and health officers found them- **383** selves in the unaccustomed role not of educating the public on a noncontroversial issue but of representing one side in a bitterly contested dispute.[9]

These three situations can be described respectively as issue consensus, issue difference, and issue dissensus. Issue consensus situations are amenable to a collaborative strategy, issue difference situations call for a campaign strategy in the sense of an educational campaign, and issue dissensus situations call for a contest strategy.[10]

While not phrased in this specific terminology, much of the reaction by so-called dissidents against "coalition strategies," as they are often called, is based on the conviction that existing community decision organizations represent not the public interest but the interests of only certain segments of the public. These organizations are interested in change, for they recognize that American communities are deeply troubled and beset with problems, and of course they desire a remedy. But the remedy must lie within bounds that will not offer any serious threat to those in positions of power, whether in the existing service agencies or in other parts of the local institutional structure.

In the past such well-to-do persons have found it quite feasible to "plan" for change within the collaborative rubric of, perhaps, a health and welfare council. But the commitment to a collaborative strategy has involved certain constraints. It has meant that many controversial issues have been avoided by the councils because the issues were "too controversial" and would burst the bubble of assumed basic agreement. It has also meant that important interest groups in the community were not a party to council decision-making, because their presence, too, might burst the bubble of assumed basic agreement. Hence, until recently, organized labor was highly underrepresented on council boards. And until now the poor or representatives of disadvantaged agency clientele, who obviously have a great stake in what the agencies do, have mainly been excluded. In other words, a collaborative strategy working toward a presumed "public interest" has been possible only at the expense of excluding from serious consideration some of the most glaring social issues and from participation in the discussion some of the people

9. Harry M. Raulet, "The Health Professional and the Fluoridation Issue: A Case of Role Conflict," *The Journal of Social Issues*, vol. 17, no. 4 (1961).

10. Roland L. Warren, "Types of Purposive Change at the Community Level," Brandeis University paper in Social Welfare, no. 11 (1965). Reprinted in Roland L. Warren, *Truth, Love, and Social Change and Other Essays on Community Change* (Chicago: Rand McNally & Co., 1971). These change strategies are given more extensive analysis in Roland L. Warren, *Social Change and Human Purpose* (Chicago: Rand McNally & Co., 1977).

whose lives are most directly affected. From this viewpoint, the frequently voiced criticism that councils really have done very little to confront the basic problems of economic disadvantage, racial discrimination, poverty, poor housing, and other types of injustice can be readily understood. These are all controversial issues that split the community into opposing interests. They cannot be addressed adequately within a collaborative framework.

In the same vein, attempts to expand the collaborative framework by including representatives of the poor on the boards of health and welfare councils or community action agencies have resulted in those representatives of the poor allegedly being co-opted into assenting to policies determined by the more well-to-do, policies that are not in the best interests of the poor.

In the light of the above developments, it is perhaps desirable to make a quick review of the field of community development, which likewise is predicated on the assumption of a public interest that is to be discovered and furthered through the community development process. In chapter 10 we defined community development as an administered process of strengthening the community's horizontal pattern. At the same time it was pointed out that an important goal of community development is usually to broaden the base of participation in community decision-making. This is especially apparent in the example from the Israeli village (pp. 307-308) and the quotation on page 325 from Sanders's definitive statement.

Community development has come under critical scrutiny in recent years,[11] and the reasons for this growing disenchantment are germane to our present discussion.

In many countries, community development was thought of as taking care of the "human aspects" of economic development, many of which were not amenable to community-level solutions. Community development was therefore overburdened with unrealistically high expectations.

Second, the conflict between the importance of task and the importance of process has continued to be resolved in experience by the ascendancy of task accomplishment over efforts to build a structure, formal or informal, to strengthen the horizontal pattern.

Third, there appears to be an inherent contradiction in the rationale of community development. The earlier belief that a broad

11. See Shanti K. Khinduka, "Community Development: Potentials and Limitations," National Conference on Social Welfare in *Social Work Practice,* 1969 (New York: Columbia University Press, 1969); Irving Louis Horowitz, "The Search for a Development Ideal: Alternative Models and Their Implications," *The Sociological Quarterly,* vol. 8, no. 4 (Autumn 1967); Charles J. Erasmus, "Community Development and the Encogido Syndrome," *Human Organization,* vol. 27, no. 1 (Spring 1968); and William L. Blizek and Jerry Cederblom, "Community Development and Social Justice," *Journal of the Community Development Society,* vol. 4, no. 2 (Fall 1973): 45-52. **385**

base of community participation equipped a community to function more effectively has been indirectly put to challenge by a number of studies, which indicate that the broader the distribution of decision-making power the less likely it is that a community will be able to take concerted action in such programs as urban renewal, manpower development, school desegregation, fluoridation, and antipoverty programs. These studies are not definitive, yet they cast grave question on the easy assumption that broad distribution of power strengthens the community's viability, that is, its ability to take concerted action on its own behalf.[12]

Whatever the ultimate resolution of this relationship may be, the conclusion seems to be warranted that community development programs that have not sought a redistribution of power have encountered fewer difficulites and less resistance than those that have. As a consequence, the temptation, once again, has been to work with the existing power structure in order to get the job done (or even in order to be able to work at the job at all) rather than to restructure the power configuration by a partial transfer of power to formerly powerless segments of the population. To the extent that programs have worked with "the same old power group," they have come to be seen as "system-maintaining" rather than "system-changing," as ways of preserving the power status quo by giving the semblance of broad participation without its reality.

Returning to our more anlytical consideration of change strategies, let us remind ourselves that community development is based on the assumption of a single community public interest and that it prescribes a process of collaboration of all important groups in the community to define their common purposes and to pursue them. It prescribes the inclusion in this process not only of groups that have exercised strong decision-making power in the past but of groups or segments of the population that have not formerly exercised such power. Through such a collaborative process, the community is to move "from a condition where one or two people or a small elite within or without the local community make a decision for the rest of the people to a condition where people *themselves* make these decisions about matters of common concern; from a state of minimum to one of maximum cooperation . . . ,"[13] in Sanders's words. Sanders

13. Irwin T. Sanders, *The Community: An Introduction to a Social System* (New York: Ronald Press Co., 1958), 407-8.

12. See Roland L. Warren, "Toward a Non-Utopian Normative Model of the Community," *American Sociological Review*, vol. 35, no. 4 (April 1970), also reprinted in Warren, *Truth, Love, and Social Change;* also, see Michael Aiken and Robert R. Alford, "Comparative Urban Research and Community Decision-Making," *The Atlantis*, vol. 1, no. 2 (Winter 1970). Recent analyses of the power structure as applied to policy outputs can be found in Roland L. Warren, ed., *New Perspectives on the American Community*, 3rd ed., (Chicago: Rand McNally & Co., 1977).

has accurately captured the intent of the community development process. The experience of recent years, both in this country and abroad, has indicated that in actual settings, these two goals have often proved to be mutually incompatible. The usual result has been that groups in power have resisted the dissolution of their power by the admission of other parties to the decision-making process except through participation that was safely controlled and that presented no threat to the existing power configuration. We have already considered some aspects of this controlled citizen participation in the preceding chapter.

Thus we have an application of the principle that change strategies must be derived from the nature of the issue under consideration. Collaborative strategies are appropriate for exploring commonalities and only occasionally result in effective action in situations of basic disagreement. The experience with the grey areas program, with the President's Committee on Juvenile Delinquency and Youth Crime, the Economic Opportunites program, and the Model Cities program has indicated that the participation of representatives of the poor in collaborative frameworks has led either to their being subtly "won over" to the position of the existing agencies or to the channeling of their participation into relatively superficial issues, with the main issues being kept beyond their control. Where such participation has avoided "cooptation" (the popular designation for the former case)[14] or "control" (what Selznick called administrative involvement as opposed to substantive participation),[15] they have had to utilize a contest strategy and have typically been fought viciously (as in Syracuse, N.Y., and Oakland, Calif., for example) by the existing power configuration of social service agencies and community decision organizations.[16]

It is interesting in this connection to note that the community development process has been taken up as a collaborative strategy for organization and action by neighborhoods within larger cities, but with a big difference in system context—namely, that a collaborative strategy is used to organize the neighborhood in order that the neighborhood may contest with other subcommunities for community-wide decision-making power as well as for decision-making

14. Philip Selznick, *TVA and the Grass Roots: A Study in the Sociology of Formal Organization* (New York: Harper Torchbooks, 1966), p. 13ff.

15. *TVA and the Grass Roots*, p. 220.

16. Stephen M. Rose has dealt with the problem of cooptation of the poor in the poverty programs in his book *The Betrayal of the Poor: The Transformation of Community Action* (Cambridge, Mass.: Schenkman Publishing Co., 1972). The same problem is also discussed in relation to the Model Cities Program in Roland L. Warren, Stephen M. Rose, and Ann F. Burgunder, *The Structure of Urban Reform: Community Dicision Organizations in Stability and Change* (Lexington, Mass.: D.C. Heath-Lexington Books, 1974).

power over the locality-relevant functions performed within the neighborhood. Thus, what is called community development turns out to be a method for organizing one of the parties to a community contest.

Let us review the discourse to this point. We started by acknowledging the growth of a viewpoint that questioned the validity of the single "public interest" and that questioned the claim of community decision organizations to operate on behalf of "the whole community," as distinguished from a particular segment thereof. We indicated a growing awareness that collaborative "citizen participation" usually stops short of a meaningful transfer of power, and that it is usually controlled in the interests of the more well-to-do of the community. As we proceeded, it seemed best to depict this point of view in analytical terms rather than in the rhetoric of current community controversy. In doing so, we left our own personal analytical thumbprint on the developments we were purporting to report. So, the reader is entitled to ask: Is the author merely describing in his own analytical terms a point of view that has been growing on the urban scene, or does he subscribe to that point of view? The answer is: both.

It is not only the poor who have learned the lesson that power is not voluntarily given up by those who possess it to those who do not. Many social scientists, including the author, have been drawing the following conclusions from the events of the past two decades:

1. Collaborative strategies will result only in programs and policies that the existing power configuration finds aceptable.

2. Power will not voluntarily be given up by elites.

3. Attempts by the poor, agency clientele, youth, and similar groups, to participate in community decision-making often will not be resisted as long as they do not pose threats to the well-being of those in power, or threaten to change the power configuration.

4. Where such threats are posed through broader participation such broad participation will be coopted, controlled, or fiercely attacked by those in power.

Two Levels of Consensus

We shall presently turn to some of the assumptions and actual historical implications of a model of community change that ignores or denies the existence of a single "public interest" at the community level.

Before doing so it may be well to note some of the characteristics of that consensus, often brought about through strategies of collaboration, within which community decision-making ordinarily occurs. As we move into this we must take note of two levels of consensus.

The first, the more superficial level, relates to consensus around the specific issue about which decision-making takes place. As indicated in chapter 10, there are many issues around which there is little basic disagreement. A new hospital is needed. Everyone concedes that. The question is whether people will give enough in the capital fund drive to provide a basis for the necessary construction funds. Or a new program is needed for the elderly. But how many people consider it important enough to do whatever has to be done in order to bring the program into existence as an operational entity? Many community change goals are of this type, and the problem is to muster enough cooperation and concentration of effort or of financial and other resources to accomplish the objective. But (and we are still on the first level) such agreement does not always accompany a change proposal. The proposal may generate considerable opposition. For example, in his book, *Political Influence,* Edward C. Banfield described seven case studies of specific change goals in Chicago, the controversy that arose around each of these, and how the contest was finally resolved.[17]

So at this first level, there may or may not be consensus on a given proposal for change. But there is a second, more fundamental level of consensus among the existing community decision organizations. There is a consensus on the manner in which the issue is to be resolved, the way in which the contest is to be conducted, and there is consensus on the legitimacy of the final outcome. The attitude of the "loser" on a given issue is something like "Well, we hated to lose that one, but we'll win the next one." There is an implicit acceptance of the legitimacy of the issue resolution and of the machinery through which the process of issue resolution takes place.

This situation, roughly, prevails within the principal components of the power configuration in American cities and includes the legitimated community decision organizations. These organizations may occasionally find themselves in vigorous dispute with each other over a particular issue, but the issues seldom are so great as to threaten the existence or viability of the organizations involved. They can afford to lose; and one of the reasons they can afford to lose on any particular issue is that they have confidence that they will win "their share" of the other issues. The system of decision-making may not be perfect for them, but it is one that is adjusted to them and to which they are adjusted—and with which they "can live." There is a division of labor among these decision organizations, each being legitimated for decision-making in a specific sector of community interests. True, these sectors overlap on certain issues; but only at the periphery, not at the core. Although these community decision organizations are not subunits of a hierarchical organization

17. *Political Influence* (New York: Free Press of Glencoe, 1961). **389**

that systematically regulates their respective endeavors, they have reached—and continue to reach through minor adaptations—a modus vivendi with each other, a relatively large degree of consensus regarding their respective domains. In the absence of an overall decision-making rubric, this consensus has been achieved crescively through a process of competitive mutual adjustment.

In sum, then, there are two levels of consensus: one on the hoped-for outcome of any particular issue; the second in the distribution of power, the allocation of domains, the acceptable procedures for decision-making, the nature of social problems and how they should be confronted, and on a set of underlying affirmations with respect to the essential soundness of the American institutional structure.

It is this second, more basic level of consensus that has partially broken down in the past decade. This breakdown has three related aspects:

First, the notion that there is a public interest that is the same for all has been undermined, with the result that the question concerning whose interests are being served under any given decision-making structure becomes highly pertinent.

Second, the existing decision-making structure is coming to be seen as serving the interests of different segments of the population differentially, and in a sense it is beginning to be recognized by large numbers of people that there are underlying systemic reasons why this is so and why it will not be otherwise.

Third, the legitimacy of these organizations to make community decisions is therefore also coming under challenge. They are being seen not as impartial arbiters of the community welfare, but as organizations well suited to preserving the existing balance of social groups and social benefits, organizations that seek and welcome change only insofar as that balance can be preserved or strengthened in the process.

To repeat, these three interrelated developments are to be considered relatively rather than absolutely. They are acknowledged by different people to different degrees, and they are seen as applying to some organizations more than to others. Although the trend described above is of the utmost importance, it represents only a modest amount of movement in the direction indicated. For the more militant elements in the population these organizations have virtually lost all their legitimacy. But for the vast majority of the population, even the disadvantaged or poor, one can speak not of a loss of legitimation but only of a relatively modest decrease of legitimation, or put the other way, of a modest but important challenge to the legitimacy of the organizations—legitimacy being the acknowledged right of an organization to claim to represent the community's interests in the decision sector that is allocated to it.

Change Modes That Challenge a "Public Interest"

My thesis at this point is that much of what is occurring in relation to community change strategies in these agitated times can be understood in the light of the challenge to the public interest described above: the challenge to the notion that there is a public interest, a community good that is the same for all; the challenge to the notion that the existing decision-making structure serves the interests of all; the challenge to the legitimacy of community decision organizations.

Perhaps the most important concomitant of these developments has been the increasing acceptance of contest, rather than collaboration, as an appropriate method for community decision-making in many types of situations. It may seem strange to note this phenomenon or even to assume that there was a time when important issues involving different points of view were solved in the community arena without contest. Municipal politics certainly presents a lively history of vigorously contested issues.

But perhaps that point lies close to the heart of the matter. Purposive change theory, as applied to the community, has confined itself largely to noncontroversial issues specifically because it was believed that the community's welfare was identical with the welfare of all groups within it. This belief led to confining community change strategies to collaborative ones, and "writing off" controversial issues as relating only to special or segmented or selfish interests rather than to community interests. Thus, politics has been seen as that morally unsatisfactory arena where selfish interests are worked out in a series of compromises and in proportion to the relative power with which different points of view are represented. The notion of purposive community change, of guiding the community's future shape, has largely been confined to those issues in which a claim was made that the community's interest was being represented, as distinguished from such selfish or segmented interests. Thus, many important issues were sloughed off by community decision organizations, and a collaborative strategy was assumed to be appropriate for finding and implementing the best interests of the community.

What seems to be new is the willingness to acknowledge that many issues that are controversial and that affect different groups differentially are issues that must be addressed but at the same time cannot be adequately dealt with in the confines of a collaborative $\qquad$ **391** strategy. Issues of inadequate housing, differential treatment of the poor, systemic racism, disputed land use, service distribution, employment practices, civil service, urban renewal, and industrial development—these cannot be left to the Olympian detachment and the presumed omniscience of the professional staffs of community decision organizations, nor can they be settled through ad hoc community actions involving only people holding similar opinions. Hence arises the willingness to accept and even to endorse contest as not only necessary but desirable if important issues are to be confronted in a purposive way and if different interests are to be represented in the decision-making.

In this context, the development of so-called *adversary models for citizen participation,* as distinguished from collaborative or "coalitional" models, is readily understandable. A recognition of an abiding difference of interests, a challenge to the legitimacy of community decision organizations, and a frank acceptance of contest as a legitimate and necessary method of resolving many community issues calls for some alternative to that of simply incorporating a component of citizen participation in the decision-making apparatus of community programs. The recognition of this relationship is implicit in the popular use of the term "cooptation" by citizen groups of various kinds who recognize that their interests and those of the community decision organizations do not coincide. If they join in collaborative planning with the community decision organizations, if they elect a member or two to the board, or if they serve through a citizens' advisory committee, things usually continue to work out in the agency's way. Somehow, the alleged benefits of collaboration do not eventuate. In this connection, the use of the term *black power* is directly relevant. There is little reason to believe that blacks as blacks are going to gain important concessions from a white-dominated power structure by supplying a little minority-group input into white-majority-dominated organizations. Many people therefore believe that in order to have leverage there must be a black point of view, which represents blacks not the public interest and which has a black constituency and a black power base. The same is true of other ethnic minority groups. This is often interpreted by whites as the unwillingness of blacks to join in collaborative efforts "for the welfare of all." And this interpretation is largely true, for many blacks believe that such collaborative efforts do not result in the welfare of all, on some equitable basis, but in the continuation of an essentially inequitable situation. Hence, the need to maintain an independent identity, an independent power base, the tendency to see the issue as resolvable not through consensus but through a hard-fought compromise that is fashioned out of the frank confrontation of different interests and different types of power brought to the situation.

Again, viewed from this context, the development of *advocacy planning* appears quite understandable.[18] For, once it is recognized that the existing planning organizations do not serve a public interest that is the same for all groups and that the interests of the poor tend to be systematically neglected, then it becomes apparent that the professional planners represent a resource that is being utilized in the interests of one part of the population. Other parts of the population with different interests that are not being adequately represented in the planning process therefore need to avail themselves of such representation. In a study made by the author of the Model Cities planning process of nine American cities, it was concluded that *all* the planners were "advocacy planners" in that they were providing professional expertise to the planning interests of a particular group or combination of groups and also were on occasion representing those interests in community decision-making arenas. What was new, then, was not the presence of advocacy planners in community decision-making but that for virtually the first time some of these advocacy planners were employed by organizations of the poor in order to represent the poor and were answerable to the poor rather than to the community decision organizations.[19] The point is that once the "myth" of the impartial, expert, noncontroversial planner who works in the interests of everyone is brought into question, it becomes quite appropriate to consider which groups are able to have their interests represented through professional planners in whatever community decision-making processes take place. As such, advocacy planning is simply a frank recognition of the existence of a plurality of opposed interests.

In this analytical context, the movement for *neighborhood control,* described in the preceding chapter, likewise seems quite understandable. For this movement involves not only the idea of decentralized control but also the idea of a transfer of power implicit in the notion of participatory democracy and in the notion of black power. It is not merely that neighborhoods are not being represented adequately in community-wide decision-making, but that neighborhoods where the poor and/or minority groups live are especially powerless in such decision-making. The whole notion of a need for "structural change," or "institutional change," implies this

---

18.   Paul Davidoff, "Advocacy and Pluralism in Planning," *Journal of the American Institute of Planners,* vol. 31, no. 4 (November 1965); Lisa R. Peattie, "Reflections on Advocacy Planning," *Journal of the American Institute of Planners,* vol. 34, no. 2 (March 1968); Marshall Kaplan, "Advocacy and Urban Planning," *The Social Welfare Forum, 1968* (New York: Columbia University Press, 1968).

19.   Roland L. Warren, "Model Cities First Round: Politics, Planning, and Participation," *Journal of the American Institute of Planners,* vol. 35, no. 4 (July 1969).

matter of power transfer, in the sense of a greater relative share of power in community decision-making by the poor, which—and this is often overlooked or ignored—can only take place at the expense of the relative share of power now exercised by groups other than the poor.

The conventional response to this line of reasoning is twofold. The first part states that as far as the various interest groups differ in their wishes, there prevails a democratic form of government that provides for periodic popular elections of officials and of legislators, with the overriding principle of majority rule. Any majority opinion or desire can become the subject for legislation. Naturally, if some proposal is against the majority will, then in a democratic system there is no justification for it. Insofar as injustice prevails in the institutional structure, the obligation and the opportunity are there to convince a majority and thus to bring about orderly legal change. The second part states that both the electoral process and the governmental machinery are subject to pressures from different interest groups in the population and that it is incumbent on people who feel their interests are not adequately represented to organize themselves and to apply their share of pressure on the legally constituted decision-making machinery.

We need not consider in detail the large amount of literature devoted to both of these points and the criticisms addressed to their validity in actual operation.[20] We need only make explicit what has been implicit in the earlier allusion to the legitimacy of community decision organizations; the same challenge that is addressed to their valid representation of a single community interest is addressed to the political structure: namely, regardless of how good it sounds in theory, in actual operation it performs in a way that systematically works injustice on the poor, on various ethnic minorities, on slum area residents. But the implications of this challenge are, if anything, even more important than the challenge to community decision organizations. For they lead fairly directly to the growth of types of action employed by the poor, by minority groups, or by radical youth movements to exert an influence on decision-making through other than the normally recognized and approved channels for such participation. These include sit-ins, various forms of demonstration,

---

20. The first point is treated in E. E. Schattschneider, *The Semisovereign People: A Realist's View of Democracy in America* (New York: Holt, Rinehart & Winston, 1960), and Theodore Lowi, *The End of Liberalism: Ideology, Policy, and the Crisis of Public Authority* (New York: W. W. Norton & Co., Inc., 1969).

The second point is treated in depth by Mancur Olson, Jr., in *The Logic of Collective Action: Public Goods and the Theory of Groups* (New York: Schocken Books, 1965). An impressive brief critique of pluralism is given by William Gamson in "Stable Unrepresentation in American Society," *American Behavioral Scientist*, vol. 12, no 2 (November/December 1968).

boycotts, vigils, and a whole array of what are often called "disruptive" tactics.[21] What such tactics all have in common is that they are attempts to influence public policies in ways that do not conform to the usual norms of how contest is conducted. They constitute a rejection of the letter to one's representative in congress, or of working through one's political party, or of organizing a pressure group to send out propaganda, and of the other ways in which contest is usually conducted within accepted social norms.[22] In this sense they can all be grouped together as norm-violating methods for engaging in contests. But in a pluralistic society such as the existing American society, the question naturally arises: *Whose* norms for contest do we refer to when we say that these norms are violated? The answer is the norms of white, middle-class American society that govern acceptable behavior in the conducting of contests or disputes.

Norm-violating social policy participation can be understood as a reaction to a sense of frustration or impatience with the rate or direction of change believed achievable by a particular group through activation of the conventional modes of participation. It is as though such groups assess the outcome of these conventional methods of participation and consider the outcome so undesirable and unjust that they begin to impugn the system of decision-making that leads so continuously to such unjust outcomes. Thus they lose their loyalty to the conventionally accepted norms in the conviction that these norms, no matter how justifiable they seem in the abstract, systematically operate to produce or continue injustice. If this is the case then why should one abide by them, particularly when one believes passionately that one's particular cause is just and cannot get a fair hearing and appropriate response within the existing acceptable channels for community decision-making? We are here asserting that it is such a line of thinking, perhaps not precisely in these terms, that provides the rationale for so-called norm-violating methods of influencing policy decisions, and that this applies specifically to the two large concentrations of such action: the one involving what we have simply called the "youth revolt" and the other, which can be called the "revolt of the poor," which has been largely, though by no means exclusively, dominated by blacks.

We cannot here treat all the pertinent aspects of norm-violating behavior—its relation to violence, its relation to statutory law, its relation to local customs and conventions, the many forms that it takes[23]—but it may be helpful to examine briefly the question of its

21. Specht, "Disruptive Tactics."

22. Warren, "Social Work and Social Revolution," *Truth, Love, and Social Change.*

23. They are treated in Warren, "Social Work and Social Revolution," *Truth, Love, and Social Change.*

efficacy, its weaknesses, and some of its other characteristics as applied by poverty area residents on their own behalf.[24]

Since norm-violating methods are utilized in complex situations, it is difficult to assess their efficacy, and so far there have been few definitive studies on the basis of which firm generalization can be made. There are many situations in which impressionistic examination indicates they have brought about tangible objectives, which the groups involved apparently were not able to secure using more conventional methods. The sit-in in the public welfare office brings an administrative concession in some of the public assistance policies; a mass demonstration at City Hall leads to the inclusion of representatives of the poor on some committee; a sit-in at a construction site leads to a temporary change in employment practices, and so on. These situations are difficult to specify and difficult to evaluate.

It is not only the desirable consequences of norm-violating social policy participation that are difficult to evaluate, but also the consequences that are undesirable from the standpoint of the participants. Most notable among these is the "backlash" effect, the presumed process in which the norm-violating tactic, regardless of its immediate efficacy, sets up a reaction of repugnance on the part of important segments of the population, which eventuates in hindering the types of reform that are being sought. Such negative response is difficult to assess even after the action is taken, and almost impossible before.

In another vein, criticism often points out that disruptive behavior such as the protesting of the location of a freeway route or an urban renewal site is largely negative in character. It indicates vigorous objection to a course of action that has resulted from considerable technical planning, has been extremely painstaking, and offers no alternative. Because it only says no, it is not constructive, is difficult to act upon, and so is often futile.

It is perhaps pertinent to observe, however, that such negative actions are customarily taken by groups of people who have neither the structured organization that could develop a set of alternative plans nor the resources with which to do so. In fact, many such activities are of an extremely ad hoc nature, bringing together people who have not been associated before, who have not gone through the process of developing a position or a set of policies or proposals, and whose only common bond is a sense of rage at the measure or condition being protested.

24. We will not here address its justification, except simply to note that since anyone who subscribes to the Declaration of Independence affirms the "right" to utilize norm-violating change strategies on some occasions, at least, the question of its justification tends to become not absolute but relative, presumably related to the magnitude of the alleged injustice and the presumed inability to correct it through norm-abiding channels.

In some instances, however, the people or organizations involved have had negative experience in previous attempts to negotiate their grievances with the officials. They may have engaged in negotiations that they thought had achieved a definite commitment for a particular change in policy only to find later that, from their standpoint, they had been deceived. They may have had negative experiences with having some of their representatives appointed to advisory committees or given what appeared to be a meaningful measure of participation only to find that their representatives could gain little or nothing for them on such collaborative bodies. It is interesting to consider in this context the practice of confronting officials with ultimatums, or with "nonnegotiable demands." These are, in themselves, viewed as norm-violating by the officials involved, officials who are used to negotiating, to hard bargaining, and who customarily have the resources with which to bargain relatively successfully. But groups of people who are not so well organized, or who fear being coopted or deceived, or who fear that they may be outmatched technically in a debate, may present their demands in nonnegotiable form simply because they fear that any other alternative will lead to their defeat.

Norm-violating social policy participation has the strength that it provides a resource for people who otherwise do not have resources pertinent to bring to bear on the situation. It gives them power through their nuisance value. But the power base is temporary. It is difficult to keep crowds of people at high emotional pitch for extensive periods of time; and while it may be possible to aggregate five thousand people to protest a particular measure, it may not be possible to get as many as fifty of them to work in concerted fashion using more usual and more norm-abiding tactics. Or, on the other hand, such tactics may have been tried but to no avail. At any rate, the usefulness of the protest gathering, the picketing operation, the sit-in, the boycott lies in the fact that it is possible to organize relatively large numbers of people around a specific issue that enrages them and that the impact may be relatively great. On the other hand, its weakness lies in the fact that the threat will soon ebb away, and those in control of more well-established organizations often have a valid sense that if only they can ride out the present crisis, perhaps by only token concessions, the episode will have disappeared and with it will have disappeared the threat posed by that particular aggregation of people.

Because of the weaknesses involved in sporadic activity and its lack of staying power, the victories that are won often turn out to be more symbolic than substantive. The concessions that have been wrested from officialdom begin to suffer attrition as soon as the disruptive activity ceases, and to reconstitute the activity would take an enormous amount of organizing effort. For this reason, the need is increasingly recognized for a type of organization of disadvantaged people that can survive beyond a particular episode and that can bring together like-minded people around a whole range of issues affecting them.

Two types of organizations illustrate these developments. One is the organization of specific groups of people in specific categorical statuses. Examples are tenants' councils and the Welfare Rights organizations. The other, more broad, is illustrated by the Black Caucus type of federation, an organizational rubric within which various organizations can keep in touch with each other, pursue their common interests over an extended period of time, and organize appropriate ad hoc action as the occasion arises. In a sense, such an organization provides a sense of continuity and focus not only to otherwise sporadic episodes of norm-violating social action but also to the more usual type of norm-abiding participation, such as collaborative participation on advisory committees, and so on. The existence of such a constituency and such a power base outside the organized citizen participation channels provides a basis of leverage independent of the control of the organization or official body in which the citizen participation is provided.

The Quest for Alternatives

We have examined some of the implications of the notion of the single public interest and also the implications of the decline in confidence in this notion for community change strategies. In the course of this discussion we have noted the pertinence of collaborative change strategies to situations characterized by consensus and of contest strategies to situations characterized by dissensus. We have noted the increase in importance of such dissensus in the minds of people concerned with community issues in the last decade or two, and of the concomitant growth of contest strategies, adversary models of change, advocacy planning, demands for institutional change involving power transfer, and the utilization of norm-violating contest strategies in some cases.

Throughout the discourse the constant theme has been the decline in the notion of the single public interest and the decline of trust in collaborative strategies as a means of shaping the course of the community's future. We have not denied the usefulness of collaborative strategies in consensus situations, nor that essential consensus does or may prevail around many specific change proposals. But at the same time we have emphasized that many important issues facing American communities today are issues that cast various groups of people against the legitimated community decision organizations and that it is doubtful whether these community decision organizations—using a collaborative strategy and without considerable pressure from outside—can be expected to take measures that will be sufficiently great to satisfy the needs and wishes of those who are challenging their legitimacy to represent all elements of the community justly. In this light, we have considered the growth of contest strategies as not only understandable historically but as having substantially valid theoretical justification, from the author's point of view at least.

Programs such as the antipoverty program and the Model Cities program, based on a collaborative strategy and designed to induce reform and greater sensitivity on the part of the existing agency structure, are likely to have minimal effect in creating meaningful or substantial change, change that is commensurate in quality and in magnitude with the demands for decent living conditions on the part of the poor.

If internal reform through collaborative techniques cannot alone be relied on to produce the desired changes, what are the alternatives? This is neither a precise question to formulate nor an easy question to answer. It is possible, though, to point out a number of developments that appear to be alternative strategies of change to those adopted by such programs as Economic Opportunities and Model Cities.

We have already given extensive consideration to what may be the most important alternative to centralized collaborative efforts for community change. To give it a summary name, let us call it *the adversary model.* We have considered its rationale and note here only that it is an alternative in the sense that rather than working in a collaborative, centralized context, it seeks to apply pressure from outside the individual agency or group of agencies through the development of an independent power base other than the citizen participation structure that the agency provides for and seeks through contest strategies to induce change in the desired direction. These strategies may include such norm-abiding ones as bargaining and negotiation and such norm-violating ones as sit-ins and other disruptive tactics.

A related alternative is the development of *alternative auspices* for the providing of various locality-relevant functions (see chapter 7). In the preceding chapter I pointed out that a broad series of facilities was being developed by radical youths as institutions of the counter-culture. A somewhat similar process is observable on the part of minority group organizations and/or organizations of the poor. Examples are the various self-defense groups, such as the Black Panthers, the Brown Berets, and the various police surveil- **399** lance organizations. The free breakfasts for children provided by Black Panthers is an example of still another function, as is the rather extensive institutional rubric incorporated by the Black Muslims. Numerous "freedom schools" have arisen outside the regular public school system, designed deliberately as alternatives or correctives to the established school system. In addition, numerous organizations have been developed to administer services in the health and welfare field, services that in a sense duplicate the existing services of the health department and the various social agencies but are provided by cooperatives or corporations or neighborhood organizations that are in the more or less direct control of the poor themselves. Multiservice centers, neighborhood health centers, and other forms of organization are frequently financed in part or in whole by federal programs. They vary in the extent to which they set themselves over against the existing health and welfare agencies as adversaries, but dependence on public monies constitutes a constant constraint. These alternative auspices (alternative, in this context, to the existing established social service agencies) are both interesting and important for they at least raise the question of the possibility that such organizations will grow in strength and numbers to the point where they would possibly supersede the existing, more conventional auspices for providing a wide range of locality-relevant functions for the poor.

A related movement is beginning to make itself known: a movement toward *greater utilization of the "market"* as a distributor of services and service facilities rather than the present emphasis on "rational" planning for their distribution through a centralized procedure. Putting this another way, the present system is based largely on the free or low-cost provision of social services to those who need them, with the funds coming from tax revenues or from donations and with the distribution of these services and facilities being centrally planned, insofar as possible, by the respective departments of government or by the United Fund. An alternative is to let the distribution of these services come to depend more on the market than on the centrally controlled planning process now utilized. The idea is that rather than avoid duplication of services, a definite attempt should be made to encourage such duplication in the form of agencies that compete with each other for their necessary clientele. It is believed this would open up more options for the disadvantaged clients in that in their search for suitable social services they are not confronted with a "monopoly" wherever they turn (for mental health services, for family counseling, for health care, for the schooling of their children, etc.) but have real choices that they are free to exercise. At the same time, the size of a service agency's budget would be made to depend at least in part on the number of clients it attracts, clients who have an option to go elsewhere, clients whose patronage the agency directly depends on for renewed budgeting. Various devices, such as scrip systems, vouchers, and bookkeeping transfers, have been proposed for such purposes. The idea has become most widely circularized through its application to the primary and secondary education field, especially through the writing of Milton Friedman.[25] But the proposal to give parents "tuition money" with which they would purchase their child's tuition either at a public school or at a private school, according to their choice, is contaminated by two somewhat extraneous issues, which may override in impact the alleged advantages of the "market" approach. One is the racial segregation issue, with the possibility that parents would utilize the arrangement as a means of continuing segregated schools or at least act more from this motive than from that of a high quality education for their children. The other is the parochial school issue.

In any event, there are in many institutional sectors the beginnings of what appears to be a growing commitment to develop patterns for utilizing the market as a distributor of services in many sectors where this is feasible, instead of providing free services and planning their distribution centrally.

In this chapter we have attempted to explain much of the current turmoil on the community scene in terms of a gradual attrition of the confidence that different groups of people place in a public interest at the community level. Viewed historically, this can be taken as a further development of the "great change," a growing product of the differentiation of interest and activity and the increasing formalization that have characterized much of modern social life. Like many other aspects of communities in earlier times, the consensus within which community people saw themselves as one, even in their differences, may continue to recede further into the murky background of irrelevance to the existing situation. It seems difficult to imagine how it could conceivably return, given the complexities of modern life and the apparent inexorability of the "great change."

But a salient characteristic of the current turmoil is the realization of the magnitude and human importance of the "great change" and the growth of a counter-trend. Out of a quiet, and occasionally noisy, sense of desperation, increasing numbers of people are seizing one opportunity or another to take a stand against this presumed inexorability. They are saying no to the despoilment of the natural environment. They are saying no to bureaucratic centralization and depersonalization. They are searching for new forms to fulfill the

25. Milton Friedman, *Capitalism and Freedom* (Chicago: University of Chicago Press, 1962).

ancient need for human association, which recognizes and involves the whole personality. In doing so, some are attempting to build adaptations within the general outlines of an advanced industrial society which is continuously given over to expanding technologies, greater differentiation, and human fragmentation. Others are more deliberate in their rejection of these main directions of crescive change. It is significant, and quite consistent, that they emphasize the search for simpler modes of social organization for the performance of locality-relevant functions. For without them it is difficult to conceive a reemergence of consensus, of more personalized relationships, and a deemphasis on technological advantage, on profitability in a narrow economic sense, and on the equating of proliferation with progress.

Postscript on the Seventies

The present chapter and the preceding one were designed not so much to afford a running commentary on "current events" in American communities as to derive from them further understanding of the nature of American communities in their aspects of both stability and change.[26] In the next two chapters, we shall return to a more specifically theoretical focus by presenting two somewhat unconventional elaborations on the principal theme that has run through this book: the analysis of the horizontal pattern and of the vertical pattern of community relations.

Before proceeding, I want to add a postscript to this and the preceding chapter in the light of recent developments. The alert reader will have noticed that events have moved past the state of affairs analyzed in these two chapters, though it is hoped that these events have in no way invalidated the analysis presented. We can continue to analyze these events within the context of the "great change" and various responses to it considered under the rubric of purposive change, as portrayed in chapter 11, and in reference to the decline in confidence in a single public interest and the increasing use and legitimation of contest strategies for change, as portrayed in the present chapter.

The changes that have developed over the few intervening years can be summarized in a few paragraphs. As will be seen, they add up to diminution in the parameters of purposive change, a diminution in the intensity or degree of change, the time frame of change, and the balance between purposive and crescive change. We have depicted various types of responses to the great change within

26. This Postscript and the next two chapters appear for the first time in the present, third, edition.

the framework of purposive change and have specified three areas in which such deliberate, purposive change has been occurring. One was in the area of *broadened citizen participation* within existing communities; a second was in the area of alternatives to existing communities in the form of *new, planned communities,* which were nevertheless within the mainstream of the great change and constituted simply further elaborations of it—the new towns; and a third was in the direction of alternatives that were in self-conscious opposition to the great change, taking the form both of *alternative institutions* within crescive communities and of the development of new alternative communities or communes.

The period of the 1970s has seen the attenuation of all three developments. In existing communities, the action that welled up from the streets has largely subsided. Like other developments, it has, in subsiding, left its residue on the institutional structure. The notion of citizen participation has been widely accepted and broadly applied but largely on a symbolic and superficial level. Along with it, the idea of "participatory democracy"—that people should participate in all decision-making directly rather than through representatives—has perhaps slightly broadened the basis of participation, but one now hears little of it as a vital new dynamic. The movement for neighborhood control has spawned a widespread network of "little City Halls" or "neighborhood centers," and other neighborhood-based organizations in many cities,[27] but as it has spread it has taken the form of an extremely mild application of the principle, as compared with the more heady aspirations for a transfer of power to the neighborhood level as depicted by Milton Kotler[28] or Alan A. Altshuler[29] or, much earlier, Saul D. Alinsky.[30]

The term *black power* has lost both its dynamic surge and its threatening quality for many whites who feared a revolutionary thrust. In the process it has left its residue in a more substantial entry of blacks and other ethnic minorities into municipal politics as organized pressure groups and a slowly growing public acknowledgement of the persistence of institutional racism.

Accompanying these developments has been a winding down

---

27. Robert K. Yin and Douglas Yates, *Street-Level Governments: Assessing Decentralization and Urban Services* (Santa Monica: Rand Corporation, 1974). See also *Neighborhood Decentralization,* a periodical published by the Center for Governmental Statistics, Washington, D.C.

28. *Neighborhood Government: The Local Foundations of Political Life* (Indianapolis: Bobbs-Merrill Co., 1969).

29. *Community Control: The Black Demand for Participation in Large American Cities* (New York: Western Publishing Co., 1970).

30. *Reveille for Radicals* (Chicago: University of Chicago Press, 1946).   **403**

of the federal government's role in the Great Society programs for the cities. One need only mention the Community Action and Model Cities programs to become aware of the extent to which such programs have either been discontinued or have hung on only as weakened shadows of their former selves. The withdrawal of federal funding from local subsidized housing programs is another example of the federal pullback, a pullback not only in funding but in "moral support" for citizen action on the part of low-income people.

While not as dramatic, there is nevertheless a leading theme that appears to have replaced "citizen participation" as a means for civic betterment. It is the new emphasis on "management." Local conditions, particularly local governmental services but also various fields of social facilities and services, are to be improved and made more effective in their service to community residents through improved management techniques, more careful planning, computerized data banks, new measures of cost effectiveness, and new technologies to improve the quality of decision-making. There has likewise been a sustained emphasis on "the need for coordination." These indicate an extension of the trend toward rationality described on page 358.

The great aspirations for moving rapidly toward the elimination of poverty and a more equitable distribution of power and income have lost much of their appeal, partly, it would seem, through a widespread loss of faith in their political feasibility and consequently in their relevance as important issues around which to organize concerted action. It is in this sense that one may speak of a diminution of the parameters of purposive change. By contrast, there has been a falling back to the idea that the way toward community betterment is through the increased health of the economy and through the operation of the "market" as opposed to administered change, crescive change as opposed to purposive.

Just as it was pointed out earlier that the implications of the urban turmoil of the late sixties and early seventies must be taken only relatively, so it needs to be pointed out that the above description of subsequent developments should also be considered relatively. Although there has been a marked attenuation in these earlier developments, things are not the same. Modest, but substantial, change has occurred, even though the dynamic for change has attenuated.

The movement toward "new towns" has likewise attenuated, to the point where there has been little activity to compare with the heady expectations of a decade ago. The attenuation is directly traceable to two specific causes. One was the withdrawal of federal support for new town starts in 1975. The other was the state of the market in terms of land values, construction costs, and interest rates for borrowed capital. They have made new town development extremely precarious as a profit venture. For the predictable future many of these new towns are in a state of arrested development at a much more modest level of population than originally planned. But again, they constitute a residue of the high-water mark of the new town movement of the sixties and seventies. More than that they constitute a body of experience that will no doubt serve as a basis for a future wave of new town development, even though there is little present indication of such a new wave.

Attenuation of the change dynamic is also apparent in the field of alternative institutions and communes. Earlier in this chapter it was indicated that the growth in alternative institutions of various kinds in relation to various locality-relevant functions showed the potential for constituting a more-or-less complete alternative society, within which people might live their lives in a mode largely opposed to the crescive developments of the great change. While many such alternative institutions still exist, there is at present less indication of their future proliferation.

It is difficult to assess whether the movement toward communes has yet reached its peak. A recent book resulting from a first-hand study suggests that they may be much more numerous than might be supposed:

> The thousands of miniature societies which exist peacefully in the interstices of American life remain invisible to the broader society. Few people except immediate neighbors are aware of their existence or of the extent of the community movement.[31]

It is perhaps plausible that their potential influence for social change is not so much a short-run result of the period of turbulence for purposive change a few years back as a long-run result of a much slower, less dramatic process. In the book just quoted, the author, who interviewed numerous veterans of the anti-Vietnam movement reported that: "They had dismissed their former activities to the point of refusing to talk or even think about them. The younger communitarians were totally immersed in the tasks at hand: putting up a fence or arranging the schedule for the care of the community's children.[32]

Thus the high watermark of a more positive attitude toward the scope and potentiality and feasibility of purposive community change seems to have been reached and passed in the areas of citi-

31. Marguerite Bouvard, *The Intentional Community Movement: Building a New Moral World* (Port Washington, N.Y.: Kennikat Press, 1975), p. 5.

32. *Intentional Community Movement*, p. 6.

zen participation activity in crescive communities as well as in new towns, alternative institutions, and communes.

What is the relationship of this development to the decline in confidence in a single public interest and to the growth of utilization and legitimation of contest strategies? In these as well, there has been an attenuation though not a complete reversal. Despite the threats to their legitimation, community decision organizations such as the health and welfare councils, the urban renewal agencies, the city planning agencies, the boards of education, the councils of churches, and the rest have withstood the threats to their continued viability; and dissident groups have apparently come to realize that they can neither be replaced nor substantially changed in the direction of broader power distribution or more equitable decision-making. A study by the author and his colleagues has sought to account for this impressive durability of the community decision organizations in terms of three processes through which they ward off threats to their viability: preventing, blunting, and repelling.[33] Much the same occurred with other organizations that form a part of the structure of American communities. Yet, the challenge to the legitimation of these organizations has not wholly disappeared. The idea that somehow these organizations, however inadvertently, tend to operate in a fashion that produces or sustains social inequity remains as part of the social climate, even though the immediate threat to their viability has disappeared. The simple notion that these organizations represent the public interest of the entire community and that opposition to them comes exclusively from selfish interests or from ignorance remains open to challenge in a way that did not exist only a few years ago.

Much the same seems to have occurred with respect to the use of contest strategies for community change. Here again there has been attenuation, but not complete reversal. There has been a marked decline in the use of norm-violating strategies of community change (see pages 396-399), but other, less dramatic forms of hard-fought contests within the conventional norms of contest strategies remain. The earlier conclusion that many important community change issues involve strongly held differences of interest and opinion and that therefore if action is to be taken it must involve some form of contest is a notion that has outlived the otherwise widespread attentuation in the developments discussed in this and the preceding chapter. This conclusion has great importance in the consideration of the horizontal pattern of community relationships, as will become apparent in the following chapter.

But before we leave this consideration of recent developments

33.   Warren, Rose, and Burgunder, *Structure of Urban Reform.*

in the field of community change, other aspects merit brief mention. The ghetto revolt, the movement for citizen participation, for participatory democracy, for neighborhood control, for advocacy planning; the decline in confidence in a single community public interest; the challenge to the legitimacy of community decision organizations; the increased recognition of the necessity for and desirability of strategies of contest for bringing about community change—all these developments characterized literally hundreds, in some respects thousands, of communities in the United States and Canada. They were obviously a phenomenon of the larger society, though they had their genesis in each community that experienced them. To most of those who participated in these dramatic developments, the issues were experienced as local issues, were locally generated, and were presumably locally changeable. Yet, as one looks at the broad sweep of the turmoil of the sixties and early seventies, it becomes apparent that these were more than local community issues, locally generated. The backdrop for the controversy was local, the actors and stage props were local, but these were all local enactments of a similar national drama. There were of course individual local variations, but the national pattern was clear. In this respect, they are reminiscent of the puzzling relationship between local and national phenomena considered earlier at two places in this book (See pp. 262-268 and pp. 297-303). We shall address this puzzling relationship again in chapter 14, but first we return to a further analysis of the horizontal pattern of American communities.

13 The Horizontal Pattern Revisited: Communities as Interactional Fields

In chapter 9 the relation of local community units to each other was analyzed in terms of the horizontal pattern. Two somewhat contrasting conceptions of this horizontal pattern have emerged in the course of community studies. Recent developments in community theory tend to assume or to imply one of these alternative conceptions or paradigms, replacing the other, more traditional approach. The more traditional approach considered the community as a collectivity, that is, as a social unit capable of decision-making and action on its own behalf and at its own level, with members subordinating their own interests to those of the larger social entity. The more recent conception of the community is not so much of a social group acting on its own behalf as of an arena or field of interaction manifesting certain systemic tendencies.

These different viewpoints are important not only for theoretical understanding but also in their implications for community action and for questions of values. They are addressed in this chapter, which affords us an opportunity to review some important contemporary developments in community theory and to relate them to the behavior of people in communities today.

Two Conceptions of the Horizontal Pattern

First, let us examine in closer detail the differences between these two conceptions of the community's horizontal pattern. We shall call them the *concrete collectivity* conception and the *interactional field* conception.

By a concrete collectivity is meant an identifiable social system that can be clearly distinguished from its environment and is capable of acting as a social entity in its own right. It has its own interests, which are clearly distinguishable from the interests of its constituent parts. It also has its own specifically identifiable shared values and norms and is capable of developing goals and taking action toward accomplishing them.

The concept of a collectivity was developed a quarter of a century ago by Talcott Parsons.[1] For him, any social system is a collectivity if the constituent parts share certain norms of interaction and feel a moral obligation to abide by these common norms It will be noticed that the description of a collectivity given above adds a number of additional characteristics to Parsons's definition of he term.

The conception of the community as a collectivity is evident r much of the conventional sociological treatment of communities Sociologists have found themselves trying to demarcate the specific geographic and sociological borders of communities, specifying who is a member and who is not, seeking a set of values and norms shared by all members of each community as distinguished from every other community in the world, and dealing with such concepts as the community interest, community goals, community values, and community decision-making. The community was treated as though it were a cerebrating "beastie" of some kind or, if not, then something pretty close to an identifiable formal organization: the most tangible kind of Parsonian collectivity.

The alternative paradigm, which is here called the interactional field approach, views the community not as a collective entity but as the simple aggregate of the clustered interaction of people and organizations occupying a restricted geographic area, whose aggregate interaction, in both structure and function, demonstrates not chaos or randomness but large areas of systemic interconnections. These connecting patterns, incidentally, show remarkable similarity as one goes from one community to another. The actions of the parts are negotiated among the parts rather than being directed by the whole. The values and norms that are shared are seldom specific to that community but rather are a part of the common macroculture according to which interaction takes place in many

1.   Talcott Parsons, *The Social System*, (New York: Free Press of Glencoe, 1951, 1964), p. 41.

communities. The community does not act, but the parts of it do.[2] The community's interest is not something in its own right but merely some aggregate of the individual interests of the parts. Collectivity orientation may be present, but strong allegiance to the specific community is not a defining criterion; rather, such allegiance varies among communities, some showing much collectivity orientation, others very little.

There is no way of validating the one or the other paradigm; rather, each is validated in terms of its own assumptions and definitions.[3] But the arena of interaction paradigm accounts for more of the community aspects that are the concern of community studies today; it appears to be more useful in examining today's community problems; and its normative implications are more congenial to today's situation. The reasoning in support of these statements will be given later in this chapter.

The interactional field paradigm is most colorfully expressed by Norton Long's classic depiction:

> The five-acre woodlot in which the owls and the field mice, the oaks and the acorns, and other flora and fauna have evolved a balanced system has no public opinion, however rudimentary. The co-operation is an unconscious affair. For much of what goes on in the local territorial system co-operation is equally unconscious and perhaps, but for the occasional social scientist, unnoticed. This unconscious co-operation, however, like that of the five-acre woodlot, produces results. The ecology of games in the local territorial system accomplishes unplanned but largely functional results. The games and their players mesh in their particular pursuits to bring about over-all results; the territorial system is fed and ordered. Its inhabitants are rational within limited areas and, pursuing the ends of these areas, accomplish socially functional ends.[4]

In a sense, the heart of community theory lies in trying to account for the dynamic processes through which these largely func-

2. A contrary position is taken by Charles Tilly, in "Do Communities Act?", *Sociological Inquiry*, vol. 43, nos. 3-4, 1973. His focus is on collective action on matters of community concern. Although he answers his question in the affirmative, he strongly delimits the conditions under which communities may act, pointing out that urbanization destroys these conditions.

3. Thomas S. Kuhn, *The Structure of Scientific Revolutions*, 2nd ed. (Chicago: University of Chicago Press, 1962, 1970). A highly important treatment of paradigms in community sociology, somewhat different from the present discourse, though not incompatible with it, I believe, is given in Jessie Bernard, *The Sociology of Community* (Glenview, Ill.: Scott, Foresman & Co., 1973).

4. Norton E. Long, "The Local Community as an Ecology of Games," *American Journal of Sociology*, vol. 64, no. 3 (November 1958). This article is included in Roland L. Warren, ed., *New Perspectives on the American Community*, 3rd ed. (Chicago: Rand McNally & Co., 1977).

tional results are brought about: how the whole thing hangs together, even though there is often little collectivity orientation and even though many of the parts are organizationally structured as integral parts of systems whose control mechanisms may be located hundreds or thousands of miles away. Corresponding to this *theoretical* or *cognitive* aspect of these alternative paradigms is a *practical* or *instrumental* aspect, namely the question of purposive community change, of conscious, deliberate inclusive-level intervention into this arena in those cases where the usual interaction processes do not produce results that are considered functional or optimal. There is, further, the *moral* or *normative* aspect of paradigm choice that is concerned with the question, For whom is the system functional?

Having briefly characterized the two alternative paradigms and indicated the direction of the shift and the ways in which the shift is important, let us now consider some current theoretical developments and relate them to these alternative paradigms.

Current Theoretical Developments

In 1968 George Hillery published his important book on *Communal Organizations: A Study of Local Societies.*[5] His theory of the vill is based on three organizing principles: locality, families, and cooperation. These are characteristics shared by the preindustrial community and the modern metropolis, as he demonstrates with a highly systematic comparison of various communities in different parts of the world. More importantly, he emphasizes that the vill is a communal organization, as distinguished from a formal organization. Communal organizations, he writes, "are heavily institutionalized systems which lack defining goals."[6] As such, they are differentiated from formal organizations, which, following Parsons, are characterized by primary orientation toward accomplishment of a specific goal. By a specific goal is meant one whose product is identifiable, whose product can be used by another system, and whose output is amenable to contract, in the sense roughly that it can be bought and sold.[7]

Although communities, or vills, contain formal organizations, they are not themselves formal organizations and they are not constituted of an aggregate of formal organizations. Hillery sees vills as consisting of families rather than of formal organizations. He tends to neglect or deemphasize formal organizations since in his estimation communal organizations are dissimilar in kind from formal

5. George A. Hillery, Jr., *Communal Organizations: A Study of Local Societies* (Chicago: University of Chicago Press, 1968).

6. *Communal Organizations*, p. 189.

7. *Communal Organizations*, pp. 156-7.

organizations. Perhaps this emphasis on the family instead of the formal organization is at least partly attributable to the fact that although he treats both folk villages and cities, his conceptual basis appears to take the folk village as its point of principal reference.

It is interesting to point out the contrast between Hillery's analysis and that given in this book. Hillery has preferred the conceptualization that emphasizes the nonformally organized aspects of the community. He does not entirely neglect the formal structure but gives relatively little attention to it. This book does the opposite: It emphasizes the formal structure of the community, as formally organized in various sectors related to the locality-relevant functions; and although the informal structure is neither denied nor ignored, it receives much less attention. The approaches are complementary rather than antagonistic.

Hillery's approach has important implications for applied sociology, only some of which he has indicated. For one thing, much community development work in small communities, as indicated earlier, can be interpreted as the attempt to convert the communal organization, the vill, into a formal organization, with all citizens participating in one or another problem committee or task force. The difficulty of community problem definition, goal setting, and community action is minimized when we realize that these are things that formal organizations do relatively well whereas communal organizations as such are not equipped to deal with them. Likewise, in a new town, we see the process through which a formal organization, the new town company or coalition, gradually devolves into a communal organization and "fades into the landscape": the sociological as well as the physical landscape.

Part of the reason why the emphasis on formal structure has gained circulation among applied sociologists and professional people working in American communities is that this approach emphasizes formal organizations and their interrelationships, which, in most tasks of community organization and change, seem to be much more suitable types of units to work with in large communities than are families. Yet, many change efforts apparently falter at least partly because they take into consideration only the formal organizational components of the change or goal they are seeking and neglect the communal aspects. Let us note, in passing, that Hillery's approach, even in his analysis of the city, tends to emphasize the *Gemeinschaft* aspects of the community, while the emphasis of the present book is largely on the *Gesellschaft* aspects.

Next, we shall consider three theoretical approaches that in various ways attempt to adapt earlier models of the community as a concrete collectivity with definite geographic borders to the present situation of diffuseness and complexity of the community field.

First, there is the conceptual path laid out most explicitly by Harold Kaufman, as described in chapter 2. Community must be differentiated from the local society, he maintains, even though it is a locality-oriented phenomenon. It is best defined and investigated in terms of community actions, actions of coalitions of local people and organizations around local concerns. Kaufman is explicit both about the components of community action and about their sequential structure.

A second alternative is simply to exclude the concept of locality as a definitional criterion of community and to define it in terms of social relationships that may or may not involve close spatial propinquity. Israel Rubin suggests that community is to be found in those social ties that bind the individual meaningfully to the larger society. Such ties are found in specific organizations situated in important institutional areas and are characterized by primary and secondary interaction of their members. Such ties may be constituted within occupational roles, ethnic group affiliations, or religious groups. Locality is thus a relatively unimportant variable in community rather than a definitional criterion.[8]

A third alternative is the seeking of community in identifiable sociometric networks. Network theory, a variant of sociometric analysis, was given a major push by Elizabeth Bott's study of *Family and Social Network*[9] and is emphasized by Jacqueline Scherer as the most useful approach to community.[10] One does not look for a collectivity called community but sees the community function performed within identifiable networks. These networks, in turn, have been found to be not random but systematically structured, so that clusters of networks can be identified that denote an empirically established set of mutual social bonds, as distinguished from the theoretically vague concept of an inclusive community based on common space. A report by Paul Craven and Barry Wellman on "The Network City" presents not only a conceptual elaboration but a methodological description of network analysis.[11]

Each of these approaches in its own way constitutes a direct challenge or alternative to the conceptualization of the community system as a concrete collectivity, emphasizing instead a selective approach to the interaction of people.

Another somewhat related approach that is significant for the-

8.   Israel Rubin, "Function and Sructure of Community: Conceptual and Theoretical Analysis," *International Review of Community Development*, nos. 21-22, 1969. This article is included in Warren, *New Perspectives on the American Community*.

9.   (New York: Free Press, 1957, 1971).

10.   *Contemporary Community: Sociological Illusion or Reality* (London: Tavistock Publications, distributed by Harper & Row, New York, 1972).

11.   "The Network City," *Sociological Inquiry*, vol. 43, nos. 3-4, 1973.

oretical understanding as well as for practical action is difficult to designate unambiguously with a single term. Perhaps the term "informal helping networks" is as good as any other. But other terms such as "informal service networks" and "the lay service system" have also been used.[12] Some writers use a slightly different conception in their research: the social economy.[13]

These terms all call attention to transactions that are often mistakenly thought of as goods or services produced only by formal organizations, firms, or agencies, either in the profit sector or in the public sector. Yet many types of services that are available commercially or through a nonprofit agency are provided by family, friends, or neighbors. They are also often provided by organizations, such as fraternal organizations or labor unions, whose primary functions may be something quite different. To be sure, a commonly accepted interpretation in the human services field is that, as society becomes more differentiated in connection with the "great change," families and neighborhoods become increasingly unable or unwilling to perform such functions. Therefore, special agencies are established to perform them, whether it be restaurant meals, nursing home care, or group recreational activities. Our national economic accounts do not include such informal goods and services in the gross national product unless they are performed by public agencies or in the profit sector. They likewise tend to be neglected in social planning for human needs, which also usually looks to the spectrum of organized agencies and to the profit sector.

In contrast, informal networks and systems of exchange of goods and services are difficult to identify and to aggregate empirically on a community basis. Yet there can be no question that they are an important aspect of the locality-oriented social activity that takes place within and among clusters of people residing in proximity to each other. These important activities get short shrift in many conceptual approaches to the communtiy, but their relative neglect in considering social policy for communities is now beginning to be rectified.

Community Power Structures

Let us turn now to a more widely recognized and fully researched aspect of community studies, that of community power structures, as

12. Donald I. Warren, personal communication.

13. Martin Lowenthal, "The Social Economy in Urban Working Class Communities," in Gary Gappert and Harold Rose, eds., *The Social Economy of Cities*, UAAR, vol. 9, (Sage Publications, 1975). This article is included in Warren, *New Perspectives on the American Community*.

described in chapter 2. Two aspects of these studies are especially germane to the present discussion.

First, the widely familiar issue of whether given communities have single or multiple power structures or pyramids is directly relevant to the two paradigms outlined earlier. Granted that communities are not formal organizations and thus do not have a single formally constituted and legitimated authority system; granted also that communities in America at least appear to be organized into sectors of activity often headed by an inclusive community decision organization such as the board of education, urban renewal agency, health and welfare council, or chamber of commerce; and granted that this sectoral interorganizational structure involves informal networks of people in various echelons with respect to the participating organizations[14]—there is still the question of whether one can find and identify in communities a single informal guidance system that can be looked on as a concrete sociological entity or leadership subsystem. The monists say yes, the pluralists say no. And, of course more recently, there is recognition that the nature of the findings depends partly on the research methods used.[15]

The notion of a single power structure is very congenial to the older conceptualization of communities as concrete collectivities. In the absence of a formally designated organizational leadership structure, the concept of the informal but unified power structure affords a ready substitute. The community as a concrete collectivity tends to be seen as having a single, identifiable guidance system, namely, the informal monolithic power structure.

It is much more difficult to conceive of the community as a concrete collectivity if one acknowledges a plurality of power structures, that is, a plurality of separate guidance systems for different sectors of community activity, for what Norton Long calls the real estate game, the education game, the housing game, and so on. On the other hand, the notion of the local community as a field of interaction is much more congenial to a plurality of power structures, with differently organized sectors comprised of interactional subfields that are more or less formally constituted and whose guidance systems may at times operate independently of each other or

14. Roland L. Warren, "The Interaction of Community Decision Organizations," *Social Service Review*, vol. 41, no. 3, (September 1967), and "The Interorganizational Field as a Focus for Investigation," *Administrative Science Quarterly*, vol. 12, no. 3. (December 1967).

15. John Walton, "A Systematic Survey of Community Power Research," in Michael Aiken and Paul E. Mott, eds., *The Structure of Community Power* (New York: Random House, 1970); James E. Curtis and John W. Petras, "Community Power, Power Studies and the Sociology of Knowledge," *Human Organization*, vol. 29, no. 3, (Fall 1970). This article is included in Warren, *New Perspectives on the American Community*.

may at other times interact in various degrees of cooperation or contest with each other.

A second aspect of power structure studies is also germane. The power structure is not usually formally constituted. You don't find it listed as such in the city directory. You have to engage in sophisticated research techniques to tease it out. But it is there. The findings of these studies of power structures constituted of a series of individuals, rather than of a series of organizations, are largely a product of their assumptions and methodologies. In any case, few if any of the power structure researchers deny the importance of organizations. Rather, they see access to organizations and to organizational resources as a source of the sanctions, positive and negative, that powerful individuals can exercise for their own purposes. In many cases, if you should cut these powerful individuals off from their ties to a single organization, or to at most two or three, their power positions would virtually disintegrate.

Nevertheless, the existence of networks of individuals in positions where they can wield inordinate influence on one or more sectors of community decision-making is an important datum that has not been adequately incorporated into community theory. This lack is partially due to the essentially theoryless orientation of many power structure researchers but also to the fact that conventional community theory has obscured the difficulties behind such vacuous terms as community leadership, opinion leaders, and elites and has not itself provided an adequate consideration of the interface of formal and informal structures.

It is difficult to see how an adequate approach to the informal structure of powerful individuals can afford to ignore the structure of organizational interaction at the local level. Interorganizational behavior is important for community analysis for another reason as well. Namely, communities don't act, despite all the attention given to "planned community change," "community action," and the rest. What are called community actions are actions of particular combinations of individuals and organizations. In large cities, these so-called community actions usually occur as the actions of specific community decision organizations within a particular sector or as a type of coalitional activity among several organizations on an ad hoc basis. In small communities, the conventional community development approach is to attempt to organize a de facto formal organization comprised of committees representing all the important institutional sectors.

Similarly, as pointed out earlier in this book, communities as such are not related to extracommunity systems (see p. 244). When we speak of the community's relationship to some larger geographic entity or some extracommunity system, we invariably speak of the

416

relationship of an organization or of individuals to an extracommunity system, such as the municipal government's relationship to the state government, the relationship of the labor union local to the national union, or that of the local Post Office to the U.S. Postal Service.

In other words, it is somewhat misleading to treat communities as concrete collectivities and much more theoretically justifiable as well as practically useful to consider them as local fields within which organizational interaction takes place. The increasing attention paid to interorganizational analysis and to coalition formation at the local level constitutes a further indication of the paradigm shift away from considering the community as a concrete collectivity and toward seeing it as a field of interaction. A recently published book, by the author and his associates, called *The Structure of Urban Reform: Community Decision Organizations in Stability and Change*, indicates something of the nature of the ecological field within which such interaction takes place among community decision organizations.[16]

Social System Theory and the Community

Turning to a brief consideration of social system theory in relation to the community, it appears that different interpretations of system theory can be adapted to the two paradigms. One can, in other words, think of the community system as a concrete collectivity, as some sort of unity in its own right, or one can think of the community system simply as an interactional field within which different degrees of structured formal and informal interaction take place between and among the owls and the field mice, which in this case are the organizations and the individuals.[17]

It is interesting that Parsons never dealt with communities as concrete collectivities.[18] Likewise, Loomis in his extensive work on

16. Roland L. Warren, Stephen M. Rose, and Ann F. Burgunder, *The Structure of Urban Reform: Community Decision Organizations in Stability and Change* (Lexington, Mass.: D.C. Heath-Lexington Books, 1974).

17. Kenneth P. Wilkinson has written a number of important papers on communities as fields of interaction, but his particular attention to the interactional field focused on locality-oriented, coordinated interests places him closer to Kaufman's relatively delimited conception of the community as distinguished from the "local society." See "The Community as a Social Field," *Social Forces*, vol. 48, no. 3, (March 1970), and "A Field-Theory Perspective for Community Development Research," *Rural Sociology*, vol. 37, no. 1, (March 1972). The latter article and Kaufman's are both included in the author's *New Perspectives on the American Community*.

18. In his article on "The Principal Structures of Community," in Talcott Parsons, *Structure and Process in Modern Societies* (New York: Free Press of Glencoe, 1960), he treated community "not as a type of concrete social unit, but as an *analytical* category."

417

Social Systems dealt with societies rather than communities.[19] But the Parsonian influence on community theory has nevertheless been in the direction of thinking of the community as a Parsonian collectivity. This direction may well be attributable to the fact that Parsons explicitly distinguished between collectivities and ecologies[20] and then defined ecologies in such a narrow way that the concept would hardly constitute an adequate model for communities.

The new interactional field model is not Parsonian and is to be distinguished from the older urban ecology, which was primarily concerned with the clustering of people and functions in geographic space. The newer paradigm draws from ecology because the ecological approach lends itself to analysis of the systemic nature of interaction and exchange patterns without making the assumption of collectivity orientation, or that the existence of systemic relationships implies a Parsonian collectivity. The newer paradigm is directed at the units that interact and looks to the systemic nature of that interaction. It does not focus on the inclusive system as the unit of analysis. In this respect, the newer paradigm is more closely akin to so-called *conflict theory*, a highly inappropriate but widely employed term, than to system theory in its usual sense of collectivity theory.

The interactional arena is an arena of social rather than physical space. It concerns itself with the systematic ways in which people and organizations interact within and across sectors of local concern. The existence of social space is implicitly recognized in terms such as *field of interaction, organizational domains,* and *sectors of activity.* But it must of course develop its own vocabulary to accommodate aspects of interaction that are nonspatial.

In one way or another, all of the theoretical developments described above reflect a movement toward the interactional field paradigm and away from the concrete collectivity paradigm. Hillery's emphasis on the nongoal-oriented nature of the communal organization, Kaufman's diffidence about equating the community with the local society taken as a collectivity, Rubin's reminder that characteristics attributed to community collectivities are preferably treated in terms of other types of human groupings, the network theorists' emphasis on the selectivity of the community phenomenon within any given geographic space, the emphasis on the informal but highly important localized function of mutual assistance and exchange, the growing preoccupation with the informal power structure and the growing conviction of the pluralism of most such localized structures, the growing attention to negotiation and exchange

19. Charles P. Loomis, *Social Systems: Essays on Their Persistence and Change* (Princeton, N.J.: D. Van Nostrand and Co., 1960).

20. *The Social System*, p. 93.

among powerful individuals rather than to their collective participation in community guidance, the growing attention to studying the interaction among local organizations, the awareness of greater organization within sectors than across sectors, the growing interest in examining the nature of the interorganizational field as an interactional arena—all these lend weight to the new interactional approach.

The new paradigm, like the old urban ecology, or even more so, recognizes the importance of culture, the existence of norms of interaction, and the importance of cultural patterns that tend to shape interaction one way rather than another. The culture and the norms, however, are not primarily those of the local community as a concrete collectivity but rather the culture and the norms of the larger society that apply in many communities. Indeed, the remarkable similarity of the social ecology as one goes from one American community to another and the similarity of the institutionalized thought structure that molds it constitute an impressive phenomenon. It points to the utter irrelevance of seeking to explain each community's culture and norms of interaction as a self-generated phenomenon, a unique characteristic of each community.

It is interesting to point out as well some of the relationships of the points of theoretical approach summarized above to the concept of *Gemeinschaft*. The horizontal ties of the preindustrial community were largely *Gemeinschaft*-like in nature, based on common sentiments, customs, commonly accepted norms, and shared institutions and values; but with the great change, there is a development of formal, *Gesellschaft*-like mechanisms, such as community decision organizations, to substitute for these earlier types of social glue, if you will. Community development, seen as a process of converting the community or parts of it into a formal organization for problem-solving and action purposes, is an attempt to achieve a substitute for *Gemeinschaft* through *Gesellschaft*-like structures and methods, as indicated in chapter 10. This raises an interesting question, to paraphrase a popular song from a few years back, "*Where Has All the Gemeinschaft Gone?*" The answer, it would seem, is that it is very much still here and always will be. But it no longer sorts itself out quite so neatly within demarcated geographic communities. Where it has gone is indicated in the extensive informal helping networks, in the ad hoc development of coalitions for local purposes, in the strength of sociometric ties, in the meaningful associations within a religious group, an ethnic group, or other groups with common bonds of interest, and in the personal bonds of affection and sentiment that spring up among people in interaction in even the most formal settings.

419

Instrumental and Normative Aspects

But to resume the main thread of the discussion, it was stated earlier that the paradigm shift has three different types of implications: cognitive, instrumental, and normative. So far, we have considered only the *cognitive* aspects. Let us turn in much briefer fashion to the *instrumental* aspects. Here I refer to the question of deliberate, purposeful intervention into the system in order to improve the aggregate output of the interaction processes already underway.

The interactional field paradigm holds definite implications for community change efforts as treated in chapters 10-12. One of the constant concerns in community planning has been the need for greater coordination and the assumption that coordination takes place only through a collective guidance system. The newer paradigm suggests that a much higher degree of coordination exists at any one time than is commonly recognized, for much of it takes place through individual interaction and negotiated adjustment without the action of a central community guidance system set up for this purpose. It also raises the question, usually implicitly answered in the affirmative by the related professions, of whether a greater degree of formal coordination centrally directed will yield a higher payoff through formal coordination. The answer must be empirically determined and should not be tacitly assumed to be invariably affirmative. Likewise, it opens up the quesion of whether cooperative intervention strategies—"on behalf of the whole"—are always to be preferred to contest strategies among partisans as a means of securing change. The newer paradigm is reflected in the growth of advocacy planning, which in turn arises from the loss in credibility of the notion that there is a single set of community interests and that the professional's job is to help formulate them or implement them. It recognizes the clash of opposed interests and suggests the negotiation of these interests for a resolution that though imperfect may be an improvement over the status quo but renounces the notion of seeking the community's interest as something existing in its own right.

All of these characteristics differentiate the principal thrust of the newer paradigm from that of the concrete collectivity paradigm, which formed the intellectual basis, however tacit, of conventional city planning[21] and community organization theory.[22]

Some of the *normative* implications of this paradigm shift are implicit in the contents of the last few chapters, especially chapter

---

21. This is an implicit theme of Alan A. Altshuler's definitive *The City Planning Process: A Political Analysis* (Ithaca, N.Y.: Cornell University Press, 1965).

22. The classic work in this field remains Murray G. Ross, *Community Organization: Theory and Principles* (New York: Harper & Brothers, 1955).

12. The most important implication is the shift in attention and credulity away from the notion of what may be termed the "single public interest" of the entire community. This concept is an important component of the older, collectivity paradigm. The older paradigm suggests that the community's well-being is an emergent, something more than merely the aggregate of the interests of the people and organizations involved: a type of community counterpart of Rousseau's general will.

The older concept had normative implications in two directions. First, it constituted the theoretical basis for the legitimation of community decision organizations, assuming that there is a single interest of the whole community and that these and other community organizations determine this interest in a rational manner and pursue this interest, thus enhancing the well-being of the whole. It lent support to the strategy of cooperative decision-making among the parts of the existing power structure, thus tending to exclude controversial issues from the decision-making agenda and important subgroups in the community from the decision-making process. It has thus had a strong conservative and elitist thrust.

Second, the normative thrust of the concrete collectivity paradigm has been toward greater managed coordination. Implying as it does a single set of community priorities, it requires for its implementation a centralized hierarchical structure that can administer the various aspects of the community in much the sense of a formal organization, maximizing the central control aspects and minimizing the free interplay of competing individuals and groups in the determination of policy and program.

Groups that are not part of the elitist consensus as to the community's interest are readily indictable as pursuing their own selfish interests as opposed to the community's well-being as this is determined by powerful, legitimated community decision organizations.

By way of contrast, the interactional field approach does not promote conflict or deny the value of cooperation in matters where all parties benefit. But it does tend to remove the veil of an alleged convergence of interests where this does not exist, and it tends to challenge the assumed unanimity as to the community interest that is brought about by a consensus of elites. In this sense I believe that it is more useful for viewing the dynamic interplay of forces, particularly in larger cities, that characterizes the determination and implementation of public action in today's turbulent circumstances.

One could apply a similar analysis to the neighborhood level and to the larger metropolitan area. They are both areas of growing importance. There has been a resurgence of interest in neighborhoods by neighborhood people. Likewise, at the metropolitan area level, there is the perennial proposal for metropolitan government as a managed guidance system to replace the panoply of special districts, intermunicipal contracts, councils of governments, and a dozen other formats for governmental negotiation and exchange across the metropolitan ecology.[23]

Finally, it would be interesting to consider some of the newer conceptions of large urban communities, which perhaps do not constitute theoretical paradigms but are nevertheless highly suggestive theoretically. There is George Sternlieb's city as sandbox,[24] Norton Long's city as a reservation,[25] succeeded by his unwalled city.[26] There is Richard L. Meier's metropolis as a transaction-maximizing system,[27] and Harvey Molotch's city as a growth machine.[28] In a different vein there is Harvey Cox's secular city[29] and Lawrence Haworth's good city.[30]

This chapter has covered some of the important new developments in community theory under a conceptual rubric, that of the gradual switch in emphasis from the concrete collectivity paradigm to the paradigm of the community as an interactional field. We have asserted that the newer paradigm seems to be more adequate to accommodate and explain recent developments in American communities than the older, more conventional paradigm. But it would be foolish to take a rigid either-or position in this matter of competing paradigms. For some purposes and in some community contexts one paradigm may be more useful, while in different contexts the other may be a superior aid to analysis and understanding. In considering the horizontal pattern, emphasis has been placed on the newer paradigm in this chapter only in order to call its advantages to the interested student's attention in a way that until now had not yet been done.

In the next chapter we turn to a further consideration of the vertical pattern, the relation of local community units to extracommunity systems.

23. Oliver P. Williams et al., *Suburban Differences and Metropolitan Policies: A Philadelphia Story* (Philadelphia: University of Pennsylvania Press, 1965).

24. "The City as Sandbox," *The Public Interest*, no. 25 (Fall 1971).

25. Norton E. Long, "The City as Reservation," *The Public Interest*, no. 25 (Fall 1971).

26. Norton E. Long, *The Unwalled City; Reconstituting the Urban Community* (New York: Basic Books, 1972).

27. "The Metropolis as a Transaction-Maximizing System," *Daedalus*, vol. 97, no. (Fall 1968).

28. "The City as a Growth Machine: Toward a Political Economy of Place," *American Journal of Sociology*, vol. 82, no. 2, (September 1976).

29. *The Secular City: Secularization and Urbanization in Theological Perspective* (New York: Macmillan Co., 1965).

30. *The Good City* (Bloomington: Indiana University Press, 1963).

The Vertical Pattern Revisited: Communities as Nodes of the Macrosystem

14

This book has emphasized the importance of the vertical ties of community units to extracommunity systems, pointing out that a large part of what takes place locally cannot be adequately understood without considering this important vertical dimension. This problem of the nature of the relationship between local communities and larger societies, or macrosystems, has had an interesting history in recent years. Only two decades or so ago the treatment of local communities by anthropologists and sociologists was almost exclusively within an implicit "closed-system" framework. Communities were treated largely as cultural islands, with only a vague, undefined relationship to the larger society; community phenomena were considered *sui generis*, as though everything of importance in the local community could be fully accounted for in terms of that system's internal dynamics.

At that time, a series of publications, including the first edition of this book, called attention to the importance of the "vertical ties" of local communities to larger national and even international social orders.[1] Attempts were made to develop a set of concepts through

---

1. Notably Julian H. Steward, *Area Research: Theory and Practice*, Bulletin 63 (New York: Social Science Research Council, 1950; Roland L. Warren, "Toward a Reformulation of Community Theory," *Human Organization*, vol. 15, no. 2 (Summer 1956), and Arthur J. Vidich and Joseph Bensman, *Small Town in Mass Society: Class, Power and Religion in a Rural Community* (Princeton: Princeton University Press, 1958).

which these ties could be analyzed. One of the important aspects of this investigation was to indicate that local communities as such have few if any traceable ties to the macrosystem but that their component parts have various ties of a formal organizational and also an informal "cultural" nature (see pages 297-303).

Nevertheless, despite the growing recognition of the importance of vertical ties in determining social processes at the local community level, the emphasis is still on the attempt to explain local community phenomena in terms of the dynamics of interaction among local actors, with some residual attention being paid to vertical ties as constituting inputs or constraints from "outside the system." Thus, local actors, in their interaction, are recognized as being constrained by norms, expectations, sanctions, and inputs from more inclusive social systems, such as national industrial, professional, voluntary, or governmental organizations. Likewise, at the social policy level, programs such as Model Cities or General Revenue Sharing are developed. These seek to give direction or resources to local communities in recognition of their acknowledged inability to face their problems without such outside help.

The growing recognition of the strength and importance of vertical constraints and inputs suggests a third mode of analysis. Instead of investigating the community as a cultural island or as an open system with some influence from vertical ties, one might consider local communities as local enactments of the macrosystem, as the nodes of implementation of the national society. This approach would constitute something of a Copernican revolution, setting on its head the relationship between community and larger society. It would represent a change in analytic paradigm. In the newer paradigm, the major thrust of explanation would be sought in the structure of the macrosystem; and emphasis would be placed on the similarities of structure and process found across communities within the same macrosystem. Variations would then be seen as comparatively minor disparities attributable to local demographic, geographic, and regional conditions as well as differences of cultural origin and traditions.[2]

One may of course argue that the proposed change in orientation represents a distinction without a difference: that much the same phenomena can be looked at from the macrosystem level or from the microsystem level with similar findings and with equal

___

2.   The two paradigms for conceptualizing the vertical pattern that are contrasted in this chapter are independent of the alternative paradigms for conceptualizing the horizontal pattern in the preceding chapter, although there appears to be a loose compatability between the two older ones in both chapters as there is between the two newer ones.

validity. Yet differences in analytic level do involve differences in findings, and different paradigms give clarity of focus to different aspects of the data. The question is not which paradigm has greater validity in a narrow sense but how useful are these alternative paradigms in accounting for what social science investigators and policymakers consider important issues: important in theoretical understanding and in addressing community problems.[3] This chapter examines the strengths of such an approach to communities as nodes of the macrosystem. There is no intention of declaring community open-system analysis to be either invalid or useless; rather there is some indication that actual empirical developments as well as current social concerns make a macrosystem approach increasingly useful for community analysis and suggest the need for its further elaboration.

Value of Pursuing the Macrosystem

Three lines of reasoning support the value of pursuing the macrosystem as the primary determinant of community phenomena. The first is the growing recognition of the importance of vertical inputs and constraints from the macrosystem. There has been considerable attention given recently to the growing impact of these impulses from the larger society. As an example, the entire 1975 annual meeting of the Community Development Society was devoted to the problem of coping with the effects on local communities of forces from the larger society. Much of the discussion at that meeting had to do with the growing extent to which these external impacts—from government, from industry, from voluntary organizations—threaten to engulf local communities in processes they cannot control and the question of what local communities can do, as it were, to stem the tide. In a somewhat different vein, the growing importance of the macrosystem's influence is perhaps most clearly illustrated in the relation of unemployment to community economic development, on the one hand, and the condition of the national economy on the other. While locality-based economic development measures may have some modest effectiveness, the fluctuation of local employment with conditions in the national economy pinpoints the massive impact of national economic conditions as compared to local economic efforts to increase the community's economic base, to provide manpower training, and the like. Clearly, anyone interested in the economic viability of local communities must turn to the economics of the macrosystem.

---

3.   Thomas S. Kuhn, *The Structure of Scientific Revolutions*, 2nd enlarged ed. (Chicago: University of Chicago Press, 1970), especially chapter 9.

A second line of support for the macrosystem approach is more inferential. It takes as its point of departure the massive similarity among American communities in their general social structures and processes and even in their physical configurations. Not every city conforms to the concentric zone pattern of the early Chicago ecologists, but anyone who has had occasion to visit many cities and has taken the taxi ride from the airport to the inner city must attest to the vast similarity in general ecological structure and in the actual patterning of different ecological areas within the metropolitan area. This is Tuesday, so we must be in Omaha. Or is it Dallas? Or Columbus, perhaps? Or Atlanta, Akron, Denver, Rochester, Buffalo? Of course there are differences, if not in physical appearance, then in social structure. But even here, one is impressed by the great similarity of social structure of these cities. Yes, some are of the city manager type, some strong mayor-weak council, and they have other structural differences. But they all have their similar community decision organizations: the chamber of commerce, the board of education, the council of churches, the health and welfare council, the welfare department. Yes, there are differences; some local welfare departments are branches of city government and others of state government, for instance. But the organizations constitute a remarkably similar "cast of characters" in most American communities.

One local variation has to do with size, of course. Not every community has a chamber of commerce, or a council of churches, or an urban renewal agency, to say nothing of a major medical center, a research library, or even a battery of large department stores. Size has something to do with all of these. Likewise, a glance at the classified telephone directories or city directories of a number of cities indicates the great similarity in availability of goods and services and organizations of all kinds in government, in the profit sector, and in the voluntary sector. As the Youngs and other investigators have pointed out in their multicommunity research, even the size dimension varies systematically, with certain types of facilities being characteristic of all communities above a given size, others of all communities above a larger size, and so on up.[4] The scalability of such data indicates once more the systemic aspects of the macrosystem as they work themselves out in community formation and growth. Such impressive similarities and observable regularities are really quite difficult to account for without acknowledging a relatively constant conformation imposed by the macrosystem. They don't just "happen" to be similar; they are similar because they rep-

4. Frank W. Young and Ruth C. Young, "The Sequence and Direction of Community Growth: A Cross-cultural Generalization," *Rural Sociology*, vol. 27, no. 4 (December 1962).

resent the working out of a similar social structure deriving from the macrosystem.

A third line of reasoning, if it may be called that, arises from a tendency within the social sciences, stimulated no doubt by social system theory, to seek to recognize the interconnectedness of any order of data within a larger, more inclusive framework. It is a tendency to look beyond the individual trees to the configuration of the forest, a tendency away from fragmentation toward holism. The recent growth of interest in political economy is in part an expression of this more general tendency, though it also has roots closely associated with the long-overdue willingness of social theorists to take Marxism seriously rather than to study it as a sort of theoretical aberration. Marx, the "conflict" theorist, has, paradoxically, had a deep influence on the increasing propensity to see the whole system, rather than merely to investigate myopically its separate, fragmented parts. In *La question urbaine*, Manuel Castells criticizes American power structure studies as exemplifying the tendency of bourgeois sociology to fragmentalize its subject matter thus permitting it to ignore the larger, systemic, class struggle aspects of power structures as well as other social phenomena.[5]

One need not be a Marxist (though some Marxian as well as non-Marxian theorists may disagree) in order to recognize the characteristics of the macrosystem that tend to channel social behavior at the micro level in ways conducive to the system's conservation and favorable to the system's powerful beneficiaries. Nevertheless, one must concede that the major thrust of interest in relating local phenomena to national systems comes from neo-Marxist "critical" sociology. It is not necessary to accept the conceptual and theoretical baggage accumulated by Marxists over the past century and a quarter in order to welcome the endeavor to pursue the way in which the macro structure shapes local social activity.

Now let us do just that: pursue the way in which the macro structure shapes local social activity. If the local community is a node of the macrosystem, what are the properties of the macrosystem that operate to structure such local nodes, that interface with local demographic, cultural, geographic, societal conditions?

Aspects of the Macrosystem

1. Let us begin with the *economic aspects* of the macrosystem. We cannot here treat all of its aspects that impact local communities, but important aspects of this relationship are readily distinguishable.

5. (Paris: François Maspero, 1973), p. 309ff.

There is, obviously, the system of private ownership, investment, control, and profits that constitutes a prescribed form for local economic endeavor, supplemented by a growing governmental involvement in what should also be recognized as "economic" activity. The form in which local economic activity takes place regarding ownership, investment, control, and profit is largely determined by this macrosystem, and only in relatively narrow areas is it susceptible to local choice. Where such local choices occur, they are sufficiently infrequent as to be considered aberrations.

In view of the above, it is readily understandable that local economic conditions, for the most part, fluctuate with the state of the national economy or at least with the state of various industrial sectors, such as mining, agriculture, finance, and specific production industries. As they go, so goes the local community in its economic activity. The local community that experiences prosperity while the nation as a whole is in a period of recession is likewise but a fortunate aberration, largely interpretable in terms of the differential components of the national economy embodied in that atypical locality. The increasing tendency for relatively autonomous units of local economic endeavor to be swallowed up by regional or national companies makes the systemic lines to the sources of power and decision in the macrosystem ever more definitely and systematically traceable.

2. As in all social phenomena, the *ideational aspects* of these ties are important and warrant special note. We need only remind ourselves that social institutions involve not only tangible organizational forms but also systems of ideas, in the broadest sense of the term *idea.* Thus, *thought systems* and their implicit or explicit values exercise major influence over and above the systemic influence that may be directly traceable through organizational connections. Local economic activity is largely determined by the macrosystem not only because of identifiable organizational linkages but because of the prevalence of the ideas and values—ideology, if you will—that support the macrosystem and the macro-level structures. The macrosystem is only partly "administered" by national-level organizations. It is also sustained through a commonly prevalent ideology regarding economic activity and the forms that it should take, even when comparatively "autonomous."

3. One other aspect of the economic macrosystem (or economic aspect of the macrosystem) may be noted briefly. The national economic macrostructure contains within it a table of *economic roles, or occupations,* which constitutes as it were the dramatis personae of the economic macrostructure. These roles are actually listed and defined, in the case of the United States, in the Depart-

ment of Labor's *Dictionary of Occupational Titles.*[6] The economic activity of local communities is carried on by people enacting these specific occupational roles. Larger communities with more variegated economic activities generally enact a larger number of these roles than smaller communities. The roles are the roles of the national economy, and the particular configuration of these occupational roles in any local community shows a remarkable degree of similarity to that of other communities. The differences are largely determined by decisions made at the macro level based on differences of geographic and demographic factors among the communities involved.

4. In connection with occupational specializations, it need only be mentioned that the *technologies* available for local community economic activity, as well as other types of activity, are similarly not generated *ab ovo* within each community; they are simply taken from the technological warehouse, as it were, of the macrosystem. The acceptance across many communities of certain technologies as appropriate for certain spheres of activity is not an extraordinary coincidence, but rather a fact flowing from the determination of local community form and structure primarily by the macrosystem.

5. What I said about the role of thought systems in connection with the economic sector applies of course *pari passu* to other aspects of the local community system. To be sure, there are differences among communities in values, norms, dominant interests, styles, and other cultural aspects. But again, if one is to watch the *public behavior* of people on a busy street corner, or at the supermarket, or in their homes, or at athletic events, one would be hard put to it to know that one is in Pittsburgh rather than St. Louis, in Bridgeport rather than in Rockland, in Atlanta rather than in Denver. Surely, the thought systems, the ideational and behavioral patterns indigenous to the locality are important, but an observer from Mars would be struck by their overwhelming similarity as one moves across the country, indicating once more that they may best be considered local enactments or implementations of thought and behavior systems of the national culture.

6. In this connection, it seems pointless to assume that, for various system-theoretical reasons, strong collectivity orientation directed at the community is necessary or even desirable for the viability of local communities. Certainly, as Parsons has stressed, some common *values and norms* governing interaction must be adhered to if a social order is to be said to exist, but the point is that these need not be conceived, as has been the conventional manner, as values

6. (Washington, D.C.: U.S. Employment Service, 1949, Supplement, 1955).

and norms specific to the individual community, but rather much more as values and norms of the macrosystem that prescribe modes of orientation of people in specific roles in *any* American community. Were this not the case, the demands of resocialization made necessary by high geographic mobility in the population would be exceedingly great, as large numbers of people move to different communities and adjust to the local social orders there. Actually, these demands are readily handled by most people, precisely because a national pattern of institutions and interaction patterns will be found to be implemented in the next community just as it was in the last one.[7]

7. The essential similarities of *land-use patterns* of American communities are dramatized for anyone who has occasion to fly over the United States and England, France, or Germany. The relation of clustered residences and other buildings to the open landscape is quite different in most parts of the United States from what one notices in any of these other countries, where patterns of open land and of community buildings are relatively clearly delineated. There is an identifiable border between the two areas. Roughly, one sees either clusters of buildings or open land. In this country, the transition is more gradual. The difference has many historical roots, but the existing difference of condition can be summed up in a single dimension: the degree of rigidity of land-use controls. In the other countries mentioned, much more control by national or district governments is exercised over the determination of which land shall be used for residences or other settlement buildings and which land shall be kept "green." The mixed use of land at the periphery of local communities in the United States indicates the lower level of control exercised, which stems in turn from the strong emphasis in the culture of the American macrosystem on individual property rights. American villages that look from the air like small English, German, or French villages are aberrant. American cities that maintain such a clear delineation between settled land and green space as, for instance, Stuttgart, Germany, are virtually nonexistent.

In this connection, as one now notes the growth of huge high-rise, monolithic apartment residences on the periphery of large and even medium-sized cities in various parts of the globe, one is reminded of the "wheels within wheels" nature of social systems, since here is a clear indication of the operation of an incipient world-wide macrosystem, which operates as an overlay on national macrosystems. In the field of economic activity, the existence of such a

7. The most forceful argument to support these statements remains William H. Whyte's *The Organization Man* (Garden City: Doubleday Anchor, 1957). See page 84 of the present book.

macrosystem, involving multinational corporations as prima donnas among the dramatis personae, has long been recognized.

8. *Social stratification* is of course an important aspect of any social macrosystem, as well as of most microsystems, including most, if not all, local communities. Like economic endeavor, thought systems, technology, and the other aspects considered above, social stratification, as indicated at the end of chapter 9, can be viewed purely from the local standpoint or can be considered within the framework of the macrosystem. Quite obviously, Marx and his followers have consistently emphasized the importance of viewing social stratification from the standpoint of the macrosystem. Interestingly, although the Lynds' Middletown studies applied this Marxian concept as central to their analysis of Muncie, Indiana, they, similarly, derived most of the dynamics of this stratification system from the internal dynamics of the community.[8] Warner, Hollingshead, and their associates made more explicit and systematic explorations of social stratification in the communities they studied.[9] Interestingly, Warner, in a small subsequent volume, used the data of stratification in various communities studied to speculate about the existence of a national system of stratification.[10] Likewise, it is interesting to note a similar sequence in Floyd Hunter's concern with power structures. When he published his *Community Power Structure,*[11] he then turned to a study of the national power structure,[12] joining a tradition implemented by C. Wright Mills,[13] Ferdinand Lundberg,[14] and others, but that stemmed back to Mosca and Pareto and is traceable in Western European thought at least as far back as Plato. Bernard Barber treated the subject in an extraordinarily perceptive article

8. Robert S. Lynd and Helen Merrell Lynd, *Middletown: A Study in Contemporary American Culture* (New York: Harcourt, Brace, 1929), and *Middletown in Transition: A Study in Cultural Conflicts* (New York: Harcourt, Brace, 1937).

9. Warner was the principal author of the monumental Yankee City studies, of which the most widely read is probably W. Lloyd Warner and Paul S. Lunt, *The Social Life of a Modern Community* (New Haven: Yale University Press, 1941). August B. Hollingshead's most well-known work in this field is his *Elmtown's Youth: The Impact of Social Classes on Adolescents* (New York: John Wiley & Sons, 1949).

10. W. Lloyd Warner, *American Life: Dream and Reality* (Chicago: University of Chicago Press, 1953, 1962).

11. *Community Power Structure: A Study of Decision Makers* (Chapel Hill: University of North Carolina Press, 1953).

12. *Top Leadership, U.S.A.* (Chapel Hill: University of North Carolina Press, 1959).

13. *The Power Elite* (New York: Oxford University Press, 1956).

14. *America's Sixty Families* (New York: The Vanguard Press, 1937), and *The Rich and the Super-rich* (New York: L. Stuart, 1968).

that differentiated between social class, family status, and local-community status.[15]

9. Such varied studies of status in the macrosystem as those of Domhoff[16] and Parker,[17] in addition to several of those already mentioned, lend support to the importance of considering local *power structures* as largely determined by position in the macrosystem and suggest the inadequacy of power structure studies that consider the macrosystem as a largely peripheral issue while concentrating on the internal dynamics of the specific local community. The new manager of the important local branch plant of the national corporation almost immediately finds himself exercising inordinate influence on local situations not because of any locally generated adulation but because his position as dictated by the national system gives him access to important resources, which can be utilized for positive or negative sanctions vis-a-vis other local actors. This is not to say that all actors occupying equal positions in the macrosystem exercise equal amounts of local power. There are differences attributable to local context and to individual personalities and sociometric networks. But in most cases one will not go far wrong in utilizing a model that assumes relatively equal or equivalent power attributable to positions in the macrostructure.

10. The question of national systemic linkages to the local community has already been touched on in much of the above. Yet it needs stressing that in virtually every aspect of local community activities, important *organizational linkages* to parts of the macrosystem are operative, whether this linkage be through religious denominations, professional associations, company branch subsidiaries, branches of federal and state government, labor unions, or whatever. All of these constitute channels through which local institutions are kept in conformity with the principal formal organizations at the macro level. Some involve direct authoritative relationships, others a much less authority-wielding kind of linkage; but in all sectors, local community social structure and activity are importantly formed and channeled through such vertical systemic linkages.

11. The last aspect of this macro-micro interface to be considered here is that of the numerous issues or problems of various types that occupy the attention, resources, and activity of local com-

---

15. "Family Status, Local-Community Status, and Social Stratification: Three Types of Social Ranking," *Pacific Sociological Review*, vol. 4, no. 1 (Spring 1961).

16. G. William Domhoff, *Who Rules America?* (Englewood Cliffs, N.J.: Prentice-Hall, Inc., 1967), and *The Higher Circles: The Governing Class in America* (New York: Random House, Inc., 1970).

17. Richard Parker, *The Myth of the Middle Class: Notes on Affluence and Equality* (New York: Harper and Row, 1972).

munities. In the field of *social problems* there has been growing awareness of the importance of aspects of these problems that transcend purely local bounds. Whether it is unemployment, drug addiction, racism, or more specifically struggles over use of methadone, school decentralization and neighborhood control, busing, or on through a long list, these issues have typically been perceived on the local scene as local issues, locally generated and therefore addressable in terms of changes in the local configuration. Yet there is growing recognition that they are in large part the product of circumstances and structures beyond the control of local people, inhering in the macrosystem. Paradoxically, despite this recognition they often continue to be addressed primarily as exclusively local phenomena, and the "solution" is sought in the locality. The relationship is adequately addressed neither by diffusion theory nor by parallel evolution theory as developed by anthropologists. Many of these issues become local issues spread across the front pages of newspapers not by diffusion and not by parallel evolution (a sort of preestablished harmony of problem emergence that would challenge the credulity of a Leibniz) but largely by developments in the national society, which find their enactment, with some variations, at the local level.

Implications of the Macrosystem Approach

Does it then make a difference whether one studies local communities as open systems subject to inputs and constraints from more inclusive systems or as nodes of the macrosystem? This chapter has examined the plausibility of the latter but without denying the value of the former. In concluding, let us draw out some of the implications of the suggested approach for theory as well as for practical efforts to change the course of events at the locality level.

Brian Taylor has recently made a trenchant critique of community studies as lacking a sociological and structural problem focus. He writes:

> To begin with, so far as problems have been examined at all, the use of a *locality framework* has tended to restrict attention to problems within the settlement-area, and thus either to miss some problems altogether or to ignore their true location, which in many cases are in social systems which extend beyond the village, parish, slum, suburb or town itself, in the context of the wider society.[18]

---

18. "The Absence of a Sociological and Structural Problem Focus in Community Studies," *Archives europeens de sociologie*, vol. 16, 1975.

His point is not that locality is irrelevant but that preoccupation with it has obscured the societal aspects of localities. Likewise, Castells emphasizes the importance of the macrosystem point of view, though from a somewhat different perspective:

> The heart of the sociological analysis of the urban question lies in the study of urban politics, that is to say of the specific artic-ulation of processes designated as "urban" in the field of class conflict and consequently in the intervention of the political instance (State apparatus)—object, center, and stake of political conflict.[19]

What stands out in Castells's entire approach is the insistence on seeing urban phenomena as a part of the macrosystem.

Certainly one theoretical implication of the newer approach is the need for further systematic analysis and more adequate concep-tualization of the interface between aspects of the macrosystem and the community subsystem than is given in this exploratory chapter. Such systematic analysis would involve much more precise specifica-tion of the nature of the linkages. The newer approach places importance on looking to the macrosystem for a greater part of the explanation of local community phenomena than it is now acknowl-edged to exercise, in part, at least, because the methods and con-cepts for such analysis are not at hand.

On the level of community intervention, the implications are numerous, but we shall limit ourselves to three:

First, the approach affords added reason for skepticism regarding the American penchant for believing that problems affect-ing local people should or must be solved by local people. The pro-totypical adaptation of this belief in the past decade was the Model Cities program. Today, in many respects, its counterpart may be considered the General Revenue Sharing program. But at the national policy level there has been little systematic basis for deter-mining what may best be done locally and what may best be done under other rubrics. The level-of-government analysis by political scientists and the economists' dictum that redistributive functions should be performed by more inclusive governmental units are indi-cations of recognition of the problem, but neither type of calculation addresses the knotty problems of the macro-micro interface indi-cated in this chapter.

Another implication of the macrosystem approach would be to suggest the desirability of utilizing community-level indicators in the assessment of national public policy, in ways in which they are not

19. *La question urbaine*, p. 307.

presently utilized. If local communities are the locus where national policies become enacted, then that is where one should look for their effects, rather than only examining the effects in macro-level terms, such as the credit system, national unemployment levels, the construction industry. Side effects of national policies may become more obviously apparent and thus be considered along with the more explicitly intended impacts of policy. As an example, the Federal home mortgage loan program was designed to stimulate home ownership and through it the construction industry. More attention to its community-level effects would perhaps have brought earlier recognition of the fact that it was also contributing to the exodus of white middle-class families from the cities and to a corresponding influx of blacks, aggravating the problem of ecological segregation along racial lines.

The changed emphasis also has implications for community development activities. First, it suggests that such efforts, based on the notion of the community as the prime mover, are bound to be limited in their effect. But perhaps more important, it suggests to community development workers that unless they are willing to be satisfied with a relatively inconsequential role and purview in attempting to influence the course of events in local communities, they will need to turn increasingly toward the macro level, for that is where, in its major dimensions, the local community's fate is primarily determined.

Because this chapter has emphasized the advantages of a theoretical conception of communities as nodes of the macrosystem, it would be easy to neglect the other side of the coin. This is the fact that although the macrosystem exercises its powerful influence, it does not by any means completely determine what happens locally. Much local structure and behavior are determined primarily at the local level. The macro-level approach is not well adapted to dealing with these primarily locally-induced variations. The relation and interaction of local units—people and organizations—with each other, that we have called the horizontal pattern of community relationships, remains an important area of investigation. We have attempted to indicate in the preceding chapter that the conceptualization of this horizontal pattern as applying to a local field of interaction is useful for many analytical purposes. The present chapter has simply pushed the concept of the vertical pattern farther than did chapter 8. Some may well say "too far." If so, at least the error lies on the side of correcting the deficiency of insufficient attention to the macrosystem that has characterized community research and theory to this date.

Again, if "too far," the following Epilogue, written for an earlier edition of this book, may help correct any notion that attention

435

to the macrosystem necessarily means "writing off" local communities as unimportant.

Epilogue

Perhaps an author's personal expression of feeling is permissible, if only as an epilogue. Mine relates to the following frequently heard line of reasoning concerning the geographic community:

In earlier days, perhaps, the concept of the geographic community had considerable validity. The local clustering of people was largely self-sufficient; it was fairly easy to identify where one community ended and another began; people tended to lead their lives within the confines of their local community and to develop strong attachment to it; and local communities showed a great deal of coherence through shared institutions and values and frequent face-to-face interaction.

But this situation has changed. In industrial society no community can be self-sufficient. Much of what occurs locally is but an embodiment of institutions of the mass society. Many of the units of social organization to be found locally are parts of large networks extending to include entire nations, and the ties of local organizations and of local people to such networks are becoming more numerous and stronger.

Community boundaries have become more difficult to delineate; overlapping service areas of all types tend to make a shambles of any notion of an inclusive community. In "megalopolis," people move toward one geographic center of activity for one purpose and toward a different one for a different purpose and often toward two **437** or more centers for even the same purpose. You cannot draw a line around groups of people and presume that they will stay within a set of abstract borders simply because they live nearer one center of activity than another or because they live within one local municipal jurisdiction or another. With people commuting fifty miles or more by car, and not infrequently commuting hundreds of miles by plane, does not the notion of a local community become absurd?

The associations that people believe to be important do not sort themselves out by local geographic areas. As an example, the pull of ethnic or religious identification, of social lifestyles, of functional interests and occupations, of political and ideological loyalties, all may be stronger that the pull of the neighborhood or the local community. The term neighborhood means less to Chicanos than the term *barrio;* and when blacks use the term *community* they are very likely referring to their ethnic rather than their geographic identifications. A combination of interests that transcend local borders and transportation and communication facilities that permit interaction among people living far apart, as well as the reciprocal depersonalization of much local social interaction, tends to make older notions of geographic communities obsolete.

As a final consideration, the type of coherence among local institutions that in earlier times was possible through personal contact and shared norms and values and behavior patterns is also largely gone. In short, the local community is no longer a valid sociological concept, lacking clarity of definition and unimportant as a type of social organization. If we are interested in the functions that local communities formerly served, we must now turn to other rubrics: to ethnic groups, to functional associations of various types, and to formal organizations that do not divide themselves up by locality.

The alert reader may have noticed that this critique of the geographic community concept is simply a repetition of the "four dimensions on which American communities differ," described in chapter 1 of this book and elaborated in chapter 3 on the "great change."

The problem, then, was to discuss how, under today's changing conditions, locality-relevant functions are performed and to describe some characteristics of this very interrelated, geographically overlapping network of people, organizations, and functions.

The orientation of this book is somewhat different from that of students of the community who have tended to study it as though it were a completely isolated phenomenon: self-sufficient, self-contained, and for most of its inhabitants the virtual container of their social universe. This book's orientation is especially distinct from the notion that the community's essential characteristic is close, face-to-face relationships based on common proximity. It was pointed out that a characteristic of the "great change" had been the increasing importance of extracommunity ties, a heightened vertical orientation. In general systems terminology, one must conceptualize the community not as a closed system but as a highly open system with borders so permeable that they are difficult to define.[1]

The dimension of psychological identification with the locality has been taken in this book as a variable on which communities differ from each other in space and time, with a general historical trend toward relatively less such identification as other meaningful ties compete with that of the locality and as important interests direct attention out of the community to extracommunity systems.

Under these circumstances, Kaufman and his associates have drawn the implication that *community* must be differentiated from the entire *local society* since it is only a small part of the local society, namely that aspect of it that is strictly oriented toward affairs of the locality (see pages 37-40). In this book we have taken a different orientation, preferring, in Kaufman's terms, to study the entire local society and not to ignore but to emphasize those aspects of the local society that are oriented to extracommunity systems.

There is a third possibility. It is to conclude from the same situation that *community*—in terms of psychological identification, an important reference group, a source of meaningful ties—has moved out of the locality, as it were, and now occurs in types of associations with little relevance to geographic localities.

Perhaps the most important statement of this third position has been made by Israel Rubin. Taking Durkheim as his point of departure, he cites the latter's assertion that residence in geographical divisions is not a highly important source of profound sentiments. "The provincial spirit has disappeared never to return; the patriotism of the parish has become an archaism that cannot be restored at will.[2] Rubin endorses Durkheim's view of the importance of groups that mediate between the individual and the larger society and agrees that the locality group no longer serves this function. Rather, he looks to "non-territorial communities" as the sources of such significant ties, and finds them in concrete organizations, situated in important institutional areas, characterized by primary and secondary interaction of the members. Such a community need not "provide for the daily needs of its members and, hence, there is no

---

1. Ludwig von Bertalanffy, *General System Theory: Foundations, Development, Applications* (New York: G. Braziller, 1969).

2. Israel Rubin, "Function and Structure of Community: Conceptual and Theoretical Analysis," *International Review of Community Development*, no. 21-22 (1969), p. 115.

reason that it constitute a microcosm of the larger sociocultural system.[3] This is in direct challenge to conceptions of the geographic community that posit a broad span of institutional organization or, in this book's terminology, that provide at the local level for the performance of the locality-relevant functions. Hence, locality itself is not essential to communities. "Communities may be organized either along residential lines or along other, non-residential boundaries, as the necessary functional and structural elements do not appear to require territorial focus."[4] Such communities have five structural characteristics: intermediate size, presence of significant primary and secondary interaction, focus on a key institutional setting, relative stability, and concreteness.[5]

In other words, the term *community* is taken to denote a concrete organization that is not necessarily residential and that mediates between the individual and the larger society. Ethnic and religious organizations, labor unions, professional societies, and other such affiliations, none of them necessarily local, are examples. It is in organizations such as these that *community* is to be found under present conditions. In the past, locality groups met these specifications. They no longer do.

It is obvious that if we define community in terms of "meaningful social ties," then its equation with the organization of local social activity in untenable. Robert Nisbet in *The Quest for Community*[6] and Maurice Stein in *The Eclipse of Community*[7] (note the implication of the titles) both emphasize in somewhat different ways the decreasing relevance of the locality group and the enduring need for such meaningful ties.

But it is one thing to acknowledge this change, another to assert or imply that the local organization of social life either does not exist or is unimportant. Even Durkheim, whose analysis is followed by both Rubin and Nisbet, footnotes the very passage quoted by Rubin, with a statement to the contrary: "The material neighborhood will always constitute a bond between men; consequently, political and social organization with a territorial base will certainly exist. Only, they will not have their present predominance, precisely

3. Rubin, "Function and Structure of Community," p. 117.

4. Rubin, "Function and Structure of Community," p. 117.

5. Rubin, "Function and Structure of Community," pp. 113-11.

6. Robert A. Nisbet, *The Quest for Community: A Study in the Ethics of Order and Freedom* (New York: Oxford University Press, 1953).

7. Maurice R. Stein, *The Eclipse of Community: An Interpretation of American Studies* (Princeton: Princeton University Press, 1960).

because this bond has lost its force."[8] It is interesting that at this much more advanced date, almost eighty years after Durkheim wrote these words, one of the current burning issues in American communities should be that of "neighborhood control."

But to repeat, the development of meaningful associational ties that are largely irrelevant to the immediate locality is hardly a sensational discovery. To derive from it the conclusion that it is therefore important to study such associational ties is certainly highly justified, even though the use of the term *community* to depict them may be unnecessarily ambiguous. To conclude that communities, in the sense of the local organization of social life, are therefore not worth studying seems palpably absurd.

Why, in an era when many different groups of people are determined to make more, rather than less, of their own neighborhoods, when they are demanding decentralization, both from the political right and the political left, is there such an emphasis among scholars on the essential irrelevance of locality? How is it possible to ignore or consider as unimportant the vast differences that exist between a Scarsdale, a Winchester, and a Grosse Point on the one hand and a Harlem, a Roxbury, and an East St. Louis on the other?

The reluctance to consider the community as an important subject for special study is largely attributable to the growth of an even more ambiguous concept—mass society—on the one hand, and to the persistence of older, pre- "great-change" images of self-sufficient primary communities on the other. The romantic conception of the community as *Gemeinschaft* has been asserted not only by students of earlier community forms, but has been advocated by members of what might be called the "community movement," that dedicated group of community specialists, professionals, and lay persons who see immeasurable value in the small, face-to-face agricultural community that became the model for their theoretical conceptualization as well as for their aspirations for social reform.

To say, with Baker Brownell, that "a community is a group of people who know one another well,"[9] is to make the logical implication that when aggregations of people in a locality come to number much more than one or two thousand, community ceases to exist. This is precisely the conclusion drawn by Brownell and by Arthur

---

8. Emile Durkheim, *The Division of Labor in Society*, trans. George Simpson (New York: Macmillan Company, 1933), pp. 28-29. This quotation and that of Rubin are from the preface to the second edition published in 1902.

9. Baker Brownell, *The Human Community: Its Philosophy and Practice for a Time of Crisis* (New York: Harper & Brothers, 1950), p. 198.

Morgan.[10] It has become the stimulus for the most varied kinds of professional activity of many city planners, social workers, and others who apparently draw the conclusion that the meaningful ties that once inhered largely in the local community can only be realized through it. In this sense, Rubin offers a strong corrective in pointing out the importance of mediating groups that do not depend on what he calls "territorial crutches." But to go on to imply that the local web of life is therefore unimportant is to throw out the baby with the bath water.

There must be some broad area of middle ground for investigation between the incurably romantic conception of the community as a focal point of virtually all meaningful social activity and the equally remote conception of a territorially undifferentiated mass society in which people's relation to the macrosystem is utterly independent of their geographic location. For in this admittedly difficult theoretical area lie numerous questions not only of theory, ideology, and social policy but also of focal issues around which people are increasingly involved. Many people want locality to be made more, not less, relevant to the administration of the police, to the operation of the schools, to the ownership and operation of business enterprise, to the operation of the sanitation department, the health department, the social agencies, the location of highways, transit systems, and on and on through some of the most hotly contested issues of the day. Like Mark Twain's comment about the fallacious report of his own death, the death of the community has been highly exaggerated. Transformed, sí—muerto, no!

The theoretical task, and also the practical one, is to determine with greater depth of analysis those areas—many of the critical issues of our time—where the local organization of social life is an integral component of the social problem.

10.   Arthur E. Morgan, *The Small Community: Foundation of Democratic Life* (New York. Harper & Bros., 1942).

Index